SPENSER STUDIES

XIII

SPENSER STUDIES

A Renaissance
Poetry Annual
XIII

EDITED BY

Anne Lake Prescott AND *Thomas P. Roche, Jr.*

AMS PRESS
NEW YORK, N.Y.

SPENSER STUDIES
A RENAISSANCE POETRY ANNUAL

edited by Anne Lake Prescott and Thomas P. Roche, Jr.

is published annually by AMS Press, Inc. as a forum for Spenser scholarship and criticism and related Renaissance subjects. Manuscripts must be submitted *in duplicate* and be double-spaced, including notes, which should be grouped at the end and should be prepared according to the format used in this journal. All essay-length manuscripts should enclose an abstract of 100–175 words. They will be returned only if sufficient postage is enclosed (overseas contributors should enclose international reply coupons). One copy of each manuscript should be sent to Thomas P. Roche, Jr., Department of English, Princeton University, Princeton, N.J. 08544 and one copy to Anne Lake Prescott, Department of English, Barnard College, Columbia University, 3009 Broadway, New York, NY 10027-6598.

ISSN 0195-9468
Volume XIII, ISBN 0-404-19213-0

Contents

NANCY LINDHEIM

The Virgilian Design of *The Shepheardes Calender*

Virgil's *Eclogues* are a specific as well as a general model for *The Shepheardes Calender,* offering eclogue-for-eclogue correspondences that suggest that imitiation can refer to structural echoes in addition to verbal and thematic ones. The measure of innovation expected from heuristic imitation is generated largely by the use of the calendar and its implication of harvest, but even these "inventions" are inflected in ways that examine and proclaim Spenser's debt to Virgilian pastoral.

I WISH TO EXAMINE in this paper how Spenser distributes and organizes the Virgilian materials that help shape his eclogue-book, *The Shepheardes Calender.* The major strand of pastoral I am calling "Virgilian" is concerned with issues that arise from *Eclogue* I (because it is the defining poem for the later European pastoral tradition[1]) and its pendant poem, *Eclogue* IX. If we generalize on the basis of these two poems dealing with the land confiscations that followed the Roman civil wars, our expectations of pastoral will be anything but "Arcadian." What the eclogues demonstrate most clearly is the shepherds' vulnerability to political power. But the exigency of their situations also allows us to see what is most valuable in their lives. Read together, *Eclogue* IX's more open awareness of the human bond connecting the members of the shepherd community underwrites Tityrus' invitation to the dispossessed Meliboeus in *Eclogue* I to share his cottage for the night, and the freedom to sing that has been granted to Tityrus becomes redefined in terms of the importance *Eclogue* IX gives to song as the measure of the human spirit.[2] These two factors—the concerns of poetry and the communal values of friendship and compassion—are central also to the *Shepheardes Calender;* they are expressed largely through its main organizing figures, Colin and Hobbinol.[3]

1

Hobbinol is not usually given such prominence in discussions of the *Shepheardes Calender,* yet he is a continuous secondary presence in the work: he appears as a speaker in *Aprill, June* and *September,* and Colin refers to him in *Januarye* and *December.* These five months place him in every season of the year; the appearances themselves occur in each of E.K.'s poetic "kinds." Uniquely designated as Colin's friend, and thus carrying special status in the work, he nevertheless functions largely as part of the shepherd community, seeming to present their pleasures and compassion. He is important for expressing some of the central values of the *Calender.* Colin, on the other hand, explores the shepherds' concern with love and pastoral's strong metapoetic interests and is the figure through whom Spenser articulates the structural correspondences between his eclogue-book and Virgil's. These correspondences simultaneously indicate the nature of Spenser's imitation and measure the extent of his innovation in reshaping the Virgilian materials for his own ends. The work's controlling innovation is apparently the use of the calendar itself, yet both the calendrical form and the idea of harvest to which it gives rise suggest interesting filiations with the Virgilian eclogue-book.

In *June,* the only eclogue of the twelve in which Colin and Hobbinol actually appear together, we are encouraged to interpret both figures in terms of their Virgilian ancestry. Because criticism is so accustomed to thinking of Colin as a pastoral persona for the poet, it is not often noticed that the traditional shepherd in the poem is Hobbinol,[4] who issues a Tityrean invitation asking the unhappy Colin to bring his flocks to live in his own more hospitable countryside. Colin's response makes Hobbinol's pastoral contentment sound Tityrean as well: "O happy *Hobbinol,* I blesse thy state" (9).[5] As John Bernard notes (p. 58), Hobbinol's later line, "O careful *Colin,* I lament thy case" (113), creates a syntactical echo that sets up a contrast between the two figures. We may expect Colin's lamentable state to remind us of Meliboeus' in *Eclogue* I, but Colin's own words define his Virgilian ancestor instead as Aeneas, the exiled hero: "But I unhappy man, whom cruel fate,/And angry Gods pursue from coste to coste,/Can nowhere fynd, to shroud my luckless pate" (13–15).[6] While Colin is in no sense actually "heroic," the effect of this allusion is to suggest alienation from the conventional life of the shepherds. His restlessness is important: in spite of the opening praise of Hobbinol's native landscape, the emphasis of the eclogue falls on the shepherds' psychological state rather than their physical place—not on the need for harmonious nature but on the mental conditions necessary for creativity. Hobbinol's "paradise," Colin says, depends on his being "withouten dread" of wolves and free to sing his songs (10–12).

Colin's own mental turmoil or "careful case" (78) shapes the poetic concerns of the eclogue into persistent "generic" uncertainties: Can a shepherd presume to equal Orpheus or Calliope (50–72)? Do the concepts "praise . . . blame . . . renown" (73–74), though rejected, still imply epic pretension merely by being acknowledged? Is the personal voice of lyric complaint with its projected audience of one (100) incompatible with the strongly communal experience of pastoral song (71–72, 79–80)?[7]

In the central two stanzas of his long speech (65–112) Colin describes the achievement of Tityrus-Chaucer as though he had reconciled these tensions within pastoral: famous (92), he expressed (yet also "slaked") his own love and told merry tales to keep his fellow shepherds awake during the long watch (84–88).[8] The Colin of *June*, on the contrary, seems defeated by the task. To be fair, however, this version of Chaucer's career, while solving the divergent claims of the personal and communal functions of poetry that Colin has foundered upon, totally avoids the thorny problem of writing epic. For Spenser, one could say, Chaucer was not caught in the anxiety of the Virgilian *rota*. But, alas, Spenser-Colin is, as these echoes of the generic self-consciousness of the opening of Virgil's sixth eclogue demonstrate: Colin, like the poet of *Eclogue* VI, considers but apparently rejects the possibility of writing on more heroic themes.[9] (Nor is it an accident, I shall argue, that *June* is Spenser's sixth eclogue also.)

By isolating Colin from some of the usual pastoral values—the framing eclogues of the *Calender,* for example, are soliloquies rather than dialogues—Spenser creates a space for another figure who can embody these traditional qualities in a less problematic way. But the relation is not a matter of opposition and does not imply the necessity to "transcend" pastoral for greater subjects. The tensions or antitheses within pastoral define the genre; they do not destroy it. The figure so created, as I have intimated, is Hobbinol. In *June* especially he is an embodiment of the classical image of the shepherd. He is said to be a poet because in pastoral herdsmen traditionally sing, just as they tend sheep or make cheese, but song and its function are not his major concerns. Freed from concentration on the poet's craft, Hobbinol is asked instead to test issues of theme and content descending from classical pastoral against the newer non-classical imperatives of the *Calender*.[10] Thus in *September* he repeats the gesture of *June*—the Tityrean invitation—in order to emphasize its validity when "Paradise" (*June,* 10) can no longer act as a guarantee, that is, when the social and moral stakes have been altered by the darkening year.[11]

Colin's restlessness, on the other hand, which we have interpreted as quasi-heroic, easily takes on the two more self-assertive themes of the pastoral repertoire: unsatisfied love and the reflexive (often defensive) concerns of poetry.[12] Spenser underlines the difference between Colin and Hobbinol by creating Colin not as an ordinary figure of the shepherd as poet or singer, but as the more vexed figure of the poet as shepherd.[13]

Let me set out some more specific ways in which Spenser's patterning echoes that of the *Bucolics*. Virgil's chief metapoetic eclogues are IV (where the thematic register changes to deal with vast cycles of time and national history), VI (both in the Hesiodic/Callimachean relation to heroic verse and in Silenus' neoteric songs), and X (whose subtext is a debate between pastoral and love elegy).[14] Spenser's chief eclogues about poetry, all centering on Colin, are also IV (*Aprill's* concern with the thematic registers and diction necesssary for national panegyric),[15] VI (*June's* restless evocation of epic and the Virgilian *rota*), and X (*October's* debate about the suitable kinds of poetry and their rewards). *August's* bravura makes it seem metapoetic; *Eclogue* VIII is not equally self-regarding, but it too consists of two separate poems about unrequited love, with the second as clearly an imitation of Theocritus (*Idyll* II) as Colin's sestina is Italianate rather than home-grown.[16] Even the most pronounced formal feature of the *Calender*—the monologues of Colin that link its beginning and end—finds a possible correspondence in the *Bucolics*. Spenser's formal or structural "frame" actually has three parts; Colin in *June* is its pivot. Virgil's parallel three-part frame is more subtle, but still perceptible. The opening of *Eclogue* VI recalls *Eclogue* I both by naming its poet-figure Tityrus and by a striking verbal echo (*Musam meditaris* becomes *meditabor . . . Musam*), while the ending of VI introduces Gallus, who will reappear as the major figure of *Eclogue* X. Virgil's 1-6-10 pattern (first, middle, last) may thus have an echo in Spenser's 1-6-12.[17] The existence of so many parallels suggests that the *Shepheardes Calender* is like a palimpsest where an earlier work has influenced the design of the overlaid text. It is a textual relation that I think warrants extending the study of imitation (of echoes of words and images in individual works, or of generic codes[18]) to include formal designs governing composite works, such as eclogue-books, that are made up of discrete parts.

Of the strategies of imitatio catalogued by Thomas Greene in *The Light in Troy*, the one most appropriate to Spenser's practice in the *Shepheardes Calender* is the kind he labels heuristic. Such imitation begins by advertising its derivation from an earlier text, but then distances itself from that text and forces us to recognize the poetic distance traversed. As Greene goes on to say, "the informed reader notes the allusion but he notes simultaneously the gulf in the language, in sensibility, in cultural context, in world view, and in moral style" (p. 40). We should not therefore be thrown off track when we perceive these gulfs between Spenser's and Virgil's texts. They are the spaces within which the humanist poem—unitary or composite—defines itself.

The speculations of this next section attempt to describe in a concrete way how the *Bucolics* can be seen as a substructure helping to form Spenser's eclogue-book. My construct is hypothetical, a simplified description in genetic terms of what can be perceived analytically. Since the difference in the number of their component poems creates an apparent obstacle to putting the two "structures" together, I shall begin here. The primary process that governs Spenser's creation of his twelve-eclogue calendar from a Virgilian ten-eclogue mold is a kind of "splitting" or breaking apart and reassembling in different configurations. The term covers some fairly specific operations: Hobbinol and Colin in *June* "split" the figure of Tityrus, Hobbinol associating with his appearance in *Eclogue* I, Colin with his appearance in *Eclogue* VI. Within the larger *Calender* they also split Virgil's Corydon; both share aspects of his unrequited courtship in *Januarye*, and Hobbinol picks up the practicality of Corydon's final position in his own last speech in *Aprill*: "*Sicker I hold him for a greater fon / That loves the thing, he cannot purchase*" (158–59). *Nor is this a Spenserian invention. Spenser is likely to have noticed that Virgil "splits" the Daphnis material of Theocritus' Idyll I* by exploiting the mythic-heroic dimension of Daphnis in *Eclogue* V and his connection to love in the Gallus-Daphnis figure of *Eclogue* X. Spenser himself appears to isolate the political from the poetic concerns found in *Eclogue* IX, taking up "politics" in *September* and "poetry" in *October*. This kind of splitting can also be seen in the generation of the last group of eclogues in the *Calender*: Spenser seems to have found the material of *Eclogues* IX and X rich enough to create four poems from them. *November*, for example, picks up the communal, *solacium* themes of IX (18) as well as the pastoral elegy conventions of X. The material from *Eclogue* X is distributed in several ways: *December* works with the alienated figure of Gallus, *October* perhaps with its implicit debate over love poetry, *September* with its formal envelope of sympathy.[19] This schematic account of Spenser's handling of the final poems of his and Virgil's eclogue-books finds interesting support in certain aspects of calendar lore.

The IX-X doubling in the *Shepheardes Calender* can be seen to arise from the anomalous names of the months themselves, a curiosity that goes back to the history of the Roman calendar (to which E. K. so ostentatiously introduces us toward the end of his "Generall Argument"). The ninth through twelfth months of the Roman calendar (like our own) are called September (meaning "seventh"), October (eighth), November (ninth) and December (tenth) because they received their names at a time when the year comprised ten months beginning in March. The same discrepancy would have been registered by the early readers of the *Shepheardes Calender:* Spenser's beginning the year with January makes September to December the ninth thorugh twelfth months; England's calendar year, which in 1579 still began in March, would make them the seventh through tenth months.[20]

This double referencing of names and numbers means that Virgil's ninth eclogue corresponds to Spenser's ninth poem, *September,* by number, but to *November* by name; conversely, Spenser's twelfth poem, *December,* corresponds because of its name to Virgil's tenth eclogue. Two poems give rise to four (and an eclogue-book of ten poems becomes one of twelve) by treating the final poems twice, once to correspond to the numbers themselves (nine and ten) and once to the names of the months associated with these numbers (November and December).[21] Spenser may even have thought that Virgil's own use of his fifth *(Quintus)* eclogue to celebrate Julius Caesar, for whom the month of *Quintilis* was renamed *Julius* in 44 BCE, represented analogous calendrical punning.

E. K.'s "learned" introduction to the mysteries of calendar formation seems designed to set his readers' minds in motion. The issue of calendar reform, we know, was being debated at this time in the intellectual circles of Europe. The Gregorian calendar was finally introduced in Catholic countries in 1582 after many years of discussion and committees; formal proposals had been sent to all Christendom in 1577.[22] England ultimately rejected the plan as Papist, but John Dee, a member like Spenser of the Leicester circle, worked out a Protestant reform proposal by the early 1580s.[23]

Spenser (and E. K.) could hardly have been unaware of the contemporary issue of calendar reform; E. K.'s account in the "Generall Argument," taken from Macrobius, suggests considerable historical awareness as well. He tells us that the Roman calendar once had only ten months, and though he later correctly credits Numa Pompilius with the addition of January and February, his syntax at one point distinctly implies that the responsibility was Caesar's:

> For from Julius Caesar who first observed the leape
> yeare which he called Bissextilem Annum . . . the
> monethes have bene nombred xij which in the first
> ordinaunce of Romulus were but tenne . . .[24]

Whether this is indeed E. K.'s error, and whether or not Spenser
shared his misconception, the fact remains that there was much excitement over calendar reform in the years just before Virgil composed the *Bucolica*—46 BCE saw the introduction of the Julian
calendar, the justification for honoring Caesar by changing *Quintilis*
to *Julius*—and this excitement makes an "antique" year containing
ten months a piece of Virgil's current knowledge. It is not outrageous
to conjecture, then, that Spenser associated Virgil's ten eclogues with
a whole calendar year, thus reinforcing the appropriateness of seeking
to imitate his design within a calendrical form.

Indeed, the number of the component poems in Virgil's book
would have been significant for both Virgil and Spenser regardless
of any association with calendars. Even the most rudimentary knowledge of numerology would make them familiar with the Pythagorean
tetractys (or 4) and its equivalence to the numbers 10 and 12, all
numbers that were thought to express complex unity or comprehensive harmony. The *tetractys,* being the Pythagoreans' spatial representation of the number 4 $\cdot$
$\cdot \cdot \cdot \cdot$, reveals its equivalence to the number
10: $1+2+3+4=10$. The properties of harmony, wholeness, and perfection that reside in the number 4 (signifying creation) therefore
apply to 10 as well, a number that allows greater magnitude and
intricacy of design. Given the likelihood that the extensive numerical
patterning in the eclogues has some significance,[25] I think it reasonable to suggest not only that Spenser thought that the number 10
gave cosmological resonance to Virgil's eclogue-book, but that Virgil
thought it too.

Spenser's decision to base his eclogue-book on the calendar offered
him the equivalent numerological significance in the zodiacal number
12, and opened the possibility of a particularly acute set of correspondences that express the same cosmological harmony. In S. K. Heninger's formulation, "Colin's life is analyzed according to the four
elements and the four seasons. The cosmos of *homo* is shown to
be correspondent to the cosmoi of *mundus* and *annus.*"[26] For these
numerological purposes the numbers 10 and 12 are equivalent because both are "sophistications" of 4;[27] for literary purposes the significance of 10 and 12 also seems interchangeable, as is suggested by

the structural divisions of Renaissance epics. Milton's first version of
Paradise Lost had ten books and Camoëns' *Lusiad* ten cantos; Tasso's
Gerusalemme Liberata has twenty cantos and the original version of
the *Orlando Furioso* forty. Presumably the authors felt these numbers
were not less suitable to express the encyclopedic ambition of epic
than were Virgil and Statius' 12 or "Homer's" 24.[28] Milton's effortless
conversion of *Paradise Lost* from a ten-book to a twelve-book work
thus gives us reason to think Spenser's 12 might bear the same significance as Virgil's 10 in the *Eclogues*.

In seeking to promote the case for seeing the *Shepheardes Calender*
as an example of heuristic imitation, the first two sections of this
paper have sought also to create a greater awareness of what might
be Virgilian in the work. Heuristic imitation, however, involves
innovation as well as allusive repetition. The interaction between
these two motives in the *Calender* will be the burden of the final
section. The examination will begin schematically again, with differences, and conclude with some important thematic resonances.

Aside from the idea of the calendar itself, which we shall return
to in several different contexts, Spenser's most obvious independent
organizational patterns are two slender narrative threads: Colin's love
story and his journey from youth to maturity. We can see in this
increased narrative, I think, as well as in the intensification of lyric
complaint in the *Calender,* the influence of Petrarch. My guess is that
the introduction of Colin Clout's passion and disappointment was
encouraged by the vague narratization found in the sonnet sequence,
where (as in Petrarch's *Rime*) the speaker's emotional state is explored
over a course of time.[29] If we look for something similar in Theocritus
or Virgil, only the latter's tenth eclogue, because it has long been
read—I think mistakenly—as Virgil's farewell to pastoral, can be seen
as planting a narrative germ by offering an "ending," even if it is to
a story that has no beginning or middle. An impulse to narrative in
eclogue books may be independent of Petrarch, however. Mantuan
imposed something like a life-scheme on his ten *Adulescentia,* though
his scheme is more a principle of division (earlier years, followed by
a conversion), than a story.[30]

But the narrative impulse in the *Shepheardes Calender,* while important and innovative, is decidedly weak. The tenuous linearity it
provides is countered and perhaps balanced by a second kind of patterning that dominates the Colin group of poems: the calendrical
or circular form insisted on in the repetition of verse scheme and
monologue that joins *December* to *Januarye.*[31] This circularity, though
a product of the calendrical form itself, raises certain problems for

maintaining the congruence between the double time schemes—of the year and of the life—that organize the *Calender*. The two schemes are more congruent metaphorically than they are narratively: the joining of December and January is a function of the yearly cycle, and has no correspondence in the stages of human life. The disparity between the two schemes gives rise to considerable aesthetic dislocation. Colin's statement in *December* that he is now an old man causes us suddenly to "revise" our reading of the work. Having all along felt more acutely the progress of the seasons than the passage of years, we must now readjust the pattern of associations to this new information. Notwithstanding such conceptual difficulties, circularity holds great interest for Spenser. He develops it with the recessed symmetry he could have observed in Virgil's *Bucolica,* probably, like Virgil, into several simultaneous patterns.[32]

The pattern in the *Shepheardes Calender* most easily reconstructed is based on E.K.'s division of the eclogues into plaintive, recreative, and moral types.[33] Thematic and formal correspondences suggest other more simple (though incomplete) symmetries: the frame monologues of *Januarye* and *December,* the contrast between life and death in *Februarie* and *November,*[34] the concern with paradise in *June* and *Julye* give us 1 and 12, 2 and 11, with 6 and 7 at the center. It may be noteworthy that E.K. ascribes incompleteness to the pattern he outlines, though it is in fact fully worked out; perhaps other schemes have been left to the reader's ingenuity.[35] The recessed symmetry of Virgil's ten eclogues is rather more consistent even to an unpracticed eye, but the numerical incongruence of the most obvious pairings—I and IX, V and X—raises ideas of asymmetry as well. The *Bucolica* too has a double structure: the circular recessive pattern coexists with a simple linear progression by which the first five poems are less dark or negative than their corresponding poems in the latter five.[36] It seems likely that the calendar itself suggested a similar darkening in Spenser, but the echo it finds in Virgil's eclogue-book could have made allusive imitation more realizable. The openness of the structure of his eclogue-book—the coexistence of various kinds of thematic, tonal and numerical patterns—should be considered a major Virgilian legacy: "The important point for us to observe," Paul Alpers has noted, "is that Virgil counteracts the tendency to look for a single-minded direction or structure in the sequence" (*Singer,* 110). Imitation of such multiplicity is a structural factor that must complicate our understanding of the *Calender*. If didacticism has a deliberately shifting foundation, it must be a less dogmatic phenomenon than we have frequently supposed. The effect is surely to open up response, to urge us to entertain possibilities of counterpointed meanings.

At least two other formal aspects of the *Bucolica* are broadly significant for the content of the *Shepheardes Calender* and should be briefly
mentioned. Servius' influential commentary emphasized the need for
variety as the hallmark of such collections, thereby allowing the poet
to think in terms of breadth—of some kind of "all" to correspond
to the numerological promise of the numbers 10 and 12. (Modern
critics, on the other hand, tend to view pastoral in terms of nar-
rowness and limit.) The paradoxical contrast between humble subject
and cosmological pretension is a facet of the coexistence of ambition
and humility present in pastoral since its Hellenistic origins; it can
be traced moving back and forth from subtext to text, from form
to theme.[37]

The second consideration is Virgil's pervasive relationship to
Theocritus. So dominant is this *imitatio* that a recessed panel structure
of the eclogues can be mapped out solely on the basis of whether
each poem is "Romano-Theocritean," "Theocritean," or "non-
Theocritean."[38] In the manner of heuristic imitation, Virgil frankly
acknowledges his debt to Theocritus while at the same time pro-
claiming his independence and innovation. We can see in this interaction a paradigm for Spenser's own relation to Virgil. However
important it is for Virgil to establish the context of his work as
Theocritean pastoral because he is introducing a new kind of literature to Rome, he seeks not only to rewrite Theocritus' material (as
in creating Corydon from Polyphemus) but to make the eclogue
form express ideas that it had not been asked to present before, as in
the golden age prophecy of *Eclogue* IV. Spenser updates the love
material by turning to Petrarch even as Virgil found it necessary to
come to terms with Roman love elegy. The "new" non-Virgilian
ecclesiastical themes are in some sense parallel to the "new" non-
Theocritean political material of Virgil's I and IX. They may express
yet another challenge: a *contaminatio* or eclecticism that tries to incorporate Mantuan's pastoral tradition into a coherent "all."[39] Concerning imitation as a factor in the total design of the eclogue-book as
well as in individual poems, then, the heuristic strategy is to provide
enough similarity to make the debt recognizable and enough dissimi-
larity to make us isolate the difference and seek its meaning.

The idea of harvest that arises from the calendrical form itself is
interesting in respect to this assertion of similarity and difference.
Although it has no apparent correspondence in the *Bucolics* (which
offer neither teleology nor summing up), Spenser develops the harvest
idea to articulate his sense that pastoral has its roots in Virgil. Harvest
is an implicit organizing principle because it does indeed connote
both teleology and summing up; it offers a metaphoric bridge for

parallels between the year and the life. The *Calender* plays off these meanings in counterpoint: the rich implications of the poems of the later harvest months—September and October, to which Spenser significantly joins the usually dreary month of November[40]—are weighed against the formal "summation" offered in the final eclogue of *December* as it charts the phases of Colin's life. *December*'s failure to acknowledge and build on the implications of harvest in the three previous poems creates a severe aesthetic dislocation: although it is the final poem of the work, it leaves us with little sense of fulfillment, promise, or transcendence.[41] Even mere closure is undercut by its patent circular connection with *Januarye*. E.K.'s "Generall Argument" has called attention to the formal calculation involved in Spenser's choice of January as his opening month by reminding the reader (who at that time presumably needed no reminding) that in England in 1579 the year begins in March. By starting with January, Spenser creates a structure for his calendar that is not synchronized with the actual seasonal pattern of the year either: his work ends at either the beginning or the middle of winter.[42] Theoretically, the more synchronized ending, in February, would permit firmer closure, but we see from the *Mutabilitie Cantos* that because of its proximity to March, February easily conveys instead the upbeat promise of renewal.[43] The January opening, on the other hand, since it neither marks nor heralds any experiential beginning or ending, offers pure cyclicity. The effect is to make Colin, as many critics have said, a figure who is locked in time.[44] I shall return to *December* after considering the harvest material that precedes it.

As a harvest eclogue *September* is full of paradoxes.[45] In a time of plenty, it is a poem of dearth (its final emblem bends the Narcissus myth to state the point: *inopem me copia fecit*); though a poem about ecclesiastical malfeasance, it offers, through its association with *Eclogues* I and IX and through its envelope of sympathy, a genuinely secular reading of experience. The darkness of Spenser's *Calender* is underscored by the failure to present a harvest celebration: *August* provides our last joyful noise, and even this is overmatched by Colin's elegant but plangent sestina. The harvest of *September* is purely conceptual, residing in what we know of the season rather than in what the poem describes. It resides also in the quality of experience related there. Diggon's "What shall I do, where shall I go?" (244) points to a moment (though an unhappy one) of "harvest," of summing up what has already happened in order to live with its implications.

Our very expectation of harvest is generically interesting since it is a georgic rather than a pastoral phenomenon, arising from the calendar form itself[46] and only indirectly related to the lives of the shepherd singers who are depicted in Spenser's work. Shepherds as such, of course, have no harvests. By focusing on herdsmen exclusively, Spenser avoids literal harvests altogether in the autumnal months of September, October and November. But he cannot avoid the reader's expectations of it. The subject comes up specifically only in the metaphorical language of *December,* where it is rather insistent. Colin talks of his personal promise as the "eare that budded faire" but now is burnt and blasted, as the seed that has become brake and bramble, then in the progressively less georgic figures of boughs that have blossomed but not borne fruit, and flowers that have withered (*Dec.* 99–112; see also 121–26). Harvests that both farmers and shepherds might benefit from are thus introduced finally in *December* only to be denied. From this point of view, then, the experience Colin recounts in *December* is indeed our experience of the *Calender* year: we as well as Colin have not known harvests.[47]

From another point of view, however, Colin's feeling of isolation is notably different from the reader's experience in the *Calender.* For us, a coalescing moment has occurred in *November,* when Colin in person sings the shepherds' lament for the death of Dido, a song he both presents to them and sings on their behalf.[48] *September* and *October* prepare the groundwork for this moment of community. *September* depicts the largest measure of accord in the three ecclesiastical eclogues: Diggon and Hobbinol, despite expressing different responses to corruption and immoral behavior, are not conceived in argument or debate terms, as were Piers and Palinode (in *Maye*) or Thomalin and Morrell (in *Julye*). Both know the behavior that Diggon describes to be examples of greed and injustice.[49] They do not react to the evil they both perceive in the same way, but the morality and sense of vulnerability they share enable them nevertheless to assert an important human and communal bond. The poem's resolution is not, like that of *Maye* or *Julye,* merely a formal papering over of differences.

The shepherd community is placed within a larger social context in *October.* As in *September* the two herdsmen in the dialogue share the same sense of what ought to be, although there is basis for debate in the contrast between Piers's idealism and Cuddie's awareness of the way things "really" are, whether the issue is how poets are ill-rewarded or how love affects inspiration. The eclogue strikes me as intentionally comic, an ironizing of the poetic issues, but other readers clearly do not agree, for it has given rise to many solemn pages of commentary. One sign of its ironic comedy is that both Piers and Cuddie get pastoral wrong,[50] Piers through converting the Virgilian *rota* into a derisive "class" statement—"Abandon then the base and viler clowne/Lyft up thy selfe out of the lowly dust" (37–38)—and Cuddie through failure to recognize what poems like *September* and *November* achieve:

But ah my corage cooles ere it be warme,[51]
For thy, content us in thys humble shade:
Where no such troublous tydes han us assayde,
Here we our slender pipes may safely charme. (116–118)

By suggesting that pastoral's function is to celebrate a place where bad things do not happen, these lines misrepresent the nature of Spenser's Virgilian tradition, especially as it has just been expressed in *September*.

I indicated earlier that *October* splits off the concern with poetry from *Eclogue* IX, but it is much more specific in its social statement than was Virgil, insisting throughout on what seems to be a social contract. Cuddie's songs, we are told, lead young people in play, feed their fancy, restrain their lust, beguile them into virtue. He would, like "Romish Tityrus" move through the *rota* to epic, but society has failed to supply him with models of epic virtue he can praise. True poetry is now disregarded, and its only avenue of acceptance, Cuddie says, is to express the folly and ribaldry that men currently value. In this way the first seventy-eight lines of the eclogue develop the social relation between poet and community, underlining the idea of "contract" by literalizing it as a transaction paid for with material goods—"But who rewards him ere the more for thy?/Or feedes him once the fuller by a graine?" (32–34)—or alternatively as transaction paid for with praise or glory. The next twenty-four lines of the poem turn inward since the poet is alienated from his society, but once there, the path is not clear: the moral and epistemological promise of neoplatonic love lures him on, but so does the equally compelling destructive "Tyrant love" of complaint poetry. The result seems to be a standoff. Colin, who became the subject of the dialogue at line 87, has both the potential to rise by love and the vulnerability (as we have seen) to be destroyed by it. Cuddie, apparently cut off from love as well as from patronage and popularity, will instead look to Bacchus for the inspiration to write high verse, but his drunken "corage" is short-lived and he feels he must settle for the protective shade of pastoral. Whether or not he understands its premises, pastoral will accept Cuddie's song: Piers pledges him a new kid when his goat gives birth—ironically, the very gesture of reciprocity or social contract whose absence Cuddie has been complaining about.

November's woodcut emphasizes the social context (the opening and closing stanzas) of this next poem by reversing the importance of its ode and frame. Colin is crowned with laurel in the foreground while a burial in taking place in the middleground (equidistant from the two shepherds and the church: death in the poem is as much a poetic as a religious event).[52] The shepherd's gesture (not enacted in the poem) acknowledges that Colin has successfully "bewayle[d]" Thenot's "woefull tene" (41); his songs both express and respond to the needs of the community. Becoming a laureate perhaps suggests the greater reach already intimated in *October*. A larger social function is suggested too by the promise of more than a traditional pastoral reward: if Colin's poem for Dido's death is as good as the ones he has composed for Rosalind, Thenot tells him, "Much greater gyfts for guerdon thou shalt gayne,/Then Kidde or Cosset, which I thee bynempt" (45–46).[53] Colin's inclusion in his society finds expression in the inclusiveness of the elegy itself. The subject is not merely Dido's death, but death as it touches all people, the reader as well as the fictional community of the poem. Nancy Jo Hoffman has analyzed how Spenser achieves this universality through a rhetoric that does not forgo its pastoral character;[54] for our purposes the aphoristic generalizations and in the simple distinction between human and other nature that she describes point to a quality of "summation." The poem finally offers an acceptance of both sadness and joy in the shape of human life and points to a harvest hereafter of the good one sows in this world.[55]

The *November* eclogue offers the most comprehensive version of pastoral in the *Calender*: the classical material is Christianized and the whole is fully communal. We are perceptibly in the presence of Virgil: the echoes from pastoral elegy from *Eclogues* V and X are particularly strong, and the poem seems a realization of the shepherds' need for Menalcas expressed in IX. Colin, whose art creates the elegy, is there to sing it himself, reassuming the social role given over in *Aprill* and *August* to other shepherds who sing his songs.[56] The public-private antithesis that exists between those two poems—since *Aprill* is a national song offered to the queen by Colin for her people, and *August* a personal love complaint—is synthesized in the *November* lament for a "private" shepherdess that is both personal and communal. The shepherds' admiration of Colin's verses in *August* of course suggests acceptance by his community, but the experience presented by the sestina remains individual pain. The pastoral elegy permits a temporary coming together of Colin's personal melancholy and his public voice; *December,* by returning to the love motif absent from *November,* returns to private pain, alienation, and disorder. It will not be until Spenser discovers marriage as a subject that he will be able to pull together these disparate forces. The *Epithalamion* allows Spenser to weave the lyric voice of the lover into a coherent social pattern,[57] but Colin's experience as it is recounted in *December* permits no hint of fertility at all. His denial of harvest is an implicit denial of the kind of death *November* depicts, one in which earthly life finds its reward.

The coalescence between Colin and his society in *November* defines a rich, satisfying poetic and thematic peak from which Colin's experience in *December* is a distinct falling off: he sits in "secreate shade alone," and make[s] of love his piteous mone" (5–6). The seasonal decorum one expects in imagery recapitulating the stages of his life is sacrificed to the "decemberness" of the season; the early as well as the late years are dominated by winter images. His "spring" takes place against a backdrop of Christmas games and gathering nuts. Decorum—or the reader's expectation—is perhaps further undermined, as his old age (if that's what it is), full of "rigorous rage," "blustering blast[s]," "careful cold" and "no sonne," is capped with a refrain having the rhythm of a lullaby.:[58] "Winter is come, that blowes the bitter blaste,/And after Winter dreerie death doth hast" (143–44). The sense and rhythm are echoed in more terminal form several lines later: "Winter is come, that blowes the balefull breath,/And after Winter commeth timely death" (149–50). Even in his time-locked[59] isolation, however, Colin's final words in the poem reinstate the bonds that have defined him: his farewells are to his sheep, his friend, and his love.

Friend Hobbinol is fittingly invoked for the final curtain; he has not actually appeared in the *Calender* since *September,* but has remained an important presence. Just as Cuddie in *August* and *October* is a figure of Colin, Piers in *October* and Thenot in *November* are figures of Hobbinol,[60] taking on his particular asssociation with shepherd values. It is important for the design of the *Shepheardes Calender* that Colin and some Hobbinol-figure come together in *November:* Thenot's strength here as a substitute is that he evokes the larger idea, "community," of which Hobbinol's "friendship" has formed the major part. The penultimate eclogue offers a momentary coalescence of the concerns of the two figures. Alone with *Aprill* (where Thenot also hears Colin's song) *November* updates the idea of the shepherd community that classical pastoral implicitly celebrates.[61] Being calendrically a moment in time, however, it yields to the next moment: the discordant *December* of a solitary Colin.[62] The play between the private and public motives of poetry that have been woven into the pastoral fabric of the *Calender* yields to the voice of lyric complaint.

Yet Colin's private pain, though the sum of his experience as presented in *December*, is not the sum of the reader's experience of the eclogue-book as a whole. At the end we must separate the alienated Colin, whose blossoms have borne no fruit, not only from his friend Hobbinol's Virgilian stance but from the voice of the Poet of the *Shepheardes Calender* as well. The epilogue presents a Post whose understanding of his art and his society allows him to hope that he has created in this poem of zodiac and time something that, like classical literature (though the nod here is to Ovid and Horace rather than Virgil), "shall continewe till the worlds dissolution." Time for Colin is the measure of frustration, but time for the Poet of the *Shepheardes Calender* is the precious medium of civilization.

University of Toronto

NOTES

1. Most notably treated in Annabel Patterson, *Pastoral and Ideology: Virgil to Valéry* (Berkeley: University of California Press, 1979).

2. See Michael C. J. Putnam, *Virgil's Pastoral Art: Studies in the Eclogues* (Princeton: Princeton University Press, 1970), pp. 309, 340.

3. I have discussed this material in "Spenser's Virgilian Pastoral: The Case for *September*," *Spenser Studies* X (1990), edd. Patrick Cullen and Thomas P. Roche, Jr. (New York: AMS Press, 1994), 1–16, especially with respect to Hobbinol's role as a classical shepherd.

4. But see Patrick Cullen, *Spenser, Marvell and Renaissance Pastoral* (Cambridge: Harvard University Press, 1970), pp. 83–84, on Hobbinol as a classical shepherd. John D. Bernard is also very good on this material—*Ceremonies of Innocence: Pastoralism in the Poetry of Edmund Spenser* (Cambridge, Cambridge University Press, 1989), pp. 52, 58–61—separating pastoral singers as contented men (Theocritus' Lycidas and Virgil's Tityrus) from noble suffers and exiles (Theocritus' Daphnis and Virgil's Meliboeus).

5. My text is from *The Yale Edition of the Shorter Poems of Edmund Spenser*, edd. William A. Oram et al. (New Haven: Yale University Press, 1989). The tendency of later poems to reinterpret E 1's situation in terms of greater sympathy is discussed in "Spenser's Virgilian Pastoral."

6. As noted in the Yale ed., intro. to *June*, 107. Meliboeus in E 1 is of course also a pastoral exile, but his view of the situation cannot be summed up in these "epic" lines. The herdsman Daphnis in *Idyll* I complicates the issue of heroism at the very inception of the genre.

7. Paul Alpers sensitively explores the extent to which shepherds sing for one another in "Theocritean Bucolics and Virgilian Pastoral," *Arethusa*, 23 (1990), 32–34.

8. "The underlying terms—solace and community—are connected with Menalcas in E 9, and though Spenser's complaining lover seems an injected note, two of the four fragments interpolated in E 9 are love poetry.

9. See the discussion of the opening of E 6 as a Callimachean *recusatio* in Wendel Clausen, "Callimachus and Latin Poetry," *Greek, Roman and Byzantine Studies*, 5 (1964), 181–96. Especially important is Clausen's insistence that E 6 denies the necessity of the very *rota* that Virgil has become associated with. Alan Cameron, *Callimachus and His Critics* (Princeton: Princeton University Press, 1995) is suggestively revisionist on the meaning of the Callimachean lines themselves.

10. See Thomas Greene, *The Light in Troy: Imitation and Discovery in Renaissance Poetry* (New Haven: Yale University Press, 1982) on *aggiornamento,* p. 41, and my discussion below.

11. Tityrus' invitation is of course originally made (E 1) at a time of political and social upheaval. Spenser's replacing the E 1-E 9 echo in *June* and *September* can perhaps be attributed to calendrical imperatives. See below.

12. Although we are likely to associate pastoral with happiness, the shepherd-lovers in Theocritus and Virgil are largely unsatisfied: of the *Idylls*, perhaps only Lycidas in his song in *Idyll* 7 is happy, and of the *Eclogues*, the two most notable lovers, Corydon and Gallus, are unhappy. Colin's inflection is Petrarchan, but the general stance has classical support.

13. See Robert Coleman, ed. *Vergil: Eclogues* Cambridge University Pres, 1977), p. 203, and Alpers, in *Arethusa*, pp. 34–37. "More vexed" because it introduces problems of masking, biographical relevance, etc.

14. See John Van Sickle, *The Design of Virgil's Bucolics,* Filologia e critica, 24 (Rome: Edizioni dell' Ateneo & Bizzari, 1974) on E 4, and e.g., Gian Biagio Conte, *The Rhetoric of Imitation: Genre and Poetic Memory in Virgil and Other Poets,* trans. Charles Segal (Ithaca: Cornell University Press, 1986), for E 10.

15. That *Aprill* is Spenser's Fourth Eclogue has been noticed before: see, e.g., Cullen, p. 112.

16. Putnam, however, considers E 8 to be a "poem about the possibilities of bucolic verse, as form and as idea" (p. 290). Insofar as *November* is "about" poetry, it repeats in a more somber mode the poet's social role of *Aprill.* My *September* piece argues a reading of that poem as Spenser's Ninth Eclogue.

17. Bernard also compares *June* to E 1 and E 10 (p. 60).

18. Important work has been done on Renaissance imitation by Thomas Greene, *Light in Troy,* and G. W. Pigman, III, "Versions of Imitation in the Renaissance," *Renaissance Quarterly,* 33 (1980), 1–33; on classical imitation by Gian Biagio Conte, *The Rhetoric of Imitation,* and Patricia Rosenmeyer, *The Poetics of Imitation: Anacreon and the Anacreontic Tradition* (Cambridge: Cambridge University Press, 1992), pp. 62–73.

19. Definition: expressions of sympathy occurring at the beginning and end of the poem. Discussed in *Spenser Studies* XI.

20. See *Complete Prose Works of John Milton,* ed. Don M. Wolfe (New Haven: Yale University Press, 1953), Vol. 1, 325n6, for a relevant September-November confusion.

21. The idea of 9–10 doubling seems to me more likely than a full correspondence of the name-number possibilities because *September* and *October* do not have strong connections with E 7 and E 8. E 7, however, like E 9, takes place in Virgil's own northern Italy, and there may be an ironic contrast intended between the duo Hobbinol and Diggon Davie and the famous description of the speakers in E 7, who are *Arcades ambo*. The specific use in E 5, 7, and 9 of Italian and Roman material may help account for Spenser's having chosen May, July and September for his ecclesiastical themes.

22. See the comments by Mary Parmenter quoted in *Variorum* VII, 243, and for somewhat more detail. Alexander Philip, *The Calendar: Its History, Structure and Improvement* (Cambridge, Cambridge University Press, 1921), pp. 21–22. Lynn Staley Johnson, *The Shepheardes Calender: An Introduction* (University Park, PA: Pennsylvania State University Press, 1990), esp. pp. 181–86, 202–40), discusses the calendear form, including a connection with the Roman calendar through Ovid's *Fasti* (p. 188).

23. Frances A. Yates, *Occult Philosophy in the Elizabethan Age* (London: Routledge and Kegal Paul, 1979), p. 104.

24. *Shorter Poems,* p. 24. Numa Pompilius of course lived hundreds of years before Caesar.

25. See, e.g., the discussion of numerical analyses of the *Eclogues* in Van Sickle, pp. 20–24. For Spenser, see Maren–Sophie Rostvig's article in the *Spenser Encyclopedia,* gen. ed. A. C. Hamilton (Toronto: University of Toronto Press, 1990), s.v. number symbolism, tradition of.

26. S. K. Heninger, *Touches of Sweet Harmony: Pythagorean Cosmology and Renaissance Poetics* (San Mariono: Huntington Library Press, 1974), p. 313; discussion pp. 311–13.

27. For the statement to this effect on p. 156, Heninger footnotes Joannes Goropius, "Hieroglyphica," in *Opera* (Antwerp, 1580), p. 154, whose "long passage unfolding the relationship of 12 to 4" has a marginal gloss that explains "the duodecad encompasses the idea of the entire universe" (p. 196 n 26).

28. Most deviations from these numbers seem likewise based on the *tetractys:* the *Argonautica* and *Paradise Regained* are in 4 books; the *Pharsalia's* 8 may be 2 × 4. Dante's 100 cantos is a comparable symbolic number. Homer himself probably predates this kind of thinking; his 24 books—and therefore the convention—are the creation of his Hellenistic editors.

29. One might also consider the importance of Sannazaro's *Arcadia* with its slight narrative. David Kalstone, *Sidney's Poetry: Context and Interpretations* (New York: 1965; W. W. Norton, 1970), describes the work as presenting a conflation of Virgil's pastoral-poet with Petrarch's poet-lover (p. 23).

30. See Lee Piepho, "The Organization of Mantuan's *Adulescentia* und Spenser's *Shepheardes Calender:* A Comparison," in *Acta Conventus Neo-Latini Bononiensis: Proceedings of the Fourth International Congress of Neo-Latin Studies,* ed. R. J. Schoeck (Binghampton, NY: Medieval and Renaissance Texts and Studies, 1985), pp. 577–82. The principle seems influenced by standard allegorizations of the *Aeneid*.

31. Discussions of the circle and line in the *Shepheardes Calender* can be found in Isabel G. MacCaffrey, "Allegory and Pastoral in the *Shepheardes Calender,* in *Critical*

Essays on Spenser from ELH (Baltimore, 1969; Johns Hopkins University Press, 1970; 117–20), and Donald Cheney, "The Circular Argument of *The Shepheardes Calender*," in *Unfolded Tales: Essays on Renaissance Romance,* edd. George M. Logan and Gordon Teskey (Ithaca, NY: Cornell University Press, 1989), 137–61.

32.   In Virgil the same basic recessed pattern supports several different grids of meaning. See the analysis in A. J. Boyle, ed. *The Eclogues of Virgil* (Melbourne: Hawthorn Press, 1976), pp. 12–14.

33.   See A. C. Hamilton, "The Grene Path Way to Life': Spenser's *Shepheardes Calender* as Pastoral," in *The Elizabethan Theatre* VIII, ed. George R. Hibbard (Port Credit, Ontario: P. D. Meany, 1982), for diagram (p. 14) and discussion (pp. 6–8). H. Neville Davies, "Spenser's *Shepheardes Calender:* The Importance of 'November,' " *Cahiers elisabéthains,* 20 (1981), 35–48, gives a slightly different diagram, taken from Marianne Brown, "Finely Framed and Strongly Trussed Up Together: A Structural Approach to Spenser's *Shepheardes Calender,"* unpubl. diss., University of Oslo, 1978.

34.   The connection between the two may find support in the old *"Fishes* haske" crux of *Nov.* (line 16), since Pisces is the sign for February.

35. And to this division may every thing herein be reasonably applyed: A few onely except, whose speciall purpose and meaning I am not privie to" ("Generall Argument," p. 23).

36.   See Brooks Otis, *Virgil: A Study in Civilized Poetry* (Oxford: Oxford University Press, 1964), pp. 128–31; Van Sickle, *Design;* Paul J. Alpers, *The Singer of the Eclogues: A Study of Virgilian Pastoral* (Berkeley: University of California Press, 1979), pp. 107–13; Alastair Fowler, *Triumphal Forms: Structural Patterns in Elizabethan Poetry* (Cambridge: Cambridge University Press, 1970); Hamilton, "Grene Path Way," p. 14.

37.   See Judith Deborah Haber, *Pastoral and the Poetics of Self-Contradiction: Theocritus to Marvell* (Cambridge: Cambridge University Press, 1994).

38.   Otis, p. 128; Boyle, p. 13.

39.   See Greene, pp. 39–40, on *contaminatio.*

40.   The *tone* of this harvest is therefore considerably darkened by its absence from what the *Shepheardes Calender* sees as the summery month of August; the *Kalender of Shepherdes* lists the autumn months as August, September, and October, and like the *Mutabilitie Cantos* talks of it as a month of harvest as well as heat (see Cullen, pp. 138–39, citing *Kal. of Shep.,* III, 10–11, 18. Spenser's scheme here seems English: L. S. Johnson, on the basis of English kalendars and almanacs from Elizabeth's accession to 1580 (p. 182 n), says that autumn or "harvest-time" meant September, October, and November (p. 184).

41.   Alternative readings are offered in David R. Shore, *Spenser and the Poetics of Pastoral: A Study in the World of Colin Clout* (Montreal: McGill-Queen's University Press, 1985), esp. p. 98, who finds Colin's acceptance "satisfying," and Paul Alpers, "Pastoral and the Domain of Lyric in Spenser's *Shepheardes Calender,"* in *Representing the Renaissance,* ed. Stephen Greenblatt (Berkeley: 1985; University of California Press, 1988), who notes the increased richness and fuller acceptance of Colin here as compared to *Januarye* (p. 176). Sophie-Maren Rostvig's exceptionally "positive" reading in *"The Shepheardes Calender*—A Structural Analysis," *Renaissance and Modern Studies,* 13 (1969), 58, can serve as a caveat against making numerological patterns govern one's understanding of a text.

42.   Several different schemes seem subterranean presences: it would be "middle" of winter for the *Kalender of Shepherdes*, "beginning" of winter for a calender which commences in March. Spenser's *Calender*, by starting autumn in September and winter in December, thus reflects March calendar divisions, which in turn correspond to the astronomical workings of the year; beginning winter at the solstice (around 12 December old style) and beginning autumn at the equinox (11 September).

43.   See especially Sherman Hawkins, "Mutabilitie and the Cycle of the Months," in *Form and Convention in the Poetry of Edmund Spenser*, ed. William Nelson (New York: Columbia University Press, 1961), pp. 76–102. Spenser's lusty old man in the *Mutabilitie Cantos* and the conflict between age and youth in *Februarie* reflect these seasonal realities. *November*, as the poem corresponding to *Februarie*, is given a similar seasonal ambiguity by its linkage to the harvst themes. See Johnson on E. K.'s gloss on the emblem for *November*: "he likens death to harvest . . . by calling it the 'grene path way to lyfe' " (134).

44.   To name several: A. C. Hamilton, "The Argument of Spenser's *Shepheardes Calender*," ELH, 23 (1956), 175–76; Robert A. Durr, "Spenser's Calendar and Christian Time," ELH, 24 (1957), 290–99; MacCaffrey, "Allegory and Pastoral," p. 121.

45.   Cullen, pp. 140–42. Note that from a "weather" point of view, this is probably a November poem. The description of lines 49–51 can hardly refer to September in England.

46.   The early calendrical work, Hesiod's *Works and Days*, is the origin of georgic. Bruce Thornton, "Rural Dialectic: Pastoral, Georgic and the *Shepheardes Calender*," *Spenser Studies* IX (1988), edd. Patrick Cullen and Thomas P. Roche, Jr. (New York: AMS Press, 1991), 1–20, is interesting on the early and constant contamination of the two traditions.

47.   Alpers, "Domain," p. 176: "Diggon Davy in 'September,' Cuddie in 'October,' and Colin Clout himself are all speakers whose experience has thwarted them."

48.   See Alpers, *Singer of the Eclogues*, pp. 127–28, on song for Gallus.

49.   For difference over such matters in *Julye*, see Morrell's statement late in the poem (209–12).

50.   Virgil's E 10, incidentally, is slyly comic about Gallus' misunderstanding of pastoral.

51.   Epic and tragedy seem specifically what "corage" is necessary for.

52.   The emblem, *La mort ny mord*, refers as much to poetry itself as to the fate of the character who is mourned. It is Marot's own emblem and signature (Renwick, in *Variorum*, p. 416).

53.   These lines are actually a translation from Marot, and in turn have their basis in *Eclogue* V. See Nancy Jo Hoffman, *Spenser's Pastorals: The Shepheardes Calender and "Colin Clout"* (Baltimore: Johns Hopkins University Press, 1977), pp. 57–58, for an analysis of the differences.

54.   Hoffman, pp. 53–61, esp. 57–59.

55.   Though this transcendence is specifically Christian, the pattern of death and apotheosis appears in Virgil's E 5. Bernard's interpretation of *November* in his generally fine reading of a Virgilian *Shepheardes Calender* is less sympathetic: "Nowhere do we have any sense that Colin has been reconciled to life, even a life that includes recognition of death" (p. 73).

56.   That others sing his songs is of course yet another, and important, social role. *November* refocuses the social energies on their source: the relation of the poet himself to his community.

57.   Narrative in *FQ* III allows Spenser to include some of the "complaint" elements that the *Epithalamion* naturally omits (unless one reads it together with the *Amoretti* as a single work).

58.   Is this a sign of the disorder of his life or–in *Erlkönig* fashion–of the seductiveness of death?

59.   The cycle of the years encourages us to read not only from January to December but to continue from December to January.

60.   See Bernard's discussion of Cuddie as a Colin-figure, pp. 73–74. Piers's communal persona in *October* may mediate the difference between Hobbinol and Diggon Davie presented in *September,* since Piers can be associated with each (with Hobbinol here, and with Diggon on the basis of his role in *Maye*).

61.   *Aprill* updates through topical allusion, local references and native literary traditions, *November* mainly through Christianizing pastoral elegy. In addition to its parallels with E 5 *November* seems particularly related to E 9's *solacia,* as I have argued above.

62.   E 10 also contrasts Gallus' alienation with the Poet's inclusion in the shepherd community.

SHERRI GELLER

You Can't Tell a Book by its Contents: (Mis)Interpretation in/of Spenser's *The Shepheardes Calender*

The ostensibly supplementary material in the 1579 *Shepheardes Calender* decenters the eclogues and emphasizes the interpretive enterprise. E.K.'s critical apparatus and the presentational strategies in the first edition are devised to implicate the reader both analogically and experientially in an interpretive *mise en abyme*: the reader, E.K., and pastoral figures encounter semantic uncertainty and attempt to impose their versions of semantic stability on another's text. Appropriative maneuvers in the apparatus and the eclogues, misinterpreting shepherds, E.K.'s dubious commentary, and the *Calender*'s equivocating presentational strategies destabilize both politically sensitive and innocuous interpretive activity in and outside of the *Calender*.

*I*N 1579, WHEN THE ANONYMOUS new poet of *The Shepheardes Calender* assigned himself the pseudonym Immerito, the first critic of the eclogues signed his prefatory epistle with the less–than–enlightening initials E.K. and thereby incited the ongoing controversy over his identity. Arguments asserting that E.K. was a real person or that he is a fictional construct range from the convincing to the convoluted, and not everyone agrees which is which. No one, of course, disagrees about who the anonymous poet really was, or that he "really was." Not too surprisingly, the consensus regarding Spenser's authorship of the eclogues has contributed to the situating of Spenser/ Immerito in an undifferentiated extratextual/paratextual realm, a realm in which the world outside of the text is collapsed into the fictive reality created in the *Calender*'s critical apparatus. Spenser and Immerito are routinely equated by those who regard the pseudonym and E.K.'s references to the new poet as no more than evasive substitutes for the name of a real person. In these critics' discussions, E.K. can be Spenser, Harvey, Spenser and Harvey, Edward Kirke, Fulke Greville, Anon., or a fiction (usually said to have been created by Spenser), but Immerito is always simply Spenser. This is so even though a related link between author and character—that between Spenser and Colin Clout—is regularly problematized nowadays. My analysis justifies the similar dissociating of Spenser and the character Immerito and further substantiates Michael McCanles's claim that "[i]t is part of the fiction of *The Shepheardes Calender* that E.K.'s glosses and commentary are not part of the fiction."[1]

I will demonstrate that the author(s) of the critical apparatus and other paratextual elements (whoever he or they were) devised E.K. and Immerito's putatively nonfictional relationship, E.K.'s textual contributions, and the presentational strategies in the first edition so that the reader would be both analogically and experientially implicated in an interpretive *mise en abyme:* the reader of the 1579 *Calender,* E.K. in the critical apparatus, and pastoral figures in the eclogues all encounter semantic uncertainty and attempt to impose their versions of semantic stability on another's text. This *mise en abyme* in the *Calender* addresses the difficulties involved in communicating meaning, and the relative ease with which meaning or intention may be misconstrued or disregarded, the discourse then being appropriated for self-interested ends.[2] E.K.'s and the pastoral speakers' appropriative maneuvers depict the consequences of the interpreter's authority over a "long time furre estraunged" author's text ("Epistle," 192)[3] and over pastoral interlocutors who are present to affirm or deny constructions of meaning. As a corollary, the 1579 *Calender* as material object and as text confronts the reader with interpretive challenges that expose the potential fallibility involved in appropriating segments of another's discourse and the virtual impossibility of uniting that discourse's disparate parts to form a coherent whole.

Although any individual gloss may be designated too blunt by one critic and obfuscatory by another, those who maintain that Spenser created E.K. (possibly with Harvey's assistance) and those who envision Spenser/Immerito collaborating with a real commentator generally agree that the apparatus guides, misguides, and otherwise interferes in the reader's interaction with the eclogues, at times restricting but not refusing access to the political and religious subtext. While for many interpretive approaches the apparatus necessarily serves a subsidiary role, and we have learned much about the *Calender* by viewing the eclogues through the veil of the glosses, the presentational strategies and content of the apparatus and other ostensibly

supplementary elements invalidate the standard hierarchizing of text
and paratext: the paratext establishes the *mise-en-abyme* structure that
decenters the eclogues, emphasizes the interpretive enterprise, and
compels the reader to misinterpret or be confused by textual appearances. The parallel interpretive difficulties experienced by the reader,
E.K., and pastoral speakers emphatically suggest that the relationship
between E.K. and Immerito is as much a part of the fiction as the
relationship between Hobbinol and Colin.

It is plausible that the *Calender* thematizes inaccurate and dubious
interpretive activity and implicates the reader in order to criticize
the mechanisms for censorship in early modern England, the prospect
or exertion of control over direct and indirect public commentary
on issues the state deemed sensitive, such as the thoroughly unpopular
proposed marriage between Elizabeth and the French Catholic Duc
d'Alençon, under consideration in 1579. Those who are familiar with
the *Calender's* history know the *Calender* was entered in the Statio-
ners' Register about four months after Johh Stubbs overtly, anony-
mously, and unsuccessfully attempted to counsel the queen in his
pamphlet entitled *The Discoverie of a Gaping Gulf, Whereinto England
is Like to be Swallowed by an other French mariage, if the Lord forbid not
the banes, by letting her Majestie see the sin and punishment thereof.* As a
response to the necessity for covert speech and perhaps to Stubbs's
imprisonment and loss of a hand,[4] the *Calender's* duplicative strategy
of indirection, pastoral accompanied by an often misleading commentary, differs in intent from and is not as conspicuous as well-
known strategies like the beast fable, allegory, historical poetry, and
pastoral without annotations, or the usually disingenuous disclaimer
of topicality so typical in the period.[5] In fact, it is such strategies and
disclaimers that the *Calender's* apparatus appears to counteract. In his
prefatory epistle, E.K. announces rather than disavows the presence
of potentially objectionable material in the eclogues: the new poet,
he says, "chose rather to unfold great matter of argument covertly,
then professing it, . . . which moved him rather in Æglogues, then
other wise to write" (147–50). Contemporary readers inured to the
traditions of pastoral hardly needed E.K. to tell them this. What may
be seen in the *Calender's* fictive reality as E.K.'s indiscretion is ampli-
fied when he at times "professes it" for Immerito, revealing an eclogue's personal, moral, or religious matter (disclosures which,
however, at times obliquely or explicitly disavow other, more politically volatile, interpretations).[6] E.K. therefore appears to be a potentially more harmful than helpful exegete, for he is not in the
comparatively innocuous position of a commentator who is tempo-
rally distant from an author and the reasons why that author implemented a strategy of fictional displacement. By revealing that the

poet is unfolding great matter of argument covertly, E.K.'s remark in effect challenges censors and other readers to search for objectionable topical comments and read or, one might say, misread into the eclogues a topicality that Immerito may not have intended. Moreover, E.K.'s own topical reading is rendered questionable when the apparatus indicates that he is not fully, and perhaps not very, informed about Immerito's intentions even though he initially claims to be "privy to [the poet's] counsell and secret meaning" ("Epistle," 188–89). The unreliability of some of E.K.'s remarks has of course not gone unnoticed, but on a larger scale, readers cannot ascertain whether many suggestive glosses, specifically those in which E.K. does not directly acknowledge his ignorance of the poet's meaning, regularly or even often impart information obtained from Immerito. The dubiousness of E.K.'s commentary, the *Calender*'s equivocating presentational strategies, and the sometimes misinterpreting shepherds destabilize both politically sensitive and innocuous interpretive activity in and outside of the *Calender*.

THE ELUSIVE PRESENTATION OF *THE SHEPHEARDES CALENDER*[7]

The reader first encounters the *Calender*'s miscommunicative strategies not in the new poet's subtext-ridden eclogues nor in E.K.'s apparatus, but rather on the peculiarly unallusive title page, and this in a text filled with allusive presentational elements. The arrangement of the woodcuts, glosses, and eclogues and the typography in the 1579 *Calender* suggest that someone, possibly Spenser, helped prepare the first edition so that it would resemble, among other things, the well-known almanac entitled *The Kalender of Sheepehards* and annotated editions of the classics. As some critics have pointed out, this unconventional and incompatible combination would have confused potential readers skimming through the book.[8] Significantly, the title page provides no clarification, for it evades rather than assists in identifying resemblances to other texts and traditions, and it contradicts the inconsistent visual clues in the rest of the volume.

Ruth Samson Luborsky, who surveys contemporaneous English and French title pages, observes that the *Calender*'s is "inappropriately bare for the kind of book it announces, when judged by contemporary standards," but "would look conventional if it had a border." "Every other element," she says, "is unremarkable: the three fonts, triadic arrangement, printer's ornament and device are all characteristic of many English books of the time and typical of Singleton's house style."[9] Although the *Calender's* title page resembles many others in some ways, its spareness disrupts the connection to the almanac: the titles are suggestively similar, and the author's name does not appear on either title page, but the illustration and the conventional decorative border on the *Kalender's* distinguish that page from the *Calender's*, which lacks both (figures 1 and 2).[10] Luborsky notes that some title pages in editions of Marot and Ronsard are also spare, but the French title pages do not vary the font size. A more crucial difference is that the title page in the 1553 annotated edition of Ronsard's *Amours,* the edition to which Luborsky refers, names both the author and the commentator (figure 3). While plenty of sixteenth-century books are anonymous, the absence of the author's and commentator's names on the *Calender's* title page disrupts the connection to early modern annotated editions, on whose title pages both names are regularly mentioned.

Unlike anonymous illuminators of medieval manuscript margins, commentators are established as significant contributors to the text when they are announced on title pages in conjunction with the author, as a brief survey supplementing the 1553 *Amours* will demonstrate. In the 1542 Antwerp edition of Virgil's works—the one that Spenser most likely referred to when he composed *Virgils Gnat*[11]—the title page privileges Virgil by placing his name at the top in an imposing type size, but it adds immediately below this the names of the commentators (figure 4). In the 1564 Venetian edition of Dante's *Comedia,* the commentators achieve prominence by means of type size, uppercase letters for their names and Dante's, and the relegation of the title, in a smaller type size, to the end of this title (figure 5).[12] In the 1578 Venetian edition of Sannazaro's *Arcadia,* whose layout of woodcuts, eclogues, and glosses is emulated in the *Calender,* the commentator's name appears after the author's name and title, and it is the only one in both upper and lowercase, but attention is drawn to it by its location on one line separated from the series of lines surrounding it (figure 6). Also, more noticeably in the 1571 edition than the 1578 reprint, boldface type differentiates the author's title and the author's and commentator's names from the other information in the complete title.[13] The title page in the 1515 Basel edition of Erasmus's *Moriae Encomium* mentions the commentator's qualifications and praises his annotations highly (figure 7).[14] Early modern readers of annotated texts would have been familiar with this type of title-page advertising.[15]

In contrast, the *Calender*'s title page does not encourage readers to expect the poetry of a famous author and the helpful annotations of a well-known or praiseworthy scholar. It names only the dedicatee and the printer, Philip Sidney and Hugh Singleton. In August 1579, Singleton printed Stubbs's *Gaping Gulf*, to which Elizabeth responded by ordering the confiscation of all copies and the arrest of the author, publisher, and printer. While Stubbs and his presumed publisher had their right hands chopped off in the marketplace at Westminster in November,[16] Singleton was for an unknown reason pardoned and released from prison in October. When the anonymous *Calender* appeared in December, Singleton's prominent name on the title page, at the bottom but in the same large type size and font as the title (figure 1), would have incited speculation about the text's topicality. His clientele probably expected the book to be like the usual fare available at his shop, which, Bruce Smith notes, included "ballads, Puritan theological tracts, and polemical pamphlets. . . . Hugh Singleton was not a 'literary' printer at all."[17] The other name on the title page would have fostered similar speculation: Sidney was a prominent member of the Earl of Leicester's faction at court, which opposed the French marriage.[18]

Like Sidney but in a different capacity, Spenser was connected to Leicester's faction,[19] and so Spenser's own relatively unknown name might have supplemented the suggestive infamy of Singleton's and eminence of Sidney's. The absence of Spenser's name performs a similar suggestive function, but the absence of both his name and the commentator's hinders rather than complements the allusiveness of the rest of the presentation. In other words, the title page does not forthrightly communicate the *Calender*'s unusual status as an annotated edition of a new poet's work.

Because of the many traditions the physical volume alludes to, and because the title page evades similar allusiveness, potential readers of the 1579 *Calender* who glanced at or even examined carefully the title page and the overall presentation could not thereby identify exactly what they held in their hands. Those who purchased the book may have related what they did (not) learn from the title page and from skimming to what they learned once they began to read, first from Immerito's prefatory poem and then from E.K.'s prefatory epistle. What they may have realized, however, is that the *Calender*'s evasive maneuvers extend into the prefatory material: Immerito's poem and E.K.'s epistle equivocate about the identification of and the distinction between the poet and the commentator.

On the verso of the title page, in the prefatory poem, the anonymous poet repeatedly prompts readers to expect his name but then substitutes epithets and periphrases. In the first stanza, where the book is referred to as a "child whose parent is unkent" (2), "whose parent is" could have been followed by a proper noun (if it rhymed). "Unkent," which means "unknown," keeps the poet's name from becoming known.[20] In the second and third stanzas, the parent/poet instructs his child/book to answer periphrastically questions about its maternity and paternity: "And asked, who thee forth did bring,/ A shepheards swaine saye did thee sing" (8–9); "But if that any aske thy name,/Say thou wert base begot with blame" (13–14). A feminized shepherd's swain brings forth or gives birth to the book, while the father who basely begot the book is excluded by the passive verb "wert begot." The poet withholds his name a fourth time when he exchanges the anonymity of the title page for the pseudonym Immerito, which alleges his unworthiness to be named. On the recto and verso of the first page, then, the book draws attention to the missing name five times. As Wendy Wall observes, "[T]he *Calender* is framed to highlight the absent presence of its author."[21]

E.K.'s epistle, which begins on the page facing Immerito's prefatory poem, is also (un)responsive to those who ask the poet's name and probably more confusing than informative for readers in 1579—except for E.K.'s good friend Gabriel Harvey. The congeniality of the "verie special and singular good friend" E.K.'s salutation to "the most excellent and learned both Orator and Poete, Mayster Gabriell Harvey," suggests that Harvey can translate E.K.'s opening references to "our Colin clout" (5) and "our new Poete" (11), but for other readers the epistle is a closed and misleading discourse. In the first sentence, the parallel phrases that follow the two colons imply that the second "whom," like the first, will precede the name of a poet or scholar, but it is instead followed by "our Colin clout," the only pastoral persona that does not have a referent:

> Uncouthe unkiste, Sayde the olde famous Poete Chaucer: whom for his excellencie and wonderfull skil in making, his scholler Lidgate, a worthy scholler of so excellent a maister, calleth the Loadestarre of our Language: and whom our Colin clout in his Aeglogue calleth Tityrus the God of shepheards, comparing hym to the worthines of the Roman Tityrus Virgile.
>
> (1–7)

E.K. links the English and Roman Tityruses to Chaucer and Virgil but does not link Colin to a poet, not even to the unidentified new poet of the salutation. We have perhaps become too used to thinking of Colin Clout as a Spenserian poetic persona to note that readers in 1579 might sooner identify him as Skeltonic, at least until "in his Aeglogue" is added, which would disrupt the reference to Skelton while not specifying one to the new poet.[22] Although readers are free to assume a connection between the new poet and "our Colin clout," the epistle withholds until the third page of footnote-sized print the information that Colin is the new poet's pastoral persona: "As for Colin, under whose person the Authour selfe is shadowed . . ." (141–42). The first sentence therefore misleads and declines to inform by means of a "missing" parallel element.

Even the salutation is misleading in that it does not admit until the last word that there are two presences in the text. The salutation's first line initially seems to be a third address to Sidney from Immerito, for it reproduces the qualities assigned to the dedicatee on the title page and in the prefatory poem: the book is "Entitled/TO THE NOBEL AND VERTU-/ous Gentleman most worthy of all titles/ both of learning and chevalrie M./Philip Sidney"; according to Immerito's poem, the book is supposed to present itself "To him that is the president/Of noblesse and of chevalree" (3–4); and the first line of the salutation is "To the most excellent and learned both." Moreover, the salutation's first line is in the same typeface as the poem and on a facing page, suggesting a continuity between the two and hence the same voice (figures 8 and 9). The second line, which names the dedicatee, disrupts the continuity by means of content and typography: the black letter type reads, "Orator and Poete, Mayster Gabriell Harvey, his." In the next two lines and the smaller typeface of the body of the epistle, someone with the initials E.K. curiously commends to his very good friend Harvey not his work but rather the "good lyking" of that work: "verie special and singular good frend E.K. commen-/deth the good lyking of this his labour." Although the reference to Harvey admits a second dedicatee into the text, E.K.'s initials and the pseudonym Immerito could at this point refer to the same person, since E.K. does not specify his labor. Readers who skimmed through the book beforehand and noted the glosses might expect to find at least two contributors as they would in most annotated texts, but since self-annotation was not unheard of they might just as well have found one, E.K./Immerito.[23] Only after two more lines are there definitely two laborers: "and the patronage of the/new Poete." It is now clear that E.K. did not write the poetry, yet the labor he has performed in connection with the poetry is not here made known.

While expecting E.K. to identify his labor in the salutation may be expecting too much from a salutation, the epistle's second and third sentences strategically continue to withhold information about E.K.'s role. Like the first sentence, which by means of a "missing" parallel element obscures the relationship between the new poet and Colin Clout, the second excludes a parallel clause that would read "it serves well my purpose" and replaces it with "so very well taketh place," which takes E.K. out of his place in the parallel construction: "Which proverbe, myne owne good friend Ma. Harvey, as in that good old Poete it served well Pandares purpose, for the bolstering of his baudy brocage, so very well taketh place in this our new Poete, who for that he is uncouthe (as said Chaucer) is unkist, and unknown to most men, is regarded but of few" (7–13). The name Pandarus is not explicitly paired with the initials E.K., just as the pastoral persona Colin was not paired with the name of a poet. Recognition of E.K.'s Pandarus-like labor as go-between for the poet and the public is further postponed in the third sentence: "But I dout not, so soone as his name shall come into the knowledg of men, and his worthines be sounded in the tromp of fame, but that he shall be not onely kiste, but also beloved of all, embraced of the most, and wondered at of the best" (13–17). The subjects "his name" and "his worthines" suppress E.K.'s agency in the act of publication. The passive constructions reveal who will kiss, love, embrace, and wonder at the poet, but not who will announce his worthiness or his name, the latter of which remains "unkent."

What appears to be E.K.'s excursus on Immerito's word "unkent" figuratively situates the poet on both the masculine and feminine sides of the relationship for which Pandarus acts as go-between, since Pandarus says, "Unknowe, unkist" to Troilus,[24] and it is Criseyde who is "unknown to most men" before her relationship with Troilus. In the third sentence, the gender-blended poet shifts toward the feminine as he, pandered to the public, becomes like the wanton Criseyde not so much of Chaucer's text as of Robert Henryson's *Testament of Cresseid,* included in early modern editions of Chaucer. The physicality of the public's (man) handling of the poet is followed in the fourth sentence by E.K.'s dismembering and admiration of the body of the poet(ry):

No less I thinke, deserveth his wittinesse in devising, his pithinesse in uttering, his complaints of love so lovely, his discourses of pleasure so pleasantly, his pastorall rudenesse, his morall wisenesse, his dewe observing of Decorum everye where, in personages, in seasons, in matter, in speach, and generally in al

seemely simplycitie of handeling his matter, and framing his
words. . . .

(17–24)

In this blazon, E.K. directs his gaze at an implicitly feminized object;
near the end of the epistle the object becomes explicitly feminine,
when E.K. speaks of "the maydenhead of this our commen frends
Poetrie" (203). "Commen frend" suggests "common woman" or
prostitute and therefore evokes the pandered Criseyde.[25] E.K.'s gen-
dering of the poet and the poetry seems to be his means of establishing
his (masculine) authority to pander/publish the work of a poet who,
like the ideologically preferable early modern woman, is reluctant to
speak in public: "I know he nothing so much hateth, as to promulgate
[his works]" (190–91). Knowledge of what the modest Immerito
hates more than anything does not deter E.K. from making the poet
a "commen frend" to all through the medium of print publication.[26]

That E.K.'s labor resembles Pandarus' is not clarified until the
informative third page of footnote-sized print:

Hereunto have I added a certain Glosse or scholion for thexposi-
tion of old wordes and harder phrases: which maner of glosing
and commenting, well I wote, wil seeme straunge and rare in
our tongue: yet for somuch as I knew many excellent and proper
devises both in wordes and matter would passe in the speedy
course of reading, either as unknowen, or as not marked, and
that in this kind, as in other we might be equal to the learned
of other nations, I thought good to take the paines upon me,
the rather for that by meanes of some familiar acquaintaunce I
was made privie to his counsell and secret meaning in them, as
also in sundry other works of his.

(178–89)

Claiming to be privy to Immerito's secret meaning, just as Pandarus
is privy to Troilus and Criseyde's secret love, E.K. panders to the
public his knowledge of "devises both in wordes and matter." Since
Immerito is, acording to E.K., "unfold[ing] great matter of argument
covertly" (147–48), some of the "devises both in wordes and matter
[that] would passe in the speedy course of reading, either as unknowen, or as not marked" may be meant to elude those who cannot
decode the words and matter without assistance. Without E.K.'s

commentary, archaisms, neologisms, and words from regional dialects, by virtue of their unfamiliarity, might have facilitated the concealment of devices in matter, some of which may be the allegorical contrivances[27] that E.K. glosses even though he asserts at the beginning of this paragraph, ". . . as touching the generall dryft and purpose of his Æglogues, I mind not to say much, him selfe labouring to conceale it" (168–70). E.K., of course, does not reveal all, and for him there may be a distinction between "generall dryft and purpose" and "devises both in wordes and matter," but the gradual shift or drift from what he won't do to what he will seems circular more than linear. E. K. says that he will not say much about "the generall dryft and purpose" and then that he will instead gloss "old wordes and harder phrases," but his subsequent reference to "matter" in the phrase "devises both in wordes and matter" seems proportionally closer to the "generall dryft and purpose" than to the "old wordes and harder phrases." In this paragraph, therefore, E.K.'s choice of words and phrases makes it difficult for readers to follow his drift.

Not until far into the diminutive print of the epistle do readers learn definitively that Colin is the new poet's pastoral persona and that E.K. has glossed the eclogues. The title page does not name the book's author or commentator, and the prefatory material does not forthrightly name or distinguish between them. In Immerito's poem and early in the epistle readers are told that the poet is "unkent" and "new," surprising adjectives for a poet whose text is annotated. The evasions at the beginning of the physical volume and the continual need to adjust to subsequent information from E.K. hinder the reader's comprehension of the text's status and its two authors. Modifying or at least attempting to modify one's impressions to account for new information can characterize the reader's interaction with E.K.'s remarks, and yet the interpretive tendency or even necessity to appropriate discrete fragments of a discourse—which is evident in some critics' reliance on E.K.'s epistolary claim to privity and their disregard of later discrepancies—resembles the appropriative maneuvers of E.K. and a number of pastoral speakers. The tendency of the *Calender*'s characters is not to adjust their perspectives to newly provided data (if such data is provided) but rather to adapt another's discourse so that it will conform to their own notions.

The Elusive Poet(ry) and the Commentator in Pursuit—of His Own Agenda

Even though E.K. says he "by meanes of some familiar acquaintaunce . . . was made privie to [Immerito's] counsell and secret meaning" (187–89), the prefatory material makes clear that E.K. did not collaborate with Immerito to produce the commentary. In the putative nonfiction presented in the epistle, after E.K. mentions Immerito's reluctance to promulgate his works, E.K. explains that he has taken it upon himself to publish the *Calender* without Immerito's knowledge: ". . . albeit I know he nothing so much hateth, as to promulgate [his works], yet thus much have I adventured upon his frendship, him selfe being for long time furre estraunged, hoping that this will the rather occasion him, to put forth divers other excellent works of his, which slepe in silence . . ." (190–94). Immerito, "for long time furre estraunged" and hence unaware of E.K.'s endeavor, addresses his book in the prefatory poem as if the gloss did not exist: "Goe little booke: thy selfe present" (1). By preventing the book from performing this action, by glossing and addressing to Gabriel Harvey a poetic text that is supposed to present itself to and communicate directly with the dedicatee Philip Sidney and other readers, E.K. thwarts Immerito's intention regarding the book's manner of expression. Moreover, the apparently benevolent foster-father E.K. has "adopted" Immerito's text in order to address poetic and political issues that, while compelling for E.K., may or may not have been significant to Immerito: the "long time furre estraunged" poet does not endorse or object to E.K.'s contributions to the *Calender*.

In contrast, the annotated second edition of Ronsard's *Amours* (1553) repeatedly asserts its status as a collaborative enterprise. The title page announces, *Les Amours de P. de Ronsard Vandomois, Nouvellement augmentées par lui, & commentées par Marc Antoine de Muret* (figure 3). There are portraits of Ronsard and Muret, as well as Cassandre, Ronsard's beloved in these sonnets.[28] At the beginning of his preface, Muret explains that he has provided a gloss at Ronsard's request: "Car outre les autres exemples, qui me venoient au devant, singulierement m'esmouvoit celuy de l'Autheur mesme, que j'entreprenois à commenter."[29] Following Muret's preface is a commendatory poem in Greek by Jean Dorat, the humanist instructor of Ronsard and other prominent French poets, which affirms the need for an annotator (the sonnets in the unannotated 1552 edition had been criticized as obscure) and praises the one that Ronsard has found: in François Rigolot's French translation,

Inspiré par l'amour de Cassandre et des Muses,
Ronsard a rendu ses oracles profonds mais obscurs.
Maintenant qu'il a trouvé en Muret un digne interprète,
Tous ces oracles sont profonds et clairs à la fois.[30]

Among the commendatory sonnets preceding the preface is one by Jan Antoine de Baif, who mentions the alliance: "Ainsi, Ronsard, de Muret t'alliant. . . ."[31] These prefatory statements attest to the cooperative effort that produced this edition.

When E.K. claims to know Immerito's "counsell and secret meaning," he leads readers erroneously to assume that he has interacted with Immerito much as Muret did with Ronsard.[32] The thoroughly informed E.K., it seems, will not need to speculate about Immerito's intentions. The "long time furre estraunged" Immerito, however, is not only uninvolved in the *Calender*'s publication and the preparation of the apparatus; he also has not provided E.K. with unrestricted access to the meaning of the eclogues. In the Generall Argument following the epistle, E.K. confesses to a few gaps in his knowledge: after he names the "three formes orranckes" (29) into which the eclogues can be divided and asserts that "to this division may every thing herein be reasonably applyed" (37–38), he immediately adds as a qualification, "A few onely except, whose speciall purpose and meaning I am not privie to" (38–39). The repetition of key words emphasizes the discrepancy between this claim and the earlier one in the epistle. Yet E.K. still is not fully acknowledging the extent to which the poet's meaning is "unkent" to him. E.K.'s confession in the Generall Argument does not adequately account for the location or number of speculations and admissions of ignorance encountered in the glosses and individual arguments.

"A few onely except" certainly seems to refer to the exception of a few eclogues, and yet the three that E.K. does not specify, "March," "Aprill," and "August," have often been placed in the category he does not enumerate, the recreative eclogues. While I agree with Harry Berger, Jr., who demonstrates that the "three formes or ranckes," plaintive, recreative, and moral, are better applied to modes within each eclogue,[33] when we dismiss or alter E.K.'s approach we disregard the pseudo-nonfictional interaction between the poet and the commentator, and the commentator and the eclogues. It is essential to keep in mind that E.K. applies these distinctions to the eclogues, not to modes within them, and that his exception of an unidentified "few onely" makes little sense given his divisions, and even less sense given what readers find in his commentary. There are interpretive speculations and admissions of ignorance in such diverse places as glosses to "Februarie" (92), "Aprill" (21, 26), "June" (18), "August" (53), "September" (180–225), "October" (1, 47), and "November" (38), and in the "March" and "November" arguments. A brief selection: "This tale of Roffy seemeth to colour some particular Action of his. But what, I certeinlye know not" ("September,"

180–225 gloss); "The worthy) he meaneth (as I guesse) the most honorable and renowmed the Erle of Leycester . . ." ("October," 47 gloss); and "The personage is secrete, and to me altogether unknowne, albe of him selfe I often required the same" ("November" argument). I am not criticizing E.K. for indulging in interpretive speculation or admitting when Immerito has refused to tell him the secret meaning; rather, I am pointing out that since the apparatus does not live up to E.K.'s claims in the epistle and Generall Argument, the *Calender*'s readers are compelled to recognize their misconception that Immerito is the source of all, and then most, of E.K.'s information. As Evelyn B. Tribble notes, "The level of knowledge E.K. possesses is markedly unstable."[34] How many other glosses in which E.K. could have included the parenthetical "as I guesse" is anybody's guess.

Readers, however, have cause to question E.K.'s claim in the epistle even before he confesses to partial ignorance and before they encounter speculations and ignorance here and there, rather than in designated, or specific undesignated, eclogues. His lengthy defense of Immerito's diction, which precedes the epistle's unqualified claim to privity, undermines that claim by indicating that E.K. does not know Immerito's reason for including archaisms, nor does he know whether Immerito actually had a reason. E.K. first maintains that the eclogues contain archaisms because the poet is so familiar with the works of earlier English authors that he unaffectedly speaks their language:

> And firste of the wordes to speake, I graunt they be something hard, and of most men unused, yet both English, and also used of most excellent Authors and most famous Poetes. In whom whenas this our Poet hath bene much traveiled and throughly redd, how could it be, (as that worthy Oratour sayde) but that walking in the sonne although for other cause he walked, yet needes he mought be sunburnt; and having the sound of those auncient Poetes still ringing in his eares, he mought needes in singing hit out some of theyr tunes.
>
> (29–38)

E.K.'s metaphors, one attesting to the poet's extensive reading and the other to his considerable memory, allege that the poet had as little intention to burn in the sun as to include archaisms in his verse. These metaphors give the poet no credit for the archaisms and suggest that speaking and hearing in one's head the language of earlier English poets is not such a positive thing. A sixteenth-century sunburn could have been a burn or tan, and although the latter is not painful, it is still a discoloration of the natural "tone," undesirable on the body and not actively sought because of the class-specific associations to working outdoors.[35] Also, although the word "tinnitus" had yet to be invented, remedying ringing in the ears was preferable to suffering with it.[36] At this point in his defense, therefore, E.K. has not endorsed the archaisms; he has only urged readers to forgive the hapless poet, who has inadvertently acquired an ideologically discomforting sunburn while walking outside "for other cause," and who is the victim of an annoying aural condition.

By repeating "needes he mought" and asserting "how could it be [otherwise]," E.K. insists that he knows what he is talking about as he eliminates the possibility that the poet included archaisms intentionally. In the next sentence, however, E.K. introduces that possibility and indicates that he is not as sure about the poet as he at first sounds:

But whether he useth them by such casualtye and custome, or of set purpose and choyse, as thinking them fittest for such rusticall rudenesse of shepheards, eyther for that theyr rough sounde would make his rymes more ragged and rustical, or els because such olde and obsolete wordes are most used of country folke, sure I think, and think I think not amisse, that they bring great grace and, as one would say, auctoritie to the verse.

(38–46)

Like the three "think's," the possibilities pile up: first is the choice between "casualtye and custome" and "set purpose and choyse"; and then between making "rymes more ragged and rustical" and imitating the way country folk actually sound (according to E.K.). The addition of an alternative to "casualtye and custome" and the supplemental alternatives within it lead to an endorsement not of the poet's "set purpose and choyse," but rather of the salutary effect of archaisms: ". . . sure I think, and think I think not amisse, that they bring great grace and, as one would say, auctoritie to the verse." It is E.K.'s opinion that whether the poet realized it or not, the "rough sounde" endows his verse with a certain grace and authority. E.K. simply does not know, or he has not bothered to ask, or the poet has declined to inform him whether the diction is a deliberate affectation or a natural ringing in the ears and eclogues.[37]

While the three "think's" in the sentence cited above unequivo-
cally declare the presence of opinion, E.K. soon blurs the distinction
between his opinion and the poet's intention by transforming effect
into intention. Moving at first further into the realm of opinion,
E.K. supports what he thinks he thinks not amiss by conferring on
Immerito's poetry purposes advocated and contested in the critical
discourse of the period, purposes which, however, conflict with those
he has just stated:

> For albe amongst many other faultes it specially be objected of
> Valla against Livie, and of other against Saluste, that with over
> much studie they affect antiquitie, as coveting thereby credence
> and honor of elder yeeres, yet I am of opinion, and eke the
> best learned are of the lyke, that those auncient solemne wordes
> are a great ornament both in the one and in the other; the one
> labouring to set forth in hys worke an eternall image of antiqui-
> tie, and the other carefully discoursing matters of gravitie and
> importaunce.
>
> (46–55)

E.K. justifies Immerito's diction by citing classical precedents and
siding with the "best learned" authorities, whose opinion is of course
the same as his own. Yet the "rough sounde" appropriate to the
"rusticall rudenesse of shepheards" has in this next sentence become
the "auncient solemne wordes" that can produce "an eternall image
of antiquitie" and are appropriate for presenting "matters of gravitie
and importaunce." While it is a pastoral convention to present "matters of gravitie and importaunce" by means of the "rusticall rudenesse
of shepheards," "auncient solemne wordes" seem distinct in tone and
in implied speaker from the "rough sounde" of "olde and obsolete
wordes . . . most used of country folke." Whatever E.K. may be trying to convey in these two sentences, as he continues his defense of
the archaisms he shifts not quite imperceptibly to another contention
that is incompatible with the two that precede it: he claims that the
"rough and harsh termes elumine and make more clearly to appeare
the brightnesse of brave and glorious words" (72–74). These "rough
and harsh termes" "bring great grace and . . . auctoritie to the verse"
not because of innate grace, as E.K.'s initial formulation implies and
as the appeal to Livy's and Sallust's practices asserts, but rather because
in E.K.'s linguistic hierarchy archaisms provide supportive contrast,
illumining by means of their ingloriousness the "brave and glorious

words" (which seem tonally similar to the "auncient solemne wordes" that are "grave" and "reverend" [59]).[38] As if this conflicting profusion of effects were not enough, E.K. then converts effect into purpose when he chastises those who would criticize the poet's diction: "But if any will rashly blame such his purpose in choyse of old and unwonted words, him may I more justly blame and condemne, or of witlesse headinesse in judging, or of heedelesse hardinesse in condemning, for not marking the compasse of hys bent, he wil judge of the length of his cast . . ." (77–82). "Purpose in choyse" echoes one of the first set of alternatives, "set purpose and choyse" (40), and E.K. is suddenly stating with certainty the presence of intention. He has exchanged his reliance on opinion for a confident but unsubstantiated expression of fact.

From opinion to surety of purpose to the chastisement of detractors: virtually the same pattern repeats itself as the sentence containing the attack on "witlesse headinesse" and "heedelesse hardinesse" continues, yet this time without the intervening appeal to Cicero and the analogies that shiftily lead into E.K.'s claim regarding the illumining effect of archaisms (55–72). E.K. again expresses his opinion but does not hesitate before adding another assertion of intentionality: ". . . for in my opinion it is one special prayse, of many whych are dew to this Poete, that he hath laboured to restore, as to theyr rightfull heritage such good and naturall English words, as have ben long time out of use and almost cleare disherited" (83–87). With this conclusion to the sentence, "purpose in choyse" becomes an ambiguous reference forward to the poet's restorative labor and back to the grace of the "rough sounde," the ornamental and tonal capacities of "auncient solemne wordes," and the ability of "rough and harsh termes" to illumine "brave and glorious words." E.K.'s second unjustifiable assertion of purpose is a second substitute for an authoritative statement from the poet, one that allows him to expound on the state of "our Mother tonge, which truely of it self is both ful enough for prose and stately enough for verse" (87–89), and to attack those who would disagree with him.

E.K. derives certainty from uncertainty, transforming the grace-conferring, ornamental, tonal, illumining, and restorative effects of archaisms into Immerito's purposes for including them. He focuses on a prominent feature in the eclogues that requires defense, as contemporary opinions of archaisms and responses to the eclogues attest, and the profuseness of his style makes it seem as if he is presenting the poet's position on this issue. What he actually presents is his own position: the poet's inadvertent or deliberate archaisms allow E.K. to situate himself in the current controversies regarding poetic practice

and the English language.[39] While one or more of E.K.'s opinions
may reflect Immerito's (and Spenser's) purposes and choices, E.K.'s
dexterous transformation of opinion into knowledge does not encourage readers to regard him as an unbiased annotator, but rather
should compel them to be wary of subjective commentary that poses
misleadingly as a definitive representation of an author's "counsell
and secret meaning."[40]

SPECULATION AND INSENSITIVITY IN THE ECLOGUES

E.K.'s intermittent admissions of ignorance in the Generall Argument, individual arguments, and glosses and his manner of justifying
the archaisms indicate that there is less communication between the
poet and the commentator than the latter readily acknowledges, and
that the commentator has consequently taken it upon himself to
speculate about intentions the poet has not specified. Similarly, some
of the characters in the eclogues speculate about what they consider
puzzling, often the sad demeanor of another. Yet unlike E.K. and
other interpreters of the *Calender,* these characters usually find out
from the source whether they are right or wrong. The incorrect
guesses in the eclogues further destabilize E.K.'s and the reader's
interpretive speculations, which are not verified or dismissed by the
"long time furre estraunged" poet, and yet even when the pastoral
producers of discourse or a sad mien are, unlike Immerito, present
and responsive, their meaning is regularly transformed. As Berger
notes, pastoral pairs talk on different levels, one interpreting the other's literal meaning figuratively and vice versa, and each appropriating
what he misinterprets in order to express his own views.[41] E.K. parallels this activity when he usurps Immerito's authority over the eclogues, appropriating them in order to present his poetic and political
opinions. I will demonstrate that the pastoral miscommunication Berger identifies is accompanied by examples of the potential for error in
interpretive speculation and, additionally, by a disjunction between
verbal and emotional understanding. In other words, even though
the pastoral speculators have greater access than E.K. does to information from the "text" they are attempting to interpret, their emotive
responses to this information mirror E.K.'s attitude toward the eclogues: as Smith describes it, "E.K. represents one way of confronting
a literary text: detached, analytical, aware of precedents, full of
schemes, but curiously aloof from the emotional force of the poetry" (89).

The first speculator in the eclogues, "Januarye's" narrator, seems at first involved in and then aloof from Colin's emotional state. With a parenthetical lament, the narrator describes "the shepeheards looke" (7): "For pale and wanne he was, (alas the while)" (8). The next line, in which the narrator suggests the alternative explanations, "May seeme he lovd, or els some care he tooke" (9), renders "(alas the while)" ambiguous: the imprecision of "some care" and the detachment of "or els" determine the interpretive line's tone, which, according to Berger, "casually understates Colin's most pressing concerns."[42] The eighth and ninth lines present a narrator who is either wavering between concern (though de-emphasized by the parentheses) and indifference or sarcastically lamenting before devaluing Colin's pain.

What appears to be certain rather than equivocal is the narrator's status: since he does not declare exactly why Colin is pale and wan, he sounds less than omniscient. According to Nancy Jo Hoffman, he is "as much in the dark as we."[43] We, however, are not in the dark: E.K. has informed us in the epistle (170–71) and, in more detail, in the "Januarye" argument that "Colin cloute a shepheardes boy complaineth him of his unfortunate love, being but newly (as semeth) enamoured of a countrie lasse called Rosalinde." Thanks to E.K., we know more than the narrator, or more than the narrator claims to know. Readers are distanced from Colin's pain by E.K., who reveals the plot, and also by the ambiguous indifference of the narrator, yet an equally important reason for Spenser to create a narrator who suggests rather than discloses is to point out that a sad look can signify any number of cares, and that only the moody person, an omniscient narrator, or a reader told by an informed commentator knows for certain what others can only speculate about.

Another speculator, Thenot in "Aprill," is not at first emotionally removed from Hobbinol's pain, but he becomes so. Nor is he vague about the reasons he suggests for Hobbinol's dejection, yet while the narrator generalizes and is right, Thenot is specific, thorough, and wrong. His specificity and tone at the beginning of the eclogue establish his concern for "good Hobbinol":

Tell me good Hobbinol, what garres thee greete?
What? hath some Wolfe thy tender Lambes ytorne?
Or is thy Bagpype broke, that soundes so sweete?
Or art thou of thy loved lasse forlorne?

Or bene thine eyes attempred to the yeare,
Quenching the gasping furrowes thirst with rayne?
Like April shoure, so stremes the trickling teares
Adowne thy cheeke, to quenche thy thristy paine.

(1–8)

Colin's remarks in "Januarye" about Hobbinol's love for him and
E.K.'s reminder in the argument to this eclogue ("the which Hobbinol being before mentioned, greatly to have loved Colin") discourage
readers from experiencing uncertainty along with Thenot. Readers
may sooner bask in the light of their superior knowledge than sympathize with Thenot's anxiety. They will not be surprised by Hobbinol's negative answer:

Nor thys, nor that, so muche doeth make me mourne,
But for the ladde, whom long I lovd so deare,
Now loves a lasse, that all his love doth scorne:
He plongd in payne, his tressed locks dooth teare.

(9–12)

What readers may not expect is the lessening of Thenot's concern
in response:

What is he for a Ladde, you so lament?
Ys love such pinching payne to them, that prove?
And hath he skill to make so excellent,
Yet hath so little skill to brydle love?

(17–20)

The elderly Thenot, who is called "lustlesse and old" (84) by Cuddie
in "Februarie," here separates himself from "them, that prove" because, one may speculate, he does not understand, does not remember, or in retrospect discounts the "pinching payne" of love and
hence has no sympathy for the pinched youths he meets. Once informed, he is as indifferent to Hobbinol's pain as the January narrator
seems to be to Colin's, and as the reader may be to Thenot's anxiety.
    In "September," Hobbinol to some has seemed concerned about
Diggon's serious misfortune, but in the course of the eclogue it becomes clear that Hobbinol is interested primarily in his own comfort

and entertainment and probably was so from his first question on-
ward. With perhaps a combination of concern and curiosity, Hobbinol begins the eclogue by inquiring and speculating about what he
finds unusual, Diggon's impoverished appearance and missing flock:

> Diggon areede, who has thee so dight?
> Never I wist thee in so poore a plight.
> Where is the fayre flocke, thou was wont to leade?
> Or bene they chaffred? or at mischiefe dead?
>
> (7–10)

In enumerating possible causes for Diggon's poor plight, Hobbinol
is less inventive than Thenot is in "Aprill." In fact, the first of Hobbinol's two alternatives seems improbable and therefore not well considered, since if Diggon had chaffered his sheep—sold them,
according to E.K.—he might not be in so poor a plight. Hobbinol
shifts from this profitable possibility directly to one that suggests that
Diggon was incapable of preventing the mischief that led to his flock's
demise. With such an invitation to speak as this, it is not surprising
that Diggon attempts to avoid Hobbinol's inquiry. It is only after
Hobbinol promises sympathy—"Eche thing imparted is more eath
to beare" (17)—that Diggon answers, "My sheepe bene wasted, (wae
is me therefore)/The jolly shepheard that was of yore,/Is nowe
nor jollye, nor shephearde more" (25–27). This unhappy shepherd-
without-a-flock is reluctant to speak of his misfortune because, he
says, he does not want to "gall [his] old griefe" (12), but what ends
up galling his grief is probably not so much the telling as it is his
listener's unsympathetic ear.

Hobbinol has little sympathy for something he has not experienced. He is the lovelorn shepherd of "Aprill" but also the reasonably
content (in all but love) and successful shepherd of "June," who
has found a safe place where wandering is not a danger: in "June,"
Colin says,

> O happy Hobbinol, I blesse thy state,
> That Paradise hast found, whych Adam lost.
> Here wander may thy flock early or late,
> Withouten dreade of Wolves to bene ytost.
>
> (9–12)

In "September," Hobbinol sounds sympathetic when he presses Diggon to talk about his pain, but he is not especially interested in the shepherd's suffering. He wants to know what has happened to the sheep, and he wants to hear stories of faraway lands: he adds to his sympathetic urging,

> And nowe sithence I sawe thy head last,
> Thrise three Moones bene fully spent and past:
> Sith when thou hast measured much grownd,
> And wandred I wene about the world rounde,
> So as thou can many thinges relate:
> But tell me first of thy flocks astate.
>
> (19–24)

That he is more curious than sympathetic soon becomes more obvious. When Diggon admits that his sheep have been wasted, Hobbinol responds not with compassion for the shepherd or sheep but rather with a complaint about his own immediate suffering:

> Diggon, I am so stiffe, and so stanck ["wearie or fainte," according to E.K.]
> That uneth may I stand any more:
> And nowe the Westerne wind bloweth sore,
> That nowe is in his chiefe sovereigntee,
> Beating the withered leafe from the tree.
> Sitte we downe here under the hill:
> Tho may we talke, and tellen our fill,
> And make a mocke at the blustring blast.
> Now say on Diggon, what ever thou hast.
>
> (47–55)

Only when Hobbinol is comfortable can Diggon continue to say "what ever thou hast." This generalization indicates that for Hobbinol, what Diggon has to say is less significant than Hobbinol's objective to "make a mocke at the blustring blast."

Hobbinol still does not respond sympathetically even when Diggon's "what ever" turns out to be a lament for his starved sheep that includes self-deprecation and two sighs (56–67). Instead of consoling Diggon, Hobbinol draws a stern moral lesson:

Ah fon, now by thy losse art taught,
That seeldome chaunge the better brought.
Content who lives with tryed state,
Neede feare no chaunge of frowning fate:
But who will seeke for unknowne gayne,
Ofte lives by losse, and leaves with payne.

                                                    (68–73)

Eche thing imparted is more eath to beare": telling a "fon" that he
should learn from his mistake does not make that mistake easier to
bear. Hobbinol's self-involvement and self-pity—"(Ah for Colin, he
whilome my joye)" (177)—along with his inexperience in flock-
losing, inhibit his compassion for Diggon. He is concerned only
about his own "stiffe" body, which seeks to evade the harsh western
wind just as Diggon wants to evade harsh criticism. In light of all
this, Hobbinol's explicit compassionate remark at the end of the
eclogue, "Now by my soule Diggon, I lament / The haplesse mischief,
that has thee hent" (248–49), seems less soul-felt than Hobbinol
claims. It instead seems primarily a forced response to a cry for help:
Diggon has just said,

What shall I doe? what way shall I wend,
My piteous plight and losse to amend?
Ah good Hobbinol, mought I thee praye,
Of ayde or counsell in my decaye.

                                                    (244–47)

Hobbinol, desirous of entertainment, listens to and appropriates Diggon's painful story in order to "make a mocke at the blustring blast"
(54); to "lament / The haplesse mischief, that has thee hent" (248–49)
is for Hobbinol secondary at best.[44]

    In "September" and other eclogues, those who are self-involved
and have not experienced certain types of pain are insensitive to the
suffering of others, and yet experience does not ensure sympathy, as
the first stanza of "Januarye" implies. Colin asks for pity from the
gods of love but then wonders parenthetically if he will receive it:

Ye Gods of love, that pitie lovers payne,
(If any gods the paine of lovers pitie:)

Look from above, where you in joyes remaine,
And bowe your eares unto my dolefull dittie.
And *Pan* thou shepheards God, that once didst love,
Pitie the paines, that thou thy selfe didst prove.

(1–6)

Colin first addresses those who, because they "in joyes remaine," do
not experience sorrows like the pinching pain of love. That Pan
"once didst love" and experienced "paines" seems more promising,
but an "Aprill" gloss suggests that Pan may not sympathize with
Colin because Pan and Colin deal with unsuccessful love in opposite
ways. Colin breaks his pipe at the end of "Januarye," while Pan,
having lost Syrinx, makes one: E.K. explains that Syrinx

> is the name of a Nymphe of Arcadie, whom when Pan being
> in love pursued, she flying from him, of the Gods was turned
> into a reede. So that Pan catching at the Reedes in stede of the
> Damosell, and puffing hard (for he was almost out of wind)
> with hys breath made the Reedes to pype: which he seeing,
> tooke of them, and in remembraunce of his lost love, made
> him a pype thereof. ("Aprill" 50 gloss)

Hobbinol, who in "Aprill" mourns for Colin (9), in a sense has
sympathy for him, but the end of that eclogue makes clear just how
far Hobbinol's sympathy extends: "Sicker I hold [Colin], for a greater
fon,/That loves the thing, he cannot purchase" (158–59). Hobbinol,
readers will recall, cannot purchase Colin either: Colin says in "Januarye,"

It is not *Hobbinol,* wherefore I plaine,
Albee my love he seeke with dayly suit:
His clownish gifts and curtsies I disdaine,
His kiddes, his cracknelles, and his early fruit.
Ah foolish *Hobbinol,* thy gyfts bene vayne:
Colin them gives to *Rosalilnd* againe.

(55–60)

Each considers the other a fool, and each pities only himself.

Interpreting a dejected look is not an uncomplicated undertaking, and identifying the specific cause of such a look is certainly not assured of success when so many causes (as in "Aprill") or such general ones (as in "Januarye") are possible. Significantly, the pastoral sufferer who informs a speculator why he is sad is not assured of understanding. A compassionate response—the response that is so important to Colin that he prefaces his lament with a request for it—is rarely, if ever really, forthcoming. Readers too are urged by various means to maintain a distance from the pain of pastoral lamenters: E.K.'s matter-of-fact exposition and explication; the ambiguously detached narrator of "Januarye"; unsympathetic listeners like Thenot in "Aprill" and Hobbinol in "September"; and the conventionality of the pastoral lament. All the *Calender's* speculators or, one might say, spectators, are in the dark even after they are made aware of the cause of another's pain. Consequently, communication fails even as it succeeds.

INTERPRETIVE PURPOSES AND METHODS IN *THE SHEPHEARDES CALENDER*

Interpretive speculation is a much practiced activity, in the eclogues, in the apparatus, in commentary in general, among censors, and in everyday situations. Insensitivity to another's moods or motives is not unusual either; one's own moods or motives often take precedence. The speculations and insensitivity in the eclogues have parallels in E.K.'s interaction with Immerito and the eclogues and also in the reader's interaction with the text: the pastoral speakers, E.K., and the reader cannot know for certain what the "demeanor" of another person or text is trying to communicate; even when meaning is revealed to them, they may depreciate or misunderstand its value, interpreting/appropriating the text for their own "set purpose and choyse." Aware that censors and authority figures might thus (mis)treat a text, Tudor and Stuart authors sometimes express their concern much as the ghost of the poet Collingbourne does in William Baldwin's *The Mirror for Magistrates* (1563). Collingbourne cautions Baldwin against attempting to amend the lives of evil magistrates: executed by Richard III for composing an obvious political slur in verse, Collingbourne complains that

wycked worldelinges are so wytles wood,
That to the wurst they all thinges construe styl.

Wyth rygour oft they recompence good wyll:
They racke the wurdes tyl tyme theyr synowes burst,
In doubtfull sences, strayning styll the wurst.[45]

The furthering of one's own purposes through the "strayning" or
appropriation of another's text may sound malevolent but of course
is not always or even often so. All commentary is appropriation, and
commentators are unavoidably influenced by the agenda with which
they approach their task, an agenda largely guided by the norms of
commentary that they inherit and the critical controversies of their
time. Such is the case with E.K.'s apparatus; E.K., then, is not so
much underhanded in his specifying of intention as he is overeager
to sound the poet's worthiness in the "tromp of fame" (Epistle," 15)
and thereby add his own voice to the critical discourse of his day.
Yet his conjectures and admissions of ignorance makes doubly apparent the fact that the apparatus lacks the authority of a collaboration,
and the transformative process in the epistle makes one wonder
whether E.K. is regularly distinguishing between information from
the poet and his own conjectures, as he does when he inserts the
parenthetical "As I guesse" into an "October" gloss.

In the *Calender*'s fictive reality, E.K.'s and Immerito's non-collabo-
rative relationship and E.K.'s methodology undermine the reliability
of the apparatus, yet notwithstanding whose intentions and opinions
are being conveyed, the commentator establishes himself as a potent
presence within the physical volume, authoritatively guiding the
reader's perceptions of the so-called primary text. What Robert A.
Kaster says of the control exerted by Servius' commentary is generally applicable:

> The commentary is often a scene of conflict, between the an-
> cients and "ourselves," between different forms and sources of
> authority, between the deference owed to the author's prestige
> and the grammarian's domination of the text. Understanding
> the commentary means in large part understanding how the
> grammarian controls such conflicts, and understanding that con-
> trol requires us to appreciate the sense of authority that the
> grammarian derives from his own institutional niche.[46]

Lee Patterson extends Kaster's explanation to other acts of commentary: "The commentary is always a power struggle," he says, "an

opportunity for rituals that are hardly disinterested," although we "assure ourselves that commentary is a way of recovering that which might otherwise be lost, a reaffirmation of the continuity of cultural traditions, an act of necessary homage to our heritage."[47] E.K. sounds altruistic when he explains that he has devoted his time to glossing "many excellent and proper devises both in wordes and matter [that] would passe in the speedy course of reading, either as unknowen, or as not marked" ("Epistle," 182–84), but he is not so disinterested a participant in the presentation of the eclogues. That he knows even in part Immerito's "counsell and secret meaning" suggests the following pseudo-nonfictional scenario: the "furre estraunged" Immerito explained, before he left town, why he wanted the text to present itself, perhaps not as a published book, but E.K. either did not understand or did not respect Immerito's wishes, for he overruled Immerito by assuming the privileges of the commentator's "institutional niche," from which vantage he indiscreetly glossed the eclogues in a disinterested and self-interested effort to make them accessible to the public.

E.K. publicizes the poet and the poetry, along with his own learned opinions, by subordinating the eclogues to his interpretive authority, taking "the maydenhead of this our commen frends Poetrie" ("Epistle," 203) and, as bawd, pandering the already interpreted text to the public for further kissing, embracing, and loving. E.K.'s overbearing presentation of a new poet reluctant to promulgate his works and hence circumspect regarding his own poetic maidenhead epitomizes the often conflicting agendas of authors and commentators and the author's loss of interpretive authority over the circulated text and its readers. However, the *mise-en-abyme* structure of the 1579 *Calender* offsets this loss by rendering questionable the methods and agenda of those who selectively appropriate material from an elusive discourse and thereby achieve a dubious form of comprehension—be they shepherds, commentators, censors, or readers attempting to understand the *Calender*'s miscommunicative presentational strategies.

Bucknell University

Notes

I would like to thank those who provided helpful suggestions as this article gradually assumed its current state: Anne Lake Prescott, David Kastan, Edward Tayler, Christopher Baswell, Catharine Randall, Jean Brink, Heather Stanford, the reader for *Spenser Studies,* and Arthur Shapiro.

1. McCanles adds that "[w]hat [Spenser] published was a fictional imitation of a humanist edition of classical texts" ("*The Shepheardes Calender* as Document and Monument," *Studies in English Literature, 1500–1900,* 22 [1982]: see 5–7).

Critics have variously suggested that E.K. is Spenser, although the initials obviously don't match; Spenser with his good friend Gabriel Harvey's assistance; Harvey on his own; Fulk(e) Greville, whom Spenser may have known through his connection with the Earl of Leicester and whose name can be identified by the initials E.K. if one takes the final letters and reverses them; Edward Kirke, whose initials are the right ones and whom Spenser may have known when they were both at Cambridge; and a persona created by Spenser, "a half-clown, half-capable exegete" as Lynn Staley Johnson describes him in The Shepheardes Calender: *An Introduction* (University Park, PA: Penn State University Press, 1990), 30. Attempts to pin down the elusive E.K. or his creator may seem to have become academic exercises in futility but continue to appear in print because E.K.'s status as a real commentator or a fictional construct is a crux in the interpretation of the *Calender.*

Paul E. McLane's identification of E.K. as Fulke Greville has not been widely accepted (*Spenser's* Shepheardes Calender: *A Study in Elizabethan Allegory* [Notre Dame, IN: University of Notre Dame Press, 1961], 280–95). Edward Kirke has never been entirely rejected (see David R. Shore's article on E.K. in *The Spenser Encyclopedia*). The most recent argument for Harvey is S.K. Henninger, Jr.'s, in "The Typographical Layout of Spenser's *Shepheardes Calender,*" in *Word and Visual Imagination: Studies in the Interaction of English Literature and the Visual Arts,* eds. Karl Josef Höltgen et al (Erlangen: Univ.-Bibliothek Erlangen–Nürnberg, 1988), 33–71; for Spenser with some assistance from Harvey, Louise Schleiner's, in "Spenser's 'E.K.' as Edmund Kent (Kenned/of Kent): Kyth (Couth), Kissed, and Kunning-Conning," *ELR,* 20 (1990): 374–407. See also Louis Waldman's "Spenser's Pseudonym 'E.K.' and Humanist Self-Naming," *Spenser Studies,* 9 (1988): 21–31.

2. Other critics have considered the malleability of meaning in the eclogues, the commentary, or both, but not with regard to the *Calender's mise-en-abyme* structure, and so I will be elaborating upon observations such as David Norbrook's, that the eclogues and "the publication of [E.K.'s] significantly inadequate commentary did draw attention to the problems, and the politics, of interpretation" (*Poetry and Politics in the English Renaissance* [London: Routledge & Kegan Paul, 1984], 74, and see also 73).

3. All quotations from The Shepheardes Calender are from The Yale Edition of the Shorter Poems of Edmund Spenser, ed. William A. Oram et al. (New Haven: Yale UP, 1989), 1–213. Parenthetical references are to line numbers within various sections of the *Calender.*

4. Suggesting the possibility that "Spenser wrote a good part of his poem in the five months prior to its licensing on December 5, 1579," McLane speculates that the April 10, 1579, date of E.K.'s prefatory epistle "was probably a fiction designed to protect Spenser from the wrath of the Queen for his allegorical portrayal of more recent events" (9). Stubbs's fate, referred to in numerous accounts of the *Calender,* is described in detail by Lloyd E. Berry in his edition of *John Stubbs's* Gaping Gulf *With Letters and Other Relevant Documents* (Charlottesville: University Press of Virginia, 1968), xxvii–xl. See also Cyndia Susan Clegg's reassessment of the censoring

of the *Gaping Gulf*, in *Press Censorship in Elizabethan England* (Cambridge: Cambridge University Press, 1997), 123–37.

5.   Numerous studies indicate that during the early modern period in England, when the authorities sought to discourage political criticism, authors regularly disclaimed topicality, implemented strategies of fictional displacement, and expressed their apprehension regarding readers or censors who might misconstrue their intentions or too easily uncover their concealed meaning. See, for instance, Annabel Patterson's *Censorship and Interpretation: The Conditions of Writing and Reading in Early Modern England,* especially the chapter entitled "Prynne's Ears; or, The Hermeneutics of Censorship" (Madison: University of Wisconsin Press, 1984. With a new introduction, 1990); and Robert Lane's chapter entitled "Labouring to Conceale It: The Hermeneutics of Protection" in *Shepheards Devises: Edmund Spenser's* Shepheardes Calender *and the Institutions of Elizabethan Society* (Athens, GA: University of Georgia Press, 1993).

6.   Many critics speak of this aspect of the glosses. According to Patterson, one of the functions of the apparatus is "to reveal *by failing to reveal* the mysteries of the text" (*Pastoral and Ideology: Virgil to Valéry* [Berkeley: University of California Press, 1987], 129). William W. E. Slights explains how the *Calender* "employed its glosses partly to direct readers outward, beyond the limits of a highly artificial poetic text into a dangerously real contemporary situation" ("The Edifying Margins of Renaissance English Books," *Renaissance Quarterly* 42 [1989]: 704). Richard Rambuss's emphasis differs: "Rather than drawing back the pastoral veil and uncovering what has been secreted in these deeply encrypted poems, E.K.'s annotations veil more than they ever reveal. *It is thus not secrets that E.K. discloses but rather secrecy itself.* Even in the rare instances where we find him denying any hidden agenda on the part of the poet . . . E.K.'s disavowal has the opposite effect of consequently raising the stakes and calling attention to what then must be concealed in the ecclesiastical and political satire it prefaces" (*Spenser's Secret Career* [Cambridge: Cambridge University Press, 1993], 53).

7.   My reason for alluding to the title of Ruth Samson Luborsky's "The Allusive Presentation of *The Shepheardes Calender,*" *Spenser Studies,* 1 (1980): 29–67, will shortly become clear.

8.   See, for instance, Bruce R. Smith, "On Reading *The Shepheardes Calender,*" *Spenser Studies,* 1 (1980): 79; Luborsky, 30, 55–56; Johnson, 24; Richard Halpern, *The Poetics of Primitive Accumulation: English Renaissance Culture and the Genealogy of Capital* (Ithaca, NY: Cornell University Press, 1991), 190–95; and Evelyn B. Tribble, *Margins and Marginality: The Printed Page in Early Modern England* (Charlottesville, VA: University Press of Virginia, 1993), 74.

9.   Luborsky, 32, 33.

10.   That Spenser's readers would have seen this title page or a similar one in *The Kalender of Sheepehards* is likely but not certain. In the introduction to the facsimile edition, Heninger notes, "This perdurable almanack retained the same format throughout its printing history with minimal modifications" (*The Kalender of Sheepehards, c. 1585* [Delmar, NY: Scholars' Facsimiles & Reprints, 1979], vii). The reproduced edition dates from 1560 or 1585: "the revised *Short Title Catalogue* changes the date to about 1585, without explanation" (v).

11.   Luborsky cites this title page (33) and includes it in her article as Figure 3. In her fourteenth footnote, she refers readers to Henry Lotspeich, who says, "No one can say that this very edition was the one Spenser had, but it can be shown that the text of the *Culex* which this edition contains is the only one among those Spenser might have seen—in so far as I have been able to examine them all,—which fulfills every requirement of Spenser's translation" ("Spenser's Virgils Gnat" *ELH,* 2 [1935]: 236). For the purposes of my argument, I will add that the listings in *The National Union Catalog, Pre-1956 Imprints,* indicate that the majority of early modern editions of Virgil name the commentator(s) on the title page.

12.   This title page is also reproduced in Deborah Parker's *Commentary and Ideology: Dante in the Renaissance* (Durham, NC: Duke University Press, 1993), 156, where I first encountered it.

13.   In "The Typographical Layout," Heninger notes the similarities in layout between Sannazaro's *Arcadia* (1571) and Spenser's *Calender* (1579). There is a photograph of the 1571 title page in Heninger's article (52).

14.   Although attributed to Gerardus Listrius, the commentary was primarily Erasmus's work. See Slights, 708–14.

15.   Sometimes, frontispieces that portray the commentator(s) along with the author intensify the impression given by title pages in annotated editions. See Patterson's analysis of two Virgilian frontispieces in *Pastoral and Ideology,* 19–27, 79.

16.   Berry notes that William Page, "who sent fifty copies of the book to Sir Richard Grenville in Cornwall, with the request that Grenville circulate them among his friends," was "credited with being the publisher of the book, but the records do not indicate that he was ever connected in any way with the book trade" (xxvi). Page's hand was chopped off nevertheless.

17.   Smith, 79.

18.   Sidney expressed in a private letter to the queen the objections that lost Stubbs his hand. See Johnson regarding his letter (152–53). The location of Sidney's name and the author's praise of him would have attracted attention also because dedications were not usually located on title pages (Heninger, "The Typographical Layout," 42).

19.   For recent considerations of Spenser's connection to the Leicester faction, see Vincent P. Carey and Clare L. Carroll's "Factions and Fictions: Spenser's Reflections of and on Elizabethan Politics" (31–44), Jean R. Brink's " 'All his minde on honour fixed': The Preferment of Edmund Spenser" (45–64), and F. J. Levy's "Spenser and Court Humanism" (65–80) in *Spenser's Life and the Subject of Biography,* eds. Judith H. Anderson, Donald Cheney, and David A. Richardson (Amherst: University of Massachusetts Press, 1997).

20.   See Paula Blank's examination of "uncouth," "unkiste," and "unkent" in "The Dialect of *The Shepheardes Calender,*" *Spenser Studies,* 10 (1989): 86; and Patterson's of "uncouth" in *Reading Between the Lines* (Madison: University of Wisconsin Press, 1993), 46–56.

21.   Wendy Wall, *The Imprint of Gender: Authorship and Publication in the English Renaissance* (Ithaca: Cornell University Press, 1993), 236.

22.   Regarding Spenser's use of the name Colin Clout, see Roland Greene's "Calling Colin Clout," *Spenser Studies,* 10 (1989): 229–44; and Robert Starr Kinsman's article on Skelton in *The Spenser Encyclopedia.*

23. See Slights, 708.

24. Geoffrey Chaucer, *Troilus and Criseyde,* in *The Riverside Chaucer,* 3rd ed., gen. ed. Larry D. Benson (Boston: Houghton, 1987), 1.809.

25. See "common" in the *OED,* especially definition #6b, and "friend," definition #4. For an account of the homosociality/sexuality connected to the early modern use of the word "friend," see Alan Bray's "Homosexuality and the Signs of Male Friendship in Elizabethan England," in *Queering the Renaissance,* ed. Jonathan Goldberg (Durham, NC: Duke University Press, 1994), 40–61. Bray says that the "public kiss" E.K. mentions "carried the same meaning as the equally public fact of being a powerful man's bedfellow" (43) and also that "The image of the masculine friend was an image of intimacy between men in stark contrast to the forbidden intimacy of homosexuality" (42). This image is in the *Calender* complicated by the gender blending I identify in E.K.'s epistle, and the distinction between the intimate masculine friend and the homosexual companion is blurred when the kiss is followed by the taking of the poet's maidenhead.

26. See Wall regarding prefatorial statements that feminize the author (169–226); and Johnson's remarks on E.K.'s bawdy references to Chaucer (27–28, 31).

27. See "device" in the *OED*: for "devises" as figures, see definition #10; for "devises" as more extensive contrivances, see #6 and #7. "Devises" may also include E.K.'s explication of the emblems at the end of each eclogue (see definition #9).

28. These portraits are reproduced and analyzed by François Rigolot in "Ronsard et Muret: Les pièces liminaires aux 'Amours' de 1553," *Revue d'Histoire Littéraire de la France,* 88 (1988): 6–8.

29. I have consulted Hughes Vaganay's 1910 edition of the 1578 text, *Les Amours de P. de Ronsard Vandomois, commentées par Marc Antoine de Muret* (Paris: Librairie Ancienne, 1910). This quotation is from page lii. Vaganay notes variants in earlier and later editions ranging from 1552 to 1604, with the exception of 1560 (see M. Joseph Vianey's preface, i).

30. Qtd. and trans. by Rigolot, 4. Vaganay does not include this poem but notes its presence in the 1553 *Amours* (447). Rigolot's source is a photocopy of the 1553 edition in the Bibliothèque Nationale. In his first footnote, he mentions that this verse is included in the introduction to the fifth volume of Paul Laumonier's 1928 Paris edition of Ronsard's *Oeuvres complètes* (3; xxvi in Laumonier).

31. Vaganay's ed., xlix.

32. For similarities between Muret's and E.K.'s commentaries, see Marjorie Adams's "Ronsard and Spenser: The Commentary," in *Renaissance Papers presented at The Renaissance Meeting in the Southeastern States* (Durham, NC: Southeastern Renaissance Conference, 1954), 25–29.

33. Harry Berger, Jr., *Revisionary Play: Studies in the Spenserian Dynamics* (Berkeley: University of California Press, 1988), 290–94.

34. Tribble, 74. See 72–87 for Tribble's account of the textual presentation of the *Calender,* which has some affinities with mine.

35. See *OED* definition #1 for "sunburnt." Ascham's *Scholemaster* is cited for "superficially learned" (#1b): "So many seeming, and sunburnt ministers . . . whose learning is gotten in a sommer heat, and washed away, with a Christmas snow againe." See also the section entitled "Sunburn: Anxieties of Influence/Anxieties

of Race" in Kim F. Hall's *Things of Darkness: Economies of Race and Gender in Early Modern England* (Ithaca: Cornell University Press, 1995), 92–107 (she comments on the *Calender* on page 100).

36. See "ringing," vbl. sb.^{2}, #3, and "tinnitus" in the *OED*.

37. Halpern also points out E.K.'s uncertainty about the purposiveness of the diction (176–77), but I do so in more detail to prepare for my ensuing discussion regarding E.K.'s transformation of uncertainty into certainty.

38. Although Lane sees E.K. "[r]epudiating linguistic elitism" (40), E.K.'s defense of the poet's diction at times supports the hierarchical notions of class that are associated with linguistic elitism: E.K.'s manner of praising the "rough and harsh termes [that] elumine and make more clearly to appeare the brightnesse of brave and glorious words" ("Epistle," 72–74) certainly appears to be subordinating the rough and harsh to the brave and glorious; and the sunburn metaphor suggests distaste for language that is "strange" ("Epistle," 25) or associated with the lower classes. In assessing E.K.'s alternative explanations, Blank points out, as I do, that "[t]he several theories E.K. lines up are conspicuously at odds" (74).

39. Regarding these controversies, see Richard Foster Jones's *The Triumph of the English Language: A Survey of Opinions Concerning the Vernacular from the Introduction of Printing to the Restoration* (Stanford: Stanford University Press, 1953), especially chapters 3 and 4; Michael Murrin's seventh chapter (see especially 177–84) in *The Veil of Allegory: Some Notes Toward a Theory of Allegorical Rhetoric in the English Renaissance* (Chicago: University of Chicago Press, 1969); Margaret W. Ferguson's *Trials of Desire: Renaissance Defenses of Poetry* (New Haven: Yale University Press, 1983); Blank's "The Dialect of *The Shepheardes Calender*"; Richard Helgerson's first chapter in *Forms of Nationhood: The Elizabethan Writing of England* (Chicago: University of Chicago Press, 1992); and Lane, 38–41.

40. In his introduction to the *Calender* in the Yale edition, Thomas H. Cain mentions the "playfully ironic exercises in the tradition of Lucian which force the reader to adapt and maintain a vigilantly defensive querying posture toward the text" and speculates that Spenser "may be playfully using the accoutrements of an edition to the same effect" (9).

41. See Berger's chapter on the moral eclogues (290–324); Patrick Cullen's related argument regarding miscommunicating shepherds and the conflict between Arcadian and Mantuanesque perspectives in *Spenser, Marvell, and Renaissance Pastoral* (Cambridge: Harvard University Press, 1970), 29–119; and Halpern's assertion that "The vision of England [in 'Aprill'] as pastoral or garden, unified politically and theologically, gives way to a sense of competing and incompatible understandings of church doctrine and discipline" (211; see 208–14).

42. Berger, 329. Berger further observes, "The understated conjecture has the effect of a stage direction suggesting that we not take too seriously what Colin is about to take terribly seriously" (330.note 7).

43. Nancy Jo Hoffman, *Spenser's Pastorals:* The Shepheardes Calender *and "Colin Clout"* (Baltimore: Johns Hopkins University Press, 1977), 44.

44. When Hoffman concludes that Hobbinol "expresses direct, genuine sympathy, a willingness to share—'as I can I will'—and a wish for the fair fortune of his friend" (117), she does not account for Hobbinol's earlier lack of sympathy. I agree with

Johnson's assessment of Hobbinol's tone: "Though Hobbinol's words are conventional enough, his offer of shelter seems flat in relation to either Diggon Davie's anguish of spirit or the pastoral conventions they evoke" (75). However, I do not agree that "[w]hat Hobbinol has to offer, in fact, is sympathy but no aid" (75). He is not truly sympathetic, and he offers what aid he can, "a vetchy bed" (256), only after Diggon has in effect begged for it.

45. William Baldwin, *The Mirror for Magistrates,* ed. Lily B. Campbell (Cambridge: Cambridge University Press, 1938), 349 (lines 59–63).

46. Robert A. Kaster, *Guardians of Language: The Grammarian and Society in Late Antiquity* (Berkeley: University of California Press, 1988), 176.

47. Lee Patterson, Introduction, *Commentary as Cultural Artifact, South Atlantic Quarterly,* eds. Lee Patterson and Stephen G. Nichols, 91 (1992), 788. For other studies of the interaction between paratext and primary text, see, for example, the articles in *Commentary as Cultural Artifact;* Christopher Baswell's "Talking Back to the Text: Marginal Voices in Medieval Secular Literature," in *The Uses of Manuscripts in Literary Studies: Essays in Memory of Judson Boyce Allen,* ed. Charlotte Cook Morse et al. (Kalamazoo: Medieval Institute Publications, 1992), 121–60; Michael Camille's *Image on the Edge: The Margins of Medieval Art* (Cambridge: Harvard University Press, 1992); and *Annotation and Its Texts,* ed. Stephen A. Barney (NY: Oxford University Press, 1991). See also theoretical explorations of the subject, such as Gérard Genette's "Introduction to the Paratext," *Seuils* (Paris, 1987), rpt. in trans. Marie Maclean, *New Literary History,* 22 (1991): 261–72; and *Palimpsestes: La Littérature au Second Degré* (Paris, 1982); Rigolot's "Prolégomènes à une étude du statut de l'appareil liminaire des textes littéraires," *L'Esprit Créateur,* 27.3 (1987): 7–18; and Jacques Derrida's *The Truth in Painting,* trans. Geoff Bennington and Ian Macleod (Chicago: University of Chicago Press, 1987).

T H E
Shepheardes Calender

Conteyning tvvelue Æglogues proportionable
to the twelue monethes.

Entitled
TO THE NOBLE AND VERTV-
ous Gentleman most worthy of all titles
both of learning and cheualrie M.
Philip Sidney.
(∵)

AT LONDON.
Printed by Hugh Singleton, dwelling in
Creede Lane neere vnto Ludgate at the
figne of the gylden Tunne, and
are there to be folde.
1579.

Figure 1: Title Page of *The Shepheardes Calender*, 1579. Reproduced
by permission of the Bodleian Library (4.F.2.Art.Bs.(11)).

HEERE BEGINNETH
the Kalender of Sheepehards:
Newly Augmented and Cor-
rected.

Figure 2: Title Page of *The Kalender of Sheepehards*, 1585. Reproduced by permission of the Bodleian Library (Malone 17).

ꝗ᷑*LES AMOVRS*
DE P. DE RONSARD
VANDOMOIS, NOV-
uellement augmétées par lui,
& commentées par Marc An-
toine de Muret.

Plus quelques Odes de L'auteur,
non encor imprimées.

Τέρπανδρος πρὶν ἔτερπ' ἄνδρας μόνον, ἀλλὰ γυναῖκας
Νῦν τέρπει, νῦν ἄρ τερπογυνής ἔσεται.

Αὐρατȣ.

ÁVEC PRIVILÉGE DV ROY.

A PARIS.

ꝗ᷑*Chez la veuue Maurice de la Porte.*

1 5 5 3.

Figure 3: Title Page of Ronsard's *Amours, 1553*. Reproduced by
permission of the Houghton Library, Harvard University.

Figure 4: Title Page of Virgil's *Opera*, Antwerp, 1542. Reproduced by permission of the Department of Rare Books and Special Collections, Princeton University Libraries.

DANTE
CON LESPOSITIONE
DI CHRISTOFORO LANDINO,
ET DI ALESSANDRO VELLVTELLO,

Sopra la sua Comedia dell' Inferno, del Purgatorio, & del Paradiso.

Con tauole, argomenti, & allegorie, & riformato, riueduto,
& ridotto alla sua uera lettura,

PER FRANCESCO SANSOVINO FIORENTINO.

*I*N *V*ENETIA, *Appresso Giouambattista, Marchiò Sessa, & fratelli.* 1564.

Figure 5: Title Page of Dante's *Comedia*, Venice, 1564. Reproduced by permission of the Department of Special Collections, University of Chicago Library.

ARCADIA
DI M. GIACOMO
SANNAZARO

NVOVAMENTE CORRETTA,
& ornata di Figure & d'Annotationi

· da M. Francesco Sansouino ·

CON LA VITA DELL'AVTTORE,
descritta dal medesimo, & con la dichia-
ratione di tutte leuoci oscure, cosi Latine
come Volgari che sono nell'Opera.

CON PRIVILEGIO.

IN VENETIA
Appresso Giouanni Varisco
M·D LXXI.

Figure 6: Title Page of Sannazaro's *Arcadia,* Venice, 1578. Reproduced by permission of the Department of Special Collections, University of Chicago Library.

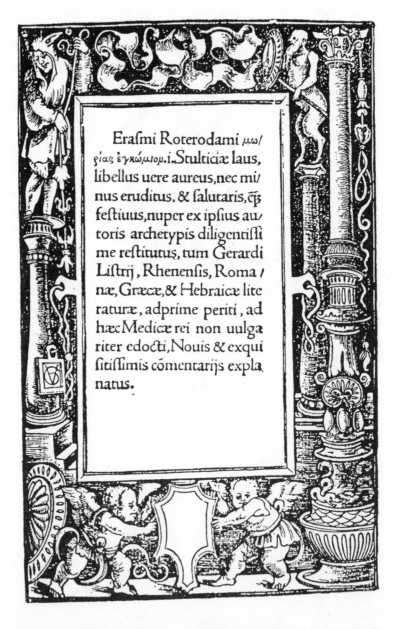

Figure 7: Title Page of Erasmus' *Moriae Encomium,* Basel, 1515; facsimile 1931. Reproduced by permission of the Department of Special
Collections, University of Chicago Library.

TO HIS BOOKE.

Goe little booke: thy selfe present,
As child whose parent is vnkent:
To him that is the president
Of noblesse and of cheualree,
And if that Enuie barke at thee,
As sure it will, for succoure flee
Vnder the shadow of his wing,
And asked, who thee forth did bring,
A shepheards swaine saye did thee sing,
All as his straying flocke he fedde:
And when his honor has thee redde,
Craue pardon for my hardyhedde.

But if that any aske thy name,
Say thou wert base begot with blame:
For thy thereof thou takest shame.
And when thou art past ieopardee,
Come tell me, what was sayd of mee:
And I will send more after thee.

Immeritô.

Figure 8: "To His Booke," verso of title page in *The Shepheardes Calender,* 1579. Reproduced by permission of the Bodleian Library (4.F.2.Art.Bs.(11)).

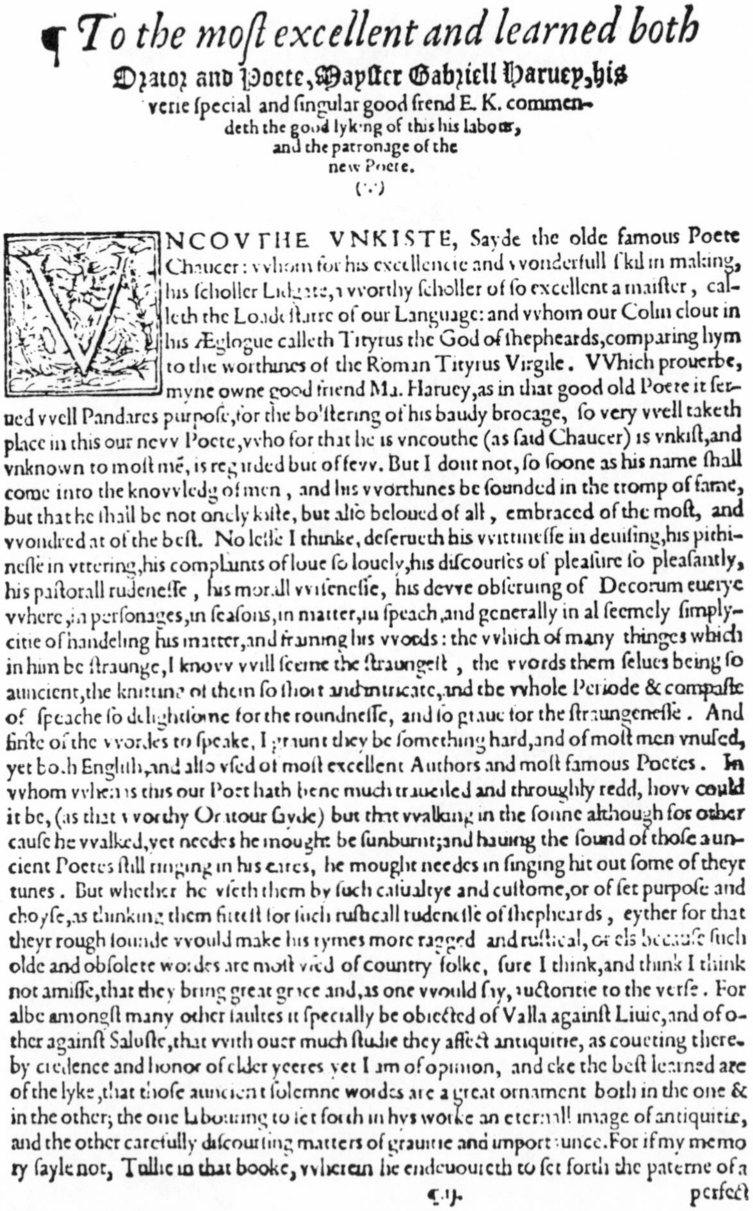

¶ *To the moſt excellent and learned both*
Ɖꝛatoꝛ and Ɖoete, Ɱayſter Gabꝛiell Ɦaruey, his
verie ſpecial and ſingular good frend E. K. commen-
deth the good lyking of this his labour,
and the patronage of the
new Poete.
(·.·)

NCOVTHE VNKISTE, Sayde the olde famous Poete
Chaucer: whom for his excellencie and wonderfull ſkil in making,
his ſcholler Lidgate, a worthy ſcholler of ſo excellent a maiſter, calleth the Loade ſtarre of our Language: and whom our Colin clout in
his Æglogue calleth Tityrus the God of ſhepheards, comparing hym
to the worthines of the Roman Tityrus Virgile. VVhich prouerbe,
myne owne good friend Ma. Haruey, as in that good old Poete it ſer-
ued vvell Pandares purpoſe, for the bolſtering of his baudy brocage, ſo very vvell taketh
place in this our nevv Poete, vvho for that he is vncouthe (as ſaid Chaucer) is vnkiſt, and
vnknown to moſt mé, is regarded but of fevv. But I dout not, ſo ſoone as his name ſhall
come into the knovvledg of men , and his vvorthines be ſounded in the tromp of fame,
but that he ſhail be not onely kiſte, but alſo beloued of all , embraced of the moſt, and
vvondred at of the beſt. No leſſe I thinke, deſerueth his vvittineſſe in deuiſing, his pithi-
neſſe in vttering, his complaints of loue ſo louely, his diſcourſes of pleaſure ſo pleaſantly,
his paſtorall rudeneſſe , his morall vviſeneſſe, his devve obſeruing of Decorum euerye
vvhere, in perſonages, in ſeaſons, in matter, in ſpeach, and generally in al ſeemely ſimply-
citie of handeling his matter, and framing his vvords: the vvhich of many thinges which
in him be ſtraunge, I knovv vvill ſeeme the ſtraungeſt , the vvords them ſelues being ſo
auncient, the knitting of them ſo ſhort and intricate, and the vvhole Periode & compaſſe
of ſpeache ſo delightſome for the roundneſſe, and ſo graue for the ſtraungeneſſe . And
firſte of the vvordes to ſpeake, I graunt they be ſomething hard, and of moſt men vnuſed,
yet both Engliſh, and alſo vſed of moſt excellent Authors and moſt famous Poetes. In
vvhom vvhen as this our Poet hath bene much trauerled and throughly redd, hovv could
it be, (as that vvorthy Oratour ſayde) but that vvalking in the ſonne although for other
cauſe he vvalked, yet needes he mought be ſunburnt; and hauing the ſound of thoſe auncient Poetes ſtill ringing in his eares, he mought needes in ſinging hit out ſome of theyr
tunes . But whether he vſeth them by ſuch caſualtye and cuſtome, or of ſet purpoſe and
choyſe, as thinking them fitteſt for ſuch ruſticall rudeneſſe of ſhepheards , eyther for that
theyr rough ſounde vvould make his rymes more ragged and ruſtical, or els becauſe ſuch
olde and obſolete vvordes are moſt vſed of country folke, ſure I thinke, and think I think
not amiſſe, that they bring great grace and, as one vvould ſay, auctoritie to the verſe . For
albe amongſt many other faultes it ſpecially be obiected of Valla againſt Liuie, and of o-
ther againſt Saluſte, that vvith ouer much ſtudie they affect antiquitie, as coueting thereby credence and honor of elder yeeres yet I am of opinion, and eke the beſt learned are
of the lyke, that thoſe auncient ſolemne vvordes are a great ornament both in the one &
in the other; the one Labouring to ſet forth in hys vvorke an eternall image of antiquitie,
and the other carefully diſcourſing matters of grauitie and import aunce. For if my memo
ry ſayle not, Tullie in that booke, vvherein he endeuoureth to ſet forth the paterne of a

¶.ij.   perfect

Figure 9: First page of E.K.'s epistle to Harvey, facing page of "To
His Booke" in *The Shepheardes Calender*, 1579. Reproduced by permission of the Bodleian Library (4.F.2.Art.Bs.(11)).

LYNETTE C. BLACK

Prudence in Book II of *The Faerie Queene*

Spenser's "allegory of prudence," far from being confined to the rooms of the three sages in the turret of Alma's castle, permeates the structure and meaning of the quest of Sir Guyon, the Knight of Temperance. Iconographic evidence prompts a reading of Guyon's journey according to the model of the scholastic Prudence, the source of the other virtues. Guyon's failures are aberrations caused by the lack of prudence and his final victory is the prudent containment of the passions. Iconographic clues direct the reader to the many manifestations of Prudence, chief of which perhaps is Wise Counsel, or Consilium, the gift of the Holy Spirit that perfects Prudence. For this reason the emblem of Prudence, rather than Temperance, appears at Guyon's visionary moment in the turret of the House of Temperance. The three sages, according to their iconographic traits, constitute Wise Counsel and also exemplify mnemonic procedure, since memory belongs to the prudent person. After his encounter with the three sages, Guyon exhibits attributes of prudence that allow him to counteract his earlier errors, so that with prudence as the eye of reason he overcomes the concupiscent eye of Acrasia and unlike Grille, who remains beast, chooses virtue over vice. It is Prudence that renders temperance effective in the struggle of the rational soul over the lower orders.

SIR GUYON, THE KNIGHT of Temperance in Book Two of Edmund Spenser's *The Faerie Queene,* experiences a visionary moment in the House of Alma, the castle representing the human body ideally governed by the temperate soul (Canto 9). In the turret, Sir Guyon visits Alma's three sages, who, according to the generally acknowledged interpretation, collectively constitute Spenser's "allegory of prudence."[1] Past, present, and future being their salient attributes, they conform to Aristotle's and Aquinas' descriptions of prudence as rational judgment and as intuition about the future resulting from memory of the past.[2]

The established interpretation of the allegory, far from explaining the complex and provocative dimensions of the three sages, provides a springboard for exploring issues raised by their very presence and by the timeliness of the visit of the Knight of Temperance to their chambers. The definition of the three sages as the allegory of prudence opens the way for the investigation of the connection between prudence, manifested at this visionary moment in the quest of Sir Guyon, and temperance, the titular virtue of Book II.

According to Renaissance views of the virtues, such as those of Spenser's contemporary Lodowick Bryskett, it is prudence that makes the other virtues effective: ". . . she [prudence] is so inseparable a companion unto them all [the virtues], as if she be taken from them, they remaine of smal valew or effect."[3] The interdependence of these virtues for the moral life belongs to the realm of commonplace thought, if the frontispiece to Cesar Ripa's *Nova Iconologia* is any indication. Here (fig. 1) prudence, with her serpent and looking glass, bears equal rank with temperance, with her bridle and set square.[4] Her location in the turret/brain of the person perfected in temperance shows that prudence is the guiding force of the temperate soul, which is by the presence of prudence naturally inclined toward virtuous action.[5] Therefore in Guyon's story prudence is not restricted to the three chambers of Alma's brain;[6] indeed, she is instrumental in Guyon's confrontation with the Bower of Bliss, the place where the rational order has lost control. As this study shows, the success of the Knight of Temperance in reversing the Circe-like effects of Acrasia, whose prisoners appear as beasts, depends on the light of reason provided by prudence.

PRUDENCE AS REASON

That Spenser would have portrayed prudence as synonymous with reason can be inferred from Bryskett, whose *Discourse of Civill Life* includes the famous persona of Spenser referring to the writing of *The Faerie Queene*. Here prudence is called "the light of reason." In his summary of Renaissance psychology concerning the three souls, Bryskett explains that prudence as reason controls the lower orders.

The three souls, in ascending order, are the vegetative, the sensible, and the rational souls. The irascible passions arise from the vegetative faculty and the concupiscent passions from the sensible soul. It is the function of the rational soul to keep the lower faculties in order through prudence, which illumines the other powers with the light of reason:

> But you must remember, that though it was said, that those morall vertues were founded in those parts of the mind wanting reason, yet were they guided by the light of reason. And this light of reason (as much as concerneth mens actions) is nothing else but Prudence, which is a vertue of the understanding, and the rule and measure of all the morall vertues concerning our actions and affects. . . .[7]

Spenser presents this role of reason/prudence in the allegory of Guyon's adventures. Jerry Leath Mills, in an article on the geometric shape of Alma's Castle, demonstrates that in the figure of the triangle contained in a square, Spenser represents the containment of the lower souls by the higher.[8] It is Prudence surmounting this structure with her guiding position in the turret that activates temperance to achieve this purpose.

According to the principle that the perfection of prudence makes temperance an active virtue, Guyon's ineffectiveness against Cymoclese and Pyroclese can be read as the inability of temperance per se to dominate over the base passions.

Before his direct vision of prudence in the House of Alma, Guyon lacks the natural inclination to temperance given by reason, although with the Palmer's aid he has seemed to understand the concept. The Palmer counters Guyon's wrath provoked by Archimago:

> His race with reason, and with words his will,
> From foule intemperance he oft did stay,
> And suffered not in wrath his hastie steps to stray.
>
> (1.34. 7–9)

Guyon acknowledges the basic principle that reason must rule the lower orders, as he points out to the Palmer the emblematic meaning of Amavia's suicide:

Behold the image of mortalitie
And feeble nature cloth'd with fleshly tyre,
When raging passion with fierce tyranie
Robs reason of her due regalitie,
And makes it servant to her basest part. . . .

(1.57. 2–6)

In spite of this understanding, however, Guyon has trouble with the "raging passions" embodied in Pyrocles, the burning emblem of Wrath (Fig. 2),[9] and Cymocles, his slothful and concupiscent complement. Before his vision of the allegory of Prudence, Guyon remains vulnerable to their assaults, at his low point when in a death-like swoon after leaving the Cave of Mammon, he is protected from the ravages of Pyrocles and Cymocles by the Palmer and by grace in the person of Arthur, who finally slays them. A. C. Hamilton's assessment that Guyon is here an "emblem of man's body dominated by the irascible and concupiscent affections"[10] is consonant with this "prudent" reading of the episode.

TEMPERANCE AND THE MEAN

Guyon's incomplete success over Cymocles and Pyrocles is foreshadowed by his confrontation with Sans Loy (of "lawless lust" [2.18.5]) and Sir Huddibras (strength without reason [2.17.6–7]) in the House of Medina. By contrast with the naturally well-regulated Castle of Alma, the House of Medina operates by an uneasy peace, which Medina imposes between warring elements exemplified by her sisters and their champions. Allegorically this would suggest the insufficiency of the mean as the best definition of temperance; without the inclination to temperance brought about by prudence, the mean can exist only through constant struggle.

The extremes with difficulty mediated in Medina's house exemplify on one level pleasure and pain. Medina stands between her sisters Elissa, who is "discontent for want of mirth or meat" (2.35.4), and Perissa, whose "pleasure and delight" (2.36.5) find no measure. Elissa and Perissa exemplify Aristotle's description of temperance "ruined by excess and deficiency": ". . . if [someone] gratifies himself with every pleasure and refrains from none, he becomes temperate, but if he avoids them all, as boors do, he becomes a sort of insensible person."[11] According to Aristotle, pleasure and pain are measures of habituation to virtue because if one is pained by the practice of the acts associated with the virtue, the virtue itself is absent: "If someone who abstaining from bodily pleasures enjoys the abstinence itself, then he is temperate; but if he is grieved by it, he is intemperate."[12] Elissa, pained by her abstinence, embodies the reverse of the ideal use of pleasure and pain in the virtuous life.

Guyon's involvement with the champions of these sisters demonstrates his reliance on the mean to make his efforts against the enemies of temperance successful. Guyon has, in fact, acknowledged the mean in his eulogy for Amavia and Mordant, exemplars of pleasure and pain ("The strong through pleasure soonest falles, the weake through smart" [1.57.9]) and in his decision to place their baby into the care of Medina:

> But temperance (said he) with golden squire
> Betwixt them both can measure out a meane,
> Neither to melt in pleasures whot desire,
> Nor fry in hartlesse griefe and dolefull teene.
>
> (1.58.1–4)

This recognition of the mean is translated into experience of it in the House of Medina. Guyon tries to fend off both Elissa's champion, the self-tormenting malcontent Huddibras (2.37), and Sans Loy, whose lawlessness takes "exceeding joy" (2.37.3) in the mirthful Perissa. As Medina steps in to stop their assaults, her action allegorically relates the effect of the mean in tempering extremes. Pyrocles' and Cymocles' association with pleasure and pain (Cymocles lost in sensuous delights with Acrasia and Pyrocles tormented by fire) echo with reverberating dimensions these extremes that have already attacked Guyon in the forms of Sans Loy and Huddibras.

ATTRIBUTES OF PRUDENCE

Since Guyon's experience at Medina's house is not enough to allow him victory, it must be the visit to Alma that prepares him for the final triumph. To discover what the House of Alma adds to the experience of temperance, we remember the traditional interpretation of Alma's sages as the "allegory of Prudence" and follow the iconographic clues to the many facets of this virtue. An exploration of the expressions and ramifications of prudence not only highlights the rich complexity of the iconography of the three sages but, perhaps more importantly, reveals the empowering aspects of that virtue in Guyon's overthrow of Acrasia.

To the Renaissance prudence, descended from classical rhetoric as filtered through medieval scholastics, belongs a complex network of attributes, not the least of which for Guyon's adventures is the ability to choose wisely. Related to Aristotle's principles concerning the habituation of pleasure and pain in the choice of virtuous action over base action, a common attribute of Renaissance prudence is the ability to discern good from evil.[13] According to Bryskett, prudence enables one "to consider what is profitable, and to apprehend it: and likewise to eschew all that is hurtful."[14] Nicholas Caussin, giving points to remember about prudence, says that prudence means "to be intelligent and able to judge well," knowing people not just "from the outward bark."[15] These definitions of prudence stem from the Macrobian elaboration of Cicero's three aspects of prudence listed by Rosemund Tuve as *memoria, intelligentia,* and *providentia*.[16] The term *"circumspectio"* appears in Macrobius's list as an expansion of Cicero's second term, *intelligentia*. Medieval iconography stresses the circumspection or discernment of prudence by giving her a sieve for sifting the true from the false, and Renaissance devices similarly represent the discernment of the bearer.[17] Ripa's figure for prudence is flanked by a stag (Fig. 3) to show that one must "ruminate before resolving on a thing;"[18] the divided hoof of the stag, according to Valeriano, shows that one must examine things separately in order

Another attribute, perhaps a corollary to discernment, is deliberation based on Wise Counsel. According to the medieval tradition described by Rosemund Tuve, Consilium comes as one of the seven gifts of the Holy Spirit. Prudence thus perfected by counsel becomes the Christian virtue depicted in medieval iconography.[20] Aquinas writes" . . . the gift of Counsel corresponds to prudence, as helping and perfecting it."[21] A second concept related to discernment is the idea that virtuous action results from choices based upon Good Counsel. Prudence is the virtue that activates the others because the person perfected in prudence naturally performs actions that are virtuous; furthermore, his deliberated choices imply action. The idea that action follows counsel underlies the balance between speed and deliberation which passes into proverb in the Renaissance.[22] In the words of Erasmus' adage *festina lente,* one combines "the speed of diligence and the slowness of deliberation."[23] The balanced tension between the opposites which characterizes the mean is implicit in this attribute of prudence.

PRUDENCE IN THE HOUSE OF ALMA

Guyon is confirmed in prudence by his encounter with Counsel in the turret of Alma's castle, the mind of the rational soul. Following the knights' vision of Good Counsel and their deliberation on national history (Canto 10), Spenser's narrative presents the prudent moment for action. Thus the battles of Arthur against Maleger and of Guyon against Acrasia take place only after prudence has been perfected by Counsel. Since Guyon is the champion of temperance, his story rather than Arthur's is the focus of this discussion, which addresses the connection between prudence and temperance in Spenser's allegory.[24]

Spenser stresses prudence as the counsellor of the temperate body by introducing the sages as Alma's advisors: "These three in these three rooms did sundry dwell,/and counselled faire Alma, how to governe well" (9.48.8–9). In making this association, Spenser participates in a tradition similarly seen in contemporary sources. Cesar Ripa in his *Iconologia* gives prudence (Fig. 3) a helmet which "signifies the Wisdom of a prudent Man, to be armed with wise counsel to defend himself."[25] The time aspects of Prudence belong similarly to Counsel. Ripa's "Consiglio" (fig. 4) carries in his right hand a book with an owl's head for the study of wisdom and a three-headed animal figure representing the Egyptian deity Serapis for knowledge of past, present, and future.[26] Alluding to this ancient god, Titian paints in his "allegory of Prudence" three animal heads beneath three human faces to represent past, present, and future.[27] Thus linked by concept and iconography, prudence and counsel overlap with respect to their temporal attributes. Further, Bryskett explains the role of counsel in the process of prudent decision making: "Next to counsell cometh judgment, and after judgement followeth election, and from election issueth the action or the effects that are resolved upon and accepted as best."[28] That the three sages "counsel" Alma indicates the prudent decision-making process beginning with the receptivity of the rational mind to spiritual perfection through Consilium and culminating in virtuous action.

The time attributes are essential to the definition of prudence, the virtue leads to action because intuition of the future comes from an understanding of the past and a clear discernment of the present. The three sages collectively provide this allegory of prudence.

The inhabitant of the first chamber of the brain, irrational as he might seem, provides insight into the future. Spenser's description of the first sage seems to undercut the rational power of the brain. The images in his chamber are disparaged as "idle fantasies" (9.50.7) even though image-making is a function of the brain. Phantastes' illusions and melancholy character hardly establish him on the surface as part of prudence. But by contrast to the illusions produced by Archimago earlier and by Pleasure's Porter later, his images transcend the senses and provide intuition for the future, the aspect of prudence represented by Phantastes, whose "sharpe foresight" (9.49.8) establishes him as the face that looks to the future. Furthermore, he is the youngest of the three, being "a man of yeares yet fresh" (9.52.3). His chamber, being "dispainted all within/With sundry colours" (9.50.1–2), shows that the rational soul creates images, which because they take their reality from the imagination, transcend the senses from which they originate. The eyes and ears are not to be relied on for pure images, which come from the rational, not the sensible soul: ". . . the chamber filled was with flyes,/Which buzzed all about, and made such sound,/That they encombred all mens eares and eyes" (9.51.1–3). The transcendent images provide a vision of the future. Phantastes brings the "Infinite shapes of things dispersed then;/Some such as in the world were never yit" (9.50.3–4), the "yit" in a final emphatic position implying future reality; and he offers "soothsayes, and prophesies" (9.51.8).

The unnamed sage of the middle chamber, who, like the present time, of which he can "best advise" (9.49.2), does not long detain his visitors. As the second face of prudence which looks to the present, that most elusive of all moments, the brevity of the visit is accounted for by the brief poise of present ripeness, another attribute of prudence.

The iconographay associated with ripeness defines the second sage as that part of prudence which teaches the appropriate moment for action. He is "a man of ripe and perfect age" (9.54.2), ripeness, or *maturitas,* being a combination of haste and caution.[29] Action comes at the perfect moment, after counsel has brought the decision to fruition. The emblems for Maturitas reveal this aspect of prudence, associated with the popular Renaissance motto *festina lente.* To depict this kind of maturity, Ripa's prudence (Fig. 3) holds an arrow for speed combined with the remora which slows down a ship to suggest "not to delay doing good when time serves."[30] Alciati's emblem "maturandum" (Fig. 5), which is indexed under the heading "Prudentia" in the Paris 1534 edition, pictures the remora and arrow with the subscriptio explaining not to delay too long nor act too soon.[31] In *The Boke Named the Governour* Thomas Elyot explains *maturitas* as an aspect of Prudence, by drawing an analogy with dancing. The tutor can teach prudence by teaching dancing; for example, the "braule" signifies "celerite and slownesse" which discord yields "an excellent vertue" for which he says he is "constrained to usurpe a latine worde, callyng it Maturitie." He further describes the concept in language that explains the importance of the word *ripe* as applied to the second sage: " 'Consulte before thou enterprise any thinge, and after thou hast taken counsayle, it is expedient to do it maturely.' Maturum in Latyn maye be enterpretid *ripe* or *redy,* as fruite when it is ripe it is at the very poynte to be gathered and eaten."[32] The second sage represents the present moment poised for action. He is like the bearded youth who represents the vitality of youth combined with the caution of age in Titian's Allegory of Prudence.[33]

In the lines describing the second sage, we find the aspect of prudence that involves comprehensive knowledge. The description of his knowledge corresponds to definitions of prudence found in contemporary dictionaries. Among the definitions for prudence in Thomas Cooper's *Thesaurus* of 1584 are "prudentia in judicando" and "knowledge of the civill law, Prudentia juris civilis," "a very deep wisdom, altissima prudentia."[34] The second sage is the skill for laws, or *juris prudence:* Painted in his room are "picturals/Of magistrates, of courts, of tribunals,/Of commen wealthes, of states, of pollicy,/Of lawe of judgments, and of decretals" (53.4–7) Further, the sage embodies the picture of prudence as the leader of the liberal arts, a concept depicted in a tapestry of 1525[35] and based on the *Anticlaudianus* of Alain de Lisle.[36] His walls are also decorated with "All artes, all science, all Philosophy,/And all that in the world was aye thought wittily" (9.53.8–9). The second sage contemplates all knowledge: "[He] did them meditate all his life long,/That through continuall practise and usage,/He now was growne right wise, and wondrous sage" (9.54.3–5). He fulfills Aquinas' advice to the prudent person to learn from the ancients.[37]

Eumnestes, the "Man of infinite remembrance" (9.56.1), like Phantastes in that his description seems to undercut the very power he represents, inhabits a chambre tainted with mortality, "ruinous and old" (9.55.1); he is "an old oldman, halfe blind,/all decrepit in his feeble corse" (9.55, 5–6). His books are "worm-eaten, and full of canker holes" (9.57.9) and things are sometimes "lost or laid amis" (9.58.6). Nevertheless, his name means Good Memory, and his shortcomings are compensated for by Anamnestes, who finds lost objects and whose youth complements his master's old age. Like the sense images transcended by Phantastes, the written materials are transcended by the memory process: all events are preserved in "his immortall scrine,/Where they for ever incorrupted dweld" (9.56.6–7).[38]

Separately, then, the extremes represented by Phantastes and Eumnestes do not signify prudence; only together and in conjunction
with the *maturitas* of the middle sage do their apparent limitations
yield the allegory of Prudence, or counsel based on an understanding
of past and future that leads to virtuous action.

Not only do the sages figure prudence, but they also represent the
way information is processed in the brain.[39] The tripartite operations
of the brain in receiving, processing, and storing information thus
described by Renaissance theorists corresponds to the three chambers
of Alma's turret. Stephen Batman describes the three divisions in
the brain:

> ... the foremost in which the vertu Imaginativa worketh.
> There are those things that the wit comprehendeth without
> be ordained and put others together . . . The middle chamber
> termed Logica: therein the reason sensible or vertu Estimativa
> is a maister. The third and the last, which is Memorativa, the
> vertu of the mind. That vertu holdeth and keepeth in the trea-
> sure of the minde. . . .[40]

The process begins with the imagination. Bryskett notes that information is received as images: ". . . without the fantasie we can understand nothing in this life, since from the senses the formes of all things
are represented unto us."[41] Next the information is organized as
knowledge. The second sage, comprehending not only jurisprudence
but many areas of learning, suggests the codification of information.
And, of couorse, Eumnestes and Anamnestes illustrate the storage
and retrieval of information. Huarte explains the way the powers
work together:

> ... It behooves that the understander go beholding the fan-
> tasmes; and the office of the memorie is, to preserve these fan-
> tasmes, to the end that the understanding may contemplat them,
> and if this be lost, it is impossible that the powers can worke;
> and that the office of memorie is none other, than to preserve
> the figures of things, without that it appertains thereto to de-
> vise them.[42]

Spenser's three sages in this way yield altogether the process of memory, which is thus not confined to Eumnestes' chamber alone.[43]

Since the memory process is embodied by the three sages, it might be worth considering Alma's turret as a lesson in the art of memory. This model would help to explain the affiliation of Phantastes with melancholy. Phantastes is

> Of swarth complexion and of crabbed hew
> That him full of melancholy did shew
> Bent hollow beetle browes, sharpe staring ees,
> That mad or foolish seemd: one by his view
> Mote deeme him borne with ill disposed skyes,
> When oblique Saturne sate in the house of agonyes.

> (9.52.4–9)

Frances Yates in her *Art of Memory* notes that Saturn represents prudence in John Ridewall's moralization of mythology, which assigns pagan gods as memory images for the use of preachers. In Camillo's memory theatre, Saturn is one of the seven pillars of Solomon's House of Wisdom. The Saturn series includes the symbol of the wolf, lion, and dog, the triceps figure described above as an emblem of Good Counsel, in three of its six steps. Further, the melancholy temperament is the one most suited to memory because of its cold and dry elements were best for saving impressions in the brain.[44] In addition, the name of the first sage recalls the Aristotelian idea, the basis for Huarte's discussion of images and memory quoted above, that phantasms form a common point between dreams and memory images.[45]

The presence of the memory process in Spenser's allegory of prudence broadens the role of the memory: it is not simply the third part of prudence but forms an essential attribute of the prudent person. In her interpretive summary of scholastic traditions of memory, Mary Carruthers brings out the view of Thomas Aquinas and others that since prudence depends on recollecting the past with deliberative judgment, a trained memory is a condition for prudence.[46] The trained memory was "coextensive with wisdom and knowledge, but it was more- as a condition of prudence possessing a well-trained memory was morally virtuous in itself."[47] The moral power of memory underlies the lessons of history which Arthur and Guyon read in the scrolls retrieved in Eumnestes' chamber.

Guyon's memory, symbolized by his reading the historical scrolls and sharpened by the visual images of prudence, signifies his progress toward internalizing that virtue. According to the theory of the artificial memory, the picture carries with it the intent to acquire the virtue placed in memory.[48] The disposition to virtue is the mark of its perfection because it evidences a natural inclination to virtuous action. Harry Berger uses the concept that "temperance can be perfected into a natural inclination of being" to show a shift in focus in the last five cantos away from an Aristotelian temperance to a Christian temperance.[49] Good Counsel as a gift of the Holy Spirit perfects prudence that activates the other virtues. The last five cantos operate fundamentally according to this paradigm in that prudence makes it possible for temperance to triumph over her enemies.

Thus Guyon and Arthur fight Alma's enemies on separate fronts after their vision of prudence. It is Arthur, not the Palmer, who has accompanied Guyon at this moment of contemplation. Following Guyon as the champion of temperance, we note that as he leaves the House of Alma, Guyon is once again accompanied by the Palmer. The Palmer's absence from the House of Alma suggests that his role as reason seen in earlier cantos is different from that of the rational mind portrayed by the sages, who, as explained above, involve the perfection of prudence as counsel.

The Palmer resumes his role as Guyon's guide with a specific mission signified by his association with Mercury, which Spenser chooses to introduce at this point. On leaving the House of Alma, Guyon launches the assault on the Bower of Bliss, the source of wrongful domination by the lower passions. His assault will restore the subordination of the lower orders to the rule of reason, as Arthur has previously done for Guyon personally in defeating Pyrocles and Cymocles. Guyon is aided by the Palmer with Mercurial powers of protection against Circe and the chimera of the underworld. The Palmer's staff puts down the threatening monsters of horror and passion (12.36–40) because it is made of the same material as Mercury's Caduceus:

> Of that same wood it fram'd was cunningly,
> Of which Caduceus whilome was made,
> Caduceus the rod of Mercury,
> With which he wonts the Stygian realmes invade,
> Through ghastly horrour, and eternall shade;
> Th' infernall feends with it he can asswage,
> And Orcus tame, whom nothing can perswade,
> And rule the Furyes, when they most do rage:
> Such vertue in his staffe had eke this Palmer sage.

> (12.41)

Mercury clears away the clouds with his staff in Botticelli's "Prima-vera,"[50] performing an allegorically similar task to that of Guyon's Palmer. Mercury is linked by long tradition and in intricate ways to the virtue of Prudence. For example, according to Servius' commentary, Mercury is called "deus prudentiae."[51] Because of his role as messenger, he is associated with eloquence.[52] Since the orator's skill implies a trained memory, which is evidence of prudence, rhetoric was equated with prudence. Thus Renaissance emblematists conflate Mercury with wisdom or specifically with Prudence. Hadrian Le Jeune's emblem 17 entitled "La Prudence joincte avec la force" portrays the concept by a double figure of Mercury looking before and after, recalling the bifrons figure of Prudence.[53] Cummings has explored the conflation of Mercury and Cupid to explain the Cupid guarding Guyon's inert body after the encounter with Mammom. If, as he suggests, Cupid and the Palmer are both spiritual guides of Guyon,[54] the Mercury association externalizes in both figures the fact that prudence guides Guyon in his confrontations with the enemies of the rational order.

Thus it is appropriate that at the approach to Acrasia's Bower, the Mercurial powers of the Palmer should be in the forefront. In his role as wisdom or reason, he clears away the monsters of Guyon's lower-order passions so that as Knight of Temperance he can overturn their effects.

The battle is waged, in the tradition of the psychomachia, in antithetical pairs. It would be too limiting to the rich imagery and the complex web of issues characteristic of Spenser's allegory to demand that all details fit this pattern, yet part of Spenser's artistry here involves elements that allegorically echo early ones, such as Acrasia's fountain and Amavia's fountain.[55] Several elements of the last episodes can be read fruitfully as fulfillments of earlier episodes. In his sea voyage, Guyon faces temptations as he did in approaching the cave of Mammon, but instead of following the broad and easy way, he follows the Boatman and the Palmer in order to keep to "the narrow way" (12.18.4). Whereas before he had naively spared Pyrocles, freed Occasion and Furor, and been moved by "pitty vayne" (5.24.6), here, heeding the Palmer's warning about "foolish pity" (12.29.2), he submits to the governance of reason: "The knight was ruled, and the Boatman strayt/Held on his course with stayed stedfastnesse" (12.29.5–6). His naive lack of self-knowledge evidenced in the Mammon episode[56] is countered at the gates of the Bower of Bliss. The self-deception offered by "Pleasure's Porter" is "quite contrary" to the celestial Genius "that is our Selfe, whom though we do not see,/ Yet each doth in him selfe it well perceive to bee" (12.47.8–9). The false genius "doth us procure to fall,/Through guileful semblaunts, which he makes us see" (12.48.5–6). In the light of Prudence as self-knowledge,[57] Guyon's overthrowing the instruments of deception, the staff and bowl, indicates his discretion in distinguishing between true self knowledge and illusion. Acrasia's bower opposes Alma's rational soul, lodged in "that heavenly towre,/That God hath built for *his owne blessed bowre*" (9.47.4–5), italics mine). Acrasia's bower conceptually and linguistically opposes God's bower, as concupiscence opposes reason.

The eye of reason opposes the concupiscent eye of Acrasia in the final battle of Guyon's quest. The eye as a hieroglyph for Prudence to which Bryskett's phrase "eye of the mind"[58] alludes, is inherited tradition. Caussin explains the tradition "that Prudence, as antiquity hath presented it unto us in their Herioglyphicks, is an hand enchased with eye."[59] An illustration of Prudence in a 1677 edition of Ripa's *Iconologie* showing a large eye radiating from her bosom, though too late to be a source for Spenser, suggests the popularity of the concept of prudence as higher vision (Fig. 6).[60] While the emphasis on vision in Book II may suggest the problem with artistic images that iconoclasts would destroy,[61] a reading of the sights of the Bower as the antithesis of the watchful eye of prudence is in keeping with the overall structure of Book II, which points toward the final victory of the rational powers over the lower orders.

The Bower of Acrasia appeals to the sense of sight. These are not monstrous shapes like those of Maleger's forces that assaulted the Forts of Alma's senses, but "the most daintie paradise on ground,/ It selfe doth offer to his sober eye" (12.58.1–2). The nymphs showing themselves through the water "th' amorous sweet spoiles to greedy eyes revele" (12.64.9). The nymph in the fountain of concupiscence threatens to replace Shamefastenesse, "the fountain of [his] modesty" (9.43.8), whose blushing she mirrors and distorts (12.68.1–3). But Guyon heeds reason's rebuke to his "wandering eyes" (12.69.2).

It is through the eye that Acrasia enchants, using her eyes as weapons against Verdant. Acrasia "with her false eyes fast fixed in his sight" takes away his power as "through his humid eyes did sucke his spright" (12.73. 2,7); "Her snowy brest was bare to readie spoyle/ Of hungry eies" (12.78.1–2). Acrasia reduces Sir Verdant to sloth (his armes are hanging on a tree) because, unlike Guyon, he has had no rebuke for his wandering eyes.

The evil eye of Acrasia, like the self-deceptive illusions that the false Genius produces, represents the vice inimical to the eye of the soul. God's bower destroys Acrasia's bower as the eye of prudence enlightening the Knight of Temperance overcomes the lust of the eye.

If the last scene shows the victory of the higher over the lower order, the example of the men-turned beasts, particularly Grille, solidifies the lesson in emblematic form.[62] Without the power of prudence these men have chosen vice over virtue, and the lower orders dominate so that human reason is no longer manifest in them. In the case of Grille, his memory, unlike that of Guyon, whose memory was restored to him in God's bower, remains fallen; his preference for bestial form testifies to his having forgotten what it is to be human. Guyon's final speech is an emblematic one, as he points to Grille and explains his significance:

> . . . See the mind of beastly man,
> That hath so soone forgot the excellence
> Of his creation, when he life began,
> That now he chooseth, with vile difference,
> To be a beast, and lacke intelligence.

(12.87.1–5)

In Grille there is an object lesson on what a creature man would be without the intellective virtue, the rational soul, of which Prudence is the central light. Without memory, that essential aspect of prudence, Grille is unable to make good decisions for the future, as he lacks prudent discernment to distinguish good from evil. He embodies the opposite of prudence, according to Bryskett's statement of the goal: ". . . a man by knowing himselfe, becommeth in this life sage and prudent, and understandeth that he is made not to live onely, as other creatures are, but also to live well. For they that have not this knowledge, are like unto bruite beasts. . . ."[63] The fact that the book ends with this emblematic figure and text is further evidence for the predominance of prudence in the narrative structure of Book II.

Guyon's story tells the victory of the eye of reason, without which temperance falls victim to excess. Prudence must accompany the knight of Temperance, therefore, in order to render temperance effective in the struggle of the rational soul over the lower orders. The visit to the three sages, the allegory of prudence, is central to Guyon's activity as the champion of temperance.

The University of Memphis

Notes

1. Walter R. Davis, "Alma, castle" *Spenser Encyclopedia*, p. 24; *Books I and II of "The Faerie Queene,"* ed. Robert Kellogg and Oliver Steele (New York: Odyssey, 1965), p. 343 n. 47.8–9; see also Jerry Leath Mills, "Prudence, History, and the Prince in *The Faerie Queene*, Book II," *Huntington Library Quarterly* 61 (1978): 86 for a summary of traditions of prudence in the sages; and for a discussion of Eumnestes, memory, and prudence, see Judith Anderson, " 'Myn Auctour': Spenser's Enabling Fiction and Eumnestes' 'immortal scrine'," in *Unfolded Tales: Essays on Renaissance Romance*, ed. George M. Logan and Gordon Teskey (Ithaca: Cornell University Press, 1989), 16–31.

2. Joseph Pieper summarizes aspects of prudence based on Thomas Aquinas in *The Four Cardinal Virtues: Prudence, Justice, Fortitude, Temperance*. (Notre Dame: University of Notre Dame Press, 1966). See especially pages 14–18 for a discussion of *memoria, docilitas, solertia,* and *providentia*, from which the temporal attributes are derived. Judith Anderson refers to the classical heritage of the three sages, p. 20.

3. *A Discourse of Civill Life* [1606], ed. Thomas E. Wright (Northridge: San Fernando Valley State College, 1970), 188–89. The reciprocity of the virtues stems from scholastic theology. Joseph Pieper explains: "Prudence is the *cause* of the other virtues being virtues at all. For example, there may be a kind of instinctive governance of instinctual cravings; but only prudence transforms this instinctive governance into the 'virtue' of temperance" (p. 6). Samuel Chew notes that some Renaissance sources follow the Aristotelian view of the priority of prudence over the virtues, whereas others assign to temperance the role of mother of virtues. See his *The Pilgrimage of Life* (New Haven and London: Yale University Press, 1962), 134–35.

4. The serpent for prudence is described by Adolf Katzenellenbogen, *Allegories of the Virtues and Vices in Medieval Art,* trans. Alan J. P. Crick (New York: Norton, 1964), plate 33. The Scriptural basis for this figure is the admonition to be wise as serpents and simple as doves (Matt. 10:16). The looking glass of Prudence, according to Cesar Ripa, "bids us examine our Defects by knowing ourselves" (*Nova Iconologia* [Padua, 1618], p. 270); Samuel Chew notes the bridle as a customary icon for temperance. For further discussion of the iconography of these virtues, see especially his pp. 135–37. (The illustrations in this article are from books in The Stirling Maxwell Collection at the University of Glasgow Library and are reproduced with the kind permission of the librarian.)

5. In his summary Pieper shows that prudence endows the other virtues with their very essence and explains the connection between goodness and virtuous action accordingly: "And so prudence imprints the inward seal of goodness upon all free activity of man. Ethical virtue is the print and seal placed by prudence upon voliton and action" (pp. 7–8).

6. See Robert L. Reid, "Alma's Castle and the Symbolization of Reason in *The Faerie Queene*," *Journal of English and Germanic Philology* 80 (1981): 512–27. Reid, noting the powerlessness of Alma and asserting that "the sages are not free to enact their wisdom beyond their cells," proposes that Arthur and Guyon serve as their agents in putting their power into action. In asserting the centrality of prudence to

the action of the last cantos, I offer a different angle on the relationship between the turret and the battles. Symbolic figures, Alma and her counselors externalize the principle of temperance informed by prudence, which pervades the allegorical actions of the knights.

7. P. 186.

8. "Spenser, Lodowick Bryskett, and the Mortalist Controversy: *The Faerie Queene,* II.ix.22," *Philological Quarterly,* 52:2 (1973): 173–86. Mills shows that since the higher faculty encompasses the lower, man is morally responsible for his actions.

9. Ripa's image of Wrath shows a figure holding a firebrand. See the *Nova Iconologia* (Padua, 1618), p. 270.

10. A. C. Hamilton, *The Structure of Allegory in The Faerie Queene* (Oxford: Clarendon Press, 1961), 101.

11. *Nichomachean Ethics,* trans. Terence Irwin (Indianapolis: Hackett Publishing Company, 1985) p. 36, 1104a20.

12. *Ethics,* p. 37, 1104b5.

13. Thomas Cooper's *Thesaurus* of 1584 and Thomas Elyot's *Dictionary Biblioteka* both note that prudence is "wisdom in eschewing and desiring of things."

14. p. 188

15. *The Holy Court in Five Tomes,* trans. Sir Thomas Hawkins, 3rd ed. (London: John Williams, 1663), 90.

16. *Allegorical Imagery: Some Mediaeval Books and Their Posterity* (Princeton: Princeton University Press, 1966), appendix. For a useful discussion of the evolving lists of attributes of prudence, see Frances Yates's summary of Aquinas's use of Tullius, Macrobius, and Aristotle. See her *Art of Memory* (Chicago: University of Chicago Press, 1966), 73–74.

17. Tuve reproduces two manuscript illustrations of prudence with a sieve. See her figures 14 and 17 and pp. 72–74. See also the sieve as the device with the motto "Ecquis discernit utrumque" in Claude Paradin's *Devises Heroiques* (Lyon, 1551), 90.

18. Fig. 3 is from the Padua 1618 edition, 428. The following English translation of the description of prudence is from the London 1709 edition (New York and London: Garland Publishing, 1976), 63: "The Helmet signifies the Wisdom of a prudent Man, to be arm'd with wise counsel to defend himself: the Stag chewing, that we should ruminate before resolving on a Thing. The Miroir bids us examine our Defects by knowing ourselves. The Remora, that stops a ship, not to delay doing good, when Time serves."

19. Jan Pierius Valerian, *Commentaire Heiroglyphiques ou Images des choses,* trans. Gabriel Chappuys (Lyons: Barthelemy Honorat, 1576), Vol. 2, 138.1.

20. See Tuve's appendix and her discussion pp. 89–102. The medieval traditions for this concept are depicted in an eleventh century gospel frontispiece reproduced by Katzenellenbogen (Fig. 38) in which Consilium in a plate to the left balances Prudence in the corresponding plate to the right.

21. *Summa Theologica,* trans. Fathers of the English Dominican Province (New York: Benzinger Brothers, 1917), II-II, 52, 3. Aquinas's argument leading to this conclusion shows further the connection of prudence to reason and to counsel: "The gift of counsel is about what has to be done for the sake of the end. Now prudence is about the same matter. Therefore they correspond to one another. . . .

A lower principle of movement is helped chiefly, and is perfected through being moved by a higher principle of movement, as a body through being moved by a spirit. Now it is evident that the rectitude of human reason is compared to the Divine reason, as a lower motive principle to a higher: for the Eternal Reason is the supreme rule of all human rectitude. Consequently prudence, which denotes rectitude of reason, is chiefly perfected and helped through being ruled and moved by the Holy Ghost, and this belongs to the gift of counsel, as stated above."

22. Edgar Wind, *Pagan Mysteries in the Renaissance,* rev. ed. (New York and London: Norton, 1968), 98.

23. Margaret Mann Phillips, *The Adages of Erasmus: A Study with Translations* (Cambridge: Cambridge University Press, 1964), 177.

24. For a discussion of Arthur, see Mills, "Prudence."

25. The translation is from a 1709 version of Ripa, *Iconologia, or Morall Emblems,* published in London, p. 63. See note 18 herein.

26. This figure for Consiglio illustrates the 1613 Sienna edition of Ripa's *Iconologia,* Part One, p. 127.

27. For a discussion of this painting and its allusion to Serapis, see chapter 4 of Erwin Panofsky's *Meaning in the Visual Arts* (Garden City: Doubleday, 1955), especially pp. 149–55.

28. p. 138.

29. See Wind, pp. 97 ff, for a discussion of *maturitas* as ripeness.

30. See note 18 herein.

31. Andreas Alciati, *Emblematum Libellus* (Paris: Christianus Wechelus, 1534), 56.

32. 1531. rpt. (London: J. M. Dent, 1907), 98.

33. For a discussion of ripeness and the *puer senex* motif, see Wind, 99–101.

34. See also Thomas Elyot's *Dictionary* of 1548.

35. Heinrich Gobel, *Tapestries of the Lowlands,* trans. Robert West (Hacker Art Books, 1974), PL. 87, "The Seven Free Arts construct the car of wisdom under the direction of Prudentia."

36. See the summary in Ernst Robert Curtius, *European Literature and the Latin Middle Ages,* trans. Willard R. Trask (New York and Evanston: Harper and Row, 1953), 119–21.

37. *S.T.* II-II 49,3. "Thus it is written (Prov. iii.5)" Lean not on thy own prudence,' and (Ecclus. vi. 35): 'Stand in the multitude of the ancients (i.e., the old men), that are wise, and join thyself from thy heart to their wisdom.' "

38. Judith Anderson notes the contrast between the books and scrolls and the scrine, which represents abstract memory: "These physically decrepit records are explicitly contrasted with the disembodied purity and seeming transcendence of the content of memory, which derives from them" (20).

39. That the sages, even the imaginative faculty represented by Phantastes, represent the rational process is argued by Reid (512–27).

40. *Batman upon Bartholome, his booke De Proprietatibus rerum* (London, Thomas East, 1582), chpt. 10, p. 15.

41. p. 196.

42. Juan de Dios Huarte Navarro, The Examination of Mens Wits [1594], *The English Experience* 126 (Amsterdam and New York: Da Capo Press, 1969): 61.

43. For a discussion of the operation of the memory in the three time aspeccts, see Bonaventure's *Journey of the Mind to God* (*The Works of Bonaventure*, vol. I, *Mystical Opuscula*, trans. Jose de Vinck [Paterson, N J.: St. Anthony Guild Press, 1960], 29): "For the memory holds the past by recollection the present by reception, and the future by anticipation. . . . In the first activity—the actual retention of all temporal events, past, present, and future—memory bears a likeness to eternity, whose indivisible presentness extends to all ages. From the second activity, it appears that memory is informred, not only from the outside by material images, but also from above, by receiving and holding in itself simple forms, which could not possibly come in through the doors of the senses by means of sensible images. From the third an unchangeable light, in which it recognizes the immutable truths." The idea of eternity in the memory process might be a helpful gloss on Spenser's treatment of the transcendence of sensual images in Phantastes and of the written documents by Eumnestes.

44. See Yates, p. 97 on Ridewall, p. 144 and insert on the memory theater, and pp. 58–59 on melancholy.

45. Mary Carruthers summarizes Aristotle on this point and cites his "On Dreams" and "On Divination in Dreams" as relevant to the art of memory in her *The Book of Memory: A Study of Memory in Medieval Culture.* (Cambridge: Cambridge University Press, 1990), p. 58 and n. 66.

46. Carruthers, pp. 69–70.

47. Carruthers, p. 71.

48. Yates, p. 64.

49. *The Allegorical Temper: Vision and Reality in Book II of Spenser's "Faerie Queene"* (New Haven: Yale University Press, 1957), 62–63.

50. See Wind's interpretation of Mercury in Botticelli's painting, pp. 122–24.

51. Qtd. in R. M. Cummings, "An Iconographical Puzzle: Spenser's Cupid at *Faerie Queene* II.viii," *JWCI* 33 (1970), p. 315.

52. Martianus Capella's *Marriage of Philology and Mercury,* still popular in the Renaissance, represents discourse as Mercury.

53. *Les Emblemes du S. Hadrian le Jeune, medecin et historian des estats de Hollande* (Anvers: Christopher Plantin, 1567).

54. p. 319.

55. For an interpretation of Amavia's fountain and baptismal regeneration, see A. D. S. Fowler, "Emblems of Temperance in *The Faerie Queene,* Book II," *Review of English Studies* 11 (1960): 144–146.

56. As he goes to Mammon in vain self-confidence, relying on "his owne vertues, and prayse-worthy deedes" (7.2.5), Guyon lacks the self-knowledge that comes with prudence. Patrick Cullen (*Infernal Triad: The Flesh, the World, and the Devil in Spenser and Milton* [Princeton: Princeton University Press, 1974], 76) has shown that Guyon follows Mammon as an innocent, unaware of the evil in his own nature. From his experiences with temptation, he learns that he is himself in a fallen condition, depicted literally by his collapse upon returning to earth. Cullen's interpretation thus supports the idea that Guyon initially lacks self-knowledge.

57. See Fig. 3 and note 18 herein.

58. ". . . counsel is the eye of the mind, by helpe wherof, men of prudence see how to defend themselves from the blind strokes of fortune, and eschewing that which may hurt them, take hold of that which is profitable" (p. 138).

59.   Caussin (vol. 1, p. 90) describes the hand as a memory device, each of the five fingers indicating a quality of prudence: memory, judgment, self-preservation, circumspection, and foresight.

60.   Cesar Ripa, *Iconologie,* trans. J. Baudoin, (Paris, 1677), part 2, p. 180. The gloss indicates that the eye means vision of final things, like the death's head she carries.

61.   Such an interpretation is offered by Ernest G. Gilman, *Iconoclasm and Poetry in the English Reformation: Down Went Dagon* (Chicago: University of Chicago Press, 1986), 71–72.

62.   Pierre Coustau's emblem "Sur le pourtrait de Grille etant encor pourceau" (*Le Pegme* [Lyons, 1560], 224) uses the picture of the man turned boar to teach the lesson that vice is pleasing to the wicked. Spenser's artistry in this instance appeals to the same general reading public as that of the emblem writers. Gabriel Harvey's letter to Spenser on changing tastes at Cambridge includes mention of emblem books in a list of "outlandish braveries" popular among scholars (qtd. in *Renaissance Letters: Revelations of World Reborn,* eds. Robert J. Clements and Lorna Levant [New York: New York University Press, 1976], 41–42). Harvey's scorn implies the general popularity of emblem books. For a study of Spenser's use of techniques common among Renaissance emblematists, see the unpublished dissertation of R. J. Manning, "Spenser's Use of Emblems in *The Faerie Queene*" (University of Edinburgh, 1978). Mason Tung notes that since Spenser and the emblem writers drew on the same materials, the issue of source remains problematic ("Spenser's Emblematic Imagery: a Study of Emblematics." *Spenser's Studies* 5 [1984]: 185). Spenser's use of the proper name "Grille" does not prove Coustau as a source, though the early date of the *Pegme* makes it possible for Spenser to have seen the emblem.

63.   p. 123

NOVA
ICONOLOGIA

DI CESARE RIPA PERVGINO
Caualier de SS. Mauritio,& Lazzaro.

Nella quale fi deſcriuono diuerſe Imagini di Virtù, Vitij, Affetti, Paſſioni humane, Arti, Diſcipline, Humori, Elementi, Corpi Celeſti, Prouincie d'Italia, Fiumi, tutte le parti del Mondo, ed'altre infinite materie.

OPERA

Vtile ad Oratori, Predicatori, Poeti, Pittori, Scultori, Diſegnatori, e ad'ogni ſtudioſo.

Per inuentar Concetti, Emblemi, ed Impreſe,

Per diuiſare qualſiuoglia apparato Nuttiale, Funerale, Trionfale.

Per rappreſentar Poemi Drammatici, e per figurare co'ſuoi propij ſimboli ciò, che può cadere in penſiero humano.

AMPLIATA

Vltimamente dallo ſteſſo Auttore di Trecento Imagini, e arricchita di molti diſcorſi pieni di varia eruditione; con nuoui intagli, & con molti Indici copioſi.

Dedicata all'Illuſtre, & M. Reu. Padre D. MASSIMO da Mantoua Decano, & Vicario perpetuo di Ciuè.

In PADOVA per Pietro Paolo Tozzi. 1618.
Nella ſtampa del Paſquati.

De la bibliotheque de Mr Pellot premier preſident du parlement de Normandie

Fig. 1. Frontispiece of Ripa's *Nova Iconology*, Padua, 1618. SM 1448.

Fig. 2. Wrath from Cesare Ripa, *Nova Inconologia,* Padua, 1618.
SM 1448.

Fig. 3. Prudence from Cesare Ripa, *Nova Inconologia,* Padua, 1618.
SM 1448

Fig. 4. Consiglio, from Cesar Ripa, *Iconologia,* Sienna, 1613.
SM 1447

56 ANDREAE ALCIATI

Maturandum.

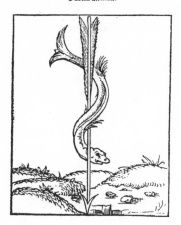

Maturare iubent properè et cunctarier omnes,
Ne nimium præceps, neu mora longa nimis.
Hoc tibi declaret connexum echeneide telum:
Hæc tarda est, uolitant spicula missa manu.

Fig. 5. Maturandum, from Andrea Alciati, *Emblematum Libellum,*
Paris, 1534. SMA 53

Fig. 6. Prudence, from Cesare Ripa, *Iconologia,* Paris, 1677. SM 1793

MATTHEW A. FIKE

Spenser's Merlin Reconsidered

The essay takes issue with William Blackburn's claim that "Spenser's Merlin, though he is well able to command demons, does not resort to them for prophecy—Spenser seems less interested than Ariosto in reminding the reader that no magic is entirely above suspicion." While appearing positive when contrasted with fellow poet-figures Archimago and Busirane, Merlin becomes ambiguous when juxtaposed with Ate. There are positive contrasts between Merlin and Ate, but he is not a lasting challenge to the discord she represents, a completely effective promoter of marital union and harmony, or an unqualified figure of goodness. Ultimately, his ambiguous nature is underscored by Britomart, who combines Merlin's beneficence with Ate's ability to act in the world.

SPENSER'S UNDERWORLDS, caves, and dungeons in Books I and II of *The Faerie Queene* suggest not only the error of failing to embrace holiness or temperance but also the punishments that result. Merlin's cave in Book III, Canto iii, has appeared to be an exception to this principle. Certainly there is nothing sinister in Spenser's most direct model, *Orlando Furioso*, Canto 3, in which Bradamante hears from Melissa about her descendants and later has a long conversation with Merlin. The positive nature of the magician is unequivocal for William Blackburn, who states that "Spenser's Merlin, though he is well able to command demons, does not resort to them for prophecy—Spenser seems less interested than Ariosto in reminding the reader that no magic is entirely above suspicion." He also says that "Spenser is at constant pains to remind us that Merlin's art is free of diabolism."[1] In Blackburn's analysis, the poem's magicians are poet-figures, and Merlin is merely the benevolent counterpart of Archimago and Busirane. "In fact," states Patrick Gerard Cheney, "*within the poem* Merlin does not practice magic at all."[2]

Merlin becomes a less positive figure, however, when juxtaposed with Ate, or discord. Ate is a logical foil not only because her own underground dwelling in Book IV, Canto i, suggests a parallel to Merlin's. More importantly, if Merlin promotes marital union, then his effectiveness must be measured against its adversary, and marriage is indeed one of discord's favorite targets. In describing the walls of her underground dwelling, Spenser mentions "the bloodie feast, which sent away/So many *Centaures* drunken soules to hell,/That vnder great *Alcides* furie fell" (23).[3] The allusion is to the marriage of Pirithous and Hippodamia, at which the drunken Centaurs tried to rape the bride. The tragedy of Oedipus and the judgment of Paris, also mentioned, are similar inasmuch as discord is domestic and attempts to disrupt relations between husbands and wives. In a part of the poem ending in the marriage of the Thames and the Medway, the union of husband and wife is a familiar target. Spenser's first mention of Ate even identifies her as the mythological promoter of marital discord, for it is she who casts the golden apple among the gods (II.vii.55).

Of course, promoting union in marriage is not the same as promoting harmony within marriage or directly opposing the discord Ate represents. While Merlin helps motivate Britomart to find Artegall, the magician's direct influence never extends beyond the walls of his cave. By contrasting Ate and Merlin, this essay attempts to show that Merlin is neither a completely effective promoter of marital union and harmony nor an unqualified figure of goodness. Underneath his attractive appearance lurks a demonic side, which deserves further exploration. Ultimately, his ambiguous nature is underscored by Britomart, who shares essential characteristics with both figures and accomplishes more than Merlin chooses to achieve.

Nevertheless, sharp contrasts between Ate and Merlin highlight his genuinely positive characteristics. To begin with, Ate's lineage is completely infernal,[4] but Merlin's is only partly so. As the son of a nun and an incubus, Merlin can draw on hell for his magical power, using it to promote harmony without any assistance from divine grace yet without serving the devil.

> And sooth, men say that he was not the sonne
> Of mortall Syre, or other liuing wight,
> But wondrously begotten, and begonne
> By false illusion of a guilefull Spright,
> On a faire Ladie Nonne. . . .

> (III.iii.13)

One legend in which Merlin is baptized immediately after birth suggests that grace is active in his life,[5] but Spenser does not include the detail. Nevertheless, Merlin's attitude toward God contrasts markedly with Ate's. Whereas "euen th'Almightie selfe she did maligne" (IV.i.30), Merlin urges reverence and submission either to God or, ironically, to Artegall: "Therefore submit thy wayes vnto his will," he counsels Britomart (III.iii.24).

Ate's family tree includes Night, and Merlin can alter the course of day and night, or at least what is both Night's descendant and one of her manifestations: darkness and the blindness to which it leads.

> For he by words could call out of the sky
> Both Sunne and Moone, and make them him obay:
> That land to sea, and sea to maineland dry,
> And darkesome night he eke could turne to day.
>
> (III.iii.12)

In spite of Merlin's demonic lineage, his "magic finds its ultimate source in Christian miracle" because the lines relate to I.x.20 where Fidelia is said to possess similar powers over the sun, the mountains, and the sea—abilities that call to mind biblical passages attributing great powers to the faithful.[6] Spenser's statement on Merlin's magic is also significant if "the forest, the sea, and the night of Books 3 and 4 are the underworld of the poem as a whole,"[7] for in stanza 12 Spenser stresses Merlin's control over two of these elements. His power over night is especially positive because Night is among the most elemental hell powers in The Faerie Queene, second only to her father Demogorgon.[8] Although Merlin's power stems from hell itself, he controls day and night for his own purposes, many of which are presumably in line with God's will for His children. Merlin commands a demonic force, rather than being subject to it, and his power, at least potentially, serves the good of human characters.

The constructive use of language in Merlin's alteration of day and night, which contrasts with Ate's use of language to promote discord,[9] makes him a poet-figure, as does his use of magical power to create objects for human use. Besides making the magical mirror and overseeing the brazen wall's construction, Merlin creates a garden mentioned in The Rvines of Time (523) and makes Arthur's arms and armor, which Merlin takes to Fairy Land where one who searches can see them (I.vii.36). The interpretation of Merlin as an artist focuses mainly on his creation of the mirror, which Spenser likens to "a world of glas," a microcosm that projects true images, as Spenser conveys poetic truths in the poem (III.ii.19). Merlin thus contrasts with Archimago, a poet-figure who projects falsehood. Both magicians use infernal power to affect the lives of other characters, and together they illustrate the contrasting drives for "revelation" and "self-deception," or for good and evil, within each person.[10] In the interaction of one's positive and negative sides, which Merlin and Archimago represent, the artist finds the genesis of creative work. Representing the positive side of this duality would seem to make Merlin not just an exception to the infernal power Ate represents but also her antithesis. Insofar as he wields his power for constructive purposes, Merlin highlights Ate's destructive intent.

As a wielder of infernal power, Merlin also appears positive by contrasting with Archimago and Busirane, poet-figures who use black magic to promote discord. Like the witch who creates the false Florimell by using a sprite to animate a mass of snow molded in her image, Archimago sends a sprite to fetch a false dream from Morpheus's house to trouble the sleeping Redcrosse Knight. In contrast, Merlin sets his sprites to a constructive task: building a brazen wall around Cairmardin, which calls to mind other brazen images in the poem—the brazen scales and tower of Book I, the brazen door of Busirane's torture chamber, and the brazen pillar to which he chains Amoret. All of these images recall the brazen gates of hell, where the Old Testament righteous are held captive until Christ liberates them.[11] In the harrowing of hell tradition, the brazen gates of hell fly open in response to the will of Christ, who at that moment wields the full power of the Godhead. In *The Faerie Queene* brazen images call to mind Christ's descent into hell and remind the reader that human beings are in thrall to demonic forces and need divine deliverance. In Book III, Canto iii. however, Merlin's actions contrast with those of Christ. Rather than using divine power to break through brazen gates, Merlin uses infernal power to force hell fiends to build a brazen wall whose very construction ensures their own bondage and whose circular shape may recall the walls around hell itself. But binding the sprites to their task also makes Merlin a contrast to Archimago and Busirane. Unlike Archimago's assaults on holiness or Busirane's on chastity, preventing sprites from roaming Fairy Land is a clear boon to human beings. What overcomes hell power in Book III, Canto iii, then, is not divine assistance but infernal might, and Merlin's brazen wall marks the bondage of demons rather than of human souls. The hell fiends are now the slaves, not the enslavers, and the construction of the wall is a clear example of Merlin's ability to use hell power without being subject to its influence. His power is so complete, in fact, that the fear he instills in his sprites endures long after his death: "Nath'lesse those feends may not their worke forbeare,/So greatly his commaundement they feare" (iii.11). Whereas Ate engenders disorder and chaos, Merlin forces hell fiends to create a structure somewhat like the spherical mirror: a circular wall whose shape symbolizes order, harmony, and marriage. Such use of hell power rather than grace to curb the forces of discord makes Merlin unique in all of *The Faerie Queene.*

For all of Merlin's positive contrasts with Ate, Archimago, and Busirane, Spenser does not depict him in entirely positive ways. To begin with, Merlin's epic role in promoting Britomart's desire for marital union, while helpful, is flawed in the same manner as the prophecy Aeneas receives in the underworld from his father Anchises. Although the prophecy fires Aeneas with zeal to fulfill his destiny, it does not include advice on how to proceed. Whereas Britomart's purpose in visiting Merlin's cave is to learn how to find Artegall, the magician provides something altogether different: a verbal prophecy of her descendants. When he says in stanza 32, "Behold the man, and tell me *Britomart,*/If ay more goodly creature thou didst see," he is not actually making Britomart's progeny appear. Either Spenser forgot that, unlike Melissa in *Orlando Furioso* and Anchises in the *Aeneid,* Merlin provides words that are not accompanied by images, or Merlin, overcome by prophetic power, is unaware that the prophecy is not visual. The further point is simply that Merlin does not help Britomart find Artegall; he resembles Anchises in never addressing the details of the quest. In contrast, Glauce, who travels with Britomart, much as the Sibyl journeys with Aeneas through the underworld, does play an advisory role. Spenser's model for the interaction of Britomart and Glauce in Canto iii, however, is Virgil's *Ciris,* in which the nurse Carme attempts to advise Scylla on her love of her father's enemy Minos.[12] As sources for the episode, both the *Aeneid* and the *Ciris* underscore the absence of practical assistance on Merlin's part.

A possible objection arises in stanza 51:

Then, when them selues they well instructed had
Of all, that needed them to be inquird,
They both conceiuing hope of comfort glad,
With lighter hearts vnto their home retird;
Where they in secret counsell close conspird,
How to effect so hard an enterprize,
And to possesse the purpose they desird:

Now this, now that twixt them they did deuise,
And diuerse plots did frame, to maske in strange disguise.

"Then, when them selues they well instructed had/Of all, that
needed them to be inquird" certainly sounds as if Merlin offers detailed advice on their journey. But the two lines are ambiguous. What
do the two women inquire about—the quest or merely the details
of the prophecy? If Merlin does provide Melissa-like advice on how
to proceed, Britomart and Glauce ought to conceive more than
"hope of comfort glad," and there would be no reason why "they
in secret counsell close conspird,/How to effect so hard an enterprize." Nor, if Merlin had shown them the way, would there be any
need for Glauce to conceive "a bold deuise" in stanza 52. For Britomart, the main benefit of her visit to Merlin's cave is not a set of
directions but her increased desire to find Artegall—desire manifested
not only as the kind of zeal Anchises's prophecy inspires in Aeneas
but also as the new awareness, symbolized by her blush in stanza 20,
of her own role in the process of sexual generation,[13] the womb-like
cave being rife with birth imagery.[14]

Although effective in these important ways, the visit to Merlin's
cave does not directly help Britomart achieve her immediate goal,
locating Artegall. As Spenser portrays him, Merlin is Anchises-like
in prophecy, but he does not achieve the advisory function of the
Sibyl, Melissa, or Carme. There is a difference between endorsing
marriage and actively helping Britomart find Artegall, and on the
latter score Merlin falls short. Although he prophesies a future that
includes the marital union Ate attempts to spoil, he remains passively
focused on his own art. In other words, the human world comes to
Merlin, who does not affect it, in immediate and concrete ways, but
with disruptive intent Ate actively enters the realm of human events.
Contrary to the general claim that "in *The Faerie Queene* evil does
not usually appear as energy,"[15] Ate, the image of evil, is more vigorous than Merlin, the image of relative goodness.

Along with revealing Merlin's passive role in promoting marital
union, the prophecy conveys a dark implication about his own nature. The prophecy moves toward the morally ambiguous martial
action of one Christian nation against another,[16] which corresponds
to a similar moral ambiguity within the seer himself, the latter made
possible by the Arthurian context with which Spenser's readers would
have been familiar. The presence of Prince Arthur in the poem and
the specific mention of the Lady of the Lake and Uther Pendragon
in Canto iii invite such a reading (10, 52). For Spenser and his Elizabethan readers, the Merlin who receives Britomart in Canto iii would

have called to mind the legendary magician who enables King Uther Pendragon to seduce Igraine, a married woman; who claims the child born of this adultery, Arthur, as the price of his service; who, like Archimago, is a shape shifter; and whose love of the Lady of the Lake renders him unable to save King Arthur from death at the hands of his nephew Mordred. Merlin, whose moral ambiguity is part of Arthurian legend, is a proper conduit for a prophecy that includes morally ambiguous currents, so that the prophecy becomes an extension and a reflection of Merlin's nature. Moreover, his susceptibility to the Lady of the Lake makes him not only a participant in the transcience his chronicle includes but also a microcosm of the passing of the Round Table and an emblem of the decay of an age. Even if the prophecy has a positive effect on Britomart, Spenser's Merlin is not only the seer who reveals the workings of divine providence for the English people but also a legendary figure who, by omission or commission, plays a role in the discord within that history. While Merlin helps legitimate the desire that drives Britomart toward union with Artegall, the "magician is indifferent to Artegall's" violent end, prophesied in stanza 28. Merlin can foster union but chooses neither to promote harmony within marriage nor to protect it from external harm.

The prophecy also suggests that Merlin's art itself is ambiguous—not entirely free of diabolism. Certainly Merlin restrains the hell fiends at work in the cave, but he also "counseld with his sprights" (III.iii.7); the phrase recalls Lucifera, who seeks the "strong aduizement of six wisards old" (I.iv.12). Perhaps the detail in stanza 7 is meant to show Merlin as a positive contrast to Lucifera: able to communicate with demons without sharing their malevolent intentions. On the other hand, communicating with fiends—however positive one's intentions—is as ambiguous as Guyon's resistance to temptation in Mammon's cave. There is nothing to suggest that either figure is corrupted, but putting oneself in contact with demonic forces is a morally ambiguous act, however strong one's resistance remains. A similar ambiguity may also be found in the prophecy itself:

But yet the end is not. There *Merlin* stayed,
As ouercomen of the spirites powre,
Or other ghastly spectacle dismayd,
That secretly he saw, yet note discoure:
Which suddein fit, and halfe extatick stoure
When the two fearfull women saw, they grew

Greatly confused in behauioure;
At last the fury past, to former hew
Hee turnd againe, and chearefull looks as erst did shew.

                                                                    (III.iii.50)

There are three possible explanations for Merlin's silence. First, although he does not *resort* to demons for his prophecy of Britomart's progeny, he is clearly in league with hell's forces, draws on hell's power and even momentarily appears to be "ouercomen of the spirites powre." Second, he may be dismayed by "other ghastly spectacle / That secretly he saw"—either a hell scene or some future human event that would extend the prophecy. Either way one reads the stanza, the magician's state is described as a "fit" and a "fury," which unsettles Britmart and Glauce until his "chearefull looks" return. While Merlin, as the son of a nun and an incubus, wields hell power without serving the devil (and probably uses magic to achieve this end), he appears to be temporarily overcome, one way or another, by the infernal power on which he draws. A third possibility arises from the word "As" in line 2, which signals the uncertainty of Spenser's narrator in determining the source of Merlin's silence. It is only *as if* he is overcome by "spirites powre" or dismayed by "ghastly spectacle"; the real reason behind his trance is mysterious and may still remain unspecified: perhaps demonic, perhaps not.

As Merlin is not completely immune to dark forces during his prophecy, neither is his power a lasting bulwark against discord. Although he fires Britomart with zeal to find Artegall, his prophecy directly benefits only her. Helping Britomart does not imply that Merlin achieves a victory over the forces of hell in a lasting or widespread fashion. After Canto iii his power does not extend beyond the walls of his cave, and elsewhere in the poem it merely resides in the devices he creates—Arthur's arms and armor, and the magic mirror. Spenser's Merlin, rather than ever directly combatting the forces of hell outside his cave in Fairy Land, remains focused on his art like a poet who lives a contemplative life. Yet his future departure from the cave, motivated by his love for the Lady of the Lake, will lead to his demise. Although Merlin's control over the sprites continues after his death, the narrator sounds an ominous note. If you come this way in the present day, he advises the reader, "dare thou not . . . in any cace, / To enter into that same balefull Bowre, / For Fear the cruell Feends should thee vnwares deuowre" (iii.8). Travellers in a later age will have to face the kind of dangers Merlin holds in check while he is alive. In the future, the completion of the brazen wall will loose the fiends to roam the earth. Whereas the immortal Ate freely wanders through Fairy Land, Merlin's power has limits not only in its geographical range but also in its effectiveness over time. Spenser never says that Merlin *promotes* discord, but he does not directly use his power to combat it. In light of this distinction, any stress on the contrast between Spenser's living Merlin and Ariosto's Merlin, a mere voice issuing from the tomb, deserves qualification. For all the delight of Canto iii, Spenser's Merlin is ultimately more like the disembodied voice in *Orlando Furioso* than one at first suspects: effective in enhancing the zeal of his human visitor, but incapable of any direct challenge to the forces of discord.

Although Merlin clearly contrasts with Ate in numerous ways and increases Britomart's desire for the marriage he does not directly enable, he is neither a completely effective promoter of harmony nor an unambiguous opponent of discord. Of course, Ate is a personification of a moral quality, while Merlin is a person, but allegorically discord is malevolent and active, whereas harmony is benevolent but passive. If a poet-figure, Merlin never gives his works a proper reading, and to the public challenge by discord he presents a private and inadequate response—the self-interest Britomart must avoid in order to found a line of kings. The magician's inadequacies become even more clearly focused in light of the nature of Britomart's action—a productive mingling of benevolent intention and purposeful action. Like a poet she is a dynamic fallen self, subject to error but able to promote virtue. Where vulnerability enables and defines strength, the Fall becomes fortunate. Like other great victories in *The Faerie Queene,* the liberation of Amoret from Busirane's dungeon can only be accomplished by one who may fail; the human susceptibility to lust that could cause a lapse of virtue makes victory possible, necessary, and meaningful. There would otherwise be no value in the defeat of Busirane. Fully human and fully tempted, Britomart achieves what Merlin does not: active opposition to Busirane, a force of discord, and (in the 1590 edition at least) the successful reunion of Amoret and Scudamore. Merlin, who is only part human and not fully subject to the Fall, is "an infernal parody of Christ" because they have contrasting fathers, divine and demonic.[17] But more importantly, Merlin parodies Christ because he does not put his power to good use by mounting an active challenge to discord in Fairy Land. He uses it mainly in ways that further his own interests, rather than promoting harmony among all persons or even helping Britomart find Artegall. Britomart transcends Merlin by effectively promoting concord, but the final measure of his inadequate opposition to discord is the transience of his power. In *The Faerie Queene,* it is characters representing infernal forces who endure despite the momentary victories of human knights: Duessa, Acrasia, Ate, the Blatant Beast. The assistance Merlin provides is individual, not corporate, and unlike Ate he will ultimately pass away.

American University in Bulgaria

NOTES

1. "Spenser's Merlin," *Renaissance and Reformation* N.S. 4 (1980): 186, 191.

2. " 'Secret Powre Unseene': Good Magic in Spenser's Legend of Britomart," *Studies in Philology* 85 (1988): 8

3. As Roche points out in his note on the stanza, it is not Hercules but Theseus who slays the Centaurs. See also *Metamorphoses* 12.210 ff., *Genealogy of the Gods* 9.28, and *The Faerie Queene* VI.x.13. All quotations are taken from Edmund Spenser, *The Faerie Queene,* ed. Thomas P. Roche, Jr. (New Haven: Yale University Press, 1981).

4. In Hesiod's *Theogony,* she is the granddaughter of Night, which would make her Duessa's cousin. In fact, it is Duessa who in Book IV "raised [her] from below,/ Out of the dwellings of the damned sprights,/Where she in darknes wastes her cursed daies & nights" (IV.i.19). As a descendant of Night, Ate is related not only to Aveugle (darkness or blindness) but also to the ignorance and malignity Lemmi calls "the night of the mind," from which all human ills descend (Edwin Greenlaw, et al., eds., *The Works of Edmund Spenser: A Variorum Edition* [Baltimore: John Hopkins University Press, 1932]: I: 231).

5. Blackburn, 182.

6. Andrew Fichter, *Poets Historical: Dynastic Epic in the Renaissance* (New Haven: Yale University Press, 1982), 172–73. Fichter cites Joshua 10:12, 2 Kings 20:10, Judges 7, and Matthew 21:21.

7. Thomas E. Maresca, *Three English Epics* (Lincoln: University of Nebraska Press, 1979): 51.

8. *Works,* I: 230.

9. Discord presents primarily a verbal threat to friendship, as the portrayal of Nimrod on the tapestry in Ate's cave attests. As the main builder of the tower of Babel, Nimrod fuels discord by actions leading to the disruption of language. In a similar way, discord in the middle books of *The Faerie Queene* manifests itself in such words as Paridell and Blandamour exchange over the false Florimell, the secret lovers' language that Paridell and Helenore speak, or Ate's own indictment of Duessa at Mercilla's court. Discord feeds on words, which is why Ate is described as a verbal cannibal:

> For life it is to her, when others sterue
> Through mischieuous debate, and deadly feood,
> That she may sucke their life, and drinke their blood,
> With which she from her childhood had bene fed.

(IV.i.26)

Her assault calls to mind otherr verbal attempts to disrupt human relations: Duessa's letter in Book I, and scandal in Book VI. Appropriately, Ate and Duessa accompany Paridell and Blandamour, and Ate's "euill wordes" (25) stem from "Her lying tongue [that] was in two parts diuided,/And both the parts did speake, and both contended" (27). The detail anticipates the Blatant Beast whose false tongues number either a hundred or a thousand (V.xii.41; IV.i.9, xii.27).

10.   A. Bartlett Giamatti, *Play of Double Senses: Spenser's* Faerie Queene (Englewood Cliffs: Prentice Hall, 1975): 120.

11.   J.A. MacCulloch, *The Harrowing of Hell: A Comparative Study of an Early Christian Doctrine* (Edinburgh: T. & T. Clark, 1930): 219.

12.   Thomas P. Roche, Jr., *The Kindly Flame: A Study of the Third and Fourth Books of Spenser's* Faerie Queene (Princeton: Princeton University Press, 1964): 53–54. For parallel passages see Merritt Y. Hughes, *Virgil and Spenser* (Berkeley, 1929).

13.   For a related point, see James Nohrnberg, *The Analogy of* The Faerie Queene (Princeton: Princeton University Press, 1976): 433.

14.   Cheney, 16.

15.   C.S. Lewis, *Spenser's Images of Life,* ed. Alastair Fowler (Cambridge: Cambridge University Press, 1965): 66.

16.   Merlin's chronicle of Briton kings, which begins with Artegall and ends with Elizabeth, completes the history of England found in Book III, Canto ix (the fall of Troy to the founding of Troynovant), and Book II, Canto x (Brutus to Uther Pendragon). As Fichter points out, Merlin's prophecy tells the story of the "exile of the Britons and the eventual restoration of their line in the person of Henry VII, the first of the Tudor monarchs." Fichter acknowledges, however, that "the last event in British history mentioned by Merlin seems strangely out of line with the prophecy of an era of 'sacred Peace' under Henry VII"—the "white rod" of war wielded against "the great Castle" (Castile), a reference to the English defeat of the Spanish Armada (175, 179). In a similar way, Harry Berger divides Merlin's prophecy into three sections, which move toward the moral ambiguity of the English people in a later age: Merlin first describes a period of history in which might prevails and moral issues are well defined (26–34); in the second section, moral issues are less clear-cut, deception plays a role in conflicts, and the reasons for war are ambiguous because the enemy is Christian (35–42); and finally, in stanzas 43–50, the Britons' supremacy has passed, and they are assimilated into a political structure uniting warring nations under Elizabeth ("The Structure of Merlin's Chronicle in *The Faerie Queen* III (iii)," *Studies in English Literature 1500–1900* 9 [1969]: 39–51).

17.   Blackburn, 182.

KENNETH GROSS

Reflections on the Blatant Beast

A picture of the damaging effects of secret slander and rumor, the Blatant Beast emerges in Book VI of *The Faerie Queene* as, apparently, the ultimate enemy of Spenser's epic project. But it is a figure of extreme ambivalence; its mode of damage is unsettlingly paradoxical. Spenser paints himself as the Beast's victim; but he also suggests that its poison inherits some of the central ambitions of his writing. Hence the difficulty of casting the Beast out, or marking it as wholly alien. The hermit who cures Timias and Serena of the festering wounds of the Beast (VI.6, 1–15) works, we are told, by orderly and "well-guided" words; but his speeches also point to an obscurely "inward" self in his patients that is at once the source of slander's poison and the final means of its cure. This hermit never really answers the question of why such a self is so strangely vulnerable to the wandering, external "noise" of slander, or why indeed it is the presence of slander that oddly helps to discover that self. In fact, this episode points to the radically ambiguous status of the energy which Spenser locates in the Beast—its paradoxical location at points of crossing between private and public knowledge, and its way of mirroring the arbitrary forms of human desire and fantasy. The Beast's appearance at the close of VI.xii re-situates such ambiguities within a more fully historical, even apocalyptic domain. Glimpsed as it sacrilegiously ravages through the monasteries, uncovering their hidden shames and corruptions (12.23–25), the "evil" Beast appears to mirror the work of violent, iconoclastic questers like Prince Arthur, even as it repeats the contaminated work of the "dissolution" which helped to found the dynasty of Elizabeth/Gloriana, and to place her at the head of an ecclesiastical state. As figured in such an episode, the moral labor of separating corruption and cure becomes at once necessary and unending. If there is any escape from mere ambivalence here, or from historical despair, it lies mainly in the extremity and risk of Spenser's fiction itself, and in the poet's ruthless, if covert, identification with the scandalous work of the Beast.

> The contempt each person feels for me is something I must make my own, an essential and significant part of the world seen from the place where I am.
>
> —Wittgenstein

I have always had a certain affection for the Blatant Beast, the barker and blatterer. I think of him as Spenser's mad pet, as a trained monster miming wildness, or else as an ordinary "bleating" sheep transformed by a wizard or mad scientist and set to ravage among the pastoral landscape of Book VI.[1] This sympathy with the Beast may resemble the incorrigible admiration some readers of Milton feel for Satan (though the Beast scarcely attracts to itself the pathos of the victim or exiled hero). But my affection comes mainly from a perennial astonishment at the *fiction* of the Beast, at the delicacy and risk implicit in Spenser's so enlarging his image of the work of slander and rumor, letting it frame some of his most extreme questions about the enchantments and corrosions of language. Spenser places himself and his poem among the victims of the Beast. But the poet also discovers that the Beast's poison inherits some of the central ambitions of his literary project.[2]

★   ★   ★

Intimations of an extreme threat from some version of slander weave in and out of the narratives of *The Faerie Queene,* emerging at the very opening of the Letter to Ralegh, with its projected fear of "gealous opinions and misconstructions" dogging the progress of the poet's "darke conceit."[3] Within the poem, slander speaks early on in Archimago's Iago-like words to Redcrosse about Una's imaginary infidelities (words that feed on the Knight's fretful dream, but that are quickly given literal form in the wizard's demonic simulacra, thus associating the poison of detraction with the seductions of idolatry). The poet's allegorical accounts of slander's origins, however, can be various. Book I, for instance, discovers words of reproach in the poisonous throat of the fifth of the sins in Lucifera's pageant, Envy (4.22), suggesting slander's origins in personal and social but also metaphysical malice; slander here starts to take on a kind of demonic agency, associated with the work of Satan, "the accuser" and "father of lies." In Book II, however—more secular in its contexts, more material in its pictures of agency—slander and "reprochefull blame" also emerges from the mouth of the hag-like Occasion (4.4–12). Beside reminding us that the danger of slanderous words lie as much in violence as in their malicious falsehood, the episode also suggests how the damages of "evil tongues" feed on more contingent, less obviously sinful accidents and opportunities.[4]

The intrusive presence of slander and slanderers becomes increasingly prominent in the second half of the poem—as if Spenser's sensitivity to slander had been heightened by the consciousness of his first three books already circulating in the world, hence subject to the kind of costly misreadings by those in power he notes in the proem to Book IV.[5] We thus see slander at work in the person of Ate, "Mother of Debate" (4.1.19–30), "fild with false rumours and seditious troubles," given a double tongue that speaks against itself and two deformed ears which each hear something different. Ate works to spread suspicions and provocative gossip as well as overt detractions, maligning all signs of concord, abetting the misrecognitions of desire, and finding even in desire's most innocent masks the material to provoke jealousy and conflict.[6] The figure of Sclaunder herself appears later in Book IV, haunting the steps of the Arthur after his rescue of Amoret and Aemylia, abusing all three with accusations of various crimes. Here the description of Sclaunder's language is markedly paradoxical. Her words, the poet tells us, are a kind of alien, inhuman noise or babble; they are words which—unlike common words—in no way express, or find their origins in, the rational meanings of the "inward mind" (4.8.26). And yet the infected, poisonous, and unanchored "wind" of slander is said at once to emerge from and to attack the "inner parts" of human beings.[7] This quasi-magical picture of the influence of slander becomes all the more uncanny insofar as one cannot tell whether Spenser is referring to the inner parts of the one who speaks or of the one who hears a slander.[8]

A more pointedly political emblem of the slanderer occurs in Book V, where the poet Bonfont, his named changed by erasure to Malfont, is discovered with his tongue nailed to a door post at the threshold of the Palace of Justice (5.9.25–26). At one level, Malfont is, like Ate, an apotropaic image of the source of linguistic and civic disorder projected from within Elizabethan culture's idealized, if often fretfully maintained fantasies, social, and political order; he is a figure that finds his cousins among all of the "lewd persons" accused in Tudor royal proclamations of spreading libel against the sovereign "full of malice and falsehood."[9] But as critics have recognized, the punished poet is also Spenser's uneasy double, his recognition of political authority's real and imaginary (possibly slanderous) designs on the ambiguously motivated tongues of poets.[10] Questions about the source of slander, as well as about the source of accusations of slander, are here written into the name of the criminal himself.[11] An accusastory re-naming in its own right, "Malfont" is also a name of uncertain etymology—marking poet as the evil source (*fons*) of damaging words, or as one whose words (intentionally or unintentionally) "did" evil (*font*, from the French *faire*). Who is responsible for the (possibly slanderous) re-naming of the poet itself remains obscure. In writing that "the bold title of a Poet bad/He on himself had ta'en" (25), Spenser even leaves open the strange possibility that this slanderous rhymer had named *himself* "Malfont."

As even so schematic a survey suggests, marking the site of slander's emergence and the nature of its damage remains a complex business in Spenser's poem. The presence of "slander" tends to indicate the presence of a "scandal" in the text (the two words, in fact, share the same etymological root).[12] And part of the scandal lies in the difficulty of locating slander's motives, objects, and means of cure, or of knowing how to accuse a mode of speech that can resemble so closely the work of moral blame and legal accusation.[13] A given episode may suggest clearly enough how a slander or slanderer constitutes a threat to certain objects of value and authority; but Spenser's figures of slanderous voice also suggest "obscure and heavily censored intimations" of perennial conflicts of value (political, erotic, poetic, philosophical). Spenser's virtuous questers often make their way through landscapes full of what seem like false accusors and detractors, and yet there are moments when what looks like slander seems to emerge from what should be sources of right judgment, pure speech, and true desire. It is often difficult to say how truly monstrous the words of a slanderer are, and how much those words's character *as* slander is a function of the way they are heard or accused by others, as happens with Malfont. (The power of a particular slander may depend on something that happens to words in the uncertain space between the mouth and the ear; "slander" is also, we should recall, a label we use to describe or indict another speaker's words, not our own.) All of these issues are fully alive in Spenser's descriptions of the Blatant Beast, the poem's most potent and elusive avatar of slander, and one whose manifestations recapitulate aspects of most earlier figures of the evil tongue.

★   ★   ★

The Beast first emerges at the end of Book V, where it is set upon
the hero Arthegall, who is returning home after being pulled away
from the work of reforming the kingdom of Irena, which he had
freed from the tyranny of Grantorto. The allegorical affiliations of
the Blatant Beast are marked at this moment with a determined,
perhaps suspect precision. There is a quasi-causal argument in the
fact that the Beast is put to work by the female monsters Envy and
Detraction. The first self-destructively directs all of her malice and
resentment inward, concealing knowledge in a way that "murders
her owne mynd," while the second projects her malice outward onto
the world: "what ever evill she conceived,/Did spred abroad, and
throw in th'open wynd," misconstruing all good intentions, turning
"to ill the thing, that well was ment" (5.12.33). The effect is to
represent the Beast as serving the purposes both of a closed, self-
destructive interiority and a vengeful, projective violence. But however stark the clarifying force of such allegorical patrons, the narrative
itself suspends our understanding of the Beast. Unaligned, highly
generalized, the creature and its rages are at this point placed beyond
the interest, as well as beyond the apparent control, of the patron of
Law and Justice: Arthegall actively tries not to regard it, holding
Talus back from attack, and the thing is left behind as the hero returns
to Gloriana's court.[14] A more complexly narrativized knowledge of
the Beast's mode of being, its poison (as well as its mythic genealogy),
is thus withheld until Book VI, the Legend of Courtesy.

The threat of slander re-emerges there in a shifted guise; its violence is traced, and control of it is sought, in a more liable, ambivalent
realm—the extra-legal, if still public, politicized domain of "Courtesy," or what Stefano Guazzo called "Civil Conversation" (a domain
in which, as both Guazzo and Castiglione point out, the wounds of
slander seem perfectly unavoidable, partly because the tools of courtly
speech—praise and blame, flattery and abuse—often touch the domain of the slanderous).[15] Spenser lends to the Beast's manifestations
in Book VI both a situational fragility and an apparently more random
virulance—as, for exmaple, in the case of Serena, who is attacked by
the Beast while simply wandering as her will leads her, gathering
flowers while Calidore talks chivalric shop with Calepine, after the
former had interrupted the lovers' private dalliance. ("Frequently in
Book VI," writes Donald Cheney, "it seems that well-intentioned
blundering is as dangerous as malice or conscious evil."[16] The Beast,
however, is not beyond being tamed, or at least set loose strategically;

hence it is employed by the (slightly satiric) triad Despetto, Deletto, and Defetto as a weird kind of courtly bait for Timias (from the Greek *tíme,* honor), for whom the creature becomes a dangerously seductive object of desire in the competitive quest for glory. (Timias, unlike Calidore, does not seem to know what kind of beast his chase has in view). There are times when the Beast seems invisible, as during Calidore's evasive pastoral sojourn, but even here recollections of its intrusive violence emerge.[17] The Beast thus becomes the image of a poison, a mode of damage, that inevitably (if irregularly) accompanies the unfolding of the quests in Book 6, I, dogging both the writing of the narrative and its being read. There are times when one starts to think of the Beast less as a discrete agent *within* the narrative than as the image of some more elusive impulse that serves to forward the "endlesse work" and "secret discipline" of the narrative itself (much as the violent and delicate energies of suspicion and jealousy help drive the writing of Proust).[18] If it figures an alien, extra-textual threat, the Beast also finds a strange home in the literary text. Hence, with the catastrophic return of the Beast at the end of Canto 12, it may seem as if Spenser's poem as a whole is participating in a strange, triumphant process of auto-destruction.

I want to focus on two passages here, which make it clear just why the Beast is so difficult to get into focus. Taken together, they suggest that Spenser makes the Beast's mode of working at once more inward or private and more violently public, even apocalyptic, in scope than the Renaissance discourse of Courtesy ordinarily allows. The first episode I have in mind is the account in Canto 6 of the nameless hermit's curing Timias and Serena of their wounds—those inward, sorely rankling and festering wounds that recall the wounds of *eros,* as described, for example, in the March Eclogue of *The Shepheardes Calender:* "and now it ranckleth more and more, / and inwardly it festreth sore" (100–101).[19] The hermit's therapy takes the form of a "talking cure" (Freud's early epithet for analysis), but more precisely a cure of talk, a disciplining of the domain of conversation, of the domain of both outward speech and inward desire.[20] This cure leaves the sources and aims of slander still ambiguous, however, except insofar as it more pointedly implicates the victims of slander in the Beast's mode of damage and attack.

The searching and well-guided words of the hermit begin by conjuring up in detail one of the two alternate genealogies Spenser provides for the monster: it was born (like the Hydra) of the mating of the fraudlike Echidna and the chthonic monster Typhaon (6.9.11). (It seems appropriate that there are two divergent mythographic rumours circulating in the text about the parentage of this monster of rumor, even as we lack any learned commentator [like E.K.?] to adjudicate between them.[21]) The hermit also describes in vivid terms the monster's rusty iron teeth, multiple tongues, and "poysonous gall," the means of its ironically *"notable* defame" against "noblest wights" (6.12). Despite the quantity of grotesque and estranging detail, however, or the linking of the Beast to mythic, archaic sources of violence and disorder, the hermit presses the point that responsibility for the monster's evil, its "seed," can be found in Timias and Serena themselves. He insists that the Beast's real power takes its origin in their "fraile affection," in their "stubborne rage of passion blinde" (6.5). The description of such a dangerous and damaged interiority is ambiguous; one cannot tell, for instance, whether the passionate rage the Hermit refers to is desire, envy, or something else. What *is* clear is that the Beaste's poisonous influence cannot be mastered, as in the case of Malfont, by nailing its tongue to the wall. Nor can the two victims be cured simply by avoiding the apparently unavoidable reproaches and "secrete shames" of the Beast, or by seeking "outward salves" (public denials? legal action? confession?) that will only "augment [the sickness] more." Rather, the allegorical monster must be recognized as part of an interior eschatology; hence the cure of its poison, the hermit insists, must "proceed alone/From your own will." The ascetic discipline involves restraining "your eies, your eares, your tongues, your talke" from "what they most affect," keeping sight and conversation "in due termes" (6.7). Or, as the hermit specifies at the end of his sermon.

> Abstaine from pleasure, and restraine your will,
> Subdue desire, and bridle loose delilght,
> Use scanted diet, and forbeare your fill,
> Shun secresie, and talke in open sight:
> So shall you soon repaire your present evil plight.
>
> (6.14)

Again, understanding what is at stake in this counsel is not easy; it seems at once practical and parabolic, secular and sacred. (The cure recalls, for example, Redcrosse's regimen in the House of Holiness, but it lacks much of the latter's systmatization and rigor, as well as the appeal to a divine authority. The hermit's is not, it seems, a cure of conscience, though conscience was at times invoked as defense against the poison of slander.[22]) The hermit's analysis of the Beast's poison and his advice about curing it suggest a crucially ambiguous stance towards inside and outside, private and public. He asks that his patients withdraw themselves from "outward sense"—which might refer both to the impulses of eyes and ears and to the "senses" of spoken language; at the same time, however, he asks them to "shun secresie" and "talke in open sight" (the sight of each other? of the hermit?). Leaving aside the matter of how rapidly this ascetic cure "works," and what *that* is a fantasy of, I would suggest that the Hermit's words point to paradoxical recognition: that the damages of slander, while contingent on the capacity of language to run abroad, to carry a defiling aggression outward into the world, also depend on the way that the language of slander takes hold of, or finds an anchor in, the space of private thought and fantasy (perhaps by "calling out" to a strain of aggression and self-doubt, even a self-loathing, which we might call "envy"). In this light, a slander's sub-tlest poison lies not simply in how it affects what I fear *other* people think of me (my "fame" or outward reputation), but in how it affects what I think of myself; it is a question of the way that "outward senses" and "fames" (in the period sense of "rumors") can gain vio-lent purchase on my ego. I would risk saying that, if Spenser's earlier description of Detraction's venom (5.12.33) suggests the workings of what psychoanalysis calls "projection"—the unconscious spitting out of inward poison onto an outward object—here we are concerned with the opposite mechanism of "introjection," that is, the taking inside the self of outward images or objects of desire in a way that can at once form, enlarge, and wound the self.[23]

Sketchy as it is, the hermit's account of slander points to a domain of self, a domain of private will, that is at once divided from and dependent upon an outward will in which images and aims of the self's desire are current, bruited about in a domain beyond the imme-diate control or knowledge of the self to which they appertain. Such an outward will is here seen to take the form of a random malice that is troublingly tied to random words, a texture of secret and not so secret verbal wounds; it is bound to that flood of dangerous speeches which Tudor proclamations against slander catalogue with such legalistic, paranoid expansiveness: "lewd and light tales told, whispered, and secret spread abroad by uncertain authors," "false and slanderous tales or news," "false, untrue, and vain rumors and bruits," and "libels full of malice and falsehood."[24] But this outward will is also something that Spenser forces back onto the self, sense, and desire of slander's victims; in the hermit's words, it becomes an interior will that he reads as the true source of both slander's poison and its cure. (I think of Montaigne here, with his sorrowful wonder at what makes human beings seek a ground for their private judgments and

beliefs in "this breathie confusion of bruits, and frothy chaos of reports and vulgar opinions."[25] The hermit's recommended therapy of
talking "in due termes," or of shunning secrecy and talking in "open
sight," thus suggests the desire for a form of conversation that avoids
being rifted either by the damages of external slanders or by the
private fears and fantasies that allow themselves to be shaped and torn
by such forms of speech. Yet even as the episode gestures toward a
form of wound-less or candid speech, a "civil conversation," it also
suggests how fragile the fiction of such a cure must be, how difficult
it is to represent. For one thing, the curing of Serena and Timias
takes place so neatly, so quickly, that one can find oneself thinking
of it as a desperate wish-fulfillment, like the hasty putting down of
Mutabilitie at the end of Book VII. The hermit's stoic, rationalistic
therapy indeed seems more like a retrospective fantasy of a means to
avoid the Beast's poison *before* it has struck—a way of outwitting the
proliferations of slander in a realm beyond the subject's control.

The uncertainty attending this fiction of cure tells us something
about the ambiguous status and origins of the energy Spenser locates
in the Beast—its wandering, archaic, yet apparently pointless rage;
its mirroring of the poisons of erotic desire; its paradoxical location
at points of crossing between interior and exterior, private and public;
its simultaneous accessibility to will and its placement beyond what
can be willed. That uncertainty only increases insofar as it is impossible to think that Spenser's poem as a whole could truly subject itself
to the regimen of the hermit—fed as *The Faerie Queene* is by shifting
investments in secrecy and dissimulation, by conflicting stories of
desire, and by ambiguous, contaminating plays on the "senses" of its
words. Insofar as Spenser does echo the hermit's ascetic advice in
Book VI's closing couplet—"Therefore do you my rimes keep better
measure,/And seeke to please, that now is counted wisemen's threas-
ure" (12.41)—it is in a fashion full of disappointment and contempt.

One further problem is that we cannot easily assimilate the hermit's
picture of slander's origins to the equally conflicted, but much more
extreme picture of the Beast's power emerging in the final canto of
Book VI—the second passage I want to examine. It is hard to imagine
Spenser sustaining an untroubled picture of an inward subject or
private mind that could either contain or survive this incarnation of
the Beast.

At the end of Canto 12, having brought to a close the romantic
narrative of Pastorella, Spenser thrusts us back into the disen-
chantments of a world in which the Blatant Beast is still at large.
After reporting that it has run "through all estates," and there left

many massacres, Spenser shows us the monster breaking into a monastery, where Calidore finds him "despoyling all with maine and might" (12.23). The perennial surprise of the episode is that the poem has here stumbled upon the wandering Beast in a quest of its own—whose ambivalences may reflect back on those of all prior quests in *The Faerie Queene*.[26] To begin with, the narrative suggests in the Beast a focused, if still anarchic will to defile and destroy: it fouls altars, speaks blasphemy, casts images to the ground, and also steals sacred objects; there seems little inherent method to its iconoclasm. But the narrative intimates that, curiously enough, the Beast is also engaged in a determined quest for knowledge, for bringing things to light. It searches through all the "cels and secrets neare" of the monks themselves, probing the spaces of what should be inward trial and private meditation (like that belonging to the therapeutic hermit)—places "in which what filth and ordure did appeare,/Were yrkesome to report" (12.24). It is hard to say *what* the Beast finds—evidences of greed, sloth, or sexual incontinence, perhaps, or indications of the suspect practices of secret confession and private masses—or to say what scruples would make "reporting" them "yrkesome." What counts is rather the troublingly paradoxical fantasy of the Beast's *mode* of knowing, or of seeking to know. At this point, it appears that the Beast works as much to uncover what is already defiled as to spread fresh defilements of its own. The poet indeed posits in the work of slander a restless, unremitting drive to uncover hidden, if not necessarily dirty secrets which cannot be pried apart from the impulses that create those secrets—at least insofar as the slanderous Beast must also spread the defilements it allegedly discovers. The process of knowledge, of drawing things into the light, is thus hopelessly contaminated, at once darkly self-sustaining (providing itself with its own objects) and self-cancelling. What is at stake in this picture of the Beast's investigations comes through more sharply if we consider the Beast in relation to certain parallel figures in the poem. For example, the scene in the monasteries echoes Spenser's description of the cave of the Ate, containing so many "altars defyl'd and holy things defast" (4.1.21). The Beast's ravages also recall the systematic depredations of the robber Kirkrapine—both a robber of churches and the Church *as* robber, a figure for both lawless violence against ecclesiastical property and for the legalized theft of alms and sacramental power which Protestants saw at work in the Roman hierarchy (not to mention, at times, the Elizabethan church itself).[27] But most remarkable, it seems to me, is to realize that the questing Beast is here in the position of Prince Arthur in Canto 8 of Book I,

investigating the dark secrets, the bloodily fouled altars and desolations, at the heart of Orgoglio's palace, dragging its monstrosities
(and its victims) into the light. Book VI's closing image of slander's
ravages thus becomes the double or dream-like mirror of the energy
of iconoclasm and reformation with which Spenser identifies the
springs of his entire epic project in *The Faerie Queene*.

Towards the end of Canto 12 we are asked to shift suddenly out
of the delicate, if often violent, pastoral narrative of Book VI and
back into something that resembles the world of Book I, with all of
its conflicts over the realm off the sacred (even though the Beast as
such is unimaginable in the earlier book). What makes this shift more
strange and scandalous (and even slanderous) is the temporal leap by
which the reader is thrust out of the hovering, idealized time frame
of the pastoral story and into a recognizable, if admittedly fantastic
version of a specific historical moment, a moment located over half
a century previous to the date of the text's first publication. For it
is not just a generalized, ironic picture of the practice of reforming
violence we see here. At this point the Beast is represented as the
agent, the allegorical memory of Henry VIII's programmatic dissolution of the English monasteries. The monster's ravages here become
a deeply troubled figure for (or translation of) the complex program
of judicial investigation, institutional dismantling, economic appropriation and redistribution, as well as organized and disorganized
physical violence, that helped found the dynasty of Gloriana. The
episode suggests (though also strategically veils) the problematic motives and carryings through of the reformation that created crucial
parts of the ideological and economic foundation of Tudor rule in
Great Britain (even as that reform created grounds for continuing
political and religious conflict).[28] The royal "patronage" of the historical event shadowed in the text may help justify the connection
between the ravages of the Beast and the violent, erotically charged
quests of Prince Arthur, Gloriana's fictive future bridegroom. But
this only complicates our attempts to construe the Beast's status as
enemy—not just because of the troubled association of iconoclasm
with the monarchy, but because the imaged activity of reform and
purification is represented through what seems at once a willful and
a strangely random occasion of violence, the work of a creature whose
quest for knowledge is, again, darkly divided against itself.

The ironies of this episode are not unprecedented in Spenser.
Gestures of iconoclastic violence in *The Faerie Queene* are very often
ambiguous, haunted by a sense of their conflicted, archaic or envious
motives, and by an awareness of their costs. Nor is Spenser the only
Elizabethan writer to recall the Tudor monarchy's founding act of

dissolution with mixed judgment, and divided sympathies towards those who possessed, scattered, destroyed, or translated the contaminated, sacred properties of the Roman Church.[29] Still, one may feel a peculiar sense of shock, a sense of some extreme or ambivalent pressure attending this moment—in the way that Spenser's wandering, slanderous Beast, with its elusive, inward poison, suddenly takes onto itself the image of a much earlier, and terribly concrete reforming violence; in the way that this image seems to thrust itself back into the eirenic present; and especially in the image's manner of muddling any obvious distinctions between sacred and sacrilegious violence, true and slanderous knowledge (a muddling which catches something at the heart of the entire epic). The blatant historical memory of the dissolution is itself rendered curiously uncanny by being so caught up in the dream-like doublings and condensations of this text—a text that yet seeks to persuade us that it is just those phantasmic, ironically ambiguous renderings of history that really count. And they count despite, or perhaps because of, the fact that the romance's internalization of the dissolution thwarts any clear historical judgment about the meaning of this event—except to remind us sharply that we are implicated in history precisely through the workings of our possibly slanderous powers of fantasy and our desire for knowing secret truths.[30]

The curious opacity, the emphatic self-referentiality of the poet's fictive machinery also comes through in the subsequent section of the canto, which describes the Beast's struggles with Calidore. At this point, moving into what might look like a more conventional romance battle between knight and monster, one still feels a marked thickening of Spenser's allegorical medium, a continuing display of self-conscious writerly ironies. When this ordinarily "mute" monster explodes into noise, Spenser tells us it cries with the tongues of numerous allegorical species—dogs that bark, cats that "wrawl," bears that "groyn," tigers that "gren," and snakes that hiss—as if to stress the inhuman, non-signifying character of its voice. But he then adds that it uses mostly the "tongues of mortal men, / Which spake reprochfully, not caring where nor when" (12.27) We are also told that the Beast first uses claws and teeth to attack Calidore but that, when bound, it uses bitter words. In both of these cases, the reader encounters a curiously double, redundant vision of the Beast's mode of violence, oscillating between figurative and literal depictions of the sources and vehicles of slander—something that tends to make one especially aware of the narrative's phantasmic and rhetorical character. This in turn can affect our reading of the narrator's own bitter, slightly stagey complaint at the end of the canto, directed against the Beast's

attacks on poets and "learned wits." In the light of the poet's display
of his figurative tools, one can feel as if Spenser is also putting vividly
on display for us the slightly paranoid motives that can feed such
allegorical projections as the Beast; he points to the fears and anxieties
that can readily convert human tongues into those of animals and
monsters. The Beast may represent a power beyond the poet's control, an image of all the myriad poet-haters that are "out there." But
Spenser's text also makes us reflect on the ways that giving such a
grotesque and externalized form to social and moral evil can answer
more private needs, salve more private wounds. His account of the
Beast's ravages points to the resentments that can be given voice, and
some satisfaction, through the poet's way of knowing his enemy
under such a monstrous guise. The Beast had earlier been seen uncovering, projecting, and diffusing a secret defilement within the space
of the ravaged monasteries. One is finally led to ask, to what degree
is it a work like that of the Blatant Beast to represent (or discover)
one's enemies in the guise of the Blatant Beast? And to what degree
does the poet's conscious, inescapable participation in such a process
of accusatory monstering trouble our ability to find out what kind
of enemy the Beast constitutes?[31]

I need to leave such questions open here. But in doing so, I don't
want to evoke too absolute or too skeptical a darkening at the close
of Spenser's poem. Tempting as this is, it risks oversimplifying the
fiction of the Beast's universal and uncontrolled ravages, a fiction
that seems to me one of Spenser's subtlest dissimulations. No doubt
the final vision of the Beast points to a force, or a reality, which
brings about the collapse of Spenser's larger project of epic and dynastic praise, moral and imaginative education, and prophetic public
mythmaking; the Beast would thus stand for a world in which Spenser
despairs of the writing of his poem. But we should remember that
the Beast's running free is, after all, a carefully staged scandal, a subtly
contrived intrusion into the fiction of what is represented as random
and uncontrollable. That is to say, Spenser needs this monster as a
tool, as a carefully trained ravager. If we remind ourselves that it is
a willful fiction, then the poet's final, disenchanting account of the
Beast may seem less a token of despair than a remarkable piece of
hybris; for one thing, by making his last enemy fundamentally an
enemy of poets, Spenser elevates those poets even in describing their
acute vulnerability to slander.[32] Again, it may seem plausible to argue
that the Beast marks the emergence of a picture of the poet's world,
of desire and language, more extreme than the poem can safely contain, the picture of a world which can only misread, or hold in

contempt, a text like *The Faerie Queene*.[33] As such, it constitutes one of the poet's most chilling knowings of the historical real. But Spenser's descriptions of the diffused, enlarged, and slanderous Beast also serve as an apotropaic defense against such final recognitions. In fact, for all that the Beast represents a threat to the poet, the story of its destructive career reads to me ultimately as a closing gesture of resistance, a way of cheating death—the poet possessing for himself and for his poem an image of the equivocal energies that exist both inside and outside that poem, that both drive and thwart the poem, which include the generosities and poisons of the poetic word. (Hence the relevance of my epigraph from Wittgenstein.[34]) Such a strategy is all the more extreme insofar as it embraces an image of the complex historical violence that stands at the origins of the Elizabethan settlement. The image of that violence here takes a form that the upholders of the settlement would presumably repudiate as a slander; but it is an image that Spenser nonetheless internalizes, or appropriates, in order to shape one of his strangest, most dream-like images of the movement of questing.[35]

★ ★ ★

The difficulties of deciphering the Beast remain massive. To start with, Spenser's poem takes as its final enemy something that one might hope would constitute a marginal, or at least managable, contamination of speech. The poem further suggests that among the most troubling points of access to such speech is not a merely external domain of fame or reputation, but rather a vulnerable interior self, a site of desire, fantasy, and memory. Even more strangely, this is a domain of self whose recognition seems strangely dependent on the very slanders that wound it, that call out to it. This inwardness or interiority indeed seems to court the slanders that wound it; the poison of such slanders can seem the product, even the aim of that inward self. At the same time, however, the force of slander seems to be sustained by an aggressivity, a seductive certainty, that works like an unhoused spectre within the uncontrollable wanderings of the word itself, as if produced by the very emptiness, the random babble, the nothing of language. It is as if the human, passional source that we think must drive slander could be extorted, pulled out into language by the aggressive play of slanderous utterance, as if the malice that spurs the slanderous word could be cut off from its source and disseminated (even recreated) by the word alone. It is in such a detached, wandering form that the aggressively driven, fantastical discoveries of slander start to attack the complexly interwoven networks of memory, knowledge, performance, and dissimulation that are the foundation, the sustenance, of the political and social world. We discover, however, that those victimized foundations are of the same substance as slander, that even the work of reforming or curing those foundations can itself mime the work of slander, that the most necessarily violent or usefully delicate reimagining of a contaminated origin seems at risk of diffusing that contamination. Yet we discover also that poet's powers of figuration, or of allegorical translation, are at their strongest in his very way of internalizing that poison.

These remarks suggest why it is so troublesome a thing to bind the Beast in a conceptual place, or to give a local habitation and a name to this defiler of names. By way of closure here, I would only add that one useful critical strategy for labelling such an extreme (even supreme) fiction might be to lend it the name of other fictions. For instance, to call the Beast "Ate," or "Archimago," or even "Arthur" can work at certain moments, as I have suggested. Breaking the circle of Spenser's fiction, we could also apply the name Iago, belonging to the subtly defamatory avatar of the monster jealousy; Iago is a demonic tale-teller who, like the Beast, seems eager to break other people's idols. It pleases me most to imagine, however, that the name which the Beast might give itself—the "deep and inscrutable, singular name" over which it sits brooding, like the one of Old Possum's cats—is a name that it would share with two other Shakespearean characters, a name that belongs to both a scandalized, slanderous, and disenchanting prince and a vengeful, poisoned, rumor-mongering ghost. We know the Beast better, I think, if we can imagine naming it "Hamlet."

University of Rochester

NOTES

All quotations from *The Faerie Queene* are taken from the edition of J. C. Smith (2 vols., Oxford: Oxford University Press, 1909).

1. The *OED* remarks that Spenser's coinage "blatant"—also spelled "blattant" —suggests an archaic form of "bleating," of which the sixteenth-century Scottish form was "blaitand." The article adds that the word may also derive from the obsolete verb, "to blatter," to speak or prate volubly (see OED, s.v.). I would stress

the echo of animal noise in Spenser's neologism, if only to suggest that the Beast is not quite as alien in the pastoral landcape of Book VI as it seems. (Thomas More's Hythlodates, one might recall, also imagined a peaceful sheep transformed into a cannibalistic monster in the first book of *Utopia,* though he was describing the desolations wrought by enclosure rather than the violences of slander.) There is no clear etymological link between the words "bleat" and "blatter"—which derive from Old English and Latin roots respectively—nor should we assume that Spenser himself thought there was. (His onomastic puns often depend on notoriously and comically false etymologies.) Had the poet glanced at the definition of *blaterare* in Thomas Cooper's massive *Thesaurus linquae Latinae et Britannicae* (London, 1570), however, he would have glimpsed the great lexicographer's attempt to conjure up the memory of some inhuman, bestial noise in the word (though from something more exotic than a sheep): "*blaterare.* To bable in vayne. to clatter out of measure. to make a noise like a cammel."

2. Among those many critics who have commented on the Blatant Beast, I am particularly indebted to Harry Berger, Jr., "A Secret Discipline: *The Faerie Queen,* Book VI," in *Revisionary Play: Studies in the Spenserian Dynamics* (Berkeley: University of California Press, 1988), 220–22; Angus Fletcher, *The Prophetic Moment: An Essay on Spenser* (Ithaca: Cornell University Press, 1970), 288–94; and James Nohrnberg, *The Analogy of "The Faerie Queene,"* (Princeton: Princeton University Press, 1976), 688–96. I should also say that this essay offers a re-thinking of the account of the Beast contained in my *Spenserian Poetics: Idolatry, Iconoclasm, and Magic* (Ithaca: Cornell University Press, 1987), 224–34.

3. Protestations concerning the dangers of "libellous" *reading* or misreading are commonplace in the prefatory letters and prologues attached to Renaissance texts. They become especially urgent in the case of literary works that invite (though also thwart) the search for topical referents hidden under general allegorical or satirical names, as do certain poems in Spenser's own *Shepheardes Calendar.* Some extreme examples of such fears of misreading, and of the kind of "apotropaic" prefaces those fears can provoke, can be found in the work of Ben Jonson. The induction to his *Poetaster,* for instance, presents us with the figure of "Envy" looking out into audience in search of those who will "traduce" the drama through "wrestings, comments, applications," spy-like "suggestions" and "privy whisperings," who will "wrest, pervert, and poison all they hear, or see, with senseless glosses or allusions." (*Works of Ben Jonson,* eds. C. H. Herford and Percy Simpson [12 vols., Oxford: Oxford University Press, 1932], 4.203–4).

4. Edward Coke, in his often-cited law report "De Libellis Famosis" (1605), in *The English Reports,* vol. 77, King's Bench Division VI (Edinburgh: William Green & Sons, 1907), 250–52, asserts that "it is not material, whether a libel be true or false"; the real issue is whether it leads to "quarrels and breaches of the peace" or brings the authority of the state into scandal. The same argument is made in William Hudson's *A Treatise of the Court of Star Chamber, Collectanea Juridica,* ed. Francis Hargrave (London: E. & R. Brooke, 1791–92), Vol. 2 of 2, page 102–103. More generally, thinking about the connection of slander with the work of "occasion" might help make sense of what remains one of the most elusive issues in *The Faerie Queene,* i.e., the connection between the depredations of Beast in Book VI and the

corrosions and defilements of the world, of history, brought about by the Titaness Mutabilitie. This complex pairing represents Spenser's most developed attempt to make sense of an issue that seems to have haunted him from the beginning of his career—as in his translation of Du Bellay, "The Ruines of Rome," which studies the ways in which different sorts of violence and entropy cooperate, how intentional and accidental "ruination" combine to produce the fragmented, unsettling landscape of history.

5. Donald Cheney observes that "in 1596 Spenser is acutely aware of being judged, especially by figures of authority . . . [He] has come around once again to his sense of the omnipresence of Envy, both in its overtly malevolent forms and also as a mis-deeming or mis-taking attendant upon any act of comprehensive vision" ("Envy in the Middest of the 1596 *Faerie Queene*," in *Edmund Spenser: Modern Critical Views*, ed. Harold Bloom (New York: Chelsea House, 1986), 282.

6. Jonathan Goldberg, *Endlesse Worke: Spenser and the Structures of Discourse* (Baltimore: Johns Hopkins University Press, 1981), 96–99, speaks very subtly of Ate's function as a picture of the misrecognitions and contradictory object-choices structured into human desire. M. Lindsay Kaplan, *The Culture of Slander in Early Modern England* (Cambridge: Cambridge University Press, 1997), 34–44, works out in greater detail the way in which "slander" haunts the career of the lovers and questers in Book IV, less as a product of intentional malice or abuse than through subtle networks of misreading and misrecognition. (Kaplan carefully and usefully places this picture of slander as "misinterpretation" against contemporary legal practices and documents, which show an acute awareness of how much the "damage" of an alleged slander depended on context and interpretation as well as on the intentions behind it.) Ate's name also suggests her function as a figure for the forces of psychological and historical violence that haunt, threaten the ambitions of the imperial itself, as is argued by Elizabeth J. Bellamy, *Translations of Power: Narcissism and the Unconscious in Epic History* (Ithaca: Cornell University Press, 1992), 251–52.

7. The image of slander's empty and yet potent wind here suggest that slander participates in a dark version of the natural magic which Agrippa called "aeromancy," in which the air becomes a medium that retains and carries the signs of human language and even human action, impressing their image in turn on the senses, fantasy, and mind of those that receive them, even without their knowledge. See Henry Cornelius Agrippa, *Three Books of Occult Philosophy*, trans. James Freake (London: 1651), 47–51. The idea that slanderous words possess a kind of infectious, demonic, or witch-like magic is something of a period commonplace, and runs throughout texts such as William Vaughan's mad and encyclopedic *The Spirit of Detraction Coniured and Convicted in Seven Circles* (London: 1611) and Nicholas Breton's *A Murmurer* (London: 1607). Elizabethan witches themselves, after all, are most often pictured as women whose own vengeful curses and insults possess a more than natural, or more than a merely social, power to harm others (even as their very status *as* witches is commonly the product of social slander and rumor).

8. It is a commonplace idea in period descriptions of slander that, besides wounding both its speaker and its intended (often ignorant victim), slander also wounds and betrays the personnn who hears it, in whom slander begets false conviction or corrosive doubt. The anonymous pamphlet, *A Plaine description of the Auncient*

Petigree of Dame Sclaunder (London, 1573), 14v–15r, for instance, describes the hearing of a slander as taking the form of a secret invasion of a walled castle or town: "For sclaunder undermindeth and casteth downe the foundation of true judgement in the outward parts, and within, trayterous confederate with their enemies, helpeth them when they brake in and receive them, and open the gates, and so endevour themselves that Madame Sclaunder may make the hearer of the tale to her servant."

9. Cf. the proclamation of 26 March 1576, which might have had Malfont in mind: "Forasmuch as within these few days there have been certain infamous libels full of malice and falsehood spread abroad and set up in sundry places about the city and court tending to sedition and dishonorable interpretations of her majesty's godly actions and purposes, and especially invented of cankered malice colorably to the destruction or ruin of some good estimation and fidelity towards her majesty by lewd persons not worthy to enjoy the benefit of this her mmajesty's quiet government, no more than evil and corrupt limbs which for lack of speedy remedy may infect more of the body; the sufferance whereof cannot but breed a further disorder to the good quietness of her majesty's most peaceable government; and because her majesty would have such villanous, treasonable, and seditious attempts both repressed and punished, and also would come to some certainty for the discovering of the authors thereof, whereby she would not enter into any scruple of suspicion of any other manner of person than the offenders or their partners: Therefore . . ." —the proclamation going on to offer rewards of 40 and 100 pounds (to commoners and gentlemen respectively) for secret information that would lead to the arrest of the libellers. *Tudor Royal Proclamations,* eds., Paul L. Hughes and James F. Larkin (3 vols., New Haven: Yale University Press, 1964–69), 3:41.

10. Cf. Angus Fletcher, *The Prophetic Moment: An Essay on Spenser* (Chicago: University of Chicago Press, 1971), 214. Jonathan Goldberg's analysis of Bonfont/Malfont, *James I and the Politics of Literature: Jonson, Shakespeare, Donne and their Contemporaries* (Baltimore: Johns Hopkins Press, 1983), 1–10, is also useful in this context—though it errs, I think, in making this image of the immolated poet speak mainly the "truth" of power's inevitable duplicity and self-destructiveness.

11. John Guillory, *Poetic Authority: Spensesr, Milton, and Literary History* (New York: Columbia University Prss, 1983), 23–68, argues that such ironic, conflicted myths of origin are common throughout *The Faerie Queene,* they point toward the equivocal, ultimately secular authority that Spenser must claim for his allegorical text. It may not be surprising then that ambiguities about origin should cluster so thickly around passages which attempt to describe the (contaminated) sources of contaminated speech.

12. On the etymology of slander, see *OED,* s.v. The shared derivation is more immediately apparent in the archaic form of the word that Spenser himself uses at times, "sclaunder"—a word which through the 1570s, at least, could be used to mean both slander *and* scandal. "Slander," like "scandal," derives ultimately from the Greek *skandalon,* meaning literally a trap or stumbling block, figuratively, a thing that gives offense. The kind of conflicts that can gather about the notion of "scandal" come through in a text like 1 Corinthians 1.23, where Paul puts off the Jewish demand for a "sign" and the Greek desire for "wisdom": "But we preache Christ crucified: unto the Iewes, a stombling blocke [*skandalon*], & unto the Grecians,

foolishness [*moria*]" (Geneva). Here the word refers to divine mysteries or truths which are *taken* as scandalous and offensive by those who failed to apprehend them. Defining both the dangers and necessities of "scandal" becomes a crucial issue for reformers like Calvin, in his struggles to make clear "how far our [spiritual] freedom must either be moderated or purchased at the cost of offense," and how much charity must be extended to those who remain unconverted (*Institutes of the Christian Religion [1536 Edition]*, trans. Ford Lewis Battles [Grand Rapids: Berdman's Publishing Co., 1975], 182). Calvin tries (pragmatically) to distinguish between scandal *given*—i.e., sinful or rash behavior that causes the faithful to stumble, or that threatens legitimate political authority—and scandal *taken*—as when an otherwise good deed, even a necessarily radical one, is "by others" ill will or malicious intent of mind turned into an occasion for offense" (181). But the distinction between scandal given and scandal (slanderously) taken always threatens to collapse—as it does, for instance, in Spenser's pictures of the iconoclastic work of the Blatant Beast.

13.   One finds in a number of period writings on slander the idea that it works to preempt, usurp, parody, and hence scandalize the "proper" legal procedures of accusation and judgement: "Whosoever backbiteth his neighboure, hee condempneth the lawe, in that it correcteth not filthynes, the office whereof the backbyter taketh upon him." (*Petigree of Slaunder,* 53r); "When slanders are presented instead of complaints [i.e., written complaints brought to a judge], that is but to set divisions between the king and his great magistrates, to discourage judges, and vilify justice in the sight and mouths of all the people" (from "Proceedings against Mr. Wrayham, in the Star-Chamber, for Slandering of the Lord Chancellor Bacon" [1608], in *State Trials,* ed. T. B. Howell, [21 vols., London: 186] 2:1065); "[Public detraction] is a process contrary to all rules of Law or equity, for the Plaintiff to assume the part of a Judg . . . 'Tis indeed sad to see how many private tribunals are every where set up, where we scan and Judg our neighbor's action, but scarce ever acquit any" (William Allestree, *The Government of the Tongue,* [London: 1671] 83).

14.   Spenser's generality here may be strategic; it allows him to evade any direct suggestion that the slanders against Arthegall—who in part represents Spenser's former patron, Lord Grey—emerge from the sphere of the royal court itself. Kaplan, *Culture of Slander,* 45–51, offers a forcefully ironic analysis of the historical allegory here. Pointing out the degree to which the fiction of Arthegall/Lord Grey's being defamed skews the historical record (official criticism of Grey was limited, and Grey himself petitioned for his return from Ireland), she argues that the allegory covertly indicts the Elizabethan state for misconstruing and defaming Spenser's own writings and politics. In effect, the Beast would represent both attacks on *The Faerie Queene's* systematically ambiguous moral allegory and (anticipated) attacks on his violent program for reform in Ireland, worked out in *A View of the Present State of Ireland* (1596).

15.   Castiglione's discussion of the courtly use of stories, jests, and word-play (*The Book of the Courtier,* trans. George Bull [London: Penguin, 1967] 44–71) makes especially clear the courtier's need to master (and survive within) the always shifting games of praise and blame at court, his need to learn the arts of subtle, often covert abuse and flattery. Guazzo's survey of the dangers that beset a public servant is typically darker, as when he talks about the various "Curre dogges, which without barking bite us privily: who must bee admitted into conversation. Some of them I

call Maskers, some Rethoricians, some Poets, some Hypocrites, some Scorpions, some Traitours, some Forgers, some Biters, some Mockers, and some unknown" (*The Civile Conversation*, trans. George Pettie [London: 1581], 67, 66–108, more generally). Frank Whigham, *Ambition and Privilege: The Social Tropes of Elizabethan Courtesy Theory* (Berkeley: University of California Press, 1984), 137–84, offers a lucid critical analysis of these problems.

16.   Cheney, "Envy in the Middest," 281.

17.   As many critics have suggested, Calidore's intrusion into Colin Clout's magic circle of dancing nymphs and Graces (6.10.17) strangely mimes the disenchanting violations of the Beast.

18.   Goldberg, *Endlesse Worke*, 99, argues that the rumor-mongering, seditious Ate represents a principle of affective contradiction and misrecognition in human desire that is nevertheless essential to keeping in motion the narrative and the poem's complex play of allegorical signifiers. Something of the same could be said about Ate's cousin, the Blatant Beast.

19.   See *The Yale Edition of the Shorter Poems of Edmund Spenser*, eds. William A. Oram, et al. (New Haven: Yale University Pres, 1989), 61. The namelessness of the hermit iin Book VI seems curiously significant—as if only someone *without* a name, and isolated from a larger network of social demands, could cure slander's violent wounding of names and selves.

20.   Freud's phrase "the talking cure" is only applicable here in a stretched fashion, since the *Hermit*'s brand of therapy tends specifically to exclude, if not repress, the sort of recollections and repetitions that characterize the work of psychotherapy.

21.   Nohrnberg (cited above, note 2), offers the most balanced and thorough account of the Beast's two explicit genealogies, as well as those genealogies established by less direct allusive suggestions. He notes its relation to classical monsters like Python, Hydra, Scylla, and most obviously to the monstrous bird *Fama* (Rumor), feathered with tongues, described in Book IV of the *Aeneid*. He also remarks, as others have, its relation to earlier Spenserian creatures like Error, Duessa's Beast, and the dragon in Book I. But Nohrnberg puts most stress on the Beast's resemblance to Cerberus, the multi-headed (usually dog-headed) guardian of the underworld who was also spawned by Typhaon and Echidna. Cerberus appears in Renaissance mythography and literature as a figure variously for cynics, rabid litigators, attackers of religious faith and political virtue, and carping critics of poetry—often provided (as in Du Bartas) with an entire menagerie of bestial heads. Nohrnberg points out that Arthegall's binding of the Beast associates him in turn with Hercules, who carried the chained Cerberus from Hell. One additional cousin of the Beast is Rabelais's satiric figure "hearsay" (*Gargantua and Pantagruel*, Book IV, Chapter 33)—an old, blind man covered by countless ears, with seven tongues split seven ways, who keeps a school for both "witnesses" and historians.

22.   The commonplace appeal to the refuge of a guiltless conscience is clear in a text like Richard Brathwaite, *Essaies on the Five Senses, with a Pithie one on Detraction* (London: 1620), 71: "As for popular opinions [i.e., slanders on his published writings], which have their foundation in no other ground than erring Repentance, I appeal from them to a firmer and faithfuller testimonie, that is, my owne conscience, which can say thus much for me in lieu of so many objections: *Non habeo in me,*

quod testetur contra me." The anonymous *Petigree of Sclaunder*, 24 34, pursues a more complex line, advising victims of slander to use the occasion of public blame and detraction to examine their consciences, to test their innocence, and to explore the degree to which they may be, however slightly, implicated in the "evils" of which the slanders accuse them. The aim of such a regimen is partly to contain self-righteous assumptions of (especially religious) virtue, but also to prevent victims of slander from too quickly seeking legal action against those who have defamed them.

23.   See especially the account of introjection in Freud's "Mourning and Melancholia," in *The Standard Edition of the Psychoanalytic Works of Sigmund Freud*, ed. James Strachey, 24 vols. (London: Hogarth Press, 1955), 14:239–58.

24.   See *Tudor Royal Proclamations*, 1.387, 388; 2.4; 3.40.

25.   Michel de Montaigne, *Essays*, trans. John Florio (3 vols., London: Dent, 1910), 2:347.

26.   Nohrnberg, *Analogy*, 693, observes that "like the Questing Beast in Malory, [the Blatant Beast's] erring course makes it a parody of the quest itself."

27.   A. C. Hamilton, ed., *The Faerie Queene* (London: Longman's 1977), 59, notes in his gloss that "the primary reference to the greed of Rome, by which the English Church was pillaged, extends to any religious greed," citing Marprelate's attack on the bishops of the church of England. The further association of Kirkrapine's "sacrilege" (etymologically, "church-robbing") with the systematic "impropriation" of church riches under Henry VIII is suggested by Nohrnberg, who extends this association to the lion that slays Kirkrapine as well: "The dissolution of the monasteries still belongs to the allegory, *pace* the rubric for this canto, for that too was an alienation of Church property. Una is wimpled like a nun at the opening of the poem, and she may in part mourn this violation, which is also found on the poem's closing pages. Therefore the lion is also guilty of sacrilege or church-robbing (equated at IV.x.53), though he is marring blind Devotion's *market* (I.iii, rubric). . . . The lion thus duplicates the Blatant Beast's violation of monastic houses in Book VI: 'into the sacred Church he broke / And robd the Chancell' (VI.xii.25)" (*Analogy*, 218n.).

28.   See the accounts of the dissolution in David Knowles, *The Religious Orders in England*, vol. 3 (Cambridge: Cambridge University Press, 1959) and Joyce Youings, *The Dissolution of the Monasteries* (London: Allen and Unwin, 1971).

29.   The memory of the dissolution clearly troubled Catholic apologists like Michael Sherbrook, whose 1596 treatise *The Fall of the Religious Houses Under Henry the Eighth* (in *Tudor Treatises* ed. A. G. Dickens [Yorkshire: Yorkshire Archeological Society, Record Series v. 125, 1959) systematically reads the legal and material procedures of the "dissolution" as the main source for political and ecclesiastical corruption in England, indeed as a founding curse on the Elizabethan settlement. But the shadow of the dissolution seems to haunt even loyalists such as Richard Hooker. For the author of the *Laws of Ecclesiastical Polity*—capable of imagining that sacred objects might themselves "loathe" being made to serve vile purposes—the memory of the dissolution helps fill out his picture of how the purest of reformations can be corrupted by willful violence, by the assumption of a narrow righteousness, by a love of accusation, of finding out sacrilege, heresy, and superstition, that itself verges on superstition. (Cf. for example, *Laws*, 5.17). (The fact that the large-scale destruction and theft of church property in England was pursued under the auspices

of the monarchy is something that Hooker tends to leave veiled, preferring to associate iconoclasm with the blind zeal of the Puritans. Spenser himself registers the ambivalence of the situation, for example, in the parallels between the quests of the Beast and those of Prince Arthur.) Earlier Tudor reformers could be equally critical of the dissolution and its aftermath, as John King notes in *Spenser's Poetry and the Reformation Tradition* (Princeton: Princeton University Press, 1990), 57; they blamed those who inherited monastic property for avarice and plunder, for failing to redistribute monastic wealth, and for continuing the "monkish" traditions of idleness and clerical pluralism. Keith Thomas suggests further that the historical guilt attached to the "sacrilege" of the dissolution manifested itself in the wide-spread superstition that persons who owned or inherited property once belonging to the violated monasteries were likely to be cursed with bad luck (*Religion and the Decline of Magic* [New York: Scribner's, 1971], 91–104). Cf. also the account of the aftermath of the dissolution in Margaret Aston, "English Ruins and English History: The Dissolution and the Sense of the Past," in *Journal of the Warburg and Courtauld Institutes,* vol. 36 (1973) 231–55.

30.   If one feels a strange intrusiveness in the Beast here, a sense that it represents the pressure of something at once violently real and violently fantastic, this may be because its work calls up not only the memory of the earlier dissolution but thoughts about the "present" chaos of Ireland, especially as it is described in Spenser's *A View of the Present State of Ireland.* Maryclaire Moroney has tried to work out this parallel in detail in a recent essay, "Spenser's Dissolution: Monasticism and Ruins in *The Faerie Queene* and *The View of the Present State of Ireland*" (*Spenser Studies* XII [1995], 105–32]. She argues that, in the context of the *View,* "Henry the Eighth's erasure of monasticism looks like a dress rehearsal for the even larger project of recon-structing—that is to say, de-constructing—Ireland" (33). The suggestion is a com-pelling one. Memories of the Henrician reformation—of its epochal ambitions, its conflicts and contaminations of motive—are clearly called up in *A View.* We can indeed sense such memories both in Spenser's setting forth of his own systematic and ruthless program of reform, and in his accounts of earlier, failed attempts at colonizing the Irish. The association of the Beast's "iconoclasm" with the equivocal violence of the dissolution becomes particularly haunting if we recall that, for Spenser, both the alien culture of Ireland and the failed colonial policies of the English are deformed by their own conflicting idolatries, including idolatries dis-guised as iconoclastic reform (an issue which I discuss more fully in my *Spenserian Poetics,* 78–109). Thinking of the apparently arbitrary occasions for the Beast's vio-lence, as well as its associations with the work of the Titaness Mutabilitie, we may also recall the *View*'s dark awareness that even useful reforms of law and custom can be betrayed, become agents of disorder, as a result of the contingencies of time and history. Even as the text calls forth such historical analogies, however, the complex fiction of the Beast's iconoclasm pulls us away from any grounding appeals to history or idology, drawing us back into the poet's own ambivalent, often opaquely self-referential phantasmagoria.

31.   The poet's curious identification with the Beast should force readers to exam-ine their trust in the creation of monsters that seems so crucial to the allegorical writing of *The Faerie Queene.*

32.　Angus Fletcher suggested this formulation to me in conversation.

33.　Donald Cheney, in "Retrospective Pastoral: The Returns of Colin Clout" (unpublished essay, delivered at the Modern Language Association Convention, New York, 29 December 1981), notes that the Beast represents the threat of "what today might be called misreading or deconstruction." (Cheney, I think, is remembering Spenser's own reference to jealous "misconstruction" in the letter to Ralegh.) Leigh De Neef, *Spenser and the Motives for Metaphor* (Durham, N.C.: Duke University Press, 1982), 176, also conjures up the thought that figures like the Beast might seem to open up a "Derridian void" in the text of *The Faerie Queene,* standing as an image uncontainable violence and slipperiness of textual "erring." But De Neef goes on to argue that the Beast ultimately figures as the poet's monitory image of duplicitous or "bad" reading, "a deliberately contrived misreader whose very challenge calls forth the activity of right reading" (156).

34.　The text is from Wittgenstein's posthumously published *Remarks on Frazer's "Golden Bough,"* ed. Rush Rhees, trans. A. C. Miles (London: Brynmill, 1979), 11e.

35.　In his writing of the Beast, Spenser possesses his text of something that threatens it; he makes that threat his own. As this essay has suggested, I am not entirely sure what to make of this act of possession (or self-possession). But I do think that Spenser's strategy resists easy moralization. Hence I find myself blankly confused when critics suggest that the Beast, like Satan in the Book of Revelation, has been loosed only for a season, and awaits an eschatological cure coming from a domain beyond the chaos of historical speech and knowledge. The problem with such a reading is not simply that it imposes on the text a vague, and otherwise unacknowledged eschatological hope (of the sort evoked so tentatively at the end of Book VII). The trouble is rather that a surmise of this sort necessarily idealizes, or (ironically) purifies, the kind of poison the Beast represents. For one thing, to cure the poem or the world of the Beast would be to cure it of the very writing which has, we might think, set about reforming that world; it would cure the world of the poet whom one imagines saying, at his most cunning and outrageous, "La Bête—c'est moi."

MARIA R. ROHR PHILMUS

The Case of the Spenserian Sonnet:
A Curious Re-Creation

As has long been known, the sonnet with the interlaced rhyme scheme usually referred to as "Spenserian" is by no means Spenser's exclusively. This sonnet form was exactly the one prevalently practiced by the poets of sixteenth-century Scotland, and, moreover, it was employed by them several years before any of Spenser's own specimens of it saw publication. This reconsideration of the question of the origin of this sonnet form, and of Spenser's relation to its Scottish exponents, argues that the duplication Spenser's sonnet involves is the fortuitous—and ironic—result of a quite personal creative process. It basically stems from the signal retrieval of a Chaucerian legacy that Spenser effected in fashioning the *Faerie Queen* stanza: his utilization in that stanza of the *Monk's Tale* octave, a verse form long forgotten in England by his time. Spenser designed his sonnet by analogy with the construction of his epic strophe, its immediate antecedent. He extended the *Monk's Tale* octave's pattern to obtain three quatrains—thereby "re-creating" the Scots sonnet, itself derived from that Chaucerian octave, a stanza immensely popular in Scotland throughout the sixteenth century.

THOUGH IT IS CUSTOMARY to find the sonnet with the interlaced rhyme scheme *ababbcbccdcdee* described in Spenser criticism and prosody manuals alike as distinctively Spenserian and as a form introduced by that poet, it has long been known that in fact this was the sonnet prevalently practiced by the poets of sixteenth-century Scotland and, further, that it was employed by them several years before any of Spenser's own specimens of it saw publication. Indeed, the whole question of the origin of this sonnet form, and of Spenser's relation to its Scottish exponents, has been the object of critical interest for nearly a century now, giving rise in the process to a fairly sizable, if fragmented, body of commentary and debate. The aim of the present essay is not so much to advance novel conclusions as to dispel at least part of the uncertainty and vagueness in which aspects of the question are still enveloped, by bringing together information that has remained to a large extent dispersed, and by adducing evidence not taken into account to date. While placing some of the issues involved in a new perspective, ultimately my reconsideration of the matter serves in the main to reinforce current emphases; on key points it lends support to views which have been variously articulated but have come forward, so far, essentially as conjectures.

Basically I propose that Spenser's sonnet form, though by no means strictly his own, can safely be regarded as being *also* his invention. In its correspondence with the sonnet favored in Scotland we witness an instance not of influence, as was formerly thought, but rather, as held more recently, of coincidental developments,[1] developments, more specifically, that occur quite independently even while proceeding, ultimately, from the same component of a shared literary heritage.

I

King James's *Essayes of a Prentise,* published in 1584, when he was barely eighteen years old, has usually occupied a central place in discussions of the history of the sonnet in Scotland, which is also, by definition, the history of the Scottish sonnet in the "Spenserian" form—henceforward the "Scots sonnet" for short. The *Essayes* comprises no fewer than twenty sonnets—fifteen by James himself and five, in commendation of the royal maker, by members of his literary circle—all in the form with the continuously interlaced rhyme scheme. It also indicates that this form was regarded by the king as being strictly the norm. When, from apprentice become instructor, he expounds the "Reulis and Cautelis to be observit and eschewit in Scottis Poesie," in dealing with the main verse forms of his country he directly stipulates that the sonnet is constituted as his two examples of it prefixed to the treatise illustrate; no other type of sonnet is admitted or even recognized.[2] To this extent the *Essayes of a Prentise* announces the emergence of the Scots sonnet as a fait accompli. It likewise suggests that this sonnet, to which it in effect gives the status of a national form, was the original one developed in Scotland.

Essayes may be the work where sonnets appeared in print for the first time in that kingdom; Thomas Hudson's *Historie of Judith,* which includes two complimentary sonnets, both in the Scots form, one by James himself, was published in the same year. But contrary to what has often been thought, it by no means marks the inception of the Scots sonnet. Nor is this a supposition that the work itself can be said to encourage. James's opening sequence of twelve sonnets of invocation to the pagan gods has all the air of a dutiful schoolboy's effort; heavy-handed in its recourse to classical mythology, it is altogether a mechanical exercise in ingenuity of conception disguising descriptive verse as a series of prayers for the gods' aid. As such, it not only appears to be earlier than some of the other contents of the volume, but points to the prior adoption of the sonnet form that James utilizes on the part of an influential tutor, the poet in charge of his literary "apprenticeship."

The earliest known sonnet in the Scots form—also the earliest known sonnet by a Scottish poet—is to be found in the Bannatyne MS, the richest manuscript collection of Middle Scots verse to come down to us, compiled in the year 1568.[3] It is the invective "Ye Inglische hursone" which, though it appears without the author's name, has been assigned to Alexander Montgomerie by both his editor and the editor of the Bannatyne MS.[4] Such a piece places the beginning of the Scots sonnet not in the days when James gathered around himself his "Castalian band" and encouraged interest in the new poetry of the Renaissance, but rather, in the days of his babyhood, or earlier still. If its traditional attribution is correct, as I think it likely is,[5] it also tends to link the origin of this sonnet form—and the introduction of the sonnet in Scotland—to Montgomerie himself, thereby reinforcing the suggestion to this effect that emerges from sundry other circumstances considered cumulatively.[6]

Montgomerie, it is well established, was King James's guide and model in his first literary efforts. Thus, characteristically, in the "Reulis" James draws examples of the verse forms he discusses (in ch. viii) from Montgomerie's poetry four times out of seven—that is, every time the illustration does not come from his own work (once) or from an unidentified source (twice). He further styles Montgomerie the "Master poet" and "maistre of our art" in a poem—the "Admonition"—which, about two years earlier than the *Essayes,* incorporates at the end a sonnet in the Scots form.[7] He also hails Montgomerie in just such terms—as "our maistre poete"—in a Scots sonnet of similarly early date, "O mightie sonne of Semele the faire."[8]

For his own part, Montgomerie took special pride in his sonnets. In the second of the five sonnets addressed to Robert Hudson in the period of his estrangement from court, as he refers to his activity as a poet and recalls nostalgically his literary association with the king, he singles out his sonnets for special mention—in "Cupid's court," he makes bold to declare, "Muses yit som of my sonets sings,/And shall do alwayis to the worlds end."[9] And, notably, while Montgomerie was in James's group of poets the one who experimented most widely with different sonnet forms, he adopted the Scots pattern for all five of these sonnets indirectly pleading to the king for reinstatement.

But where does this sonnet form that was to remain by far the dominant one among sixteenth-century Scottish poets come from? If the arrangement of the fourteen lines into three symmetrical quatrains and a closing couplet distinctly reflects the influence of the English sonnet—presumably as exemplified in *Tottel's Miscellany*—the rhyme scheme of the quatrains as distinctly suggests "influences" of a less external order. It points to the Scots poets' characteristic predilection for complicated verse forms and, more particularly, to their peculiar attachment to a specific stanza form, namely the octave rhyming *ababbcbc* that King James in his "Reulis" calls "Ballat Royal." As has often been observed, the interlinked quatrains of the Scots sonnet are in effect an extension of the pattern of this stanza, a stanza whose pronounced popularity constitutes a distinctive phenomenon of Middle Scots verse.

When it is given a name other than "Ballat Royal," this stanza is mainly referred as the "French octave" and the "ballade octave" or the "ballade stanza,"[10] obviously because it corresponds to the decasyllabic *huitain* of French poetry. Such designations, however, in suggesting French models, obscure its more immediate provenance and, with it, what must be Chaucer's most enduring and most widespread legacy to Scots verse. This is, of course, the stanza that Chaucer used in the "Monk's Tale" as well as in the "ABC" and in short poems, whether in ballade form or not; and it distinctly enters Scottish poetry as part of the earlier Middle Scots poets' zealous imitation of Chaucer's verse forms, the aspect of their work that perhaps best justifies the characterization of them as "the Scottish Chaucerians." It is used by Robert Henryson, the first of the great makaris, in the majority of his short poems—in eight of them out of thirteen. It is likewise the strophe favored by William Dunbar; despite his great metrical variety, as many as seventeen of his ninety poems are in this form. So too, it occurs again in Gavin Douglas. To this extent, its diffusion parallels, somewhat belatedly, the ample use made of it in

England by Chaucer's immediate successors—by Lydgate and Hoc-
cleve, for example. However, while in England it was to all intents
and purposes abandoned subsequently, so that not a single specimen
of it appears, for instance, in *Tottel's Miscellany* nor in a collection
such as the Arundel Harington MS, in Scotland it fully retained its
popularity throughout the sixteenth century, thus emerging in effect
as altogether a staple form of Middle Scots verse. That is the role it
clearly has in the Bannatyne MS where, by far the commonest form
among poets both old and new, it is employed six dozen times—that
is, in over a sixth of the total number of poems that MS comprises.[11]
Interestingly, an early poem by King James that I have had occasion
to refer to, his "Admonition to the Master Poet"—the poem from
which he draws the illustration of "Ballat Royal" in the "Reuli-
s"—relates this very traditional form of "Scottis Poesie" to the Scots
sonnet as closely as it could. Made up as it is of *Monk's Tale* stanzas
leading to a Scots sonnet, apart from the further stanza appended by
way of envoy, it literally shows that sonnet issuing from this
stanza—this stanza issuing in a Scots sonnet.[12]

II

To pass from the Scots sonnet to Spenser is in the first place to
dispose of possible suspicions of dependence on the latter's part. The
earliest known Scots sonnet—the one in the Bannatyne MS ascribed
to Montgomerie—clearly antedates any of Spenser's own efforts in
sonnets of this interlaced type. Indeed, from it it appears that this
sonnet arose in Scotland even before Spenser developed an interest
in the sonnet as a distinct form; among his contributions to Van der
Noodt's *Theatre*, only two of the "Epigrams" (the first and the third)
are sonnets—of the standard English kind—and the "Sonets" are
simply unrhymed (nor are they always of fourteen lines). Yet none
of the biographic information we have about Spenser suggests that
he could have access to manuscript collections of Scottish verse. Scots
sonnets, on the other hand, did appear in print in 1584, in both
James's *Essayes of a Prentise* and in Thomas Hudson's *Historie of Judith;*
and it is conceivable that either volume reached Spenser even in
Ireland. But there are more than adequate indications that by that
time Spenser hardly needed such productions as models for the sonnet
form that has come to be known by his name.

Discussions of the relation of the Spenserian sonnet to its Scottish
counterpart have sometimes cited the poet's sonnet to Gabriel Harvey

dated "Dublin, this xviij, of July, 1586" as evidence that he adopted this sonnet form quite early in his career.[13] More recently, they have also pointed occasionally to a still earlier sonnet of the same type, the one dedicating the *Gnat* to the Earl of Leicester, a sonnet that, it is usually agreed, dates, like the translation it prefaces, from about 1580.[14] Yet though this sonnet has figured—if at all—as a precariously lone exemplar in treatments of the subject, it by no means constitutes an isolated "first." It represents, rather, only an instance of Spenser's earliest uses of this form—the one that seems capable of being identified as such the most readily. Just how many of Spenser's sonnets in this form belong to a comparably early period may indeed be more than we will ever know for sure. Among the works included, like the *Gnat,* in the *Complaints* volume, *The Visions of the Worlds Vanitie,* consisting of twelve Spenserian sonnets, can at best be regarded as a plausible candidate; while it has all the appearance of early work in both matter and method, its date remains entirely elusive. Probably the same has to be said also of the Spenserian sonnet that closes a companion piece in that volume, *The Visions of Petrarch,* the refurbished version of the "Epigrams" Spenser had published in Van der Noodt's *Theatre.* But unquestionably, it is roughly to the period of the *Gnat* that are to be assigned some of the sonnets comprised in the work which is primarily associated with Spenser's "distinctive" sonnet form, the *Amoretti* sequence.

The idea that not all the *Amoretti* sonnets were written for the occasion the sequence ostensibly refers to, Spenser's courtship of Elizabeth Boyle, is nothing new. First advanced at the beginning of the century, and then militantly elaborated by J. W. Lever in *The Elizabethan Love Sonnet,* it has been in the air ever since.[15] In so far as I know, however, no attempt has been made to assign specific early dates to specific sonnets, whereas for some sonnets there are definite clues relating them to a time a good deal earlier than that of the apparent occasion of the sequence. I shall restrict my comments to the more obvious instances among such sonnets, sonnets that can be dated to the period of Spenser's association with the Sidney circle during the last year or so before his departure for Ireland in August 1580.

To begin with a sonnet that can be dated on the basis of purely external evidence is to begin with *Amoretti* 8, the only *Amoretti* sonnet in the standard English form. As is well known, its opening lines are echoed almost verbatim in the opening lines of a poem by Fulke Greville, *Caelica* 3, a piece belonging to the part of the collection written during the period that saw the composition of the original version of the *Arcadia* and Sidney's enthusiasm for quantitative verse (witness the quantitative sapphics of *Caelica* 6). Thus it seems certain that *Amoretti* 8 was composed before Spenser left England, and, more specifically, at the time when he was in contact with Sidney and his group, as he reported in his letters to Harvey of October 1579 and April 1580.[16] This implication is in turn reinforced by the fact that three of the earliest manuscripts in which the sonnet is found draw most of their texts from the courtly poetry of the late 1570s and 1580s.[17] Interestingly too, its attribution itself in the earliest of these manuscripts relates the sonnet directly to Sidney's coterie; in Bodleian MS Rawlinson Poetry 85 it is ascribed to "Mr Dier" (while in the other manuscripts it is anonymous). *Amoretti* 8, however, does not stand by itself. It makes part of a triad of sonnets on the lady's eyes, *Amoretti* 7–9, which was obviously conceived as a unit inspired by Petrarch's three songs on Laura's eyes (Nos. 71–73), poems from which Spenser in the first two of these sonnets insistently draws images and motifs. The approximate date to which *Amoretti* 8 can be assigned must, then, apply also to the rest of the group. Nor does *Caelica* fail to offer evidence relevant in this respect too. For the *Caelica* poem following the one where Greville borrows verbatim from *Amoretti* 8 points to the early circulation in Sidney's milieu of the other two sonnets as well. *Caelica* 4, where Greville himself deals with the subject of the lady's eyes (for the first time), is simultaneously a compliment and a plea, like *Amoretti* 7, and furthermore is based on just the same conceit that *Amoretti* 9 is built upon, the comparison raising the lady's eyes to the status of cosmic—in fact, supernatural—forces. Thanks to these three sonnets, it is in turn possible to attach to the same early date a few others—themselves from the first part of the sequence—on the strength of affinities they exhibit. *Amoretti* 10 surely stands out in this connection. Distinctly inspired by a Petrarch madrigal (No. 121), it essentially performs on that poem exactly the mischievous kind of operation that *Amoretti* 7–9 do on Petrarch's three companion songs; it recalls a Petrarchan text to effect a total *bouleversement* of Petrarchan sentiments.[18] Sonnets 3, 16 and 24 likewise bespeak a time of composition close to that of the triad on the lady's eyes. For they are related both to that triad and to one another by what can but be a telling network of elements—by recurring phrases, images, and conceits, as well as by their basic conception: their ironic manipulation of Petrarchan motifs.

On the whole, then, it seems certain that, though none of Spenser's sonnets in his "characteristic" form saw publication until the 1590s, he in fact began employing that form a good deal earlier, and, specifically, too early to have the benefit of the Scots poets' example. His use of it about half a decade before any Scots sonnets became available in print is instanced not only by the dedication prefixed to the *Gnat* but also by sonnets included in the *Amoretti* sequence. So, if he evolved his sonnet on his own, whence its correspondence to the Scots sonnet's pattern? How did Spenser, working independently from the Scots poets, arrive at a sonnet form that coincides with theirs? The *Amoretti* sonnets I have singled out as being early pieces bear upon this question, and help toward its resolution.

One of the things that can be gathered from those sonnets is that that they comprise some of Spenser's very earliest uses of the form: *Amoretti* 8, as a standard English sonnet, reveals uncertainty on Spenser's part about the form he was to adopt. Thus it appears that the Spenserian sonnet is chronologically close in its origin to the development of the *Faerie Queene* stanza, just as it is unmistakably close to that stanza in point of structure. The period in which it came about is very much that which saw the inception of Spenser's magnum opus. Those sonnets, however, also intimate that, of the two cognate forms, the *Faerie Queene* stanza is the one that came first: *Amoretti* 10, which (like the probably later *Amoretti* 45) ends with an alexandrine, points to the practice of closing a strophe with a verse of that kind. This makes the *Faerie Queene* stanza the Spenserian sonnet's immediate antecedent. Accordingly, it seems useful to look for an understanding of the formation of Spenser's sonnet through consideration of his epic stanza, itself the subject of no small amount of commentary over the years.

The *Faerie Queene* stanza has often been seen as derived from ottava rima, and, more specifically, as itself part of that endeavor to "overgo" Ariosto that according to Gabriel Harvey was Spenser's express epic program.[19] In reality, however, Spenser's stanza departs too widely in its details from the octave of Italian epics to be considered a modification of it. In its first eight lines, on the other hand, it corresponds exactly to the *Monk's Tale* stanza, which, as a result, has just as often been regarded as its possible model.[20] This view, I believe, is very much encouraged by Spenser himself. Indeed, *The Shepheardes Calender,* parts of which are also contemporary with the beginning of Spenser's epic project, goes a long way, it seems to me, towards explaining the make-up of the *Faerie Queene* stanza as a whole, including its final line, prominent as a hexameter.

Spenser casts "June," an eclogue where he both eulogizes Chaucer as his teacher and gives notice of his epic enterprise, in stanzas rhyming *ababbaba*. It seems difficult, in view of Colin's reference to Chaucer as the Tityrus "[w]ho taught me homely, as I can, to make" (l.82), not to see the octave Spenser utilizes as consciously an adaptation of the *Monk's Tale* stanza—rather than, for instance, as a version of the

French *huitain*. Further, and more particularly, it seems difficult not to see in it, given the allusion to Colin as epic poet in the making (ll. 57–64), a deliberate semblance of the Chaucerian stanza with which the first eight lines of Spenser's epic strophe coincide. To this extent, "June," I am suggesting, implicitly designates the *Monk's Tale* stanza as the verse form on which the body of Spenser's own strophe is based. By the same token, I think it can be added, it also identifies as specifically a *Monk's Tale* stanza the octave in that form that appears on two occasions in *The Shepheardes Calender,* both times, interestingly, in contexts related, whether more or less directly, to the creation of *The Faerie Queene.* That octave is to be found in "April," the eclogue that contains, in Colin's lay of fair Elisa, the most explicit announcement of Spenser's epic understanding, and indeed a figuration of it; Hobbinol, before he recites Colin's poem, is made to speak, twice, in quatrains that, linked by the rhymes, give rise to the format of the *Monk's Tale* stanza (ll.9–16 and 21–28). Likewise, that octave occurs again in "November," an eclogue wholly centering on the royal mistress, and figuring her under a name that inherently recalls Colin's celebration of her in "April";[21] set apart by their rhymes from the scheme of continuously linked quatrains that in the first part of the eclogue Spenser imitates from his model, Marot's "Eglogue sur le Trespas de ma Dame Loyse de Savoye," Thenot's eight opening lines themselves introduce the *Monk's Tale* stanza's pattern. But Chaucer, of course, is only one of the poets whose inspiration Spenser acknowledges expressly in *The Shepheardes Calender.* He is accompanied in this respect by the Roman Tityrus, the poet on whose career Spenser, as "October" intimates, consciously modelled his own. And this earlier Tityrus too, it seems inevitable to observe, was present in Spenser's mind when he designed the *Faerie Queene* stanza; for the closing alexandrine reproduces, in iambic meter, Virgil's epic measure of six feet.[22] Thus with it the stanza comes to unite inextricably the two Tityri of *The Shepheardes Calender,* framing what is, in effect, simultaneously a joint tribute to both of the poets whom Spenser, at the time he devised it, envisaged as his precursors and an assertion of his kinship with them.

When Spenser's sonnet, then, is viewed in the light of what can be gathered about the origin of the *Faerie Queene* stanza and about this stanza's chronological relation to it, it does not seem hard to see how it came into being. It essentially presents itself as a further utilization of the structure of the Chaucerian octave on which the body of that stanza is based. Practically, proceeding by analogy with the construction of his epic strophe, Spenser extended the *Monk's Tale* stanza's pattern to obtain three quatrains, and completed them with

the requisite couplet rhyming separately. Hence, to be sure, the duplication he incurred: his sonnet's exact correspondence with the
form developed by Scots sonneteers. Hence, too, the ironies of that
correspondence, resulting, as it does, from a wholly autonomous
process. There is no escaping in the end the near-perverse ironies
that Spenser's sonnet involves, as an invention he had to share with
the Scots poets, when regarded from the standpoint of literary history.

Doubtless, the crucial factor in that correspondence, Spenser's reliance on the pattern of just the Chaucerian stanza that, dear to Scottish
poets, furnished likewise the basic matrix of their sonnet, represents,
historically, the most fortuitous of coincidences—in effect, a coincidence going against all odds. Recourse to that stanza entails after all,
for an English poet of Spenser's time, an act of resuscitation proper.[23]
But it is not simply that Spenser failed, through most fortuitous circumstances, to fashion a sonnet he could properly call his own. While
to all appearence he devised his sonnet, with its obvious resemblance
to the *Faerie Queene* stanza, as a markedly individual structure, one
bearing a distinct personal imprint, the form he hit upon was one
not only already in existence but peculiarly "other" in its nature and
its course. It was a form that, practiced in a different country, had
largely arisen there with a distinct national identity, a form to a
considerable extent representative of characteristic features of that
country's own poetic tradition. It was, indeed, a form whose diffusion
largely depended on the influence of a monarch who was to regard
Spenser as a personal enemy—a form all too closely associated in its
career with the figure of the very monarch who would have had the
poet prosecuted for his treatment of "Duessa" in the fifth book of
The Faerie Queene.

Concordia University (Montreal)

NOTES

1.   For suggestions to this effect see, e.g., Murray Markland, "A Note on Spenser
and the Scottish Sonneteers," *Studies in Scottish Literature,* 1 (1963): 136–140; Ian
Ross, "Sonneteering in Sixteenth-Century Scotland," *Texas Studies in Language and
Literature,* 6 (1964): 255–68; Michael Spiller, *The Development of the Sonnet* (London
and New York: Routledge, 1992), 144.
2.   See "Ane Schort Treatise" in *The Essayes of a Prentise, in the Divine Art of
Poesie,* ed. Edward Arber (London: Constable, 1895), 68. The treatise is also included
in *Elizabethan Critical Essays,* ed. G. G. Smith (Oxford: Clarendon Press, 1904) 2

vols; see 1, 223; in that edition, however, the significance of the passage is not clear since Smith omits James's two prefatory sonnets. Throughout I modernize archaic typographic conventions.

3. R. D. S. Jack, in *Alexander Montgomerie* (Edinburgh: Scottish Academic Press, 1985), 77, is incorrect in putting together the two sonnets contained in the Bannatyne MS as "the two earliest known Scottish sonnets." The second one, "Lyke as the littil Emmet" (rhyming *ababbcbcbdbdee*) is not part of the original collection compiled by George Bannatyne but one of the later insertions. It is marked "Inserted in MS. by a later hand" by W. T. Ritchie, ed. *The Bannatyne Manuscript,* The Scottish Text Society (Edinburgh and London: W. Blackwood and Sons, 1928–34), 4 vols.; see his note to No. CCXXXIX in the Table of Contents, III, xi.

4. The sonnet is "Miscellaneous Poems," No. LIII in *The Poems of Alexander Montgomerie,* ed. James Cranstoun, The Scottish Text Society (Edinburgh and London: W. Blackwood and Sons, 1887), and No. CCXXXII in Ritchie's edition of *The Bannatyne Manuscript;* for the attribution to Montgomerie in this text see the Table of Contents, III, ix.

5. In *Alexander Montgomerie*, p. 77, Jack questions Cranstoun's attribution of the sonnet to the poet on the ground that the Bannatyne MS does not name him as its author while it clearly identifies other poems as his. As Jack acknowledges, however, the poem "displays the sort of ingenious word play which characterizes many of his sonnets" (ibid.). Moreover, in the Bannatyne MS it immediately follows another invective, "Fyndlay McConnoquhy," which is signed "montgummary," and it is not unusual for this MS to group together poems by the same author without attaching his name to each. (Groups of poems by Dunbar are an example.) It is also worth observing that a lyric by Montgomerie included in the MS, "Irkit I am with langum luvis lair" (No. CCCXXIX), indicates, through some of the motifs it incorporates, that by this period the poet was acquainted with Petrarchan sonnet-eering.

6. The invention of the Scots sonnet has been variously assigned to Montgomerie, to King James, and to his whole coterie working collectively. See respectively Oscar Hoffmann, "Studien zu Alexander Montgomerie," *Englische Studien,* 20 (1895): 51; Allan F. Westcott, ed., *New Poems by James I of England* (New York: Columbia University Press, 1911; rpt. AMS Press, 1966), li; and James Craigie, ed., *Thomas Hudson's Historie of Judith,* The Scottish Text Society (Edinburgh and London: W. Blackwood and Sons, 1941), xcvi—xcvii.

7. No. LI in Westcott's edition. The date of the "Admonition" is established by its direct allusions to Montgomerie's *Flyting,* which is usually placed in 1582; see George Stevenson, ed., *Poems of Alexander Montgomerie,* Supplementary Volume, The Scottish Text Society (Edinburgh and London: W. Blackwood and Sons, 1910), 266–67. In ch. viii of the "Reulis" James quotes from both the *Flyting* and the "Admonition."

8. Westcott was obviously mistaken in thinking that this sonnet, No. XLV in his edition, was written after Montgomerie's death (cf. his Introduction, pp. xiv and xxxii). The reference to the poet's demise from overdrinking in the closing lines appears facetious, and is at any rate in the future tense; moreover this motif links the sonnet to the "Admonition," in the final stanza of which James refers to both

himself and Montgomerie as votaries of the "God of wine" (l. 115); likewise the allusion to the myth of Semele and of Bacchus' untimely birth relates this sonnet to that which opens the sequence in the *Essayes,* just as its form of an address to a god associates it with those compositions generally. James's epitaph on Montgomerie is the sonnet "What drousie sleepe" which, addressed to the "sacred brethren of Castalian band," commemorates Montgomerie as "the Prince of Poets in our land"; No. XXXIV in Westcott's edition.

9.   "With mightie maters mynd I not to mell," Sonnet XXVI in Cranstoun's edition.

10.   See, e.g., Westcott, ed., *New Poems by James I of England,* p. li, n. 2, and Janet Smith, *The French Background of Middle Scots Literature* (Edinburgh and London: Oliver and Boyd, 1934; rpt. Norwood Editions, 1978), 49–50, 57, 162.

11.   I rectify the estimate of the incidence of this stanza form in the Bannatyne MS offered by Craigie, ed., *The Historie of Judith,* p. xcviii ("nearly a third of the whole"); also the detailed list he provides on the same page is quite inaccurate, as it both omits poems which are in this stanza form and includes others which are not.

12.   Craigie, ed., ibid., c–ci, (followed by Kurt Wittig in *The Scottish Tradition in Literature* [Edinburgh and London: Oliver and Boyd, 1958], 117–18) suggests that the Scots sonnet evolved from two intermediary developments of "Ballat Royal": the ten-line stanza formed by the addition of a couplet, used by Montgomerie, Fowler, and Scott in one poem each, and the twelve-line stanza consisting of three quatrains interlinked by rhyme, used once by Montgomerie and once by Fowler. However, it is by no means certain that the poems Craigie cites in fact antedate the earliest known Scots sonnet, of whose existence in the Bannatyne MS Craigie is unaware. Surely, the two assigned to Fowler (born 1560), if they are his, do not.

13.   "Harvey, the happy above happiest men," printed in Harvey's *Foure Letters, and Certaine Sonnets,* 1592: *Spenser. Poetical Works,* ed. J. C. Smith and E. De Selincourt (London: Oxford University Press, 1969), 603 and 659. The sonnet is noted, for instance, by Stevenson, ed., *Poems of Alexander Montgomerie,* xlvi, and Westcott, ed., *New Poems of James I of England,* l–li.

14.   This sonnet is pointed out, e.g., by the editors of the *Variorum* edition of Spenser's works (Baltimore: Johns Hopkins University Press), *The Minor Poems,* II, 643, and by Markland, "A Note on Spenser and the Scottish Sonneteers," 137, n. 4.

15.   See J.W. Lever, *The Elizabethan Love Sonnet* (London: Methuen and Co., 1956; rpt. 1968), 97–103; cf. e.g., Spiller, *The Development of the Sonnet,* 219, n. 7.

16.   *Spenser. Poetical Works,* 635–38 and 611–12 respectively. Both letters comment on the "reformed [i.e., quantitative] versifying" promoted by Sidney, and contain specimens of Spenser's own experiments in it. The earlier one suggests that his connection with the Sidney circle was, by that time, of some duration: "Master Sidney, and Master Dyer, they have me, I thanke them, in some use of familiarity" (635).

17.   See William Ringler, Jr., ed., *The Poems of Sir Philip Sidney* (Oxford: Clarendon Press, 1962), xxxiii, n.1.

18.   The inverted order of the comparisons in *Amoretti* 9, which crucially undermines the logic of the lofty closing compliment, thus leading the triad to a mockingly subversive climax, seems generally to have escaped attention. *Amoretti* 7–9 and 10

are the only sonnets where Spenser in effect frames a bold response to Petrarch himself, though elsewhere he similarly "plays" with, or rewrites, texts by other poets. Compare, e.g., *Amoretti* 30 and 72 with their "sources" printed in the *Variorum* edition, *The Minor Poems*, II, 430 and 446 respectively.

19.   See the letter of Harvey to Spenser dated May 1580 in *Spenser. Poetical Works*, 628. One of the more recent exponents of this theory about Spenser's epic stanza is Thomas H. Cain, in *Praise in* The Faerie Queene (Lincoln: University of Nebraska Press, 1978), 39-ff.

20.   See, e.g., Susanne Woods, *Natural Emphasis* (San Marino: The Huntington Library, 1984), 148 and 178–79, n. 18.

21.   On the interchangeability of the names "Dido" and "Elisa," and its currency in Spenser's time, see Paul E. McLane, *Spenser's Shepheardes Calender* (Notre Dame and London: University of Notre Dame Press, 1961), 52–53.

22.   It is usually assumed that Spenser derived the alexandrine from French verse; cf. e.g., Woods, *Natural Emphasis*, 148. But, to be sure, this was also a native meter; iambic hexameters occur not only in combination with heptameters, as in poulter's measure, but also by themselves; for two poems in alexandrines in *Tottel's Miscellany* see Nos. 182 and 200 in Hyder Edward Rollins' edition (Cambridge, Mass.: Harvard University Press, 1966). Above all, I am suggesting, Spenser's closing alexandrine was inspired by Virgil, just as was Surrey's blank verse in his translation of Books II and IV of the *Aeneid*.

23.   The notable exception to the near-total oblivion that in England overtook the *Monk's Tale* stanza in the sixteenth century is Mary Sidney's use of this octave—with variations in the distribution of masculine and feminine rhymes—in three of her Psalms, Nos. 45, 80, and 89. Did she get the idea for it from *The Shepheardes Calender*? Stephen W. May, in *The Elizabethan Courtier Poets* (Columbia and London: University of Missouri Press, 1991), 209, proposes that she derived both the *Monk's Tale* stanza and the Spenserian sonnet, which she uses in Psalm 100, from James's *Essays of a Prentise*. But he is obviously wrong in assuming that the *Essayes* would have been Mary's sole source for the Spenserian sonnet before 1594, when she is thought to have finished her translations of the psalter. She would have readily found that sonnet form in Spenser's *Complaints* volume, which opens with a work inscribed to her, as well as in the dedications accompanying the first three books of *The Faerie Queene*. That she took Spenser as a guide in matters of versification is indicated by the fact that she also utilized the modified form of the *Monk's Tale* stanza that he employed in the "June" eclogue (Psalm 104), and the adaptation of rhyme royal that occurs in *Daphnaida* (Psalm 106).

MARK DAVID RASMUSSEN

Spenser's Plaintive Muses

The Teares of the Muses has been perhaps the least commented-upon of Spenser's minor poems. This essay proposes that the laments of the nine Muses may best be understood as a series of reflections on the paradoxes of poetic complaint, and especially on the ambivalent energies of the plaintive will: the urge to exert oneself upon the world through the process of lament. These reflections are self-critical, for at the heart of the poem stands an analogy between the condition of the plaintive Muses and the situation of the non-aristocratic poet who mourns their plight. This essay traces that analogy as it is developed over the course of the poem, showing how Spenser uses it to touch on some of the main concerns of the *Complaints* volume as a whole.

*P*UBLISHED IN 1591 AS part of the omnibus volume of *Complaints,* Spenser's *The Teares of the Muses* has been perhaps the last commented-upon of his minor poems. Up to the time of the *Variorum,* critical discussions of this six-hundred-line poem mainly focused on the question of its date—early 1580s or closer to 1590?—as well as on such topical matters as the identity of the comedian "pleasant *Willy*" (208) whose recent death Thalia mourns.[1] The only article-length study of the poem to appear since then has been Gerald Snare's valuable account of the Renaissance background of Spenser's Muses, published in 1969; more recent commentary has been limited to a few scattered remarks by critics mainly concerned with other matters, as well as William Oram's helpful introduction to the poem in the Yale edition and Hugh Maclean's entry in *The Spenser Encyclopedia.*[2]

Nor is one tempted to speak here of unwarranted critical neglect. On its surface, at least, *The Teares of the Muses* seems a forbiddingly unlovely work. Rehearsing the laments of the nine Muses at their own plight in the barren world of Spenser's England, it is unrelievedly doleful in mood and numbingly repetitive in subject matter—not a poem likely to bring new readers to Spenser. Yet upon more careful examination this proves to be an oddly engaging text. For once you start looking closely at them, you soon find that the laments of the nine Muses do not all tell precisely the same story; rather, over the course of the poem several distinct versions of the Muses' fall can be seen to emerge and reflect upon one another. In what follows, I would like to trace the details of these different accounts and show how the poem's meaning evolves from the play among them. My emphasis in these remarks will be two-fold. First, I will show how the various accounts of the Muses' fall offer a series of self-critical perspectives on the paradoxes of poetic complaint, and especially on the paradoxes of what I will call the plaintive will: the urge to exert oneself upon the world through the process of lament. To some extent, my comments here will be an attempt to catch up with a stray insight of Harry Berger's—not an unfamiliar experience for a Spenserian. Speaking of the Muses' plaintiveness in one of his influential articles of the late sixties, Berger remarks: "If the monotony of the Muses' stance makes for a fairly low-grade poem, and fairly low-grade poetry, it is yet functional: endless complaint implies willed passivity to the external world as it is (as bad as it is)."[3] "Willed passivity"—an assertion of the will through endless suffering and lament—is an oxymoron worth holding onto in engaging this poem. In the following pages, I will attempt to fill out Berger's insight by showing how the various accounts of the Muses' fall combine to offer a detailed anatomy and critique of this plaintive will. But following more culturally specific lines of analysis than Berger would have pursued thirty years ago (though not, I hope, in a manner foreign to the spirit of his work today), I will also want to propose that Spenser's representation of the plaintive Muses is meant to reflect upon the situation of the non-aristocratic poet writing in Elizabethan England, anatomizing both his weaknesses and his strengths. Tracing this analogy between the plaintive will of the Muses and the attempts of contemporary authors to manage their own plight will be my second main emphasis in the pages that follow, for through this analogy the poem touches on some of the main concerns of the *Complaints* volume as a whole.

* * *

Spenser takes both the title of his poem and the conceit of the Muses lamenting in sequence from his friend Gabriel Harvey, whose Latin verses *Smithus, vel Musarum Lachrymae* (1577) had recorded the laments of the nine Muses at the death of Harvey's patron, Sir Thomas Smith.[4] Like Harvey, Spenser has his Muses appear in the order given by some Latin mnemonic verses, *de Musarum inventis,* that were printed in Comes and in the 1542 Dumaeus edition of Virgil, among other places.[5] But where Harvey's Muses eulogize his patron, Spenser's poem offers a glum reversal of Du Bellay's *Musagnoeomachie* (1549), which celebrated the triumph of the arts and their royal patrons over the forces of barbarism led by the personified monster, Ignorance. Spenser's Muses mourn their own defeat by these same adversaries, some of whose features are drawn from du Bellay's poem.[6] Moreover, as Snare has shown, the English poet follows Du Bellay, Erasmus, and many other Renaissance writers in making his Muses the vehicles of human-ist instruction, rather than simply the patronesses of verse. As Snare puts it, the "whole encyclopedia of knowledge which men need in order to know God and to know themselves . . . is under the aegis of the Muses."[7]

In form, Spenser's poem appears to be strictly, not to say relentlessly, additive. After a nine-stanza introduction relating the narrator's en-counter with the group of nine wailing Muses, each Muse steps forward to lament for—what else?—nine stanzas, with each lament rounded off with a refrain-like tenth stanza shifting attention to the next of the mourning sisters "in rew." (The pun on row/rue neatly condenses the process of grief-by-number). The one exception to this scheme is the lament of Euterpe, which lasts for ten stanzas rather than nine, but whether this slight irregularity is meant to reflect the brokenness of the Muses' world, as the Yale editor suggests, or is due to some other cause, the overall additive pattern is clear, and seems designed to evoke (as it does) the potential endlessness of the Muses' woe.[8]

However, to a degree that has not yet been recognized, thematic connections among the Muses' laments work to offset this overall pat-tern. The central three laments—those of Euterpe, Terpsichore, and Erato—are quite closely linked in theme, as are those of Clio and Calli-ope, and of Melpomene, Thalia, Urania, and Polyhymnia. This gives three main groups, and a roughly concentric structure, as follows:

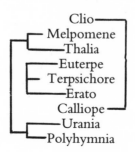

In what follows, I will organize my discussion of the poem around
these three groups, glancing as well at the nine-stanza introduction
that precedes them, and summarizing the account that each group
has to offer of the Muses' fall.

1.   Euterpe / Terpsichore / Erato

The three central laments relate the central myth of the poem, that
of the overthrow of the gentle Muses' kingdom by the rude forces
of Ignorance. We will want to look closely at how this story is told,
for it is here that Spenser sets the terms for his analysis of the plaintive
will. Terpsichore's lament opens with three stanzas that contrast past
joys with her present woes:

> Who so hath in the lap of soft delight
> Beene long time luld, and fed with pleasures sweet,
> Feareles through his own fault or Fortunes spight,
> To tumble into sorrow and regreet,
> Yf chaunce him fall into calamitie,
> Findes greater burthen of his miserie.
>
> So wee that earst in joyance did abound
> And in the bosome of all blis did sit,
> Like virgin Queenes with laurell garlands cround,
> For vertues meed and ornament of wit;
> Sith ignorance our kingdome did confound,
> Bee now become most wretched wightes on ground:
>
> And in our royall thrones which lately stood
> In th'hearts of men to rule them carefully,
> He now hath placed his accursed brood,
> By him begotten of fowle infamy;
> Blind Error, scornefull Follie, and base Spight,
> Who hold by wrong, that wee should have by right.

(301–18)

Nothing in these lines, or anywhere else in Terpsichore's lament,
links her to any particular function, much less that of the Muse of

dance with which modern readers associate her name.[9] Rather, she is said to exercise her rule within "th'hearts of men" and seems to stand for the capacity of knowledge to orient human beings within their own experience, bringing order and balance to their lives.[10] This is, of course, one of Renaissance humanism's great defenses of its own enterprise—"my mind to me a kingdom is"—but what we need to notice here are the specific terms of the Muses' sovreignty. For Terpisichore's image of the Muses "like virgin Queenes with laurell garlands cround" is a specifically Elizabethan vision of aristocratic rule, recalling nothing so much as the poet's own April eclogue in praise of "Eliza, Queene of shepheardes," to whom the Muses themselves had borne "Bay braunches" ("Aprill," 104). Like Eliza, Spenser's prelapsarian Muses rule within the chaste feminine seclusion of the bower. Euterpe, whom Spenser associates with pastoral song (278–82), speaks with a similar nostalgia of her "chast bowers, in which all vertue rained" (269) and bewails the razing of that "pleasance" (281) by Ignorance and his brood, while Erato, depicted as presiding over love poetry, describes her acolytes as resting in the "securitie" (365) of "Venus silver bowre" (362) before the goddess herself is rousted and her scepter broken in two (400).

We need at least to register the potential incongruity between a humanist defense of knowledge and the framing of such a defense in the pastoral fictions of Elizabethan rule, for the incongruity is one between two pairs of linked class and gender terms—non-aristocratic/masculine versus aristocratic/feminine—whose conflict is central to this section of the poem. In all three laments Spenser draws repeatedly on the specialized class terms of Elizabethan English to portray the destruction of the Muses' bowers both as the masculine invasion of feminine space and as a social upheaval. While the Muses are represented as queens and are described, together with their followers, as "gentle" (334, 345, 361), "noble" (331), and "loftie" (394), their masculine antagonists are regularly characterized as 'base" (317), "base-borne" (392), "vulgar" (319), and "rude" (328). Ignorance and his brood aim not just to usurp the Muses' kingdom, but to stain their "chast bowers" with "brutishness and beastlie filth" (269–70), to "spot" (333), "deface" (399), "mar" (281), and "despoil" (238).

This, then, is the chief story that the poem's central section has to tell: that of the gentle Muses' ruin at the hands of the vulgar, a ruin figured as the invasion and destruction of their bowers. As the story of masculine intrusion into a feminine space, it reads most immediately as the narrative of a rape. But there is more to the Muses' fall than this. For as is so often the case in Spenser's poetry, the lost place of delight is also represented here as a place of escape, a retreat from the world. Where Eliza in the April eclogue had been accompanied by a host of attendants, including the lowly figure of Colin Clout, Spenser's Muses occupy their bower alone, and their delights seem distinctly regressive. We see this in the stanzas just quoted from Terpsichore's lament, where she looks back nostalgically to the Muses' former life "in the bosome of all blis" and likens it to the experience of being lulled "in the lap of soft delight" and "fed with pleasures sweet," and similar images recur both in Erato's description of her followers in "*Venus* silver bowre" as being "with pleasure fed" (364) and in her subsequent reference to Cupid sprung "pure and spotles" from "th'Almighties bosome where he nests" (388–389). Throughout this section of the poem innocence is presented as a condition of narcissistic feeding and self-enclosure. By contrast, the masculine forces of Ignorance and his "accursed brood" are portrayed as alarmingly, obscenely prolific. Spenser dwells repeatedly on the ever-multiplying numbers of Ignorance's offspring—Error, Folly, and the rest—and speaks of their engendering among their followers of the "vulgar sort" the "fruitfull spawne of their rank fantasies" (319–22). One is reminded here of similar figures of loathsome male fecundity in *The Faerie Queene,* such as Mammon, playing onanistically with the mass of coins in his lap and pouring his plenty "out unto all" (2.7.5, 8), or the simile of "father *Nilus*" in the Error episode, whose "fattie waues do fertile slime outwell" (1.1.21).[11] Spilling their "beastlie filth" into the chaste sisters' bowers, Ignorance and his brood represent the same sort of procreative evil. Yet the contrast between their copiousness and the closed-in, regressive quality of the Muses' retreat offers a suggestive counterpoint to the sisters' account of their fall, for it at least raises the possibility that the Muses need the disruptive energies of their foes to make them prolific. After all, to find a greater burden of one's misery, in Terpsichore's phrase (line 306 above), is both to feel the weight of sorrow and to discover in sorrow a fruitful topic for song, taking "burthen" as both musical refrain and a loading of the womb; it is to be made fertile by one's griefs. Erato's lament develops this suggestion even further. She presents her function as that of ruling over passion "in measure moderate" (379), or rechanneling desire into verse. But when she appeals to her followers to mourn her overthrow by those that "rime at riot, and do rage in love" (395), it is precisely their own past unruly desires that she calls upon them to "renew":

Such as ye wont whenas those bitter stounds

Of raging love first gan you to torment,
And launch your hearts with lamentable wounds
Of secret sorrow and sad languishment,
Before your Loves did take you unto grace;
Those now renew as fitter for this place.

(373–78)

The pangs of "raging love" that Erato asks her followers to revive directly mirror the disruptive excesses of her opponents, who themselves "do rage in love"; once again, the suggestion is that of a circulation of energy between the Muses and their foes.

The central section of the poem, then, both mourns the defeat of the Muses and shows how they rely on this defeat to quicken their song. Viewed in this light, the Muses' retreat into the bower seems designed to elicit the responding attack of their enemies: the retreat invites the violation that gives the Muses a voice. This cycle of retreat, violation, and lament serves as the Muses' life support system, prolonging their existence as vehicles of woe. The cycle itself obeys the rhythms of what Harry Berger has called the "paradise priciple" and which he identifies as the "organizing motif" of *The Shepheardes Calender:* that is, a dialectic between recreative and plaintive attitudes involving "an obsessively repeated alternation between paradisal expectations and bitterness, or . . . a 'fall' from the first to the second followed by an effort to return."[12] Here, the recreative retreat seems primarily driven by the need to keep the cycle going; where Berger spoke in his earlier article of the Muses' "willed passivity," we might want to speak instead of "willed regression," for the movement into the bower represents the first stage in the working of the plaintive will. That retreat in turn excites the "spight" (303, 317) of Ignorance and his crew, who must destroy what they cannot possess; and the Muses' grief, their own "mischievous despight" (46), then takes the form of a ceaseless "pouring forth" (4, 230, 415, 595) of tears and lamentation that mimics the masculine copiousness of their foes.

This, then, is Spenser's anatomy of the plaintive will as an asserting of the self through the process of lament. By insisting on the dependence of the Muses on the conditions of their own victimization, he highlights the paradoxical combination of passivity and aggression, of weakness and strength, that is at the heart of the psychological and poetic dynamic of complaint. He does so, moreover, by drawing on a highly charged set of class and gender terms whose full significance will become clearer after we have looked at the paired laments of Clio and Calliope. Before turning to that portion of the poem, though, I would like to glance briefly at its opening section, the nine-stanza introduction that relates the narrator's first encounter with the grieving Muses, for much that we find there confirms what we have seen so far. Most immediately relevant, perhaps, are the stanzas where the narrator recounts the devastation of the Muses' fallen world:

> For all their groves, which with the heavenly noyses
> Of their sweete instruments were wont to sound,
> And th'hollow hills, from which their silver voyces
> Were wont redoubled Echoes to rebound,
> Did now rebound with nought but ruefull cries,
> And yelling shrieks throwne up into the skies.
>
> The trembling streames which wont in chanels cleare
> To romble gently downe with murmur soft,
> And were by them right tunefull taught to beare
> A Bases part amongst their consorts oft;
> Now forst to overflow with brackish teares,
> With troublous noyse did dull their daintie eares.

$$(19–30)$$

What is most striking here is how emphatically the language characterizes the sisters' grief as an act of will—shrieks thrown up to the skies, streams forced to overflow with tears. When the sisters lament that the noise of the swollen streams offends their ears, they both complain of and perpetuate a sound that is of their own making. Moreover, as we saw in the poem's central section, the action of the plaintive will begins at the moment of the Muses' retreat. Here, the chiasmic sequence "heavenly noyses" /"silver voyces"/"rebound"/ /"rebound"/"ruefull cries"/"troublous noyse" suggests a continuum between retreat and lament rather than a rupture—suggests, that is, that both the "redoubled Echoes" of the Muses' pastoral voices and the "yelling shrieks" of their grief represent a single exertion of their will upon the world. This suggestion is further developed two stanzas down, where the harmonious relation between nature and the Muses before the fall is specifically characterized as one where the world of nature was "made . . . to serve their will" (40), as well as in the lines just quoted about the Muses' teaching the streams to sing their parts, for these lines significantly reverse one of the most familiar *topoi* in Spenser's poetry, that of the singer tuning his song "unto the gentle sounding of the waters fall."[13] Instead of the poet bringing himself into accord with the natural world, here nature is shown receiving instruction from the goddesses of song. In the process, class energies that are hopelessly polarized elsewhere in the poem are figuratively brought into accord, as the gently rumbling stream is taught to sing "a Bases part" in the Muses' consort, but both this state of prelapsarian harmony and the Muses' fallen griefs are presented as parallel enactments of the sisters' will.[14]

In other ways, too, the opening section confirms much that we have seen before. The second and third stanzas, for instance, offer mythopoeic accounts of prior occasions of the Muses' grief—their mourning over the death of Phaethon and over the murder of Calliope's twins by the Fates—that suggest that the Muses depend on either the transgressive breaking of limits (Phaethon's taking the Sun "beyond the compasse of his pointed path" [10]) or the mimetic "spight" (16) of others (the three sister Fates "unkindly" mirroring the nine sister Muses) to provide them with matter for song.[15] So, too, the unnamed, presumably masculine narrator of this opening section assumes a stance that is at once deferential and commanding, self-effacing and self-assertive. Acknowledging that the sisters' grief is solely their concern, he nonetheless demands that they "display" its "secret causes" and orders them to sing (49–54). In his ambivalence he reflects the condition of the Muses as we have seen them so far: passive and aggressive, recreative and plaintive, suffering and "impatient" of their "plight" (44).

2.   Clio / Calliope

With the laments of Clio and Calliope, we get a rather different perspective on the Muses' fall. While the laments of the central group had recounted the usurpation of the gentle Muses' kingdom by the vulgar race of Ignorance, Clio and Calliope complain of the failure of the aristocracy to live up to its own ideals, and portray the Muses' downfall as the result of this aristocratic failure. In the process, they focus much more directly on the place and function of the poet within the Elizabethan social order and so reflect back on the laments of the poem's central section in some extraordinarily suggestive ways.

As the Muses of history and epic, both Clio and Calliope serve the nobility by recording the virtuous deeds of its members. To do so is to sustain a social hierarchy that depends on a link between nobility and virtue; indeed, as Calliope suggests, it is virtually to put such a hierarchy into place:

> What bootes it then to come from glorious
> Forefathers, or to have been nobly bredd?
> What odds twixt *Irus* and old *Inachus*,
> Twixt best and worst, when both alike are dedd;
> If none of neither mention should make,
> Nor out of dust their memories awake?
>
> (445–50)

Irus is the beggar who challenges Odysseus at the door to his own palace and gets his teeth knocked out, much to the delight of the suitors; Inachus, the father of Io, was the legendary first king of Argos whose name had by the time of Horace become synonymous with "old money" (see *Odes* 2.3.21). The difference between them of "best and worst" is more obviously social or economic than moral, and this perhaps is the point: the value of the link between virtue and nobility is that it serves to confirm hierarchical norms. So long as the nobility does not absolutely forfeit its claim to virtue, the Muses can continue to underwrite that claim through their celebrations, making it worthwhile to have been nobly bred. But when a degenerate aristocracy loses all "desire of worthie deeds" (437), so that the link between virtue and nobility becomes thoroughly implausible, the Muses can no longer ratify the social order, and their function is at an end.

Clio, too, laments that a slothful aristocracy leaves her with "nothing noble" to sing (108), but she particularizes her complaint in some additional ways. For one thing, she takes pains to distinguish between two classes of nobles: a new generation of courtly *arrivistes*, unjustly promoted to honor by Jove (69–70), versus the older aristocracy of birth, the "honorable race/Of mightie Peeres" (79–80). Moreover, Clio not only represents the members of each group as heedless of their own virtue, but characterizes them as actively hostile to the attentions of the Muses. The new generation has quickly learned to "Despise the brood of blessed Sapience" (72) and works to keep the Muses and their followers down, while the older nobles, deeming learning itself "a base thing," have shown themselves to be "Base minded" (87–88).

In this section of the poem, we find ourselves much closer to the world of "October," with its explicit concern for the place of the

poet within the Elizabethan social order, than to that of "Aprill,"
with its recreative celebration of aristocratic rule. The dilemmas of
the Muses and their followers here are recognizably those of the
humanist poet at court, charged with celebrating the virtues of a
nobility that is either indifferent or hostile to his enterprise. As with
the central section, though, the terms of the Muses' account will
repay attention, for in this case a single motif links the two laments,
that of the sisters' ability to lift up the subjects of their song. Epic
praise, says Calliope, spurs men on to perform heroic deeds:

> Therefore the nurse of vertue I am hight,
> And golden Trompet of eternitie,
> That lowly thoughts lift up to heavens hight,
> And mortall men have powre to deifie:
> *Bacchus* and *Hercules* I raisd to heaven,
> And *Charlemaine*, among the Starris seaven.
>
> (457–62)

And Clio makes a similar claim for the proper use of history, that
the wisdom derived from it lifts human beings toward the divine:
"For God himselfe for wisedome most is praised,/And men to God
thereby are nighest raised" (89–90). Rather than rely on the Muses'
support, though, the members of a degraded nobility vainly attempt
to elevate themselves: "But they doo onely strive themselves to raise,/
Through pompous pride and foolish vanitie . . ." (91–92).

If, then, the terms of a hierarchical social order resolve themselves
into a polarity between high and low, Clio and Calliope sustain that
order by lifting up the subjects of their song. It is telling, therefore,
that the reaction of the nobility against the Muses and their followers
is portrayed in Clio's lament as a suppression of aspirations that directly parallel the nobility's own:

> The sectaries of my celestial skill,
> That wont to be the worlds chiefe ornament,
> And learned Impes that wont to shoote up still,
> And grow to hight of kingdomes government
> They underkeep, and with their spredding armes
> Doo beat their buds, that perish through their harmes.
>
> (73–78)

Clio's metaphor of the plant shooting up describes the activity of the humanist poet at court in terms that recall two moments from the October eclogue: first, Cuddie's image of the "buddes of Poesie" that spring up only to wither; and, second, Piers' earlier injunction to Cuddie to move from pastoral into epic: "Lyft up thy selfe out of the lowly dust: / And sing of bloody Mars, of wars, of giusts" ("October," 73–77, 36–39). But here the poets' shooting up also clearly recalls the vain self-raising of a foolish nobility, and this in turn suggests that the "underkeeping" of the Muses' followers may be less an act of gratuitous malice than a reciprocal response to their own ambitious desires; their shooting up compells the nobility to push them down. The lines, in other words, imply that the Muses' wish to lift up the aristocracy in song masks a competitive urge to emulate noble behavior and so to raise themselves "to hight of kingdomes government." As the lines also make clear, the mimetic competition with the nobility is one that the Muses and their followers can never hope to win, unless through a mourning of aristocratic failure that now looks less like a response of sympathetic bereavement than like an act of aggression, one that allows the Muses to re-classify noble as base and to cloak the lofty in "darknesse" and "slime" (106).[16]

There are some obvious points of contact here with what we saw in the poem's central section, particularly in the mirroring of energies between the Muses and their opponents, as well as in the veiled aggressiveness of the Muses' laments. But the emphasis in these stanzas on the condition of the poet also allows us to view the reiterated class and gender terms of the central section in a new light. For it is, of course, precisely the masculine, non-aristocratic poet who is left out of account when humanist knowledge is celebrated by means of a feminine fiction of aristocratic rule—when Colin Clout, so to speak, is excluded from the bower. If what drives that poet is the competitive urge unmasked in the laments of Clio and Calliope, then in the poem's central section his agency may find its displaced expression in the masculine energies of Ignorance and his brood, as well as in the further displacement of those energies into the voices of the plaintive Muses. The poet himself steps forward as the absent source of the base masculine spite that destroys the Muses' world and engenders their song.

We are now in a position to grasp the analogy that stands at the heart of this poem, the analogy between the plaintive will of the Muses and the condition of the poet who mourns their plight. As we have already seen, the Muses as portrayed in the central section exemplify the paradoxical workings of the plaintive will, with its cycling between passivity and self-assertion. But these paradoxes apply equally to the situation of the masculine, non-aristocratic poet.

On the one hand, that poet may identify himself so closely with the fictions of aristocratic rule that he literally vanishes from the scene, as in the poem's central section, or functions solely as a vehicle of celebration, as in the laments of Clio and Calliope. Or, on the other hand, he may assert his will through a ruthless act of destruction that unleashes his own competitive drive. The paradoxes of complaint directly express, then, the dilemma of the non-aristocratic poet's state: his conflict between passivity and self-assertion, and his anxiety about exerting his will. While one side of the dilemma is played out through his identification with the masculine forces of Ignorance, ultimately the poet seems most fully invested in the ambiguously powerful voices of the plaintive Muses themselves, both in their regressive retreat into the bower and in the copious pouring-out of their "musick of hart-breaking mone" (6).

3.   *Melpomene / Thalia / Urania / Polyhymnia*

Together, the two sections of the poem discussed so far offer a composite picture of the psychological impasse faced by a non-aristocratic poet working in an aristocratic milieu, with his vacillating urges toward passivity and a self-consciously transgressive assertion of will. The laments of the third section present a somewhat more miscellaneous group, but they too are held together by a shared account of the Muses' defeat. That account is presented in two stages. First, the linked laments of Melpomene and Thalia, the Muses of tragedy and comedy, portray the withdrawal of the Muses and their followers from the spectacle of an impure world. Then the laments of Urania and Polyhymnia inflect that withdrawal upwards into a motif of Astraean flight. In all four instances, the Muses' departure is presented as an alternative that has been forced upon them, but the equivocal terms in which that alternative is portrayed suggest that it can also be read as an act of will originating with the sisters themselves. Once again the claim of victimization and neglect modulates into an assertion of will, as the Muses try to sustain their autonomy by marking their difference from the world. This urge finds its final expression in the lament of Polyhymnia, where the Muse presents herself as set off from her surroundings by her possession of a single empowering secret.

With Melpomene, plaintiveness initially takes the form of a refusal to engage the fallenness of the world. Her opening stanzas strike a penitential note:

> O who shall powre into my swollen eyes
> A sea of teares that never may be dryde,
> A brasen voice that may with shrilling cryes
> Pierce the dull heavens and fill the ayer wide,
> And yron sides that sighing may endure,
> To waile the wretchednes of world impure?
>
> Ah wretched world the den of wickednesse,
> Deformd with filth and fowle iniquitie;
> Ah wretched world the house of heavinesse,
> Fild with the wreaks of mortall miserie
> Ah wretched world, and all that is therein,
> The vassals of Gods wrath, and slaves of sin.
>
> (115–26)

Where Clio and Calliope wished to celebrate worldly deeds, the attitude of Melpomene is that of contempt for the things of a "world impure"; the condition of 'wretchednes" represents a bondage to sin that is intrinsic to the fallen universe. As the Variorum notes, the opening two lines of the passage echo verses from Jeremiah, and the hammering repetitions of the word "wretched," combined with the final reference to mortals as the "slaves of sin," give the stanzas a decidedly Pauline cast.[17] At the same time, Melpomene's opening plea to receive the voice of another and yet to have that voice pierce the sky evokes the now familiar passive/aggressive dynamic of complaint, whereby an insistence on the world's impurity may serve as a vehicle of the Muse's will.

The second section of Melpomene's lament marks a significant change of direction. Her third stanza begins in the penitential mode of the first two—"Most miserable creature under sky" (127)—but then veers off: "Man without understanding doth appeare" (128). And the third through sixth stanzas go on to counsel the Stoic recourse to reason as a bulwark against "Fortunes freakes" (130) and "dolours darts" (134), counsel that "foolish Men" ignore in banishing the Muses (145–48). This shift of emphasis, from a Pauline insistence on human sinfulness to an opening up of the possibilities of Stoic consolation, is potentially of great importance, for it allows for an understanding of tragedy as a mode of active participation in the world. As the tragic Muse, Melpomene can serve mortals by providing exemplary instances of human ruin to guide them in their plight. The shift amounts to one between two different versions of complaint—the *de contemptu mundi* lament over the sinfulness of a fallen world versus exemplary lamentation in the *de casibus*, or "fall of princes," tradition—but this second possibility is raised here only to be discarded.[18]

In her seventh stanza, Melpomene offers her own understanding of her proper role, and for the first time her thoughts turn toward the stage:

> My part it is and my professed skill
> The Stage with Tragick buskin to adorne,
> And fill the Scene with plaint and outcries shrill
> Of wretched persons, to misfortune borne:
> But none more tragick matter I can finde
> Than this, of men depriv'd of sense and minde.
>
> (151–56)

Nothing in these lines explicitly contradicts the *de casibus* justification for tragedy implied in stanzas three through six, but the invocation of "wretched persons, to misfortune borne" slips back into the *contemptus mundi* mode, and the lines as a whole evince a veiled contempt for theater—"My *part* it is and my *professed* skill"—that seems to undercut Melpomene's claim for the utility of her displays. This attitude carries over into the final two stanzas of her lament:

> For all mans life me seemes a Tragedy,
> Full of sad sights and sore Catastrophees;
> First coming to the world with weeping eye,
> Where all his dayes like dolorous Trophees,
> Are heapt with spoyles of fortune and of feare,
> And he at last laid forth on balefull beare.
>
> So all with rufull spectacles is fild
> Fit for *Megera* or *Persephone;*
> But I that in true Tragedies am skild,
> The flowre of wit, finde nought to busie me:
> Therefore I mourne, and pitifully mone,
> Because that mourning matter I have none.
>
> (157–68)

In a fallen world, Melpomene claims, every moment of mortal experience is tragic, and this leaves the tragic Muse with no function to perform, since the "rufull spectacles" of the world itself pre-empt representation. Melpomene's only recourse is to the *mise en abîme* of her final couplet, an endless mourning of her own lack of "mourning matter."

These concluding stanzas bring us back full circle to Melpomene's opening rejection of the "world impure," now become a world of theatrical spectacle. The possibility conspicuously raised in stanzas three through six, that of tragedy as a means of engaging the world, has now subsided in favor of allegiance to those "true Tragedies" whose proper home is in the mind ("the flowre of wit"). The power of Melpomene's voice comes from her rejection of the world in favor of this unrepresentable ideal.

Given Melpomene's aversion to theater, it comes as something of a surprise that Thalia, the next of the Muses to speak, begins her lament with a nostalgic celebration of the charms of theatrical display. It is precisely spectacle's demise that Thalia mourns:

> Where be the sweete delights of learnings treasure,
> That wont with Comick sock to beautefie
> The painted Theaters, and fill with pleasure
> The listners eyes, and eares with melodie;
> In which I late was wont to raine as Queene,
> And maske in mirth with Graces well beseene?
>
> (175–80)

Thalia's commitment to the "delights" of "painted Theaters" (a phrase perhaps meant to evoke the glittering "heavens" of the Elizabethan stage) is also a commitment to representation—the fit task of comedy is that of sketching "mans life in his likest image" (201), and the late comedian "pleasant *Willy*" is praised for his ability "Truth to imitate,/With kindly counter under Mimick shade" (206–07)—but her defense of her own function relies less on any of the conventional moral justifications for comedy than on the sweetness of the delight and "goodly pleasance" (200) that she is able to provide. She must therefore distinguish the greater seemliness of her mirth from the "follie" (193, 212, 220) thrown forth by Ignorance and his crew, and this she does in two ways. First, she underwrites the distinction between good and bad theater, and good and bad pleasure, by introducing the class terms familiar to us from the poem's central section. Not only do we have a return of the usurpation myth (Thalia, ruling over a recreative court of Graces, is dispossessed by foes who "in the mindes of men now tyrannize" [191]), but the Muse's own "joyous gentle dalliaunce" (186) is explicitly contrasted to the "rudenes" (192) of her antagonists and their appeal to "the vulgare" (194). Stanzas six through eight further underwrite the distinction by representing the departure of two poet-figures from the scene.[19] First comes the comedian "pleasant *Willy,*" already mentioned, whose death leaves "idle wit" holding the field; and then a second, more patently aristocratic, figure:

But that same gentle Spirit, from whose pen
Large streams of honnie and sweete Nectar flowe,
Scorning the boldness of such base-borne men,
Which dare their follies forth so rashlie throwe;
Doth rather choose to sit in idle Cell,
Than so himself to mockerie to sell.

(217–22)

Not only in this unnamed figure explicitly marked off as "gentle" in opposition to the "base-borne" dramatists who hold the stage, but the flow of "honnie and sweete Nectar" from his pen associates him with the world of courtly literary practice rather than that of the commercial theater. Certainly part of what is at stake both here and at the close of Melpomene's lament is Spenser's own anxious response to the phenomenon of the public theater as a sphere of non-aristocratic cultural production; the retreat of the "gentle Spirit" allows Spenser himself to keep his distance from the stage.[20] What is most striking about this retreat, though, is how equivocally it is portrayed. The key word here is "idle." As no less an authority than Camille Paglia reminds us, this is always "a big word in Spenser," connoting narcissism and sterile self-abuse.[21] Given that the word had been used only six lines previously to characterize the "wit" of Thalia's enemies, its presence here seems to call into question the very distinctions that the departure of the gentle Spirit has been asked to sustain. In his quasi-monastic seclusion, this figure mirrors both the self-enclosure of the Muses of the central section and the freely flowing copiousness of their foes, blurring rather than confirming boundaries between good and bad theater, good and bad pleasure, and noble and base, distinctions further conflated by the sameness-in-difference of the concluding homophones "Cell" and "sell."[22]

In several ways, then, the laments of the tragic and comic Muses present a matched pair. Not only does the departure of the two poet-figures named by Thalia literalize the rejection of the world that is

the burden of Melpomene's lament, but in each instance the movement of withdrawal is represented in ambivalent terms that evoke
the willfulness that it dissembles. In the case of Melpomene, the
conspicuously raised possibility of tragic engagement with the world
ensures that we recognize the Muse's final claim of allegiance to "true
Tragedies" as an evasion, noting the disingenuousness of a tragic
Muse who bewails her own inability to find topics of song within a
tragic world; while in the case of Thalia the equivocal nature of the
gentle Spirit's retreat similarly ensures that we read his departure from
the scene as an attempt to shore up distinctions that cannot ultimately
be sustained. What surfaces in both cases is quite simply the strain
involved in the Muses' efforts to mark their own purity; like the
retreat into the bower in the poem's central section, the withdrawal
of Melpomene and Thalia from the spectacle of an impure world is
driven by the self-assertive energies of the plaintive will.

   The last two Muses to speak, Urania and Polyhymnia, redirect the
movement of withdrawal upwards into one of flight.[23] Spenser's Urania is the Renaissance "Christian Muse," and her first four stanzas
characterize the world that refuses her tutelage as one infected by
"pestilence" (483) and hopelessly lost in "darkenesse" (486).[24] References to "hell . . . and the grislie grave" (496) and to the power of
ignorance to "debace" the "mindes of men" (498) implicitly contrast
the lowness of earth to the height of heavenly contemplation, and
this contrast becomes explicit in the fifth stanza, as Urania speaks of
her and her followers' elevation: "From hence wee mount aloft unto
the skie,/And looke into the Christall firmament" (505–06). The
movement here, of course, is that of the Neoplatonic ascent through
contemplation toward the divine, and can be paralleled by such passages in Spenser's poetry as "October," 91–96, and "An Hymne of
Heavenly Beautie," 126–40. Urania's eighth stanza, however, offers
a slightly different perspective on this movement of ascent, presenting
it as a flight fueled by the scorn of those who remain below:

   How ever yet they mee despise and spight,
   I feede on sweet contentment of my thought,
   And please my selfe with mine owne selfe-delight,
   In contemplation of things heavenlie wrought:
   So loathing earth, I looke up to the sky,
   And being driven hence I thether flie.

                                             (523–28)

While the first version of the Muse's flight portrayed it as the natural outcome of a process of thought, these lines suggest that the Muse's departure from the world has been driven by the "spight" of her enemies. Given the reference in Urania's opening stanzas to the "noyous pestilence" afflicting the world after her fall, her "loathing" of the earth closely resembles the "disdaine" of Astraea, whose flight back to heaven in a time of "plague pestilence, and death" opens *Mother Hubberds Tale* (1–8). In each instance, the goddess' departure can be read as a moment of competitive self-assertion, a reciprocal response to the world's disdain. In the case of Urania, the end-point of the movement of ascent is the by now familiar condition of "selfe-delight" and solipsistic complaint ("and for my selfe complaine" [533]).

It is worth noting here that the movement of Neoplatonic ascent often has the potential in Spenser to serve as a vehicle of personal ambition. A particularly telling instance comes in the course of *Colin Clouts Come Home Againe,* where Colin rapturously praises Cynthia (or Elizabeth) for the loftiness of her own contemplation, whereby she beholds in "high aspiring thought,/The cradle of her own creation" (612–13). To this Cuddy offers the following rebuke:

> *Colin* (said *Cuddy* then) thou hast forgot
> Thy selfe, me seemes, too much, to mount so hie:
> Such loftie flight, base shepheard seemeth not,
> From flocks and fields, to Angels and to skie.
>
> (616–19)

As John D. Bernard notes, Colin's response that he has been lifted up by Elizabeth's "excellence" (620) rather than by his own ambition, "cannot explain away the element of self-aggrandizement implied" in celebrating the loftiness of his Queen, a self-aggrandizement that is hardly diminished by Colin's own reference at line 622 to the "furious insolence" of his inspired state.[25] The example is particularly relevant to our concerns, because the lament of Polyhymnia, the next (and last) of the Muses to speak, similarly links poetic flight and praise of the Queen. Polyhymnia's lament concludes with three stanzas that first celebrate the virtues of "Divine *Elisa,* sacred Emperesse" (579), and then recount the ascent of a select coterie of poets, "Admirers of her glorious excellence," who are "lifted up above the worldes gaze,/To sing with Angels her immortall praize" (587–88). As Spenser depicts her, Polyhymnia has special authority over the realm of poetic craft, understood here as especially involving technical skill in meter and rhyme. Her opening five stanzas mourn the loss of the "naturall delight" of verse, now that poetry has been usurped by those who lack the "skill to rule" her "sweet numbers and melodious measures" (547–52). In place of the Muse's "tunefull Diapase of pleasures" (549), the verses of contemporary poetasters run amuck, too much "at libertie," clanging "with horrid sound" and "little sence" (550–54). Even the Muse herself echoes these discordant accents in the "ragged rimes" of her own "dolefull" laments (541–45).

In Polyhymnia's fourth stanza, the lost skill at verse-making is described in highly significant terms:

> Whilom in ages past none might professe
> But Princes and high Priests that secret skill,
> The sacred lawes therein they wont expresse,
> And with deepe Oracles their verses fill:
> Then was shee [Poetry] held in soveraigne dignitie,
> And made the noursling of Nobilitie.
>
> (559–64)

While today Polyhymnia's rhymes echo the cacophony around her, in times past she was fostered by the nobly born. It is natural to read these lines as Simon Shepherd does and view them as portraying the poet as the servant of ideology and preserver of "the mystique of power."[26] But this misses the essential point that the "secret skill" that has been lost is that of technical facility in making verses. In these terms, Spenser's lines may be read as claiming grounds for the poet's authority in his "rule" over his craft, establishing the poet in a position, not of subservience to, but of rivalry with, the dominant order.[27] And now the concluding stanzas praising Elizabeth begin to look more than a little equivocal:

> One onelie lives, her ages ornament,
> And myrrour of her Makers majestie;
> That with rich bountie and deare cherishment,
> Supports the praise of noble Poësie:
> Ne onelie favours them which it professe,
> But is her selfe a peereles Poëtresse.
>
> Most peereles Prince, most peereles Poëtresse,
> The true *Pandora* of all heavenly graces,

Divine *Elisa,* sacred Emperesse:
Live she for ever, and her royal P'laces
Be fild with praises of divinest wits,
That her eternize with their heavenlie writs.

Some few beside, this sacred skill esteme,
Admirers of her glorious excellence,
Which being lightned with her beawties beme,
Are thereby fild with happie influence:
And lifted up above the worldes gaze,
To sing with Angels her immortall praize.

                                                          (571–88)

This last stanza points toward the question that will later be raised more explicitly in *Colin Clout*: to what extent is the poet's praise simply a vehicle for his own ambition, the claim of being passively "lifted up" by the celebration of Elizabeth masking the aggressive desire to rise? More to the point, though, to praise Elizabeth for her abilities as a "peereles Poëtresse" is to praise her for virtues that the poet himself possesses in his privileged access to the secret of his skill. If like Pandora Elizabeth is herself the bearer of secrets, she mirrors her servant in this. Nor is it necessary to appeal to outside sources to confirm that any comparison to Pandora must cut more than one way. For the nineteenth sonnet of Spenser's *Ruines of Rome,* published together with *Teares* in the volume of *Complaints,* describes Pandora as the source of "mishap" and "good hap" mixed indistinguishably together (257–58). The compliment has an unmistakably aggressive edge: once again, poetic praise of the dominant order shifts into rivalry and *ressentiment*.

As with the movements of withdrawal and flight represented in the other three laments, Polyhymnia's claim of access to an empowering secret serves the purpose of asserting her own autonomy, of marking her special status. In all four laments, we see again the paradoxical combination of passivity and aggression, of self-effacement and self-assertion, that characterizes the working of the plaintive will. Fittingly enough, the poem concludes with Spenser's signature image of poetic frustration, as the Muses break their instruments and subside into silence: "The rest untold no living tongue can speake" (600).[28]

*   *   *

Spenser's *The Teares of the Muses* brings together an extraordinarily heterogeneous body of Renaissance discourse, including pastoral,

Neoplatonism, anti-theatricality, and hermeticism, not to mention several varieties of poetic complaint. No one would want to argue that this is a great, or even an entirely coherent, poem. But in the preceding pages I have tried to show how many of its details are animated by Spenser's wish to explore the conflicts of his own experience through his representation of the plaintive Muses. It is in keeping with the paradoxical nature of poetic complaint that the sketching of an analogy between poet and Muses should itself be a form of poetic self-assertion; that Spenser's own identification with the fallen Muses is both with their weakness and their unappeasable strength.

In conclusion, I would like to suggest some ways that the issues of plaintiveness and the poetic condition raised in *The Teares of the Muses* are central to the other poems of the *Complaints* volume. Some of the connections are obvious enough and do not need to be belabored—the malign self-fashioning of the Fox and the Ape in *Mother Hubberds Tale,* for instance, has obvious parallels with the mimetic competition between poet and nobility that we see sketched in the laments of Clio and Polyhymnia. But the extent to which other poems of the volume structure themselves around the alternatives of excessive passivity and excessive willfulness is really quite striking, and worth taking a moment to explore. I will limit my remarks here to three of the other poems of the volume: *Muiopotmos, Virgils Gnat,* and *The Ruines of Time.*

In *Muiopotmos,* the conflict between the embittered Aragnoll, the "bondslave of spight" (245), and his enemy, "the careles Clarion" (375) fitting aimlessly about the flower beds, seems to re-enact the opposition between Ignorance and the Muses in all of its ambivalence. Clarion's delight in the "pleasaunce" is linked to aristocratic fiction both through his own status as inheritor of "his fathers throne" (32) and through his inclusion by proxy on the margins of Minerva's tapestry, a work celebrating the emblems of political rule. By contrast, the tapestry of Arachne, Aragnoll's mother, has woven into it images of the desires of the gods and is enlivened by her own imaginative sympathy for their victims. The poem's conclusion reenacts the destruction of the Muses' bowers by the brood of Ignorance, with Clarion made prey to Aragnoll's "spight" and his dead body left as "the spectacle of care" (436, 440).

The opposition between "care" and "carelessness" is central to *Virgils Gnat,* where the two words and their variants occur no fewer than sixteen times over the course of the poem's 687 lines. This poem rewrites the opposition between passivity and aggression as the contrast between the carelessness of the shepherd and the care of the gnat who seeks to wake him from his slumbers, first with his sting, and then with his embittered plaint. As in both *Teares* and *Muiopotmos,* the condition of passivity, or carelessness, is associated with aristocratic delight, both by means of the poem's references to the shepherd as "Lord of himself" (113) and "that flocks grand Capitaine" (268), and more comprehensively through the dedicatory sonnet's implicit identification of the shepherd with Leicester, whom Spenser addresses as "the causer of my care." This last reference would seem to identify Spenser himself with the aggressively biting gnat, with the poet's sting consisting of the secret meaning that his sonnet at once conceals and promises to unfold. But Spenser can also be identified with the careless shepherd, for in the guise of Virgil the narrator expresses his wish to celebrate Augustus at a "season more secure" (9)—that is, at a time when the poet himself has achieved the shepherd's freedom from care (*cura*). As with *Teares,* then, the poet's condition mingles passivity and aggression in an unstable compound. But, strikingly, at the poem's conclusion the shepherd adopts the gnat's "cares" (462) as his own, and monumentalizes them through the construction of a tomb. In this sense, the shepherd appears to provide a model for moving out of the double bind of aggression and passivity through the act of taking on the sorrows of another.

In the first poem of the volume, *The Ruines of Time,* we see a similar move toward an indirect investment of authorial will aimed at resolving the poetic impasse depicted in the other poems of the volume. Here, the mournful Verlame clearly recalls the grieving Muses, but her plaintiveness, though felt to be excessive, does not make her into a figure of aggressive spite. Instead, midway through the poem the plaintive voice of Verlame merges with that of the sympathetic narrator of the poem, a merging that allows Spenser to celebrate Sidney, Leicester, et al. without falling into aggressive poetic rivalry on the one hand, and yet with an indirect authorial investment that avoids the loss of will that accompanies a sheerly passive response. The authorial presence, finally, leaves its trace, not in the closing plaintiveness of the narrator, but in the significance of the pageant of images and signs that appears at the conclusion of the poem, a pageant whose meaning the narrator fails to grasp, but whose availability for the reader's interpretation represents another way of solving the impasse presented over the course of the volume. In this sense, both *Virgils Gnat* and *The Ruines of Time* depict the poetic dilemmas played out over much of the volume as problems that in 1591, after the publication of the 1590 *Faerie Queene,* have already been confronted and resolved.

Centre College

Notes

1. Passages from Spenser's poetry, except for *The Faerie Queene,* are cited from *The Yale Edition of the Shorter Poems of Edmund Spenser,* ed. William A. Oram et al. (New Haven: Yale University Press, 1989) and are indicated by line numbers within the text. Oram's introduction to *Teares* in this edition, 263–64, summarizes the arguments on dating; the issue is considered further in Harold Stein, *Studies in Spenser's Complaints* (New York: Oxford University Press, 1934), 42–53, and most thoroughly in *The Works of Edmund Spenser, A Variorum Edition: Volume 8, The Minor Poems, Part Two* (Baltimore: Johns Hopkins University Press, 1947), 533–50. The Variorum commentary, 317–21, surveys the candidates that have been put forward for the role of "pleasant *Willy.*"

2. Gerald Snare, "The Muses on Poetry: Spenser's *The Teares of the Muses,*" *Tulane University Studies in English* 17 (1969), 31–52; *Yale,* 263–67; and A. C. Hamilton, gen. ed., *The Spenser Encyclopedia* (Toronto: University of Toronto Press, 1990), 182–83. References to comments on the poem by Harry Berger, Jr. and Simon Shepherd will be found below.

3. Harry Berger, Jr., *Revisionary Play: Studies in the Spenserian Dynamics* (Berkeley: University of California Press, 1988), 50. The sentence comes near the end of an essay, "Archaism, Immortality, and the Muse in Spenser's Poetry," that originally appeared in 1969. Also relevant are some remarks by Louis Montrose in the course of his fine essay on "Spenser's Domestic Domain," in Margreta de Grazia, Maureen Quilligan, and Peter Stallybrass, eds., *Subject and Object in Renaissance Culture* (Cambridge: Cambridge University Press, 1996): "Throughout Spenser's poetic corpus, the poet's voice is characterized by an oscillation between self-aggrandizement and self-abasement, between vaunting and wailing. This oscillation is inadequately explained by recourse either to literary convention or personal psychology; it is the literary inscription of a lived contradiction that is indissolubly social and subjective" (102). In tracing the "literary inscription" of complaint over the course of *The Teares of the Muses,* I attempt to follow the examples both of Berger and of Montrose.

4. The text of Harvey's poem can be found in Alexander B. Grosart, ed., *The Works of Gabriel Harvey* (privately printed, 1884; repr., New York: AMS Pres, 1966), Volume 1, xxv–xxxv. In his commentary on the September eclogue, E.K. mentions the work in his commendation of Harvey/Hobbinoll as Immeritô's "especiall good freend."

5. The verses, which may also have suggested some of the traits of Spenser's Muses, are cited in the Variorum, 312. Spenser probably used the Dumaeus edition of Virgil in composing *Virgils Gnat,* the translation of the pseudo-Virgilian *Culex* that appeared along with *Teares* in the 1591 *Complaints.* The Variorum, 545–50, cites the arguments in favor of this edition, which *The Spenser Encyclopedia,* 183, accepts as "the Renaissance text Spenser probably used."

6. As the Variorum notes (322), the closest parallel comes at lines 253–64 of Spenser's poem, where the genealogy given for Ignorance borrows several details from Du Bellay's text.

7. Snare, 45.

8. See Oram's comment, *Yale* 267: "Like the world it portrays, the form of the complaint is broken."

9. The whole question of when and how individual Muses became identified with distinct functions is enormously complex. The nine sisters are first named in lines 77–79 of Hesiod's *Theogony,* but other than the fact that Clio is cited as their leader, no differentiation is made among them; the association of various Muses with particular functions begins in late antiquity. In a work in progress, Thomas P. Roche, Jr., is tracing the iconography of the Muses from Hesiod through the Renaissance, both literary and pictorial. Until his study becomes available, it seems prudent to assume nothing about what Spenser "would have known" about the Muses, other than what can be directly gleaned from the lines of the poem.

10. Compare Oram's comment, *Yale* 266, on "the Muses' power to discipline men, guide them, enable them to keep proper *measure* in their lives."

11. Passages from *The Faerie Queene* are cited from J. C. Smith and E. de Selincourt, eds., *Spenser: Poetical Works* (Oxford: Oxford University Press, 1912), and are indicated by Book, canto, and line numbers within the text.

12. Berger, 278. This definition of the "paradise principle" is drawn from Berger's "Introduction to *The Shepheardes Calender,*" published for the first time in *Revisionary Play.*

13. This line is quoted here from its earliest version in *The Theatre for Wordlings* (1569), page 467 in *Yale.* The *topos* of the singer harmonizing with the water's fall occurs at one other point in that volume, as well as in the revisions of both passages in *Complaints,* and resurfaces as a Spenserian signature in both *The Shepheardes Calender* ("Aprill," lines 55–56) and *The Faerie Queene* (twice, once at 2.12.71 and once at 6.10.7). John Hollander's fascinating account of Spenser and Milton's use of the *topos* does not note its reversal in the lines cited from *Teares.* See "The Footing of His Feet: On a Line of Milton's," in Richard Waswo, ed., *On Poetry and Poetics* (Tübingen: Gunter Narr, 1985), 11–30.

14. On the question of a pun on "Bases," note the recurrence of Spenser's signature image in Acrasia's Bower, 2.12.71.6, where a pun is certainly intended, as Hamilton notes in his commentary on the line. See A. C. Hamilton, ed., *The Faerie Queene* (London: Longman, 1977), 294.

15. As the footnotes in *Yale* indicate, both myths are original with Spenser. In Ovid, Phaethon is mourned "not by the Muses but by his sisters the Heliades," and the Palici are not the children of Calliope but "the twins of Jupiter and the nymph (not the Muse) Thalia" (*Yale,* 270).

16. On the phenomenon of aggressive sympathy and its bearing on Spenser's work, see Jonathan Crewe, *Hidden Designs: The Critical Profession and Renaissance Literature* (New York: Methuen, 1986), 66–69.

17. *Variorum,* 314, noting echoes of Jeremiah 9.1, John 8.32–36, and Romans 6.12–23, to which might be added Romans 7.24; *Yale,* 245, cites this last verse in a note on line 293 of *The Ruines of Time,* glossing "wretched" as a "Pauline word for man's fallen state."

18. In chapter 3 of her unpublished dissertation, "The Poetic Unity of Edmund Spenser's *Complaints*" (University of Western Ontario, 1985), Linda Mary Vecchi provides an admirably detailed survey of the development of *de contemptu mundi* and *de casibus* laments as separate branches of the complaint genre.

19. Many of the commentators cited in the Variorum, 317–21, take the two passages to refer to a single figure, but as the Yale editor, 277, notes, this is unlikely, since the "gentle Spirit" is represented as still living.

20.   Simon Shepherd makes this point about the passage in the course of his book-length study, *Spenser* (Atlantic Highlands, New Jersey: Humanities Press, 1989), 107. Pages 106–11 of Shepherd's monograph comment on Spenser's poem from an avowedly Marxist perspective, focusing on how contradictory elements of Spenser's position within the Elizabethan patronage system find expression in the work. Shepherd's is literally the only detailed interpretive reading of the poem that I have come across, and many of his observations are clearly relevant to my own interpretation, but like many Marxist critics he is not overly concerned with attending to the nuances of the text. So here he argues plausibly enough that through the figure of the "gentle Spirit" Spenser "condemns the rewards that come from a mass market," but fails to note how ambivalently the figure is portrayed. See also his similarly one-sided reading of Polyhymnia's lament cited in note 25 below.

21.   Camille Paglia, *Sexual Personae: Art and Decadence from Nefertiti to Emily Dickinson* (New Haven: Yale University Press, 1990), 189; see also her entry on "Sex" in *The Spenser Encyclopedia*, 640.

22.   "Idle" is used only one other time in the poem, at line 335 ("idlenes"). In this context, it is worth noting the parallel between the equivocal description of the "gentle Spirit" here and the equally equivocal praise of Raleigh's "sweet verse, with *Nectar* sprinckeled" in the proem to Book Three of *The Faerie Queene*.

23.   The *topos* of flight as a metaphor for poetic aspiration is pervasive in Spenser's poetry, and is considered extensively by Patrick Cheney in *Spenser's Famous Flight: A Renaissance Idea of a Literary Career* (Toronto: University of Toronto Press, 1993), where Spenser's images of poetic flight are integrated into a four-stage model of his career.

24.   See Lily B. Campbell's classic article, "The Christian Muse," *Huntington Library Bulletin* 8 (1935), 29–70. As the Variorum notes (330), whether or not Spenser drew on Du Bartas' *Uranie* in writing *Teares,* the two authors share a common conception of the Muse.

25.   John D. Bernard, *Ceremonies of Innocence: Pastoralism in the Poetry of Edmund Spenser* (Cambridge: Cambridge University Press, 1989), 130.

26.   Shepherd, 109. Richard Rambuss, *Spenser's Secret Career* (Cambridge: Cambridge University Press, 1993), argues that much of Spenser's early work deliberately advertises his ability to serve as the bearer of secrets, and so serves to advance both his poetic and his professional ambitions. Rambuss does not comment on the stanza from Polyhymnia's lament.

27.   It may be relevant to recall here Spenser and Harvey's experiments with quantitative verse, in which they were preceded and encouraged by Sidney and Dyer, among others. As Derek Attridge points out in his entry on "quantitative verse" in *The Spenser Encyclopedia*, such experiments, because they conceived of meter "as an intellectually apprehended formal arrangement" rather than an ordering of natural word stresses, tended to make poetry "the exclusive property of the learned" (575). In other words, they established a metrical secret to be shared among the initiated. The analogy to Polyhymnia's lament consists of the hermetic authority that in both instances comes to be associated with technical skill.

28.   The text of the line as quoted here adopts the Folio variant, "living," over the Quarto's "loving" printed in *Yale*.

CRAIG RUSTICI

Muiopotmos: Spenser's "Complaint" against Aesthetics

Edmund Spenser, who claimed to have addressed the "contempt of poetry" in his lost text *The English Poet,* uses the mock epic *Muiopotmos* to critique the aesthetic theories of Plato's *Republic.* The poem's main plot depicts in narrative Plato's account of artistic imitation. The butterfly Clarion represents a Platonic ideal form, which acquires material reflection through an arming scene. The spider Aragnoll, represents an imitative artist and attempts to "capture" or render the butterfly in his deceitful web. However, he ultimately procures only a carcass, devoid of the creature's true essence. In a digression that retells the mythic weaving contest between Pallas and Arachne, Spenser exposes the inadequacy of this Platonic view of artistic endeavors. Pallas displays her superior artistry by fashioning an extraordinarily lifelike butterfly within her tapestry's decorative fringe. Although this brilliant ornament distracts attention from the tapestry's more meaningful central tableau, the narrowly mimetic criteria employed in judging this contest rewards the butterfly's scene-stealing splendor. Ultimately, by employing the mock epic genre, Spenser defies such inadequate Platonic aesthetics, since rather than attempting to copy accurately an extraliterary reality, he settles for mimicking Homer and Virgil and casting insects as "mightie ones."

*T*HE ARGUMENT TO THE *October Eclogue* of *The Shepherds' Calendar* (1579) refers to *The English Poet,* a book which Edmund Spenser reportdly "at large discourseth" concerning "the contempt of Poetry, and the causes thereof" (456). Although this book has been lost, I propose that the troublesome poem *Muiopotmos: or The Fate of the Butterflie* (1590) expresses one likely component of such a work: a critique of the aesthetic ambitions attributed to poets in Book 10 of Plato's *Republic* and of the difficulties they pose for "Poets historicall" such as Spenser (Letter to Raleigh, 407).[1] One need only look to *The Defense of Poesy* (1595), penned by Sir Philip Sidney, to whom Spenser dedicated *The Shepherds' Calendar,* to see that Plato's "contempt of poetry" troubled Elizabethan literati.

Like Spenser's longer works, *Muiopotmos* seems invested with multiple meanings. References to envy and daring in several of the poem's different episodes have prompted Ronald B. Bond to pursue a moral interpreation of the butterfly's adventures. In light of linguistic and iconographical associations between butterflies and the soul, spiders and the devil, Don Cameron Allen has proposed a more specifically Christian reading. Allusions to spectacle and to ladies at court have also encouraged critics like Robert A. Brinkley to argue that the poem comments on the fates of Elizabethan courtiers. Since such multiple allegorical levels conform to the Renaissance poetic theories that Michael Murrin has explicated in *The Veil of Allegory,* without denying the merit of moral, theological, or political readings, here I propose to pursue a different, art-critical approach that scholars, like Harry Berger, Clark Hulse, and Judith Dundas, have explored, but not exhausted.[2]

Through numerous references to artistic competitions and comparisons, the poem foregrounds questions of aesthetic value. Spenser devotes more than a fifth of *Muiopotmos* to retelling the weaving contest between Pallas Athena and Arachne, a classical and Renaissance figure for the human artist. He also observes in passing that no painter could match the beauty of the multicolored wings worn by the poem's butterfly protagonist and that no human handiwork could compare with the "curious networke" woven by his spidery nemesis (89–91, 361–68). Even in the pleasant garden that Spenser describes, "Arte" contends with "Nature" to produce the greater delights (163–66). As Judith Dundas has put it, the poem "shows art reflecting about itself, turning back on itself, and delighting in itself."[3]

In his very brief account of *Muiopotmos,* Harry Berger identifies the butterfly Clarion, frolicking in "his womblike garden of pleasure," as a symbol of the apprentice poet. According to Berger, this creature exhibits the sensibility that characterizes the first of three stages of artistic development: "recreative thesis, plaintive antithesis, [and] moral synthesis." Although intriguing, this interpretation poses difficulties. First, the butterfly is an awkward symbol for a poet in Berger's "initial phase of recreative innocence, a self-concerned and self-delighting period of *incubation,*" since, biologically speaking, the butterfly is itself the product of the caterpillar's previous incubation (my emphasis). More importantly, according to Berger, the apprentice poet produces (admittedly derivative and fragmentary) poetry. However, in a poem that Spenser densely populates with makers such as Jove, Pallas, and Arachne, Clarion stands out as a consumer who "casts his glutton sense to satisfle" (279) but produces nothing. The bee, gatherer of nectar and maker of honey, would better symbolize the stage of artistic development that Berger has in mind—although it would pose the same difficulty with respect to incubation.[4]

Clark Hulse too has studied Clarion's explorations in the "gay gardins" (161). In this episode, Hulse expects to find "the philosophical center that raises the whole narrative from concrete fable to abstract signification." Like other critics, he notes Spenser's apparently ambivalent moralizing in this passage; consequently, he contends that, like the "Sermon of Pythagoras" in Ovid's *Metamorphoses,* the garden episode "twists and turns" but ultimaterly and anticlimactically "tells us nothing." Hulse concludes, therefore, that by travestying the epic, *Muiopotmos* "gently" questions the didactic use of poetry.[5]

I find, however, that Spenser's conflicting assessments of Clarion's conduct in this episode signify, rather than "nothing," a shift in the protagonist's behavior, most specifically in his approach to variety. At first, Clarion pursues an orderly experience of variety. His "choicefull sense" leads him away from "common things" and the random pleasures of meadows and fens toward the artfully crafted garden (159–60). As Spenser's fourteen-line herbal set-piece demonstrates, the diverse plants there have been "fetch from farre away" (202) and "set in order" (172). Clarion examines and respects that order. He surveys the garden and probes its borders, presumably acquiring a sense of its shape and structure (169–72); he neither "disorder[s]" nor "deface[s]" its contents (173–75). However, once Spenser begins a new stanza at line 177, Clarion begins to gratify his "glutton sense" more carelessly and "To spoyle [despoil] the pleasures of that Paradise" (179, 186). Whereas he earlier avoided treading on plants' "silken leaves" (175), he now, less delicately, bathes his feet in the same fonts from which he drinks (180–82). Most importantly, he fails to distinguish between "good or ill" among the flora but rather "of euerie one he takes" (201–03). As Hulse rightly insists, Clarion does not seem clearly to have earned his death by sinning; he has, however, invited it through recklessness. Survival in the hazardous world of *Muiopotmos* demands not only innocence but also circumspection. At once, "faultles" (418) and "foolish" (389), Clarion finds himself entangled in Aragnoll's web. According to one lesson that Spenser extracts from the garden: "He likest is to fall into mischaunce,/That is regardles of his governaunce" (383–84).

Clarion becomes perilously "regardles' as he lingers among the floral delights.

"Governaunce" is an aesthetic as well as an ethical virtue. Appropriately, then, the garden episode includes the poem's most direct aesthetic statement: "for all change is sweete" (178). But, as Spenser's subsequent lament over the transience of earthly delights suggests (217–20), among sixteenth-century literati the value of change and variety was a thornier question than he at first implies.[6] In the Proem to Book VI of the *Faerie Queene,* a passage that sometimes echoes the garden episode, Spenser states his position most clearly. Like Clarion, the speaker of the Proem journeys in a "spacious" and "delightfull" land whose "sweet variety" "refreshes his sprights" (VI.-Proem.1; *Muiopotmos* 162). The speaker in each poem also insists upon the need for guidance in such an environment. In *Muiopotmos,* he warns, "That none, except a God, or God him guide" may escape the "thousand perils" that surround living beings (223). In the Proem, he entreats the muses:

Guyde ye my footing, and conduct me well
In these strange waies, where neuer foote did vse,
Ne none can find, but who was taught them by the Muse.
(VI.Proem.2).

For Spenser, variety is at once delightful and potentially disorienting. The "variety of matter" that attracts most readers to "historicall fiction[s]" like *The Faerie Queene* might also distract them from the allegory's "darke conceit," making the discourse seem "confused"—according to Michael Murrin, poets sometimes intended both effects at once (Letter to Raleigh, 407). In the garden episode, then, Spenser illustrates the importance of the poet's employing "learnings threasures" to "govern" their readers' experience of variety (VI.Proem.2). In fact, according to Judith Dundas, Spenser found a model for this poetic activity in the bee, which, like Clarion at his best, employs "choicefull sense," as it selects and arranges the delicious contents of its orderly honeycombs. Whereas Hulse detects in Spenser's tale of insects and gardens the poet's "subtle bemusement with the high purposes of the *Faerie Queene,*" I find in it his reflection on the techniques and theoretical foundations of such a didactic enterprise.[7]

Unlike Berger and Hulse, who concentrate on Clarion, Dundas considers the world of the poem as a whole. By emphasizing parallels and correspondences between elements within the poem, Dundas derives a reassuring view of the "world of art" depicted in *Muiopotmos:* "All the gods, it must be noted, are supreme artists, from Venus, who fashioned the butterfly, to Jove, who weaves the tapestry of life. And because they are artists, we can rest assured that, in spite of either their caprice or mortal folly, the final pattern will be beautiful." This view obscures potentially important distinctions between creation and imitation, between artisan and artist. Contrary to Dundas's assertion, beauty in the poem does not depend "finally upon craftsmanship which achieves a fine degree of finish and *imitative* artifice," since not all the craftsmanship depicted in the poem is mimetic (my emphasis). The "workmanship of the heavens hight" does not, as Spenser describes it, copy any other heavens. Similarly, the "arte" that framed Clarion's breastplate is a craftsman's skill rather than "imitative artifice"—Spenser emphasizes this point by comparing the armor to the handiwork of Vulcan, the Olympian blacksmith. Thus, Dundas blurs the distinction between artisans, such as Jove and Venus, and imitative artists, such as Pallas and Arachne, a distinction that she does explore in a later study of *The Faerie Queene* and one that is central to certain aesthetic theories. For example, according to Plato's well-known argument, the craftsman makes "something that resembles real being but is not that." If, in turn, artists imitate the craftsman's work, they produce something that resembles the truth even less than does the craftsman's "dim adumbration in comparison with reality" (*Republic* X. 597–98).[8] If, as I propose, *Muiopotmos* addresses Plato's account of art, Dundas's failure to observe this distinction seriously limits her interpretation.

As I understand it, the main plot of *Muiopotmos* depicts in narrative Plato's account of artistic creation—or more precisely artistic imitation. Clarion represents a Platonic form, a product (through his ancestor Astery) of divine creativity. Through the arming scene the form acquires material reflection, and Clarion assumes the physical characteristics of a butterfly. His nemesis, the spider Aragnoll, representing the imitative artist, attempts to capture Clarion, that is, to render him artistically, in his deceitful web but ultimately possesses only a lifeless husk quite distant from the Platonic form.

Clarion, as described at the beginning of the poem, is a curious creature. Although in the past he has taken up wings with which "To mount aloft vnto the Christall skie" (44), the subsequent arming scene reveals that at present he lacks the physical characteristics that distinguish the "race of silverwinged Flies" (17): wings, horns, hairy back, and exoskeleton. He seems, in fact, nearly immaterial. Spenser mentions his "heart," "shoulders," "back," and "head" principally as shapes or bare structures to be enclosed by his butterfly armor. Yet, the earliest references to Clarion in the poem assert that he is essentially a butterfly—indeed a paragon of butterflies: "Was none more fauourable, nor more faire" (20). Thus, as essence with little or no matter, Clarion resembles a Platonic form—and the qualities of clarity and brilliance evoked by his name's Latin roots further enhance that resemblance.[9]

Once embodied as a physical object through Clarion's arming, the form represented by this butterfly is vulnerable to the devices of the imitative artist represented by Aragnoll. Elements in Spenser's description of this anthropomorphic spider suggests a particularly Platonic version of the artist. References to Aragnoll's "false hart" (395) and "deceiptful traine" (398) recall Plato's contention that "mimetic art is far removed from the truth" (Republic X. 598B). Similarly, the description of Aragnoll as "th' author of confusion" (244) recalls Plato's charge that imitative poetry "seems to be a corruption of the mind of all listeners who do not possess . . . a knowledge of its real nature" (Republic X. 595B). Finally, according to Spenser, Aragnoll dwells in a "cave" (358) or "den" (398, 435), an apt symbol of the artist's imprisonment in the obscure, deceptive world of sense impressions.

Moreover, following the example of his mother Arachne, Aragnoll acts as a very literal-minded version of Plato's mimetic artist. Whereas Ovid's Arachne succeeds so well at the weaving contest that she ultimately provokes Pallas to transform her into a spider, in Spenser's version Arachne silently concedes defeat and transforms herself.[10] As she examines Pallas's tapestry, she passes over its subject and composition and fixes upon the decorative fringe, where an ornamental butterfly "seem'd to live, so like it was in sight" (332). This mimetic tour-de-force overwhelms Arachne, and the defeat so perturbs her that she "inly fret[s], and felly burne[s],/And all her blood to poysonous rancor turne[s]" (343–45), as she mutates into a venomous insect. By assailing Clarion, her son attempts not only to exact vengeance for the butterfly's slight role in Arachne's misfortune but also to redress her defeat by surpassing Pallas's verisimilar accomplishment. This second-generation weaver fashions a "curious networke" (368) to contain a butterfly that, unlike Pallas's, is not merely lifelike but alive. He thus attempts to reform his race's myth of origin and to claim victory for Arachne and her descendants.

But Aragnoll's attempt ends in failure. At the moment of his success, when Clarion's resistance is exhausted and his capture is complete, Aragnoll, "the bondslave of spight" (245), strikes out, dispatching the butterfly and releasing his "spright" (438) into the air that is his "Empire" (18). The animating force, the essence passes out of Clarion's corpse leaving Aragnoll in possession of a mere "spectacle of care" (440). Even on the literal, biological level the butterfly's death is a defeat for a spider, which, according to Aristotle, eats its prey alive and consequently has no use for such a lifeless carcass.[11] The imitative artist who seeks to render a form but lacks true knowledge achieves only a similarly dissatisfying "spectacle," an imitation of the illusory appearances of the physical world.

Spenser aptly describes Aragnoll as "the foe of faire things" and "the shame of Nature" (244–45). A narrowly mimetic conception of the artistic enterprise sets the artist, represented by Aragnoll, against objects of natural beauty, such as Clarion, in a contest to materialize forms. This competition is as hopeless for the artist as the contest of weavers is for Spenser's Arachne. The plot of *Muiopotmos* suggests that, like Arachne and her descendants, some artists are poisoned by frustration that arises from inevitable defeat and consequently turn against nature. They become nature's traitorous "shame," and the "foe[s]" of the "faire things" with which they compete (244–45). In this light, Spenser's choice of anthropomorphic antagonist seems doubly appropriate: through the Arachne myth the spider represents artists, and, as Ronald B. Bond has demonstrated, in early modern iconography it represents envy, the destructive emotion that mimetic artists might well feel, if they pursued the futile ambitions attributed to them in *The Republic*.[12]

Through his descriptions of the tapestries that Pallas and Arachne weave, Spenser implies further commentary on the aersthetic questions that Aragnoll's attack raises. At first glance, Pallas's tapestry seems to demonstrate that, contrary to the Platonic charges, imitative artists can accurately convey essential traits of their subjects. The faces alone of the gods who witness the weaving contest are sufficient to identify them:

Each of the Gods by his like visnomie [visage]
Eathe [easy] to be knowen; but Jove above them all,
By his great lookes and power imperiall.

(310–12)

Evidently, symbolic objects, like Hermes's caduceus or Aphrodite's Cestus, would be superfluous. Pallas has found concrete means to manifest more abstract qualities, such as Jove's majesty. We must recall, however, that Pallas is a goddess, who, as the subject of her tapestry suggests, can create an olive tree just as successfully as she can imitate one. Sharply contrasting details in Arachne's tapestry suggest that only divine artists might be capable of such mimetic feats. As Leonard Barkan has noted concerning Spenser's Ovidian source, the suggestion that Arachne's tapestry depicts a "so liuely scene,/ That it true Sea, and *true Bull* ye would weene" is pointedly ironic, since the beast depicted is not a "true Bull" but Jove's disguise (my emphasis; 279–80).[13] By imitating an appearance that itself reflects a divine masquerade, Arachne interposes an additional remove between imitative artist and Platonic form and compounds Plato's charge of artistic falsehood. Whereas Pallas conveys Jove's essential majesty, Arachne captures only his deception.

As my argument thus far implies, Spenser shares Plato's dissatisfaction with imitative illusion as a principal artistic objective. However, since Spenser embraces poetry rather than dismissing it, his response to that dissatisfaction obviously differs from Plato's. As he confronts the challenge of portraying his chaste sovereign in the Proem to Book III of *The Faerie Queene,* Spenser asserts the imitative inadequacy of both visual and poetic arts:

> But liuing art may not least part expresse,
> Nor life-resembliIng pencill it can paint, . . .
> Ne Poets wit, that passeth Painter farre
> In picturing the parts of beautie daint,
> So hard a workmanship aduenture darre,
> For fear through want of words her excellence to marre.
>
> (III.Proem 2.)

To solve his dilemma, Spenser determines to "shadow" Queen Elizabeth in "colourd showes" and in the "mirrours more then one" provided by several characters in his narrative (III.Proem.3, 5) As Judith Dundas has observed, here Spenser resorts to metaphor to portray virtue and convey truth. In contast, as Plato defends the exclusion of poets from his republic, he does not address poetic metaphor and moreover denies that even Homer, "the most poetic of poets," possessed "genuine knowledge" to convey in any form. Whereas Plato spurns poetry—"save only hymns to the gods and the praises of good men"—Spenser looks beyond mimesis for more adequate means and criteria of poetic accomplishment (*Republic* X. 599B, 607A).[14]

In *Muiopotmos,* he uses the description of Pallas's tapestry to demonstrate that a narrowly mimetic conception of art not only dooms the artist to failure and Platonic condemnation but also hinders or even distorts perceivers' appreciation of art works. The source of Pallas's victory, the woven butterfly, is literally and figuratively marginal. It appears within the "wreathe of Olives" (328) that encompasses the "storie" of Pallas's tapestry. After surveying medieval and Renaissance manuscripts, Andrew Weiner has argued that such marginal butterflies frequently signified "absolutely nothing." Consequently, we might suspect that Spenser is punning when he reports: "Emongst those leaves she made a Butterflie,/With excellent device and wondrous slight" (329–30). Perhaps, "sl(e)ight" describes both the means of the butterfly's composition and its significance within the tapestry. Unlike the surrounding olive leaves or the four trial scenes that frame the tapestry in Ovid's account, this slight ornament draws attention to itself without referring inward to the principal subject and content of Pallas's work. If Spenser's *ekphrasis* reflects the perceiver's cognitive experience of the tapestry, the diminutive butterfly claims as much of the perceiver's attention as the assembly of Olympian gods (305–12), Neptune's creation of the horse (313–20), and Pallas's creation of the olive tree (321–28), since each of these elements garners stanza-length descriptions. Thus, the viewer who prizes illusionistic "slight" above all else mistakenly equates the significance of peripheral ornament and central content.[15]

The danger that narrowly mimetic criteria of appreciation will distort the perceivers' experience of an art work is particularly troublesome for works like allegorical epics that are both mimetic and didactic. In his "Account of the Allegory of the Poem [*Jerusalem Delivered*]" Torquato Tasso asserts that "Heroical Poetry . . . is compounded of Imitation and Allegory: with the one she allureth unto her the minds and the ears of men, and marvellously delighteth them; with the other . . . she instructeth them." Although the imitation of "the pattern and image of human action" may in itself be instructive, "it doth not consider the customs, affections, or discourses of the mind as they be inward, but only as they come forth . . . being manifested in words [or] in deeds. . . ." Consequently, in Heroical Poetry, "Allegory" complements imitation by considering "the passions, the opinions and customs, not only as they appear, but principally in their being hidden and inward."[16] In the Letter to Ralegh, Spenser adopts the terms "ensample" and "doctrine," as he characterizes *The Faerie Queene* as a similar compound of mimetic and didactic art (407). Since imitation is only part of the compound, a narrowly mimetic criterion of artistic evaluation will necessarily minimize the accomplishment of allegorical poetry. Similarly, readers who attend

only to the mimetic delights of allegorical poetry will fail to comprehend fully or appreciate the work that they experience. In *Muiopotmos,* the *ekphrasis* of Pallas's tapestry depicts such flawed evaluation
and appreciation. Enthralled by the mimetic tour de force embodied
in the decorative butterfly, the perceiver whose cognitive experience
is recorded in the *ekphrasis* fails to observe or appreciate the "doctrine" conveyed in the tapestry's central scene of the creative contest
between Pallas and Neptune and consequently fails to recognize the
superiority of peace and productivity over war and destruction. This
tendency to appreciate or comprehend allegorical art incompletely is
a serious flaw in a narrowly mimetic theory of art.

The mock epic characteristics of *Muiopotmos* perform a powerful
rhetorical function within Spenser's critique of such theories, since
several of those characteristics flout principles that foster Plato's "contempt of poetry." First, by insisting upon its flawed imitation of
other literary works, mock epic flagrantly disregards Plato's concerns
about the deceitfulness of art. Mock epic presupposes an epic to be
mocked, and *Muiopotmos* draws much of its humor from the readers'
recognition that the poem's opening and closing stanzas parody classical epics (the *Iliad* I.1–7 and the *Aeneid* I.11 and XII.350–52).[17] By
unabashedly imitating poetry, which in Platonic terms is itself an
imitation of illusory appearances, Spenser, as a mock epic poet, defies
Plato's concerns and the mimetic theory that underlies them.

Second, mock epic, by definition and in pursuit of humorous
effect, violates decorum and disregards its verisimilar function. As
Artistotle explains in the *Rhetoric,* treating "weighty matters . . . off-
hand" or "trifling matters with dignity" creates comedy and undermines plausibility, since: *"Appropriate style also makes the fact appear
credible; for the mind of the hearer is imposed upon under the impression that the speaker is speaking the truth, because, in such circumstances, his feelings are the same . . ."* (my emphasis; III.vii). In
Muiopotmos, Spenser chooses comedy over verisimilitude and digni-
fies trifles like the titular "Fate of the Butterflie." By intentionally
selecting an inappropriate, indecorous style Spenser, as a mock epic
poet, rejects credible illusion and convincing imitation as ultimate
and sufficient aesthetic goals.[18] In a sense, then, Spenser uses the
experience of reading *Muiopotmos* to persuade his audience that the
Republic proposes a reductive understanding of the poetic enterprise.
Readers who enjoy the mock epic elements in *Muiopotmos* will likely
also question the aesthetic objectives that those elements disregard.

Hofstra University

NOTES

1. Although the references to poetic inspiration in the Argument to the *October Eclogue* recall aspects of other Platonic dialogues (such as *Phaedrus* and *Ion*) that describe poetry more favorably than the *Republic,* I do not believe that these dialogues are particularly relevant to Spenser's critique of mimesis in *Muiopotmos.* All quotations from Spenser's works refer to *Poetical Works,* ed. J. C. Smith and E. de Selincourt (Oxford: Oxford University Press, 1912) and will be cited parenthetically in the text. Spenser's poetry will be cited by line number.

2. Ronald B. Bond, *"Invidia* and the Allegory of Spenser's *Muiopotmos," ESC* 2 (1976): 144–55. Don Cameron Allen, *Image and Meaning: Metaphoric Traditions in Renaissance Poetry* (Baltimore: Johns Hopkins University Press, 1960), 20–41. Robert A. Brinkley, "Spenser's *Muiopotmos* and the Politics of Metamorphosis," *ELH* 48 (1981): 668–76. For a summary of several earlier interpretations of *Muiopotmos* as a poliltical allegory, see the *Variorum,* ed. E. A. Greenlaw, et al., 11 vols. (Baltimore: Johns Hopkins University Press, 1923–49) vol. 7, part 2, appendix V, 599–608. Michael Murrin, *The Veil of Allegory: Some Notes toward a Theory of Allegorical Rhetoric in the English Renaissance* (Chicago: University of Chicago Press, 1969), 98–134.

3. Eve D'Ambra, *Private Lives, Imperial Virtues; The Frieze of the Forum Transitorium in Rome* (Princeton: Princeton University Press, 1993), 103; Pamela Royston Macfle, "Ovid, Arachne, and the Poetics of Paradise," *The Poetry of Allusion: Virgil and Ovid in Dante's Commedia,* eds. Rachel Jacoff and Jeffrey T. Schnapp (Stanford: Stanford University Press, 1991), 159–71. Judith Dundas, *The Spider and the Bee: The Artistry of Spenser's* Faerie Queene (Urbana: U. of Illinois Press, 1985), 191.

4. Harry Berger, "Biographay as Interpretation, Interpretation as Biography." *College English* 28 (1966): 112. For an examination of the bee as a conventional emblem for the artist, see Judith Dundas, *The Spider and the Bee,* 1–14.

5. Hulse somewhat overstates the literal centraility of the garden episode (lines 161–208), which concludes before the midpoint of *Muiopotmos* (lilne 220), when he locates the relevant stanzas "precisely in the middle of the poem." Clark Hulse, *Mtamorphic Verse: The Elizabethen Minor Epic* (Princeton: Princeton University Press, 1981), 254, 258–59. Judith Dundas, Judith Anderson, and Andrew Weiner have all noted the ambivalence in this passage. Judith Dundas, *"Muiopotmos:* A World of Art," *The Yearbook of English Studies* 5 (1975), 33; Judith Anderson, "'Nat worth a butterflye': Muiopotmos and The Nun's Priest's Table," *The Journal of Medieval and Renaissance Studies* 1 (1971): 98–101, 104; Andrew D. Weiner, "Spenser's *Muiopotmos* and the Fates of Butterflies and Men," *Journal of English and Germanic Philology* 58 (1985): 208–10.

6. Because Aristotle had deprecated variety by insisting upon unity of action and denouncing episodic plotting (*Poetics* 1451–52), writers and critics like Torquato Tasso and Giambattista Giraldi Cinthio felt compelled to defend "diversity of actions" as "the spice of delight" and to argue that Aristotle's guidelines applied to tragedy but not to romance or epic. Tasso, *Discourses on the Heroic Poem,* trans. Mariella Cavalchini and Irene Samuel (Oxford: Clarendon, 1973), 42–45, 54; Cinthio, *On Romances,* trans. Henry L. Snuggs (Lexington: U of Kentucky Press, 1968), 20, 23.

7. Dundas, *The Spider and the Bee,* 3–4; Hulse, pp. 261–62; Michael Murrin, pp. 14–15.

8. Dundas, "*Muiopotmos:* A World of Art," 33, 38. All quotations from Plato refer to *The Collected Dialogues of Plato Including the Letters,* ed. Edith Hamilton and Huntington Cairns (Princeton: Princeton University Press, 1961). In the *The Metamorphoses,* Ovid repeatedly depicts Vulcan as an artisan, who constructs, for example, Apollo's chariot in Book 2 and the net that snares Venus and Mars in Book 4. Further, in the preface to his translation of Ovid, Arthur Golding contends that Vulcan represents "smythes and such as woorke in yron, tynne, or lead," whereas "*Pallas* and the famous troupe of all the Muses nyne" represent. "Such Folke as in the sciences and vertuous artes doo shyne." See *Shakespeare's Ovid Being Arthur Golding's Translation of the Metamorphoses,* Arthur Golding, ed. W. H. D. Rouse (Carbondale: Southern Illinois University Press, 1961), 16. Judith Dundas argues that as models for the poet the bee exemplified patient industry and careful arrangement, and the spider represented illusionistic skill. See, *The Spider and the Bee,* 1–14.

9. In books 6 and 7 of the *Republic,* Plato's use of metaphors of sun and sight to describe the ideal forms (especially the Good) and their influence on human beings effectively associates clarity and brilliance with those forms.

10. Concerning Pallas's reaction to Arachne's tapestry, Ovid writes, "doluit successu flava virago" (the golden-haired goddess was indignant at her success). Ovid, *Metamorphoses,* trans. Frank Justus Miller, 2 vols., Loeb Classical Library (Cambridge: Harvard University Press, 1984), I, 296–97.

11. Aristotle explains that a spider "sucks out the life-juices" of its immobilized prey in *Historia Animalium,* Vol. 4 of *The Works of Aristotle,* trans. D'Arcy Wentworth Thompson, ed. J. A. Smith and W. D. Ross, 12 vols. (Oxford: Clarendon, 1910), 623.

12. Bond, 147–53. I use the phrase "narrowly mimetic" to distinguish Plato's description in the *Republic* of the precise imitation of sense impressions from the mimetic theories of other thinkers, such as Plotinus, who asserts in a passage that seems to answer Plato directly:

> It has been attempted to degrade the arts by saying that to create they imitate nature. This may be answered by pointing out that the nature of beings are themselves the images of other beings (or essences); besides, the arts do not limit themselves to the imitation of objects which offer themselves to our view, but that they go as far back as the (ideal) reasons from which are derived the nature of objects. Further the arts independently create many things, and to the perfection of the object they add what is lacking, because they possess beauty in themselves.

Plotinus, "Fifth Ennead, Book Eight," *Complete Works,* trans. Kenneth Sylvan Gurthrie, 4 vols. (London: George Bell, 1919), II, 552.

13. Leonard Barkan, *The Gods Made Flesh: Metamorphosis and the Pursuit of Paganism* (New Haven: Yale University Press, 1986), 10–11.

14. Dundas, *The Spider and the Bee,* 59–60.

15. Weiner, 210–11. Michael Baxandall argues that *ekphrasis* offers "a representation of thinking about a picture more than a representation of a picture." Baxandall,

Patterns of Intention: On the Historical Explanation of Pictures (New Haven: Yale University Press, 1985), 1–5.

16.   Torquato Tasso, "Account of the Allegory of the Poem," *Jerusalem Delivered,* trans. Edward Fairfax, ed. Henry Morley (London: George Routledge, 1890), 436.

17.   James H. Morey identifies Spenser's Imitation of the *Aenied* I.11 in his article "Spenser's Mythic Adaptations in *Muiopotmos,*" *Spenser Studies: A Renaissance Poetry Annual* 9 (1988): 56.

18.   Aristotle, *The "Art" of Rhetoric,* trans. John Henry Freese, Loeb Classical Library (Cambridge: Harvard University Press, 1926), 377–79. Spenser's technique here resembles the absurdity principle that Michael Murrin has described: poets might render their stories incomplete or somehow absurd in order to "draw attention away from an illusionary, surface realism, to an inward truth." Murrin, 147.

MARY JOAN COOK

The Other Meaning of "Bridal Day" In Spenser's *Prothalamion*

It has long been noted that Edmund Spenser in *Prothalamion*, his last complete published poem, struck an elegiac note, an apparently discordant element in a poem which declares itself "A Spousall Verse" and which celebrates the "brydale day" of two young couples of Elizabeth's court. If, however, in reading *Prothalamion* one allows "brydale day" a second meaning, that of "final bridal of the soul in eternity," the elegiac note, as well as several otherwise perplexing passages in the poem, can be explained.

*I*T WAS A. KENT HIEATT who wrote some years ago that Edmund Spenser's mode of composition demands a particular critical approach since it is a mode which "requires before everything else a pursuit of an integral meaning, integrally expressed, below the surface of discourse" (81). It is a meaning which, according to this mode of composition, is hidden and must be discovered. Spenser's *Prothalamion,* which has long perplexed critics, seems to illustrate Hieatt's observation. Comments on the poem often begin with a recognition that the work presents a problem. Harry Berger, for instance, opens his article with the following question:

> *Prothalamion* is a simple-seeming poem and the particular problem it poses for interpretation appears to be straightforward: in a poem of ten stanzas nominally celebrating the double marriage of "two Honourable & vertuous/Ladies" to "two worthie/ Gentlemen", why are two stanzas devoted to the poet's own life and troubles, and a third to some patron-seeking praise of Essex?
>
> (363)

Not surprisingly, Berger himself takes up the challenge and seeks to resolve the "straightforward" problems with his own integrative interpretation. Thus, critics continue to study the poem, seeking what Hieatt calls "an unexpected nexus of meaning, gradually intuited through large-scale effort, [which] becomes a permanent and aesthetically valid possession for all readers" (82). The present essay, indebted to the many critics who have already commented on the poem, is one more contribution to the "large-scale effort" of those who believe that arriving at the "nexus of meaning" is a proper critical goal. Although Berger does not mention it in his introductory passage quoted above, there is a line in the refrain of each stanza in the *Prothalamion* which is particularly problematic. The line refers to a "Brydale day." In the Variorum Edition of Spenser's *Works*, three critics are quoted who call attention to this refrain's contradictory aspects.[1] More recently, M. L. Wine, in "Spenser's 'Sweete Themmes': Of Time and the River," focuses particularly on the "Brydale day" refrain, noting that the "effect of the refrain in *every* stanza—and this may be one of the reasons for its appeal—is somewhat ambivalent, and in this ambivalence may lie the clue to the much vexed problem of the poem's organization and meaning" (112). Although Wine's analysis of the refrain is painstaking and perceptive, there is no mention in it nor in the writing of any earlier critic of a meaning of "Brydale," used elsewhere by Spenser, which may well shed light on the problematic refrain and therefore on the entire poem.

It is in Spenser's *Daphnaida* that the word "bridale" occurs with a figurative meaning which it could have in the *Prothalamion*. In that earlier poem, the dying Daphne speaks to her beloved Alcyon in these words:

I, since the messenger is come for mee,
That summons soules unto the bridale feast
Of his great Lord, must needes depart from thee,
And straight obay his soueraine beheast:
Why should Alcyon then so sore lament,
That I from miserie shall be releast,
And freed from wretched long imprisonment?

(7.267–73)

She continues in the following fourteen lines to contrast "the worlds sad care" with the "happie quiet" of a blessed eternity. Spenser's explicit connection here of the term "bridale" with the joyous celebration of heaven makes the reader wonder if he could be making a comparable connection in the *Prothalamion*. If he is, then in that later poem the term "Brydale day" carries two possible meanings: first, "wedding day" in the expected sense and, second, that final joyous bridal to be experienced in eternity.

It is fairly easy to build an argument that, as a contrast to the enduring joy of eternity, motifs of sorrow, time passing, and mortality or death are present in the poem. Before proceeding to that, however, a brief explanation of the poem's occasion and a summary of its ten stanzas will be helpful. The poem celebrates the spousal or betrothal of Elizabeth, daughter of Edward Somerset, Earl of Worcester, to Sir Henry Guildford and of Catherine, her sister, to William, Lord Petre, at Essex House. The wedding itself took place on November 8, 1596, also at Essex House.

The poem opens with the poet's describing a calm day on which he, saddened by his "fruitlesse stay/In Princes Court," takes a walk along the Thames. He sees a "Flock of Nymphes" gathering flowers "To decke their Bridegromes posies." Next he sees two lovely swans on the water. The nymphs, having hastened to view them, cast their flowers on the swans and water. Then one of the nymphs addresses the birds in song. It becomes clear, as she sings to them, that the maiden swans are entering into marriage. The birds continue on their way, approaching Essex House. At this point, the poet touches on his own family, his birth in London, and the changing residents of the dwellings bordering this section of the Thames. He is reminded of the loss of friends, especially Leicester. Nonetheless, he continues with his own song, focusing especially on Essex, England's present hero. The maidens arrive at their destination and are received by the two knights whom they are to marry. Each stanza closes with a two-line refrain mentioning a "Brydale day." The first of these two lines focuses on this day. The second is the haunting "Sweete Themmes runne softly, till I end my Song."

To return to the argument that motifs of sadness, time passing, and mortality or death are present in the poem: one can note first that Spenser speaks of "sullein care," "discontent," and "idle hopes" as the mood in which the poetic vision begins. And, later, in stanza 8, he expresses the need to turn himself from thoughts of "old woes" to the "ioyes" of this poem's occasion. Alastair Fowler, commenting on this mood in the poem, speaks of "a melancholy sense, perhaps, of the fugacity of life and of patrons. . ." (77). The motif of time passing is, of course, clearly emphasized in the two-line refrain. In the first of these lines, the poet describes the bridal day as "not long." In the second line of the refrain, the poet bids the Thames (figuratively, the river of life) to flow softly or gently until he ends his song.[2] In addition to these examples in the refrain, words and phrases referring to time, such as "did delay/Hot Titans beames," "happie hower," "whylome," and "ages following" suggest the passing of time.

Both M. L. Wine and Harry Berger have considered this motif of time passing in detail since it is basic in their interpretations. Wine, for instance, concludes that Spenser's *Prothalamion* says: "A world of ruinous decay gives marriage and fame and song their brilliance and desirability; love and noble deeds and art being most godlike and most enduring, they make a brazen world golden" (4). Berger, too, writing on the poet's achievement, draws his essay to a close with the observation that "as the poem ends, the opposed stresses of the poem merge in tensional embrace. Time may flow as usual because this is the nature of things, and nothing can be done about it, also because the occasion has been *used,* poetry has done its work and made a symbolic form which/infolds all such occasions and manifests their true importance" (378–79). Both critics see that the passing of time is a significant motif in the poem and both develop interpretations which include it.

If "Brydale day" in *Prothalamion* is to suggest to the reader the final joyful bridal, which will be experienced in eternity, a motif of mortality or death in the poem would help to open the mind (at least, the Christian, Renaissance mind) to thoughts of a life beyond death. Images of death do, in fact, occur repeatedly. A strong instance is the poet's mention of the loss of Leicester, his former patron, in stanza 8. Another is the combination of the swan imagery with the refrain "Sweete Themmes runne softly, till I end my Song." The line brings to mind the mythic connection between the swan and a death-song. That Spenser was mindful of that connection can be easily demonstrated. In *The Ruines of Time,* the following passage referring to the recently-deceased Sir Philip Sidney occurs:

Vpon that famous Riuers further shore,
There stood a snowie Swan of heauenly hiew,
And gentle kinde, as euer Fowle afore;
A fairer one in all the goodlie criew
Of white Strimonian brood might no man view:
There he most sweetly sung the prophecie
Of his owne death in dolefull Elegie.

(8.589–95)

Another instance of the death motif can be found in stanza 2 wherein the nymphs are pictured gathering flowers. They, "with fine Fingers, cropt full feateously/The tender stalkes on hye" (27–28). Life is thus brought to a close in this image. Finally, in stanza 10, Spenser likens the two young bridegrooms to Castor and Pollux, adding that these two sons of Jove now "decke the Bauldricke of the Heauens bright" (174). In so saying, Spenser is alluding to their death, after which the twin heroes were translated into the constellation Gemini.

Clearly Spenser has introduced into his *Prothalamion* the motifs of sadness, of passing time and of immortality, strange elements in a poem *simply* celebrating the pre-wedding spousal ceremony of two young couples. But in a poem in which this spoual is to be seen, as we are suggesting, as the veiled image of the unchanging joy of a soul united to God, these apparently discordant motifs actually warn the reader that the "simply celebrating" reading is inadequate. Attributing to "Brydale day" two meanings—first, wedding day in the usual sense and, second, the final bridal in heaven—resolves the problem of the elegiac tone in the *Prothalamion*.

That tone, however, is not the only critical problem to be considered in interpreting the poem. There are also, as mentioned earlier, several seemingly contradictory passages involving the "Brydale day." Allowing "Brydale day" its other, veiled meaning eliminates the contradictions. In order to develop this claim, it will be necessary to analyze, at some length, the lines in which "Brydale day" occurs. A close examination of the lines in which "Brydale day" appears brings to light variations in its wording, variations which can be explained if "brydale day" has an alternate meaning. The occurrences of the line follow, each preceded by the number of the stanza in which it is found. The line occurs twice in stanza 7; its first use there is enclosed below in parentheses.

1. Against	the	Brydale	day,	which	is	not	long:
2. Against	the	Brydale	day,	which	was	not	long:
3. Against	their	Brydale	day,	which	was	not	long:
4. Euen as	their	Brydale	day,	which	was	not	long:
5. Against	their	Brydale	day,	which	was	not	long:
6. Vpon	your	Brydale	day,	which	is	not	long:
(Which said	their	bridale	daye,	should	not	be	long:)
7. Against	their	wedding	day,	which	was	not	long:
8. Against	the	bridale	daye,	which	is	not	long:
9. Vpon	the	Brydale	day,	which	is	not	long:
10. Against	their	Brydale	day,	which	is	not	long:

The variations in the line occur (a) in the introductory preposition; (b) in the modifier preceding "Brydale day"; (c) in the substitution of "wedding day" in stanza 7, and (d) in the tense of the verb. In addition, the phrasing of the line as it occurs early in stanza 7, omits the introductory preposition and substitutes "should be" for the indicatives "is" and "was." Although "not long" remains a constant element, both Wine and Berger have suggested that it may have two meanings here. Berger, for instance, explains that " which is not long' may mean the bridal day is not far off, but also, it is a very short day" (368). This suggestion, incidentally, that Spenser intends a double meaning in this part of the poem, seems to strengthen the possibility that a double meaning is also intended with "Brydale day."

Of the four variations listed, that of the modifier immediately suggests a distinction in the meaning of "Brydale day." In four instances, Spenser uses "the Brydale day"; in seven, "their" or "your." In the poem, "their Brydale day" and "your Brydale day" limit the day to one which explicitly concerns the two young couples. In the remaining four uses, "the" distinguishes the day from "their[s]." This distinction leaves the reader free to consider "*the* Brydale day," as possibly unattached to that of the young couples. In stanza 1, "the Brydale day" seems to refer to that of the undetermined "maydens" and "their Paramours"; in stanza 2, to that of the "Nymphes" and "their Bridegromes." Its two other occurrences, in stanzas 8 and 9, will be dealt with later.

Examination of a second type of variation; that is, the tense of the verb, reveals a noteworthy pattern. The verb "was" occurs five times; "is" occurs five times, and "should be" once. The one time that Spenser writes "wedding day," rather than "Brydale day," he uses "was." In four of the seven times that he uses "their" or "your" to modify the bridal day, the verb following is also in the *past* tense. In stanzas 6 and 10, where he uses "is," reading "Brydale day" as "'wedding day" raises a question. The variation in stanza 7 will be considered later. Analysis of the variation between "was" and "is" suggests that when Spenser is speaking of the young couples' wedding day, "Brydale day" is followed by "was'"; when the term has some other meaning, it is followed by "is." That other day is yet to come.

Applying this thesis to stanzas 6 and 10 eliminates the seeming contradictions referred to earlier. In stanza 6, one of the nymphs addresses the swans, wishing them well. She ends with a prayer that they may be blessed with "Peace," "Plentie," and "fruitfull issue." These, she continues, "may your foes confound/And make your ioyes redound/Vpon your Brydale day, which is not long." Of these lines, Edward Marsh has written: "Spenser has so little control over the refrain which ends every stanza that he lets it force him into wishing his two young couples 'fruitful issue *upon their Brydale day*' regardless of the inconvenience and even scandal which would result"

(300). Marsh is reading "Brydale day" here as "wedding day." If, however, "Brydale day" means the day of entrance into eternal joy, then the nymph is praying that on that day the fruitful issue of their blessed married life will be a cause of honor and joy. This reading obviates the problem of fruitful issue giving joy on their wedding day.

In the following stanza Spenser refers to this prayer of the nymph in what could be cryptic words:

> So ended she; and all the rest around
> To her redoubled that her vndersong,
> Which said, their bridale daye should not be long.
>
> (109–11)

Daniel H. Woodward in "Some Themes in Spenser's 'Prothalamion' " says of this: "Possibly 'undersong' suggests by a pun the serious undertones which are found throughout this poem of happy celebration," adding "such a meaning, however, is not reported by the OED until 1631" (41–42). To look at this in another way, the fact that the OED does give the recorded usage of "An underlying meaning; an undertone" in 1631 may also support the possibility that Spenser was using the term figuratively in 1596. The only other meaning given is "A subordinate or subdued song or strain, esp. one serving as an accompaniment or burden to another." For this meaning, a clear example from Spenser's 1579 *Shepheardes Calender* is used in which two shepherds are engaged in a rhyming contest: "And Willye is not greatly ouergone/So weren his undersong well addrest." The use of "undersong" in stanza 7 could, in fact, easily fit either definition. In a poem in which word play does occur, the word play suggested by Woodward would not be surprising.[3] If the nymph's use of "Brydale day" in stanza 6 carries the meaning of "day of entrance into eternal bliss," the figurative use of "undersong" as "underlying meaning" fits in well.

In stanza 10, as in stanza 6, interpreting "Brydale day" as wedding day results in a problem. An apparent contradiction occurs. In the final lines of stanza 10, Spenser writes that the two young men

> Receiued those two faire Brides, their Loues delight,
> Which at th'appointed tyde,
> Each one did make his Bryde,
> Against their Brydale day, which is not long.
>
> (176–79)

J. D. Manly, in an effort to explain this problematic passage, argued that "'at th'appointed tide' refers to the spousal ceremony, while 'their bridal day' in the refrain refers forward to the wedding, which did not take place until November 8."[4] Given this explanation, though, one asks two questions: (1) why does Spenser say "Bryde" in line 178 and, more significantly, (2) why does he speak of *their* "Brydale day" in the *past* tense in stanzas 3, 4, 5, and 7? His use of "is" here in Stanza 10 suggests that the meaning of "Brydale day" is distinct from the day on which the maidens became the brides of these young men. Reading "Brydale day" as the final bridal day in eternity would resolve the questions. The couples' wedding day ("th'appointed tyde") has taken place; the other "Brydale day" still lies before them.

In stanza 9, as in stanzas 6 and 10, "Brydale day" is followed by "which *is* not long." It is preceded, however, by "the" which, according to our analysis, distinguishes this "Brydale day" from the wedding of the two young couples. The stanza as a whole has been a focal point of critical writing on the *Prothalamion*. In the Spenser *Variorum,* Dan S. Norton's commments on it are given at considerable length. "Either the conclusion of the stanza is clumsily forced or it contains a hidden significance," he observed and then argued that the bridal day of this stanza is to be understood as a future celebration of the Queen's Accession Day on which she (seen as the virgin bride of England) with Essex would be praised in song (8.503).

Berger has also found this stanza problematic. He recognizes that the change of tense is significant and sees it as an indication that "is not long" in this instance means a bridal day "is in general a very short day" (377). This ties in with Berger's thesis that the poet is able both to accept the shortness and to immortalize the moment. He writes: "A wedding, like a poem, is 'for a short time an endlesse moniment' " (378). Although Berger notes the tense change, he does not suggest that "Brydale day" itself could have a second meaning here. The change in tense, in fact, is not his major problem with the stanza; rather, it is the high praise given to Essex. Near the conclusion of his interpretation of the poem, Berger notes that "the praise of Essex may still cause uneasiness because it is so conventionally hyperbolic and so blatant a piece of patron-seeking" (375). Berger then integrates this "piece" into the poem, "hyperbolic" though it remains: "If this is degrading to a pure poet, still the poet as man must stoop, must compromise his purity and be realistic in order to survive" (375). It is, according to Berger, as if Spenser were saying in this passage that this is an example of what is demanded of the paid poet.

It seems clear that both Norton and Berger were impelled to seek some deeper meaning in the stanza on Essex. Does the possibility that "Brydale day" in this stanza alludes not to the couples' wedding day but to the unending joy of eternity shed new light on Spenser's praise of Essex?

In the stanza immediately preceding the one which highlights Essex, Spenser reflects on his family's "auncient fame," on his birthplace, on the "bricky towres" where the "Templer Knights" dwelt (until their decay) and where the "studious lawyers" now dwell, and on the "stately place" where his patron Leicester had lived. The themes of time passing, change, and mortality are unmistakably present. As the stanza closes, Spenser is thinking of his own "freendles case," but at the thought of "the bridal day" he says, "But Ah here fits not well/Old woes but ioyes to tell/Against the bridale daye, which is not long" (141–43).

Having introduced and lamented the loss of Leicester, a lament which Herbert Cory referred to as "his winningly tactless and pertinacious mood of loyalty to Leicester even after death," (476) Spenser begins stanza 9 with the line, "Yet therein now doth lodge a noble Peer." Essex *now* dwells in Leicester's home. The poet proceeds to paint a picture of Essex as "Great Englands glory and the Worlds wide wonder" (146) and to pray for him as the nymph prayed for the two young couples. He asks that Essex may have joy, fame, and victory of "Which some braue muse may sing/To ages following,/Vpon the Brydale day, which is not long" (159–61).

If "the Brydale day" here alludes to a heavenly celebration which is to come, what does it do to this passage on Essex? What happens to the "conventionally hyperbolic . . . piece of patron-seeking"? Basically, it becomes a passage in which the admiring but "sage and serious" Spenser notes that this young hero's hour of worldly glory, like that of others, will pass but that there lies ahead in the not too distant future the "Brydale day" of "endlesse happiness." The passing of time, mutability, and death seem to permeate this stanza also. That opening line, for instance, in which Spenser writes, "Yet therein now doth lodge a noble Peer" suggests that the past abode of Leicester is only for the time being that of Essex. The use of "Yet" here leads the reader to wonder "How long?". Later in the stanza Spenser calls Essex "Faire branch of Honor, flower of Cheualrie." This seems appropriate enough as praise, yet one thinks back to stanza 2 in which the fragility of flowers appeared as the nymphs "with fine Fingers, cropt full feateously," flowers which are later referred to as "the honour of the field" (74). Midway in this stanza, the poet, like the nymph in stanza 6, voices a prayer, saying "Ioy haue thou of thy noble victorie,/And endlesse happinesse of thine own name/That promiseth the same" (152–54). There is, however, an echo here of the poet's own "expectation vayne/Of idle hopes" (7–8) and, therefore, the implication that "endlesse happinesse" is a state connected with eternity. The stanza concludes with the prayer that of Essex's deeds "some braue muse may sing/To ages following,/Vpon the Brydale day, which is not long." On the occasion of Sir Philip Sidney's death, Spenser himself had sung his *Astrophel*. Now in the *Prothalamion,* he speaks of "some braue muse" who will sing of Essex. It seems unlikely, given the swan-song motif here, that Spenser is implying that he will be the "braue muse." Rather, the poet, whose own approaching "Brydale day" is suggested in stanza 8, seems to be foreseeing that it will be for another to elegize Essex.[5]

Reading the passage in this way does not detract from Essex's right to glory. He is justly praised for his deeds. Spenser is, however, prophetically calling him to place all within the context of eternity, for earthly glory, especially in sixteenth-century England, is passing.[6] If one argues that Spenser would not dare to address Essex thus, one is denying him the courage to voice his faith and Essex the faith needed to accept the poet's words. Moreover, reading the passage as Spenser's honest tribute to Essex with the young hero's good in mind is less demeaning to Essex than reading it as an example of "hyberbolic . . . patron-seeking."

There are, then, at least three places in the *Prothalamion* where reading "Brydale day" as "the young couples' wedding day" has presented problems. In stanza 6, it gives the bridal pairs fruitful issue on their wedding day. In stanza 9, their "Brydale day" seems to be the future occasion for praising the deeds of Essex in particular. In stanza 10, the brides are made so "Against their Brydale day, which is not long." Reading "Brydale day" in each of these instances as "the ultimate heavenly bridal" yet to come obviates the problem.

In addition, allowing "Brydale day" this other meaning casts a new light on the title of the poem. J. Norton Smith in "Spenser's *Prothalamion*: A New Genre" comments that Spenser has "gone out of his way to coin an entirely new word, a genre term" (174), adding that he did this because the "theme of criticism, deeply connected with the poet's own fortunes, as well as the nation's, . . . would make the Epithalamion the wrong form to attempt" (175). One could add that, if Spenser is playing on "Brydale day," the title *Prothalamion,* a song *before* the wedding day; that is, the final bridal, helps to suggest the veiled second meaning.

It has long been puzzling to critics that Spenser struck an elegiac note in the *Prothalamion*. Such an elegiac note seemed discordant in a poem which declares itself "A Spousall Verse." Yet if for the poet, discouraged at life's disappointments and sensing that his days are drawing to a close, the beauty and joy of a spousal ceremony translate into the eternal joy of union with God, then the elegiac tone is an appropriate preliminary to this consoling vision.

Saint Joseph College

NOTES

1.   The three critics are Dan S. Norton, Edward Marsh, and J. M. Manly. Excerpts from th eir writing are quoted in *The Minor Poems*, vol. 8 of *The Works of Edmund Spenser: A Variorum Edition*, edited by Edwin Greenlaw et al. All quotations of Spenser's poetry will be taken from this volume or the preceding one (vol. 7). Quotations from the *Prothalamion* itself will be identified by line number. Quotations from others of Spenser's poems will be identified by the *Variorum* volume number followed by line number.

2.   According to the *Concordance to the Poems of Edmund Spenser*, the adverb "softly" occurs 57 times in Spenser's poetry, excluding its use in the *Prothalamion*. Very frequently the word illustrates the first meaning recorded in the OED; that is, "Gently, carefully, tenderly; in such a manner as to avoid causing pain or injury; without force or violence; with gentle action." This meaning would fit readily into Spenser's "Sweete Themmes runne softly, till I end my Song." The poet is asking that the river of life or time flow "gently, carefully, tenderly." By "my Song," the ·reader could understand (1) the *Prothalamion* itself, (2) Spenser's magnum opus, *The Faerie Queene*, or most probably (3) figuratively, Spenser's life. Given the tone of personal disappointment and sadness in the poem, Spenser's plea that the river of life flow gently is a touching one.

3.   The play on "Somers-heat" in line 67 is an example. And of lines 153–54, Einar Bjorvand notes: "A pun on his name, Devereux, as dev (enir) (h)eureux, i.e. to become happy" (768n).

4.   The *Variorum* (8.664) quotes from Manly's *English Prose and Poetry*, p. 703, a revised edition of which was published by Ginn, 1926.

5.   In stanza 8, Spenser uses "the" and "is" in the "Brydale day" refrain. Since the stanza touches on *his* life and *his* loss of Leicester, it seems probable that his use of "the" and "is" signals that the "Bridale daye" is not the young couples' wedding day but, in this instance, Spenser's own approaching final bridal day.

6.   The story of Leicester himself exemplifies, of course, this changing fortune and also intertwines with that of Essex, whose widowed mother Leicester married. Writing of this passage in the poem, Richard C. McCoy comments that "Spenser's praise for Essex is lavish and hopeful, and he anticipates still greater victories and a renewal of chivalric virtue. But despite these triumphant expectations, the mood remains profoundly elegiac" (154).

Works Cited

Berger, Harry. "Spenser's *Prothalamion:* An Interpretation." *Essays in Criticism*
15(1965): 363–80.

Bjorvand, Einar. "Introduction" to the *Prothalamion,* in *The Yale Edition of the Shorter
Poems of Edmund Spenser.* Ed. William A. Oram et al. New Haven: Yale
University Press, 1989. 755–60.

Cory, Herbert Ellsworth. *Edmund Spenser: A Critical Study.* University of California
Publications in Modern Philology 5. Berkeley: University of California
Press, 1917.

Fowler, Alastair. *Conceitful Thought: The Interpretation of English Renaissance Poems.*
Edinburgh: Edinburgh University Press, 1975.

Hieatt, A. Kent. *Short Time's Endless Monument.* 1960. Port Washington, NY: Kenni-
kat Press, 1972.

Marsh, Edward. "An Emendation in Spenser's *Prothalamium.*" *London Mercury*
9(1924): 300.

McCoy, Richard C. *The Rites of Knighthood: The Literature and Politics of Elizabethan
Chivalry.* Berkeley: University of California Press, 1989.

Osgood, C. G., comp. and ed. A. *Concordance to the Poems of Edmund Spenser.*
Gloucester, MA: Peter Smith, 1963.

Smith, J. Norton. "Spenser's *Prothalamion:* A New Genre." *Review of English Studies*
ns 10(1959): 173–8.

Spenser, Edmund. *The Works of Edmund Spenser.* Ed. Edwin Greenlaw et al. 10 vols.
Baltimore: Johns Hopkins University Press, 1932–45.

Wine, M. L. " Sweete *Themmes':* Of Time and the River." *Studies in English Literature*
2(1962): 111–17.

Woodward, Daniel H. "Some Themes in Spenser's 'Prothalamion.' " *English Literary
History.* 29(1962): 34–46.

KENNETH BORRIS

Elizabethan Allegorical Epics: The *Arcadias* as Counterparts of *The Faerie Queene*

In this century, Sir Philip Sidney's *Old Arcadia* and *New Arcadia* have been defined largely in opposition to *The Faerie Queene,* as non-allegorical texts that present exemplary models for emulation, through Aristotelian mimesis. Such interpretation of the *Arcadias* assumes that Sidney's *Defence of Poetry* opposes literary allegory, so that his Arcadian fictions must practically exemplify the anti-allegorical poetic of the treatise. However, as recent critics have rightly resituated the *Defence* within allegorical poetics, so additional textual evidence from not only the treatise itself but writings by Sir William Temple, Sidney's personal secretary, and Abraham Fraunce support allegorical redefinition of Sidney's poetic, and we should now thus reconsider the *Arcadias* themselves. Both texts extensively involve allegory, as in the attacks of the beasts and rebels, which involve psychomachia; the allegorically self-reflexive addresses of Musidorus to Pamela through Mopsa, and thus through "second meaning," as Sidney calls it; the episodes of the Giants of Pontus and Cecropia's temptresses in the *New Arcadia;* and the whole siege and captivity in Book Three of the *New Arcadia*. The *Arcadias* involves broad psychological allegory concerning the inner conflicts experienced in the heroic pursuit of virtue, and correlative political allegory, so that both texts treat themes associated with epic in the Renaissance, and do so in the allegorical mode hitherto linked especially with Spenser in England, and propounded by Tasso in his account of heroic allegory that was appended to most editions of the *Gerusalemme liberata*. Spenser's and Sidney's creative enterprises are much more congruent than previously assumed, for both dedicated their most substantial literary endeavours to the production of allegorical heroic poetry, and share many codes and conventions of the genre. The conventional "Spenser-Milton" line of "visionary epic" in English literary history should be expanded to include Sidney: within England, Sidney introduced many of the most fundamental techniques and features of that form.

*T*HOUGH SIDNEIANS COMMONLY consider the *New Arcadia* an epic, and many find the *Old Arcadia* at least a nascent epic, in the expanded, heroico-romantic sense current in the sixteenth century, these texts are almost never approached as allegories in any sense. Edwin Greenlaw's essay of 1913, "Sidney's *Arcadia* as an Example of Elizabethan Allegory," actually only identified some broad analogies with Elizabethan topical situations, and showed that Sidney provides non-figurative behavioural examples, as when a hero who appears to act with fortitude may be said to instance or demonstrate heroic fortitude. Yet, in what we would now consider fully developed allegories of the period, such as Spenser's, action can be exemplary, but in any case figuratively expresses further moral, psychological, ecclesiastical, or other meanings. Elements of the story thus serve conjointly as vehicles for figurative representation of, for example, some conceptual scheme or complex of topical references. That tenor, as we may call it, is not simply integral or equivalent to the action as such, as with exemplification (the exemplar of fortitude acts with fortitude anyway), but adumbrated by a pattern of allusion that effects a general transposition of significance. The adventures of Spenser's errant damsel Una, in which she displays much fortitude, also partly allegorize various vicissitudes of the Church, which Una to some extent signifies. Whatever the exemplary functions of certain incidents involving Spenser's Guyon, Pyrochles, and Cymochles, their interactions also broadly allegorize potential challenges of irascible and concupiscible capacities encountered in quest of the temperate ideal, so that the story partly constitutes an extended symbolic inquiry into the characteristics of the psyche and its moral implications.[1]

Since Greenlaw, the *Arcadias* have been defined largely in opposition to *The Faerie Queene,* as non-allegorical texts that just present exemplary models for emulation. Though first advanced by R. W. Zandvoort and Kenneth Myrick in the 1920s and 1930s, this view still governs Jean Robertson's note on Sidney in *The Spenser Encyclopedia*, S. K. Heninger's recent *Sidney and Spenser*, and many other critical texts, so that, as Annabel Patterson recently observes, allegory remains "a dreaded term" for Sidneians. However, the *Arcadias* involve much allegory, and Sidney's usage of the mode, like Spenser's in *The Faerie Queene*, reflects diverse resources of Elizabethan culture, including iconographical programs and prior allegorical or semi-allegorical romances and court pageants. Just as the *Arcadias* have widely attested heroic affinities, I focus here on their correspondences with allegory in Renaissance heroic poems such as Tasso's and Spenser's. As our knowledge of Arcadian allegory increases, the norms of that generic context will likely prove to have the broadest and most decisive importance. Though Sidney and Spenser each treat heroic poetry and allegory very differently, both are nonetheless fundamentally alike in dedicating their most substantial literary labours to the production of allegorical heroic poems, and share many codes and conventions of that genre, despite differences of focus, emphasis, and elaboration.[2]

ALLEGORICAL POETICS AND SIDNEY'S *DEFENCE OF POETRY*

Dissociation of Sidney from allegory largely stems from assumptions that his *Defence* excludes or rejects it. In 1899, J. E. Spingarn declared that "the allegorical interpretation of imaginative literature" is "minimized" in Sidney's treatise, but later decided that the *Defence* indeed has "an allegorical substratum." Yet, in 1922, his student Donald Lemen Clark claimed that the *Defence* "remains conspicuously aloof" from allegorism so as to promote exemplary imitation instead, in which actions and characters only serve to exemplify virtues and vices, without any figuration of further meanings. Then Zandvoort and Myrick imposed Clark's principle on the *Arcadias*: in Myrick's words, "allegory of any sort" has "little importance" in them, and "may safely be ignored." For Myrick, Sidney's characters are types and exemplars, not allegorical, so that Arcadian narrative is simply " 'an imitation of men in action' " (what happened to the women?), and not at all like *The Faerie Queene*. In the two most authoritative current editions of the *Defence*, Geoffrey Shepherd's commentary follows Clark's exemplarist interpretation, while Jan van Dorsten and Katherine Duncan-Jones avoid allegory altogether, and refer readers to Myrick's exemplarist account, which remains standard for Sidney studies.[3]

However, although Clark assumed that allegory and exemplary fiction were somehow mutually exclusive, very distinct alternatives in Sidney's time, exemplars were commonly subsumed in allegory or deemed complementary. Quintilian, for example, had declared that "illustrative examples involve allegory if not preceded by an explanation." Whereas the anti-allegorical exemplarist program that Clark and his inheritors ascribe to Sidney would commit this poet-theorist to distinguishing clearly between allegory and exemplification, rejecting the former, and privileging the latter both in theory and practice, no-one has provided evidence that Sidney does so. He repeatedly endorses allegory in the *Defence,* and never states his supposed displacement of the mode with exemplary imitation.[4]

Perplexed by Clark's lack of evidence, even Myrick wonders "whether . . . or not" Sidney actually distinguished allegory from exemplary fiction, which would be necessary for Sidney to privilege the latter, and concedes that "he does not call attention to the distinction." Actually, Sidney's treatise never makes this imputed distinction, and fluidly associates allegory and doctrine "by ensample," like Spenser's "Letter to Ralegh," Harington's commentary on the *Orlando furioso,* and Renaissance allegorization of the *Aeneid.* Nevertheless, Myrick decides that "we *must suppose* him to have seen a distinction" anyway. Whereas Myrick further assumes that Sidney's interest in Aristotle's literary theory necessarily entails aversion to allegory, many critics of the time with Aristotelian interests, such as Jacopo Mazzoni, Torquato Tasso, and Giovanni Viperano, eagerly assimilated Aristotle to allegorical poetics. Especially in relation to heroic poetry, that approach remained compelling even well after 1675, when it was further institutionalized in René le Bossu's widely influential *Traité du poëme épique.* Perceived not as a stable frame of reference, but as an incomplete collection of lecture notes to be understood and perfected through recourse to other literary theorists, the *Poetics* was so freely conflated with diverse doctrines and authorities, including many aside from Horace, Plato, and "Longinus," such as Plutarch, Strabo, and Maximus of Tyre, that its reception and influence remained highly pseudo-Aristotelian long after Sidney. Sidney's own literary theory further absorbed much Platonic, Horatian, and Augustinian thought favorable to allegory.[5]

Rather than just adducing characters and actions that exemplify specific qualities such as wisdom, cruelty, and ambition, Sidney's *Defence* praises biblical parables and fables such as Aesop's, "whose *pretty allegories,* stealing under the formal tales of beasts, make many . . . begin to hear the sound of virtue" (*Prose* 86–87; emphasis mine). That epithet accords esthetic and pleasure-giving values to allegory, as various literary theorists had argued, and the prestige of fables as fictions that yet impart figurative truths had been very high ever since patristic times. Defending poetry with a Horatian allegorical argument, Sidney affirms that poets "draw with their charming sweetness the wild untamed wits to an admiration of knowledge, . . . as Amphion was said to move stones with his poetry to build Thebes, and Orpheus to be listened to by beasts—indeed stony and beastly people" (*Prose* 74). Sidney further deploys long-standing critical arguments that apparently unedifying stories can well have allegorical meaning of profound worth. So, "under the pretty tales of wolves and sheep," pastoral "can include the whole considerations of wrong-doing and patience": hidden significance underwrites Sidneian literary value (*Prose* 94–95). Likewise, "the heroical, which is . . . the best and most accomplished kind of poetry," sets out "virtue," yet so as "to make her more lovely in her holiday apparel, to the eye of any that will deign not to disdain *until they understand*" (*Prose* 98; emphasis mine). Poems that may possibly seem to deserve rejection, Sidney avers, come to yield enlightenment to patient understanding of indirect or veiled meaning, and his claim reflects and appeals to fundamental Renaissance assumptions about the literary value and appropriate application of allegory.[6]

Sidney's ensuing declaration that poets are not liars involves a corollary of that claim: 'If then a man can arrive to that child's age to know that the poets' persons and doings are but pictures *what should be,* and not stories what have been, they will never give the lie to things not affirmatively but *allegorically* and *figuratively* written." Besides asserting that poets are not liars because they do not seriously claim to report actual events, the wording also reflects the once-common critical doctrine that indirect expression of some higher truth or ideal (what should be), typically accomplished through allegory, justifies the invention or feigning of fictions. Fabulous events may be figuratively imbued with edifying significance, which readers had best attend to, in Sidney's view: "as in history looking for truth, they may go away full fraught with falsehood, so in poesy, looking but for fiction, they shall use the narration *but as* an imaginative *ground-plot* of a *profitable invention*" (*Prose* 103; emphasis mine). In accord with basic principles of allegorical poetics, Sidney assumes the importance of profit or utility as a criterion of literary value and justification of literature, and treats poetic narrative as a pretext for the unfolding of implied beneficent perceptions. The role of allegory in literature had long been comparably defined by the common hermeneutic tropes of chaff and fruit, or husk and kernel, which privilege inner content and its discernment. The *Defence* treats literature as a figuring forth of wisdom that is to be "allegorically" conceived. Many other Sidneian passages favourable to allegory could be adduced, including positive usages of the term; some have begun to redefine Sidney's poetic allegorically, and Margaret Ferguson and M. J. Doherty now even find the treatise itself an allegory.[7]

Sidney's grand summation deploys the authority of ancient Cornutus, the prestigious basis of much mythological allegorism in the Renaissance, who considered Homeric texts allegorical repositories of primal wisdom: "believe, with Clauserus, the translator of Cornutus, that it pleased the heavenly Deity, by Hesiod and Homer, *under the veil* of fables, to give us all knowledge, logic, rhetoric, philosophy natural and moral, and quid non?; . . . *believe with me,* that there are *many mysteries* contained in poetry, which of purpose were *written darkly,* lest by profane wits it should be abused . . ." (*Prose* 121; emphasis mine). While the local context is disarmingly light and rhetorical, these complementary statements are fundamentally serious, for they accord with earlier positions and passages of the treatise: the *Defence* as a whole—and poetry itself, as Sidney defines it—is not merely a joke. Like many literary theorists of the time, Sidney himself repeatedly insists that the intellectual disciplines sprang from poetry; citation of Hesiod and Homer as primordial wellsprings of narratively veiled knowledge was almost *de rigeur.* Sidney variously recommends hidden meaning throughout the *Defence,* and also repeatedly associates poetry with "sweet mysteries" containing "true points of knowledge," or "sacred mysteries" (*Prose* 107, 121).[8]

Sidney's crucial promotion of the right poet over historians and philosophers indeed depends on just such a claim that literature has a mysterious capacity to impart or reveal hidden wisdom: "with a tale forsooth he cometh unto you. . . . And, pretending no more, doth intend the winning of the mind from wickedness to virtue—even as the child is often brought to take most wholesome things *by hiding them* in such other as have a pleasant taste. . . ." While seeming to proffer only delight, the poem inwardly manifests the irresistible "form of goodness," which steals upon even immoral readers "ere themselves be aware" (*Prose* 92–93; emphasis mine). Essential to Sidney's poetic, the means of achieving such ends include allegory, just as this passage echoes numerous preceding theorists' recommendations of the capabilities of allegory to mediate hidden wisdom attractively. Insisting on the potential of literature to convey exalted significances obscure to the unworthy, the *Defence* finally condemns earth-creeping minds deaf to "the planet-like music of poetry," and blind to its "sky" (*Prose* 121). Ideas of cosmic harmonies and correspondences provided a metaphysical foundation for literary allegorism.

Consideration of the *Defence* as an allegorical poetic began with Sidney's own private secretary, Sir William Temple. His logical analysis of the *Defence,* apparently written for Sidney alone, assumes that the argument rests on "definition of poetry" as "an allegorical fiction" (*allegorica fictio*) of "truth." How could Temple have made that claim if Sidney defined his own poetic in contradistinction to allegorical poetics and literary practices? Such writers as Coluccio Salutati, Spenser, and, in the final phase of his theoretical development, Torquato Tasso, similarly conceived poetry as "total allegorical metaphor," in Mindele Anne Treip's phrase. The writings of Abraham Fraunce also associate Sidney and his circle with allegory and hermetic modes of discourse. Since Sidney's connections with allegory are extensive, Clark's and Myrick's rush to dissociate him from the mode seems a function of its anathematization in orthodox Anglo-American critical ideology of their time, and well afterward. By accommodating Sidney to that ruling perspective, their approach easily came to dominate study of his texts, while the ascendancy of formalism discouraged culturally informed interpretation, indispensable for identifying complex allegories in Renaissance literature.[9]

ARCADIAN HEROIC ALLEGORISM

Since Clark, Zandvoort, and Myrick, Sidney's supposed rejection of allegory in the *Defence* has conventionally entailed its exclusion from the *Arcadias,* so that, with few exceptions, studies of them typically either do not mention the mode or deny it has any Sidneian relevance. Yet the *Arcadias* are very likely to involve extensive allegorism, for Sidney's innovative, complex construction of "Arcadian epic" broadly combines pastoral and epic, the prime loci of allegory in sixteenth- and seventeenth-century literature. Sidney clearly endorses generic mixtures in the *Defence,* such as mingling "matters heroical and pastoral," and argues that heroic poetry is the pre-eminent literary vehicle for apprehension of knowledge, for the heroic poem "doth not only teach and move to a truth, but teacheth and moveth to the most high and excellent truth." Likewise, "under pretty tales" pastoral can figuratively involve "whole considerations" of moral and political philosophy (*Prose* 94–95, 98).[10]

Whereas the pastoralism of the *Arcadias* can be taken for granted, and the heroic development of the *New Arcadia,* the relation of the

Old Arcadia to epic, in the broadly heroico-romantic sense of Sidney's time, has become occluded. But as A. C. Hamilton observes, the *Old Arcadia* strongly impinges on epic according to Sidney's *Defence,* by focusing on justice and magnanimity in the trial. Moreover, in assessing ideals of personal development at the highest social levels, the *Old Arcadia* approximates heroic poetry, and exploits its generically encyclopedic qualities by incorporating a large selection of elements from other genres, such as pastoral romance and comedy. The *Odyssey* prestigiously warranted epic without warfare. And just as the *Iliad, Odyssey,* and *Aeneid* deal extensively with love and friendship, some widely influential theorists, such as Torquato Tasso, found those subjects "entirely suitable for the heroic poem," so that "actions performed for the sake of love" were even "beyond all others heroic." Sidney himself adduces Heliodorus's "sugared invention of . . . love," the *Aethiopica,* as "an absolute heroical poem" in the *Defence* (*Prose* 81). Converting much of the epic repertoire, especially marital conflict, to treat the inner strife of love in the Old Arcadia, Sidney represents his story as an *Iliad, Odyssey,* and *Aeneid* of love's impact on the mind, through implicit and explicit analogies. Infatuated Gynecia, for example, hourly suffers "whole armies of mortal adversaries" within, and rushes upon trysting Pyrocles and Philoclea "with as much rageful haste as the Trojan women went to burn Aeneas's ships." Enamoured Pyrocles is himself "blown . . . with as many contrary passions as Aeolus sent out winds upon the Trojan relics guided upon the sea by the valiant Aeneas." Even in his transvestism, Pyrocles corresponds to Hercules, a main paradigm of heroism. The princes' former exploits, recounted in the Second Eclogues and somewhat in the narrative, exalt their stature, as do their rescuings of Basilius's family; like Euarchus himself, they display " 'heroical greatness,' " at least from the viewpoint of Kerxenus, Sympathus, and the Mantineans, among others. In the *New Arcadia,* Sidney fully manifests the nascent epic alignments of its precursor through more direct and expanded use of the heroic repertoire, as with the new *in medias res* opening, and the princes deliberately aim to surpass "Ulysses and Aeneas" in their "exercises of . . . virtue" and "heroical effects," so that "all Asia" resounds with Musidorus's "heroical enterprises." Cecropia directly compares the relation of Amphialus and Philoclea to that of Paris, Menelaus, and Helen. Comments of sixteenth- and seventeenth-century readers show that this text widely satisfied contemporary expectations of epic.[11]

The credibility of textual allegoresis most depends on a shared sense that the diction has a polysemous capacity to convey figurative as well as literal meanings at once, in such a way that, within a substantial segment of the discourse, a variety of details extensively evoke or correlate with one or more tenors. Although comparison of Arcadian imagery to iconographical and other symbolic conventions would quickly reveal many extended patterns of figurative significance, in keeping with Sidney's great interest in creating enigmatic *imprese*, I will focus here on adducing Arcadian verbal devices, such as significant names, diversely meaningful phrasings, and techniques of narrative construction, that form protracted combinations inviting a relatively programmatic figurative analysis. Though definition of allegory is controversial, this is a main feature that distinguishes the mode from relatively incidental analogies, parallels, symbols, and exempla, just as allegorical discourse was commonly defined as *extended* metaphor in the Renaissance. Most of my argument thus concentrates on related incidents that form a general expressive pattern in both *Arcadias*. In the *Old Arcadia,* the assaults of the wild beasts and rebels address the relationship of the "higher" and "lower" natures of humanity, broadly comparable to mind on one hand, and senses and appetites on the other. The *New Arcadia* retains these incidents and adds the more insidious threat of Artesia's deceptive entertainments that enable abduction of Pamela, Philoclea, and Zelmane. Moreover, Sidney newly attributes all these challenges to the machinations of Cecropia, which culminate in the great siege of her fortress to free her kidnapped victims. Most clearly in the *New Arcadia,* but also in its predecessor, we find correlative events that together allegorize inner conflicts of heroic development. Both texts reflect the strong association of allegorical epic with moral philosophy and related theories of the psyche in the Renaissance. Sidney's Arcadian heroic poems incorporate the general allegory of moral progress through temptation, trial, and discipline of the "lower nature," that was commonly ascribed to Homer's *Odyssey* and Virgil's *Aeneid,* and thus strongly conditioned the scope and applications of allegorism in Renaissance heroic poetry.[12]

As Tasso and Spenser recognized, allegorical epic depends much on pervasive wordplay, so that the telling of the story evokes and plays on the figurative meanings it expresses. Hence the heroic poet can negotiate between the narrative and the ambitious encyclopedic content prescribed for epic, without detracting from lively presentation of the action. Spenserians look for "allegorical pointers" in the language of *The Faerie Queene,* or multivalent words and phrases that both advance the action yet also allude to and amplify the allegory, and Sidney's Arcadian diction supports such interpretation as well as Spenser's, for they are both allegorical heroic poets.[13]

Sidney's account of the Giants of Pontus in the *New Arcadia* contains various phrases that, if the episode were written by Spenser, would be quite commonly taken to indicate a particular allegorical meaning. As Nancy Lindheim mentions, though without explanation, these Giants allegorize the tyrannical potential of irascible inner powers. When they "obeyed a master," Sidney's text states, "*their anger* was *a serviceable power of the mind* to do public good"; but "now, *unbridled,* and *blind judge* of itself, it made wickedness *violent*" (NA 178; emphasis mine). In conjunction with "anger," this reference to a mental capacity to do good, if properly disciplined, indicates the episode involves a moral and political allegory about the once-standard concept of the irascible appetite, which was exactly so defined.[14]

The Giants' characterization further evokes such allegoresis, for they have main traits ascribed to that appetite. "Full of inward bravery and fierceness," and prone to "effects of anger," "faults of rage," and impatience at personal injury, the Giants are so dominated by the irascible appetite that they readily figure forth its abusive potential. Their size and strength aptly reflect the great power attributed to that psychic capacity, and in this figurative sense too, then, they are "jewels to a *wise* man, considering, indeed, what wonders they were able to perform." The irascible appetite was thought a great personal asset if ruled by reason and wisdom, but otherwise tended to become destructively wrathful, much as Sidney's figurative Giants revolt, delighting only "in slaughter" and "others' wrack" (*NA* 177–78); emphasis mine). As Arthur finally kills Spenser's Pyrochles, whose meaning is similar to that of Sidney's giants, so Sidney's heroic princes slay them both, thus expressing censure and disciplined transcendence of such destructive potential within, in furtherance of Sidney's definition of heroism. The allegory of the Giants is not only psychological but also political, for it examines the correlation between internal conditions and social situations. However, this victory is allegorically proleptic, like Redcross's defeat of Error, rather than final, for the Giants prefigure the yet greater challenge of irascible Anaxius.

According to epic norms of the late sixteenth century, the presence of such allegory in the *New Arcadia* is much to be expected, for theorists of epic and heroic poets often privileged allegorization of moral philosophy and related psychological concepts, and rationally apt governance of the irascible appetite was one of the most important heroic principles. It is a central issue in Tasso's "Allegoria del poema" ascribing allegory to the *Gerusalemme liberata,* and in Book Two of *The Faerie Queene.* Moreover, in demonstrating the psychological meanings of Goffredo and Rinaldo himself, Tasso's main vehicle for figurative exploration of irascible potential, the "Allegoria" cites allusive phrases very like those I quote from Sidney's account of his Giants, that mediate between the narrative and its conceptual configurations. Spenser similarly advises interpreters to track the hidden senses of his faery according to "certaine signes here set in sundry place" (II.pr.4). I subsequently adduce further Arcadian allegorical pointers of various kinds such as are normally taken to demonstrate allegory in *The Faerie Queene*.[15]

Not only various episodes of the *New Arcadia* involve allegory, as with the Giants, but also the main action of both versions. In both, Book One climaxes with the attack of a marauding lion and bear, and Book Two with that of a rebellious mob; in the *Old Arcadia*, the rebels reappear to assault Pamela and Musidorus during their elopement. This narratively important series of events expresses potential inner challenges of disordered appetites and passions through external conflict, and the figurative techniques at play are certainly allegorical in their extent, detailed development, and programmatic significance, and comparable to the complex allegory of Spenser and others. A most adept and enthusiastic composer of such narrative. Sidney even developed his own distinctive repertoire of verbal and narrative devices for presenting allegory.[16]

Most obviously, various passages following the attacks indirectly indicate the beasts' and rebels' figurative significance through allusive homologies. For example, shortly after the beasts' assault, Gynecia laments that, since her heart has become replete with fierce desires, it fills the Arcadian wilderness, in effect, with "wild ravenous beasts" that do not exist there otherwise (*NA* 120; *OA* 91). Likewise, after the rebels' assault, the Second Eclogues begin with "a dance . . . called the skirmish betwixt Reason and Passion," which terms passion a "rebel vile" (*OA* 135–36). Moreover, the sections involving the beasts and rebels all repeat a common formula of phrasing that provides an expressive transition between the impassioned psychic states of the main characters, and external conflict that figures forth those inner conditions. An initial clause describing some impassioned state typically precedes another clause beginning "when" or "at what time," which describes an immediately violent external challenge that must be combatted. Thus Sidney correlates the inner turmoil with the ensuing external turmoil, so that inner and outer conditions become mutually expressive.

Just before the rebels first attack, Philoclea finds that her devoted Amazon is a disguised male lover, Pyrocles, and he begins kissing and caressing her. Meanwhile, Gynecia, already upset by guilty conscience and a nightmare about her own infatuation with him, hears of their tryst from Miso, whose name significantly means "hatred" (μῖσος). Gynecia thus finds herself an inner battleground of love for Pyrocles and "rage of jealousy," possessed by those passions as if by "devils." In this "frenzy" or "inflaming agony of affection" which renders her "powers prostrate," Gynecia races to the amorous couple:

> *THEN began* she to *DISPLAY* to Zelmane [i.e., Pyrocles] the *storehouse* of her *deadly desires—WHEN suddenly* the confused rumour of a *mutinous multitude* gave just occasion to Zelmane to break off any such conference . . . , and to retire . . . towards the lodge. Yet . . . they were overtaken by *an unruly sort* [i.e., crowd, mob] of . . . *rebels*, which like a violent flood were carried. . . . (*NA* 276–80, my emphasis; similarly *OA* 120–24)

As the rebels focus potentials for inner disorder of the passions or, in Elizabethan terms, the "affections," so Pyrocles's subsequent account of the situation as a "matter . . . of a vehement, I must confess *over-vehement, affection*" reflects that tenor (*NA* 287, emphasis mine; similarly *OA* 131). The allegory assumes that heroic discipline requires rational mastery of such impulses, both internally and within the state.

After Pamela and Musidorus elope in the *Old Arcadia,* having agreed to postpone sex until marriage, rebellious impulses and some of these same rebels again become jointly manifest, as she sleeps defenceless in his arms:

> *overmastered with the fury of delight,* . . . *he was bent to take the advantage. . . . And NOW he began to make his approaches WHEN . . . there came by a dozen clownish villains,* armed with divers sorts of weapons, and for the rest, both in face and apparel, so forwasted that they seemed to bear a great conformity with the *savages.* . . . *(OA* 202; emphasis mine)

Returning to this incident after some entrelacement, Sidney again emphasizes joint manifestation of the attacking rebels and Musidorus's powerful libidinal urges:

> the braying cries of a *rascal company* robbed [Pamela] of her quiet, *AT WHAT TIME* she was in a shrewd likelihood to have had great part of her trust in Musidorus deceived. . . .

But . . . the every way enraged Musidorus rase from her—*enraged betwixt a repentant shame of his promise-breaking attempt and the tyrannical fire of lust* (which, having already caught hold of so sweet and fit a fuel, was *past the calling back of reason's counsel).* . . . *(OA* 306; emphasis mine)

In Musidorus's phrase from the First Eclogues, the situation expresses the "wretched state of man in self-division" (*OA* 63). The rebels figure forth insurgent aspects of his furious delight or loss of reason's counsel, and the human potential for those conditions; the ensuing struggle expresses typical inner conflict, just as Musidorus, we are told, experiences diverse conflicting impulses. In this case, sexual desire entails the figurative manifestation of villainous savages who inconveniently threaten to usurp the lover's role: according to the allegory, the lover cannot truly enjoy the beloved through lustful violation of trust, for that brings on a de-humanizing or savage transformation of personal identity.[17] Pamela's sleep may well express some passivity, incaution, or lack of appropriate vigilance against rising passions, both as typical inner conditions of both persons involved in such predicaments, and on her own part.

At least until Sidney set aside his manuscript of the *New Arcadia,* this situation was to have been included. In the *New Arcadia,* some rebels still escape to the woods after the attack on Basilius's retreat, and in the *Old Arcadia,* those same fugitives assail Pamela and Musidorus during their elopement (*OA* 132, 306–07; *NA* 290). Apparently to prepare for inclusion of this scene, Sidney removed his former attribution of rapacious lust to Musidorus. Since that hero is no longer compromised when the rebels materialize, the allegory of the conflict focuses yet more on a typical inner potential to be combatted, without indicating its partial enaction due to some culpable acquiescence of the will.[18]

Like Spenser, Sidney also uses beasts for allegory about the passions: mainly the ravening lion and bear that appear at the end of Book I in both *Arcadias.* Just as the protagonists intensely experience irrational impulses, so the action figuratively manifests the challenges of that general inner potential, anticipating the allegory of the rebels:

WHILE Gynecia walked hard by them *carrying many unquiet contentions about her,* the ladies sate them down. . . . But Zelmane [i.e., Pyrocles], . . . taking the hand of Philoclea, and with *burning kisses* setting it close to her lips . . . *began* to speak these words: "*O love,* since thou art so *changeable* in men's estates, *how art thou so constant in their torments*"—*WHEN* suddenly there came out of a wood a monstrous lion, with a she-bear not far from him of little less fierceness. . . . (*NA* 111, emphasis mine; similarly *OA* 46).

Whereas inner rule of reason was especially definitive for humanity, the powers of love to effect change include theriomorphic metamorphosis, as it were. Impassioned loss of reason, the allegory indicates, can inwardly savage or devour specifically human qualities; bestial transformation through indulgence of appetite and desire was a topos of Renaissance moral philosophy, psychology, theology, and literary allegory.[19]

These four passages from important and diverse parts of both *Arcadias* show that at least some agents and actions with a substantial presence in the main plot body forth internal states, and produce lively allegorical images of the trials attending pursuit of heroic virtue. In both *Arcadias,* the general characteristics of Sidney's rebel townspeople further confirm that conclusion, for they broadly correspond to Plato's representation of appetites, passions, and pleasures in the *Republic.* Despite the wide diffusion of the Platonic imagery of inner conditions in Renaissance culture, the correspondences of Sidney's rebels with such elements of the *Republic,* which Sidney knew well, are so extensive, significant, and concentrated that this dialogue constitutes not only an intertext but a main source of both the narrative and its allegorical content. When disordered or insufficiently subject to reason, Plato argues, the appetitive part becomes like an irrational and wanton crowd or mob that displays madness, bestial savagery, fury, gluttony, confusion, drunkenness, and chaotic strife even amongst its own members. Sidney converts that imagistic repertoire into his narrative realization of the rebels, so that his description of them involves many allegorically resonant details, and evinces the extensive and programmatic allusiveness that we conventionally associate with allegory as polysemous discourse.[20]

In the *Old Arcadia,* the "mad" or "many-headed multitude" of frenzied rebels comes from Phagona, and Sidney's allegorical agenda apparently governed his invention of this place-name. Alluding to φάγών, "gluttony," φαγο, "eating, devouring," and φαγεῖν, "to eat, devour," the "Phagonian" rebellion springs from festive consumption of excess food and drink, which figures appetitive self-indulgence (*OA* 126–32). Likewise, Plato's *Republic* closely links passions, instincts, and appetites with "pleasures of nutrition and generation and their kind," and designates hunger and thirst the "most conspicuous" and paradigmatic desires. Lacking rational discipline, the appetitive part of the soul indulges, in effect, in revelries, and becomes "replete with food and wine," endeavouring "to sally forth and satisfy its own instincts," like a motley "mob." Drunkenness in the *Republic* both induces and figures irrational subjection to appetite.[21] In a complementary passage in the *Timaeus*, the appetitive part of the abdomen is like a "manger" that is best removed from the "counselling part" of the head; the Phagonian rebellion arises when, after "banqueting" and "wine," a "proud word did swell in their stomachs," setting "fire to their minds" (*OA* 126–27).[22] Just before they appear, Gynecia herself "did . . . eat of her jealousy," and, in turn, that passion and love "feed on" her until she is "consumed," burnt, and frenzied (*OA* 118, 233–23). The townspeople are also "like enraged beasts" (*OA* 124; cf. 307), and Plato associates the appetites with bestiality too; Sidney concentrates this aspect of appetitive imagery in the earlier attack of the lion and bear.

While the imagery, diction, and action defining the rebels remain much the same in the *New Arcadia,* Sidney replaces his invented Phagona with a town that actually existed, Enispus, presumably for enhanced verisimilitude. However, Enispus was so obscure that its location within Arcadia was controversial even in antiquity, and so Sidney probably selected it to enable some witty negotiation between geographical constraints and his allegorical requirements.[23] Sidney's usage of this name likely plays on ἐνίσσω, "attack, maltreat," associating the passions with abusive contention; and οἶνος, "wine," οἰνωπός, "flushed with wine," or οἰνωσις, "drunkenness," which Plato, among others, had associated with impassioned states.

Though the rebellion still springs from a drunken banquet that produces irrational frenzy, rage, and bestiality in the *New Arcadia,* Sidney's revisions use Platonic images and attributes of the passions even more extensively. Also, since Clinias now instigates the uprising with rumours promoting tyrannical Cecropia's plots against Basilius, the *New Arcadia* assimilates the rebels into extended allegorical analysis of inner and outer tyrannies (*NA* 290–93, 319). According to the *Republic*, tyranny within the soul similarly arises from some desires goading and inciting the others to "run wild and look to see who has aught that can be taken from him by deceit or violence," especially at the behest of the ruling passion. Within the state, such unreasonable persons, if "fluent speakers," "become sycophants and bear false witness and take bribes," much like Clinias himself; they and their dupes or allies may "create a tyrant out of that one" who, like Cecropia, has "the greatest and mightiest tyrant in his own soul" (573E–75D).

The *New Arcadia* further amplifies the Platonic allegory by appending the story of Antiphilus, a commoner who assumed rule, as if one of the more amorous Enispians were to become king. "Swayed . . . as every wind of passions puffed him," his weakly licentious rule travesties good government, demonstrating the political consequences of inner disorder resulting from such a ruling passion (*NA* 298–306).

Analogues of drunken, rebellious, or otherwise unruly mobs representing undisciplined appetite or passion appear in Tasso's, Spenser's, and Ariosto's heroic poems; thus Ariosto's Alcina, for example, marshals disorderly forces against Logistilla, symbolic of reason and wisdom. As such allegories were fundamental for epic analysis of heroic virtue, so they appear also in the *Arcadias*. In the *Discourse of Civill Life,* Sidney's friend Lodowick Bryskett contrasts those who live according to the passions and senses, who become "like brute beasts," as Sidney describes the rebels, with those who endeavour to cultivate the "part of man" most akin "unto the divine nature" by pursuing reason, and thus constitute inspirational exemplars "aunciently . . . called *Heroes.*" The psychological significance of the Arcadian beasts and rebel townspeople is not casual or intermittent, but highly programmatic, encompassing their basic characteristics and behavior over lengthy sections of narrative, and numerous details of the imagery and action, such as place-names, particular wounds, and gestures. The various engagements with the beasts and rebels are complex allegory, and so are most of the *Arcadias,* which display much technical accomplishment in the allegorical expression of internal states.[24]

Sidney's new connection of the beasts and rebels to tyrannous Cecropia in the *New Arcadia* shows that his revisions partly aimed to deepen, expand, and extend the existing allegory; his subjects for figurative treatment tend to be jointly psychological and political, along the lines of Plato's analogies between the psyche and state in the *Republic.* Cecropia's role, which dominates Book III of the revised text, allegorically addresses the origins and nature of tyranny. As in Plato's analysis, Sidney's allegory assumes that tyranny arises from unleashed ferocity of lawless desires within the populace, especially the tyrant, and the inner dominance of any passion amounts to a psychic tyranny conducive to the political equivalent. However, Sidney goes beyond Plato in relating tyranny not simply to inversion of reason and passion, but also to corruption of reason itself, and effects of the Fall.

Just before the kidnapping of the princesses according to Cecropia's further plot, Musidorus attempts to kiss Pamela, who thus rejects him; so, he declares, "*reason to my passion yielded.*" While Musidorus thus remains tormentedly *"half mad* for sorrow *in the woods,"* which are symbolic as in *The Faerie Queene,* the princesses and Pyrocles are entrapped by Cecropia, and this situation expresses general implications of the abeyance of reason (*NA* 313, 309, 316; emphasis mine). Promising entertainments, six maidens sent by Cecropia lure the sisters, Pyrocles, and Miso into *"the midst of the thickest part of the wood"* where they are then abducted by "twenty armed men" who rush *"out of the woods."* As the allegory expresses conditions lacking presence of mind, so the victims take direction from foolish Miso, associated with irrational, impassioned aspects of the psyche, like the family of Dametas in general. Because Miso desires *"to lead her . . . senses abroad to some pleasure,"* she urges following the maidens (*NA* 316, 315; emphasis mine); yet, in moral philosophy and allegorical epic of the time, pursuit of sensory pleasure requires great prudence.[25]

This Arcadian predicament allegorizes the adverse potential of such pursuits, and the psychic process of delusion by an apparent good through "oblectation" of the senses, as an Elizabethan moral philosopher might put it. In effect, the narrative portrays misleading tendencies of the lower part of the soul, focused in Miso, when indulged through impassioned inattention or confusion of reason. This ultimately leads to a debilitating act of the will and some consequent "spiritual bondage" or captivity of the self, in effect, figured forth by the incarceration in Cecropia's castle.

Whereas the armed kidnappers from the woods correlate with the former rebels in their role and significance, the five tempting maidens signify the five senses or sensory temptation, and their leader Artaxia either the superior common sense or delusory imagination, both of which were held to represent sensory perceptions to the mind. A close analogue, at least, that indicates some currency of such allegory is Francesco Colonna's *Hypnerotomachia Poliphili,* in which five attractive nymphs figuring forth the five senses appear in the forest and lead the hero away. Sidney's portrayal of Cecropia's temptresses concentrates sensory and sensual allures. Festooned with garlands and playing "well-pleasing tunes," they wear scarlet with "naked" legs, their breasts "liberal to the eye." Phoebus has kissed them "over-often and hard," and their modesty itself is "wanton," their soberness "enticing." At the scene of the ambush, the victims find "pleasantest fruits," drink wine, and "taste . . . of swelling grapes which seemed great with child of Bacchus." Sidney's description features appeals of all five senses: sight; hearing (music); smell (flowers); taste (food, drink); and touch (bodily sensuality), with the cumulative effect of euphoric intoxication focused in wine "which seemed to laugh for joy" (*NA* 314–16). The allegory reflects various *topoi* of literature and the visual arts: sensory temptations of personified Pleasure; the cautionary case of Circe's blandishments; and the "banquet of sense" motif. Since all this is Cecropia's trap, the allegory represents sensory pleasures as inducements to incaution with possibly harmful consequences.[26]

In dealing allegorically with this subject matter, the *Arcadias* are comparable to the *Orlando furioso,* the *Gerusalemme liberata,* and Book II of *The Faerie Queene,* with their stories of Alcina, Armida, Acrasia, and fortified Alma, who opposes assaults upon the senses. Tasso's "Allegoria" defines the allegorical significance of imagery like that of Sidney's context: "the Flowers, the musical instruments, the nymphs, are the deceitful inticements, which . . . [figuratively] set down before us the pleasures and delights of the sense, under the shew of *Good."* Narratively and allegorically following from impassioned loss of reason in the typical case of Musidorus, the Arcadian ambush culminates in a symbolic reification of that kind of problem, expressed in the predicament of the sisters and disguised Pyrocles. As the victims' captors "put *hoods over"* their "heads," and *"night"* conspires in the subsequent abduction, so the situation expresses occlusion and incapacitation of reason, mind, or clear insight (*NA* 316; emphasis mine).[27]

In the *New Arcadia,* Cecropia thus launches three initiatives that allegorize challenges to reason: she trained and set on the wild beasts, arranged the attack of the rebels, and devised this ambush. We have already found allegory extending through much of the narrative, and she herself, her castle, and other agents are also allegorical. Extrapolating from Musidorus's impulsive kiss, in which he never stayed "to ask reason's leave" (*NA* 309), the following imprisonment and conflict figuratively explore the psychic and political implications of losing rational control. Much as in *Astrophil and Stella,* the *New Arcadia* comes to turn on a kiss which epitomizes felt conflict of the body with high, Platonizing aspirations associated with supremacy of reason. The kiss ushers in a general allegorical confrontation with the potential dangers of acquiescence to irrational impulse.

From a psychological perspective, Cecropia's schemes and forces figure forth potential for psychic disorder through corruptions of faculties, and inverted relations between them. Sidneians have long recognized that the account of the captivity and siege distinctively features an extensive reciprocity of metaphor, whereby internal and external conflicts are mutually expressive; but that characteristic of the discourse signals and helps articulate the psychological allegory. Conceptions of human capacities were highly generalized, and the engagement with Cecropia's power has general significance. Notions of a fundamental human condition were culturally prevalent in the Renaissance, on account of common assumptions such as the creation of humanity in the divine image, and yet the subjection of the entire race to the effects of the Fall. Though the protagonists' loves embroil them in "great war" within, as with Pyrocles (*NA* 258), the ultimate confrontation with Cecropia's forces is much less a consequence of those characters' actions, allegorically, than a climactic and summary projection of challenges considered intrinsic to the human condition. In other words, the allegory displays the context for the protagonists' human implication in fault, and its potential extent. In the initial kidnapping, Cecropia's lure of physical indulgences focuses possibilities for descent to commitments of the body, passions, and material concerns, which were routinely condemned in moral philosophy and theology. The full consequences of such an orientation are finally reified in their most destructive form in Cecropia herself; the allegory of the kidnapping implies that incautious attention to physical or sensory needs and desires readily causes some subjection within the domain of Cecropia's meaning, just as it brings imprisonment within her castle.

The characterization of Cecropia goes much beyond Plato's analysis of tyranny in the *Republic,* for she herself does not simply express the inner dominance of a ruling passion, of which the *New Arcadia* provides various tyrannical examples earlier, such as Antiphilus, but the condition of inner perversity that Renaissance moral philosophers considered most extreme: corruption of the rational faculty itself. That is also the state of Plexirtus, and, like him, Cecropia spins diverse ingenious plots and rationalizations of wrongdoing with her "malicious wit" (*NA* 418). As Pamela observes, rebuking Cecropia's atheism, she is "so wicked," "so rotten," and "miserably foolish" because "wit" itself makes her so (*NA* 359), and "wit" was a common term for the rational faculties themselves. In her inveterate perversity of mind, Cecropia is "like a bat which, though it have eyes to discern that there is a sun, yet hath so evil eyes that it cannot delight in the sun," and thus rejects "truth" even when she finds it (*NA* 363). Pierre Charron, for example, considers Cecropia's very knowing kind of wickedness the worst and most incorrigible: "some are incorporated into evil, by discourse and resolution, or by long habit, in such sort, that *their understanding it selfe* approveth it and consenteth thereunto. This falleth out, when sinne having met with a strong and vigorous heart, is in such sort rooted therein, that it is there formed and as it were naturalized, and the soule infected and wholly tainted therewith."[28]

This "hopelesse" condition of "corrupted judgement" or "vicious mind" arises, Sidney's friend Lodowick Bryskett explains, through habituation to "false opinions, vices, wickednesse, disordinate appetites, ambitions, greedie desires of wealth, . . . wanton lusts and longings."[29] Cecropia constitutes an end point and summation of human possibilities for inner corruption, expressing such challenges in their most acute form. From a political viewpoint, her story also expresses the inner and outer conditions of tyranny at its worst.

Reflecting this character's significance, "Cecropia" primarily refers to Athens and its ancient legendary founder, Κέκροψ, for whom that city was sometimes called Κεκροπία. Cecrops and Sidney's Cecropia are obvious opposites, for he was celebrated as the pious and just ruler who introduced civilized life to Greece, and an enlightened religious reformer who ended sacrifices of living things.[30] Selection of this name for the main exemplar of evil in the *New Arcadia* insists on the limitations of human projects for civilized reform. Against the positive potential that Cecrops and the achievements of Athens epitomize, Sidney adduces, in effect, their contrary; the homology of names stresses the co-existence of these opposite potentials in life, and the consequent difficulty of maintaining the values of Cecrops and Athens at their best. From a Protestant standpoint, the ancient civilizations of Greece and Rome overestimated the power and good of natural human capacities, contrary to enduring effects of original sin resulting from the Fall. Sidney's representation and naming of Cecropia allegorically focuses these issues in his Greek context, as a critique of values and perceptions associated with pagan culture.

Some mythic and iconographical correspondences probably stimulated Sidney's creativity here. According to legend, mentioned in Ovid's *Metamorphoses,* for instance, Cecrops had the upper body of a man conjoined to a serpent's tail; by Sidney's time, coincidentally, "artistic conceptions of the Fall" had been "dominated . . . for three hundred years" by the "vastly popular" anthropomorphic image of the Edenic serpent, with a human head and sometimes torso as well, usually feminine.[31] That was also a standard image of sin and evil during the Renaissance, as with Spenser's Error and Milton's Sin. From a mythologically informed viewpoint, "Cecropia" evokes these kinds of associations, and just as the character is emphatically "wicked," her name in Sidney's context probably also plays on κακουργία,"sin, wickedness," and κακός, "bad, evil." This "damnable creature" ends with a spectacular fall that may well symbolize such states of being, and she thus receives "her death's kiss at the ground": a fate comparable to that of the serpent condemned to eat dust and have its head crushed upon the ground, in Genesis 3:14–15 (*NA* 440).[32]

Cecropia's castle is a deathly house of horrors where the princesses and Pyrocles are imprisoned, tormented, and tempted to succumb to her vicious influence, or despair. Sidney extrapolates this allegory from once-common metaphoric motifs of the body as prison, tomb, or underworld of the soul. In the *Defence,* he promotes poetry as the intellectual discipline best able to yield "*knowledge to lift up the mind from the dungeon of the body* to the enjoying of his own divine essence" (*Prose* 82; emphasis mine). The climactic final book of the *Old Arcadia* explicitly broaches these issues, using the same metaphors, and the repertoire of such figurative discourse constitutes the allegorical basis of the great confrontation with Cecropia. Our intellectual part, the princes affirm, derives from God, but is "many times *rebelliously* resisted" within, and "always with this [bodily] *prison* darkened" (*OA* 372–73; emphasis mine). In the *New Arcadia,* the imprisoned characters, especially the sisters, broadly figure forth potential for human good and spiritual value; Cecropia's symbolic realm figures forth inner challenges that can arrest or jeopardize its development within, and outwardly in society. The narrative itself explicitly engages these issues, for the debates about virtue, vice, and atheism express inquiries, engagements of doubt, and psychic conflict related to the allegory and its conceptual content, while the representations of death and carnage question conditions and appraisals of mortality. The allegory broadly corresponds to Pierre de la Primaudaye's chapter "Of the diseases and passions of the bodie and soule," in his encyclopedic *French Academie:* in sum, "the soule, . . . being filled with infinite perturbations, . . . is carried away with inconstancie and uncertaintie into a streame of troublesome passions, which if they be not cut off and maistred by reason, draw a man into utter destruction." Attention to bodily needs and desires obscures "the light of the soule," which "aspireth unto the true Good." This predicament results from the Fall, and consequent "provocations and allurements of the flesh." The soul within the body, Ficino comparably explains, "is seized by the senses and lust, as though by police and a tyrant"; similarly, in Sidney's story, the sisters, who most focus textual ideals of virtue and wisdom, become tyrannically imprisoned through an ambush expressing dangers of sense and passion.[33]

Drawing on extensive traditions of psychomachia and castles of the self, the siege and struggles within the castle allegorize spiritual conflict, much as in Tasso's contemporary *Gerusalemme liberata,* where he says the siege of Jerusalem by his forces of good signifies endeavor to overcome "imperfection of humane nature," "inward difficulties,

and . . . outward impediments, . . . noted unto us by Poeticall figures."[34] Though, from a literal viewpoint, the Arcadian sides involved
are clearly divided, the division is nonetheless blurred allegorically,
for psychomachia implies some entanglement of potentials, some ambiguity of allegiance that must be clarified or resolved. In effect,
confrontation with Cecropia's forces is most broadly a figurative
encounter with human tendencies towards disorder and depravity, as
obstructions to pursuit of heroic love and achievement. The allegory
assumes that social and inner conditions are fully reciprocal, as in the
Republic: "injustice and . . . all turpitude" spring from a "civil war"
within, "and the revolt of one part against the whole of the soul that
it may hold therein a rule which does not belong to it" (444B).

Nevertheless, by comparison with conventional Protestant accounts of the inner predicament of humanity, such as those of La
Primaudaye's *Academie* and Philippe de Mornay's *Trewnesse of the
Christian Religion,* the Cecropia allegory seems relatively optimistic.
Just as La Primaudaye, for example, insists that reason is the medicine
of the soul, "by curing the passions and perturbations thereof," so
Musidorus and Pamela, often respectively linked with mind and wisdom in the text, are the mainstays of serious opposition to the forces
of Cecropia. Yet La Primaudaye stresses that the effectiveness of reason in such a role involves "the grace of God, to resist all the assaults
of unbridled desires, and the froward affections of this flesh."
Through Pamela's refutation of Cecropia's atheism, the allegory implies that, as La Primaudaye assumes, reason "is a divine guide, and
wisedome inspired from above." But, even though the protagonists
virtually attain victory by the point that the narrative breaks off, and
frequently invoke providence, the allegory does not feature supernatural aid in any clearly decisive way. The effect is as if Spenser's
Redcross nearly quelled the dragon without any apparent recourse
to the well or tree of life, or as if Guyon finally defeated Pyrochles
and Cymochles without the aid of his guardian angel and Arthur.
Whereas Redcross in Orgoglio's dungeon is wholly in the giant's
power, with the possible exception of the symbolic dwarf who flees
for aid, Cecropia's prisoners have some impressive powers of resistance. This heterodox tendency may account for Sidney's suspension
of his story, pending some further consideration. So long as Cecropia's castle remains finally unconquered in these circumstances, the
allegory does not decisively break with Elizabethan Protestant orthodoxy of the time: the action is frozen, in effect, as unresolved, continuing spiritual warfare. The progress in liberation of the castle may
well constitute a proleptic allegory of overcoming inner challenges,
since it applies generally to the human condition; in that sense, it

would express the strengthening of human good through extended processes of personal and cultural development in history. Cecropia seems destroyed in that anticipatory allegorical sense; Plexirtus, who has similar meaning, remains to express the persistence of such dangers meanwhile.[35]

The *Arcadias* not only involve much allegory, as we have seen, but also implicitly reflect upon its assumptions and techniques. In both *Arcadias,* for example, Musidorus must court Pamela in Book Two through apparent attentions to her chaperone, Mopsa. Sidney correlates the situation with allegory, in effect, by calling this courtship a delivery of "*second meaning.*" Likewise, on the disguised manner of Musidorus's courtship, Pamela herself remarks, "*under that veil* there may be *hidden things* to be esteemed" (*OA* 99, 106; emphasis mine). Similarly, the gift that Musidorus gives Mopsa in Pamela's presence to symbolize his indirect approach is "the figure of a crabfish, which . . . *looks one way and goes another.*" As Plato's *Republic* maintains that the Ideas must be sought by means tolerable for hjuman perception, like looking at the sun reflected in water (516A-C, 532A-C), so Musidorus must look to Mopsa in order to pursue Pamela, in whom the text invests various ideals of virtue and wisdom, as if seeing his "*sun shine in a puddled water*" (*NA* 139, 129; emphasis mine). Just as Mopsa's family are often projections of appetite in a relatively non-threatening, comically bumptious aspect, Mopsa's presence figures forth obstacles of sense and flesh that higher aspirations are to overcome or circumvent in quest of fulfillment, and the situation mocks such predicaments and compromises of desire. Also, as allegory in Sidney's period tends to approach ideals indirectly, so that we only encounter Spenser's Gloriana through reflections and covert veils, so, in one sense, Musidorus's indirect courtship of Pamela in Book Two of both *Arcadias* constitutes a ruefully self-reflexive figure for the predicament of such allegorical endeavours themselves.

In addition to many topical analogies, the *Arcadias* involve broad psychological allegory concerning the inner conflicts experienced in the heroic pursuit of virtue; correlative political allegory dealing with the appropriate relations of inner and outer modes of rule; and also some local theological allegories about the extent to which natural capacities can contribute to heroic endeavour. In exploring such matters, the *Arcadias* treat themes associated with epic in the Renaissance, and do so in an allegorical heroic mode quite comparable to that explicitly propounded by Tasso in his "Allegoria" appended to most editions of the *Gerusalemme liberata;* yet in Elizabethan literary studies, such approaches have been almost exclusively identified with Spenser. Like Spenser's most amply developed heroes, Musidorus,

Pyrocles, and the daughters of Basilius are neither personifications nor novelistic characters, but focus allegorical meanings as part of their complex textual development.[36]

In keeping with Sidney's claim in the *Defence* that poetry figures forth the grounds of wisdom, and his fascination with esoteric *imprese,* he stresses the elevated, oblique, or ingenious significance of the *Arcadias* even from the outset: the muses bestow "their perfections so largely here" that even the "shepherds have their fancies *lifted* to so *high conceits* as *the learned of other nations are content to borrow* their names and *imitate their cunning*" (*NA* 16; similarly *OA* 4). Besides acknowledging the previous literary role of Arcadia, and the allegorical associations of pastoral, these comments promote Sidney's distinctive production of Arcadian epic and imply some felt attainment of the general literary and generic principles of the *Defence*. The poet, Sidney argues, surpasses the historian "in moral doctrine, the chief of all knowledges," virtually matches "the philosopher" for "instructing," but "for moving leaves him behind"; and "if anything be already said in the defence of sweet poetry, all concurreth to the maintaining the heroical, which is not only a kind, but the best and most accomplished kind of poetry," in which "the image of each action stirreth and instructeth the mind" (*Prose* 98–99). Hence Sidney immediately invokes the long-venerated paradigm of Homer's enlightening profundity, "even as Horace saith, '*melius Chrysippo et Crantore,*' " and, much as Milton later applauds Spenser's *Faerie Queene* through a parallel betterment of Scotus and Aquinas, Sidney extends Horace's observation to Virgil's *Aeneid* as well. Remembrance of the adventures of Aeneas, Sidney declares, surpasses representative philosophers in illuminating all the diverse conditions and vicissitudes of life, even within the "inward self," and in "outer government" (*Prose* 98). Insofar as the *Arcadias* themselves have comparable aims, they should be considered in relation to the contemporary norms of Homeric and Virgilian reception that privileged the values of allegorical content, and to the thematic, structural, and expressive codes and conventions of heroic allegorism.[37]

Even though Sidney's and Spenser's treatments of the heroic poem differ greatly, with Spenser opting for an extravagantly Italian romantic-epic model, and Sidney for a more strikingly distinctive and "naturalistic" synthesis of Heliodoran, pastorally romantic, chivalric, and epic materials, their creative enterprises are much more congruent than previously assumed. Both were committed to producing heroic poems, especially, in Sidney's case, in his revisions. Although Sidney has been radically differentiated from Spenser, in this century, as an exponent of "exemplary imitation" averse to allegory, both were also committed to heroic allegorism. Further research can extend our knowledge of the structure and content of Arcadian allegories, and begin defining the particular characteristics of Sidney's own allegorical poetic and technique, in relation to other sixteenth-century allegorists such as Ariosto, Tasso, and Spenser. Now requiring broad reassessment, the *Arcadias* feature language, for example, that densely expresses various literal and allegorical meanings at once, and thus involves much allusion and wordplay. Abraham Fraunce was very close to the Sidneys, and his *Arcadian Rhetorike* features not Spenser but Sidney as his exemplar of allegory and continued irony, which he associates with allegory. Yet Fraunce had already seen substantial portions of *The Faerie Queene* in manuscript. Moreover, Fraunce's writings dedicated to the poet's siblings shortly after Sir Philip's death indicate that the Sidney circle had a deep and abiding commitment to esoteric symbolic lore, allegorical mythography, and literary allegorism. Fraunce's *Third Part of the Countesse of Pembrokes Yvychurch, Entituled, Amintas Dale,* dedicated to Sidney's sister, commemorates the death of the poet himself, as Amintas. In this volume, Fraunce advocates a traditional allegorical poetic and mythography in which stories of the "exploites of renowmed *Heroes*" disclose, to discerning capacities, an inner "morall sence" and "hidden mysteries of naturall, . . . or divine and metaphysicall philosophie." If Sidney had based his literary career on abjuring such notions, as most Sidneians have assumed in this century, Fraunce, who knew the Sidneys well, and was highly indebted to them, would not likely have chosen to provide the poet with a textual memorial advocating contrary principles; to dedicate it specifically to Sidney's sister and literary collaborator, who edited the 1593 composite *Arcadia;* and to link Sidney with allegory in the *Arcadian Rhetorike*. Instead, Fraunce sought to provide a literary commemoration that would support and promote Sidney's major advancement of allegorical poetics.[38]

The conventional "Spenser-Milton" line of "visionary epic" in English literary history should be expanded into a "Sidney-Spenser-Milton" line: within England, Sidney introduced many of its most fundamental techniques and features, such as the characteristic emphasis on heroic development through intensive trial of personal capacities, and the use of epic action to reflect inner conflict, so that epic becomes, in effect, internalized. Since Spenserians have long been researching the conventions of allegorical epic, much can be learned about the *Arcadias* from Spenser studies. That would in turn further elucidate *The Faerie Queene* by helping to define Spenser's particular selection and treatment of generic options in comparison and contrast with Sidney's.

McGill University

Notes

1. This essay amplifies a paper I delivered in a Sidney session at Kalamazoo in May 1995. I am thankful to that audience, and especially to Gerry Rubio and Thomas Roche, for encouragement. Anne Lake Prescott was both respondent for the paper and an evaluator of this essay, and her comments were invaluable. Cf. Greenlaw, in *Anniversary Papers by Colleagues and Pupils of George Lyman Kittredge* (Boston: Ginn, 327–37. There are basically three Arcadian texts: (1) the *Old Arcadia,* the only completed version; (2) Sidney's incomplete revision published in 1590, after his death, and breaking off just before the capture of Cecropia's castle (commonly now called the *New Arcadia*); (3) the composite *Arcadia* published in 1593, which adds Books III and V of the first version, with some authorial and other revisions, to the second. I leave the latter text aside: exploring the interpretive problem of the narrative splice is not a priority here.

2. Myrick, *Sir Philip Sidney as a Literary Craftsman* (Cambridge, Mass.: Harvard University Press, 1935); Zandvoort, *Sidney's "Arcadia": A Comparison between the Two Versions* (Amsterdam: Swets and Zeitlinger, 1929), 121–35; Robertson, "Sidney, Philip," in *The Spenser Encyclopedia,* ed. A. C. Hamilton et al. (Toronto: University of Toronto Press, 1990), 656–67; Heninger, *Sidney and Spenser: The Poet as Maker* University Park, Penn.: Pennsylvania State University Press, 1989); Patterson, *Censorship and Interpretation: The Conditions of Writing and Reading in Early Modern England* (Madison: University of Wisconsin Press, 1984), 33.

3. Spingarn, *A History of Literary Criticism in the Renaissance,* rev. ed. (New York, 1908; rpt. New York: Columbia University Press, 1930), 276; Spingarn, "Introduction," in Spingarn, ed., vol. 1 of *Critical Essays of the Seventeenth Century* (Oxford: Clarendon Press, 1908), xviii; Clark, *Rhetoric and Poetry in the Renaissance* (New York: Columbia University Press, 1922), part two, ch. 4, quoting 148; Zandvoort, 123n1; Myrick, chs. 6–7, quoting 241–43. Shepherd, ed., *An Apology for Poetry* (London: Nelson, 1965), 75. Van Dorsten and Duncan Jones, eds., *Defence of Poetry,* in *Miscellaneous Prose of Sir Philip Sidney* (Oxford: Clarendon Press, 1973), 63n1, 202. I cite the *Defence* from this latter edition, hereafter cited parenthetically within my text as *Prose.*

4. Quintilian, VIII.vi.52; trans. H. E. Butler. I cite this and all subsequent classical texts from the Loeb edition. On the convergence or symbiosis of exemplary imitation and allegory, see O. B. Hardison, Jr., *The Enduring Monument: A Study of the Idea of Praise in Renaissance Literary Theory and Practice* (Chapel Hill: University of North Carolina Press, 1962), 54–67; Baxter Hathaway, *The Age of Criticism: The Late Renaissance in Italy* (Ithaca, N.Y.: Cornell University Press, 1962), ch. 9; and William Nelson, *The Poetry of Edmund Spenser* (New York: Columbia University Press, 1963), 129–30. Means of conveying didactic expression in general tended to be assimilated to allegory.

5. Myrick, 206–07; emphasis mine. On Aristotle's pseudo-Aristotelian literary role in the Renaissance, cf. Bernard Weinberg, "From Aristotle to Pseudo-Aristotle," in Elder Olson, ed., *Aristotle's "Poetics" and English Literature: A Collection of Critical Essays* (Chicago: University of Chicago Press, 1965), 192–200; and his *A History of Literary Criticism in the Italian Renaissance,* 2 vols. (Chicago: University of

Chicago Press, 1961). Paul R. Sellin shows that late sixteenth-century literary criticism actually depended on a very broad mix of classical and late-classical authorities in "Sources of Julius Caesar Scaliger's *Poetices libri septem* as a Guide to Renaissance Poetics," in *Acta Scaligeriana* (Agen: Societé Academique d'Agen, 1986), 75–86. On Tasso's neo-Aristotelian allegorism, cf. Mindele Anne Treip, *Allegorical Poetics and the Epic: : The Renaissance Tradition to "Paradise Lost"* (Lexington, KY.: University of Kentucky Press, 1994), chs. 5–7. On assimilation of allegory to Aristotelian poetics, see, e.g., Hathaway, *Marvels and Commonplaces: Renaissance Literary Criticism* (New York: Random House, 1968), 49, 57, 106.Cf. also Lawrence C. Wolfley, "Sidney's Visual-Didactic Poetic: Some Complexities and Limitations," *Journal of Medieval and Renaissance Studies*, 6 (1976): 221; in Sidney's theory of imitation, by contrast with Aristotle's, "life and art" are both an "ongoing, transcendent allegory." On Renaissance Horatian allegorism, cf. Weinberg, *Italian Renaissance*, I, 101, 109.

6. On fables as traditional exemplars of literary inventions that are figuratively estimable, see Philip Rollinson, *Classical Theories of Allegory and Christian Culture* (Pittsburgh: Duquesne University Press, 1980), ch. 2. Sidney's allegoresis of the Orpheus and Amphion myths here derives from Horace, *Ars Poetica*, ll. 391–96. Compare Landino on veiled literary meaning: when poetry "most appears to be narrating something most humble and ignoble or to be singing a little fable to delight idle ears, at that very time it is writing in a rather secret way the most excellent things of all." *Opera Horatii cum Commentario* (Florence, 1482), p. clvii; cit., trans. Weinberg, *Italian Renaissance*, I, 80.

7. Compare Chapman, introducing his translation of the *Odyssey*: "Nor is this all-comprising Poesie phantastique, or meere fictive, but the most material and doctrinall illations of Truth. . . . To illustrate both . . . ,the Poet creates both a Bodie and a Soule in them—wherein, if the Bodie (being the letter, or historie) seems fictive and beyond Possibilitie to bring into Act, the sence then and Allegorie (which is the Soule) is to be sought—which intends a more eminent expressure of Vertue . . . and of Vice," beyond what "any Art within life can possibly delineate." "To the Earle of Somerset" in *Chapman's Homer*, ed. Allardyce Nicoll, 2 vols. (London: Routledge and Kegan Paul, 1967), II, 5. On the *Defence* as an allegorical rather than exemplarist poetic, cf. D. M. Beach, "The Poetry of Idea: Sir Philip Sidney and the Theory of Allegory," *Texas Studies in Literature and Language*, 13 (1971–72): 365–89; Edward A. Bloom, "The Allegorical Principle," *ELH*, 18 (1951): 163–90; A. Leigh Deneef, "Rereading Sidney's *Apology*," *Journal of Medieval and Renaissance Studies*, 10 (1980): 175; M. J. Doherty, *The Mistress-Knowledge: Sir Philip Sidney's "Defence of Poesie" and Literary Architectonics in the English Renaissance* (Nashville, Tenn.: Vanderbilt University Press, 1991), 252; Margaret Ferguson, *Trials of Desire: Renaissance Defenses of Poetry* (New Haven: Yale University Press, 1983); Maureen Quilligan, *Milton's Spenser: The Politics of Reading* (Ithaca, N.Y.: Cornell University Press, 1983), 31–37; Treip, 45–47; Wolfley: 221.

8. In Sidney's own practice, he himself shields controversial meaning with purposefully oblique discourse, as when, for example, he uses myth to allegorize topical ecclesiastical satire in the poem to Mira, "Now Was Our Heav'nly Vaulte Deprived of the Light." William A. Ringler, Jr., ed., *The Poems of Sir Philip Sidney* (Oxford: Clarendon Press, 1962), pp. 119–20.

9. Temple, *William Temple's "Analysis" of Sir Philip Sidney's "Apology for Poetry,"* ed., trans. John Webster (Binghamton, N. Y.: Medieval and Renaissance Texts and Studies, 1984), 138–39. Treip, Index, s.v. "Allegory," "total or global."

10. The only substantial prior investigations of Sidney's Arcadian allegorism are Franco Marenco's. Cf. *Arcadia Puritana: L'uso della tradizione nella prima Arcadia di Sir Philip Sidney* (Bari: Adriatica Editrice, 1968); "Per una nuova interpretazione dell' *Arcadia* di Sidney," *English Miscellany,* 17 (1966): 9–48; and "Double Plot in Sidney's Old 'Arcadia,' " *Modern Language Review,* 64 (1969): 248–63. In *Arcadia Puritana,* Marenco claims the *Old Arcadia* is a severe Calvinist allegory addressing pagan deviation from the four cardinal virtues and condemning Renaissance literary genres. Alan D. Isler accepts Greenlaw's misleading equation of Sidneian "allegory" with exemplary fiction, and thus reduces allegory to the latter, in "Heroic Poetry and Sidney's Two *Arcadias,*" *PMLA* 83 (1968): 368–79; and "The Allegory of the Hero and Sidney's Two *Arcadias,*" *Studies in Philology,* 65 (1968): 171–91. Though defining the content of the *Arcadias* in a way that implies presence of intricate philosophico-religious allegory, Walter Davis only mentions the mode incidentally, so that its relevance remains obscure, in *A Map of Arcadia: Sidney's Romance in Its Tradition* (New Haven: Yale University Press, 1965). Nancy Lindheim's *The Structures of Sidney's 'Arcadia''* (Toronto: University of Toronto Press, 1982) at least allows for the existence of Arcadian allegory (pp. 56, 62, 91, 151–52, 199n12). On pastoral "as a species of allegory" in the Renaissance, cf. Barbara Kiefer Lewalski, *"Paradise Lost" and the Rhetoric of Literary Forms* (Princeton, N.J.: Princeton University Press, 1985), 173, 201, 342n32; and Giovanni Antonio Viperano, Poetry, trans. Philip Rollinson (Cambridge: James Clark, 1987), pp. 71–73, 145–52. C. S. Lewis differently applies the term "Arcadian Epic" to the 1593 composite text, in *English Literature in the Sixteenth Century Excluding Drama* (Oxford: Clarendon Press, 1954), 355.

11. Hamilton, *Sir Philip Sidney: A Study of His Life and Works* (Cambridge: Cambridge University Press, 1977), 49–50. Quoting Tasso, *Discourses on the Heroic Poem (Discorsi del poema eroico),* trans. Mariella Cavalchini and Irene Samuel (Oxford: Clarendon Press, 1973), pp. 47–48. *The Old Arcadia,* ed. Jean Robertson (Oxford: Clarendon Press, 1973), 203, 122, 232, 325, 357; subsequently cited within my text and notes as *OA. The Countess of Pembroke's Arcadia (The New Arcadia),* ed. Victor Skretkowicz (Oxford: Clarendon Pres, 1987), 179, 152, 402; subsequently cited within my text and notes as *NA.* Most Sidneians find the *Arcadias* broadly akin to the romantic epics of Ariosto, Tasso, and Spenser. Cf. Isler, "Heroic Poetry": 368–79; and Robert W. Parker, "Terentian Structure and Sidney's Original *Arcadia,*" *English Literary Renaissance,* 2 (1972): 61–78. For an overview of Arcadian generic issues, see Michael McCanles, *The Text of Sidney's Arcadian World* (Durham, N. C.: Duke University Press, 1989), Index, s.v. "Genre."

12. On Sidney's emblematic interests and composition of *imprese,* see, e.g., Katherine Duncan-Jones, "Sidney's Personal *Imprese,*" *Journal of the Warburg and Courtauld Institutes,* 33 (1970): 321–24; and Norman K. Farmer, Jr., *Poets and the Visual Arts in Renaissance England* (Austin, Texas: University of Texas Press, 1984), ch. 1. On the Virgilian paradigm of developmental moral-psychological allegory in Renaissance heroic poetry, cf. Treip, Index, s.v. "Virgil."

13. For discussion of such wordplay in Tasso, Spenser, and Milton in relation to the characteristics of epic and allegory, see Kenneth Borris, " Union of Mind, Or

in Both One Soul': Allegories of Adam and Eve in *Paradise Lost,"* in *Milton Studies,* 31 (1995): 54–64.

14. Lindheim, 199*n*12; I reached the same conclusion independently.

15. Cf.Tasso, "The Allegorie of the Poem," in *Godfrey of Bulloigne,* ed. Kathleen M. Lea and T. M. Gang, trans. Edward Fairfax (Oxford: Clarendon Press, 1981), 89–92; and Borris, 54–56. Quoting Spenser from *The Faerie Queene,* ed. A. C. Hamilton (London: Longman, 1977).

16. Though some have noticed that the attacks of the beasts and rebels have figurative implications, such discussion has been very cursory, and all, except for Marenco, avoid using the term "allegory," so as not to challenge the dominant exemplarist theory. Cf. Davis, 152; Hamilton, *Sidney,* 51–55; Richard Lanham, *The Old Arcadia* (New Haven: Yale University Press, 1965), 208, 215–216; Jon Lawry, *Sidney's Two "Arcadias": Pattern and Proceeding* (Ithaca, N.Y.: Cornell University Press, 1972), 57–58; Marenco, "Double Plot": 248–63; and Andrew D. Weiner, *Sir Philip Sidney and the Poetics of Protestantism: A Study of Contexts* (Mineapolis, Minn.: University of Minnesota, 1978), 74–75, 156, 160–64.

17. Spenser's allegory of Lust works similarly, in *The Fearie Queene,* Book IV. Lust himself never makes love to Aemylia, but only to a hag who substitutes for her in the act, so that Lust is always debarred from "knowledge," as it were, of Aemylia's representative person.

18. These and other significant alterations of the original plot appear in the latter part of the *Old Arcadia* that was incorporated in the composite *Arcadia* published in 1593. On their Sidneian provenance, see Ringler, ed., *Poems,* 375–78; and Robertson, ed., *OA* lx–lxii.

19. On bestiality as the opposite of heroic or superhuman goodness, see Aristotle, *Nicomachean Ethics,* VII.i.1–3. Compare Philippe de Mornay: ". . . man doth covertly carie in his breast all maner of Beasts, the which it behoveth him to kill in himselfe, according to this saying of the Platonists, That the readiest way to returne unto God, and consequently to a mans first nature, is to kill his owne affections." *A Woorke Concerning the Trewnesse of the Christian Religion,* trans. Sir Philip Sidney (?) and Arthur Golding (London, 1587; facs. rpt. Delmar, N. Y.: Scholars' Facsimiles, 1976), 318. Cf. Sir Thomas Elyot, *Of the Knowledge which Maketh a Wise Man,* ed. Edwin Johnston Howard (Oxford, Ohio: Anchor, 1946), 64–65; Erasmus, *Enchiridion,* trans. Charles Fantazzi, in *Spiritualia,* ed. John W. O'Malley, vol. 66 of *Collected Works* (Toronto: University of Toronto Press, 1988), 50; Carlos G. Noreña, *Juan Luis Vives and the Emotions* (Carbondale, Ill.: Southern Illinois University Press, 1989), 214; Marcello Palingenio, *The Zodiake of Life,* trans. Barnaby Googe (London, 1576; facs. rpt. New York: Scholars' Facsimiles, 1947), 143–44; and John Woolton, *A Treatise of the Immortalitie of the Soul* (London, 1576), 32ᵃ–32ᵇ.

20. Without discussing the correspondences between Sidney's rebels and Plato's *Republic,* Davis and Lawry trace other relations between the *Arcadias* and that Platonic text.

21. 431B, 436B–7D, 571C–3A; trans. Paul Shorey. Compare 439D: a "companion of various repletions and pleasures," the "irrational and appetitive" part of the soul is that which "loves, hungers, thirsts, and feels the flutter and titillation of other desires." For economy, I provide subsequent references within my text, do not

cite Shorey hereafter, and dispense with dialogic quotation marks for Socrates or his perspectives.

22.   *Timaeus* 70E–71A; trans. R. G. Bury.

23.   Compare Pausanias on Arcadia, *Description of Greece,* VII.xxv.12–13: "Those who have thought that Enispe, Stratia, and Rhipe, mentioned by Homer, were once inhabited islands in the Ladon, cherish . . . a false belief. For the Ladon could never show islands even as large as a ferry-boat" (trans. W. H. S. Jones).

24.   Bryskett, *Discourse of Civill Life,* in *Literary Works,* ed. J. H. P. Pafford (Farnborough: Gregg, 1972), 206–07; a text mostly translated from treatises on moral philosophy by Giraldi and Piccolomini. Bryskett was one of Sidney's companions on his grand tour in 1572–74.

25.   Dametas' heart, e.g., is "never . . . without a passion," and when Musidorus disposes of Miso in the *Old Arcadia* by inventing a tale of her husband's infidelity, she almost comes to personify certain passions like Spenser's Malbecco, who becomes Jealousy: "in the very anatomy of her spirits one should have found nothing but devilish disdain and hateful jealousy" (*OA* 53, 189–93, 269–70).

26.   Colonna, *Hypnerotomachia Poliphili,* ed. Giovanni Pozzi and Lucia A. Ciapponi, 2 vols. (Padua: Editrice Antenore, 1980), I,67–72; Anne Lake Prescott advised me of this correspondence. On the *topoi,* see Frank Kermode, "The Banquet of Sense," *Bulletin of the John Rylands Library* 44 (1961–62): 68–99. Analogous allegories include Spenser's *Faerie Queene* II and Milton's *Comus.* Compare Elyot's strictures on sensory indulgence in *Wise Man:* "if manne do forgette to sette Wyll under . . . rayson," "the senses do prepare them selfes eftsones to rebell," with "craftye perswasions." "And affectes whiche *as wanton girles be flexible . . . , do prepare them with wanton countenaunce and pleasaunt promyses* to allure eftesones Wille to their appetite: whereby the soule shalbe ageyn in daunger to perysshe. . . ." The mind must rationally scutinize "inclynations . . . conceyved in the sences" however apparently pleasant, or else the soul "being abandoned of understanding, loseth hir dignite, and *becomith ministre unto the sences / which before were her slaves"* (129–30, 118–20; emphasis mine). Allegories of Sidney's period are often exploratory narrative developments of the moralists' and psychologists' figures of speech. Cf. Thomas Rogers, *The Anatomie of the Minde* (London, 1576), 5ᵃ–7ᵇ; Pierre de la Primaudaye, *The French Academie,* trans. T. Bowes, R. Dolman, and W. P. (London, 1618), 417; and Pierre Charron, *Of Wisedome,* trans. S. Lennard (London, 1608), 72–73.

27.   Tasso, "Allegoria," 90; trans. Fairfax.

28.   Charron, 268, emphasis mine; trans. Lennard. Compare Cecropia's bat-like rejection of truth to Mornay, 27: in the soul, "evil . . . is a kind of darknesse, for want of looking up to the light of the sovereyne mynde which should inlighten it; and through suffering it selfe too bee caried too much away to the materiall things which are nothing" (trans. Sidney? and Golding). See also *NA* 423.

29.   Bryskett, *Discourse,* 164, 221.

30.   Cf., e.g., Pausanias on Arcadia VIII.2. Mornay discusses Cecrops, 412.

31.   Cf. Roland Mushat Frye, *Milton's Imagery and the Visual Arts: Iconographic Tradition in the Epic Poems* (Princeton, N.J.: Princeton University Press, 1978), 102–05, 118–22 (quoting 104). Davis differently explicates the Christian implications of Sidney's captivity sequence, 73–83.

32. Compare Genesis 3:14–15: "God said to the serpent, Because thou hast done this, thou art cursed . . . above everie beast of the field: . . . dust shalt thou eat" and "thine head" shall "breake." In kissing the ground, as Sidney ironically puts it, due to her terrible fall, Cecropia, with her serpentine affinities, suffers a similar kiss-off, and she is the main exponent of evil in the *New Arcadia. The Geneva Bible,* introd. Lloyd E. Berry (Geneva, 1560; facs. rpt. Madison, WIS.: University of Wisconsin Press, 1969.

33. La Primaudaye, 12–13; trans. Bowes. Ficino, *Commentary on Plato's "Symposium" on Love,* trans. Sears Jayne, 2nd, rev. ed. (Dallas, Tex.: Spring Publications, 1985), 76. Cf. Mornay, citing Seneca: "these bones, these sinewes, this coate of skin, this face . . . , are fetters and prisons of the Soule. By them the Soule is overwhelmed, beaten downe, and chased away. It hath not a greater battell than with that masse of flesh" (268; trans. Sidney? and Golding). Also pp. 309–10, citing Plato. For such allegorization of the *Aeneid,* cf. Landino's commentary, as in the translation of Thomas H. Stahel, S. J., "Cristoforo Landino's Allegorization of the *Aeneid:* Books III and IV of the *Camaldolese Disputations* (Ph.D. diss., Johns Hopkins University, 1968), 198–205.

34. Tasso, "Allegoria," 89–90; trans. Fairfax.

35. La Primaudaye, 14–15; trans. Bowes. The proleptic implications of Cecropia's fate, relative to the continuing threat of Plexirtus, are comparable to the relation of Spenser's progressive Elfin Chronicles to the continuing struggle expressed in Briton Moniments, in *The Faerie Queene.*

36. Or as Lindheim puts it, "Sidney created characters to serve thematic ends," yet they "yield complex psychological insights that transcend and complicate the purely schematic factors in their conception" (62).

37. For Horace's famous dictum on Homer, a main basis for pedagogical valuation of literature and thus for allegorical poetics in the Renaissance, cf. *Epistles,* I.ii.

38. Fraunce, *The Arcadian Rhetorike,* ed. Ethel Seaton (Oxford: Luttrell-Blackwell, 1950), 10–12, 20–21. Cf. Fraunce's *Insignium, Armorum, Emblematum, Hieroglyphicorum et Symbolorum Explicatio* (London, 1588); and *The Third Part of the Countesse of Pembrokes Yvychurch* (London, 1592), quoting sig. B1ᵃ.

STEPHEN M. BUHLER

Pre-Christian Apologetics in Spenser and Sidney: Pagan Philosophy and the Process of *Metanoia*

One problem tackled by Spenser and Sidney was how to convince members of a Reformed Church that moral reformation is an on-going process. Drawing upon a strategy at work in Mornay's *De la Vérité de la religion chréstienne,* both use pagan systems of thought–notably Epicureanism—to point out where Christian piety needs to be reformed and disciplined further. The figures of the Atheist and the Epicure can serve as indirect representations of those aspects of the Christian which remain unregenerate. In Book III of the *New Arcadia,* Cecropia's calculating skepticism finds expression in cruel and treacherous behavior; readers are asked to consider what "creed" their own conduct figures forth. In Book II of *The Faerie Queene,* Guyon's encounter with Amavia and his celebrated swoon combine to dramatize how attitudes toward the divine translate into action either compassionate or callous. Sidney's formulation of the poet's objective as helping the reader in "well doing" and "well knowing" is realized in his and Spenser's practice of exploring the interrelation between action and doctrine. Pre-Christian apologetics could enable Reformed readers both to consider their own "falles" at an aesthetic distance and to bridge that distance by recognizing aspects of the Self in a supposedly absolute Other.

IN HER STUDY of Spenserian philosophy, *Plato Baptized,* Elizabeth Bieman distinguishes between what she terms the participatory and the dichotomizing modes of mimesis inscribed within metaphor and metonymy. Drawing upon the work of historian Karl E. Morrison, she applies the distinction to anxieties at work within the culture of the Reformed Church over understanding and representation of the sacred:

> Metaphors are unavoidable in religious texts, but doctrinal inter-preters find metaphors embarrassing. They attempt to settle the questions metaphors raise, to tame their unpredictability, by imposing explanations on them in narrow and incontrovertible codes. Limits must be established—right thinkers must always be separated from wrong thinkers, the sheep from the goats.[1]

Bieman sees Edmund Spenser, and Sir Philip Sidney to a lesser extent, as energetically negotiating between the metaphoric and metonymic, with each poet endeavoring to rediscover the participatory metaphor latent even within a dichotomizing parable or metonymic gloss. Spenser's reluctance to separate definitively the sheep from the goats in his fictions, however, is shared by Sidney to a far greater degree than Bieman suggests, and this reluctance shows itself most clearly in a didactic strategy employed by other writers within the Reformed Church.

While the parable of the sheep and the goats (Matthew 25:31–46) can strongly reinforce a sense of dichotomizing in Christianity, other parables undermine one's sense of being a redeemed Self in opposi-tion to a reprobate Other: as one example among many, the story of the Good Samaritan (Luke 10:30–37 retains its power—too often latent, it must be observed—to upset comfortable notions of who is worthy or unworthy; of who exhibits signs of grace or not; of who, most distressingly, are *we*? The story reconfigures relations of identity in, to use Bieman's terminology, metaphoric ways, establishing inten-tionally shocking correspondences between the familiar and the alien. Both parables, however, provide answers to the question of identity, of how one understands and represents oneself as a follower of Christ, in action. Marked by poverty, disease, imprisonment, and foreign-ness, the Other is nonetheless treated by the sheep in Matthew 25 with compassion; the goats respond with indifference. In this parable, the teller not only claims identity with the Other but encourages his followers to do the same: the regenerate Self is dependent upon an active, participatory identity. While the alien Samaritan in his compassion represents one's better self, characters more familiar to the parable's original audience figure forth the estrangement which threatens persistently to come between the professedly devout and their God. But who has ears to hear, over and over, the news of that estrangement and the call to regenerative action, especially when one is in church, and in the Church? Once one has painfully and sincerely repented, can one readily accept that *metanoia* — repentance — is not once and for all, but for all one's earthly existence?

One problem faced by the authors of both *The Faerie Queene* and the *New Arcadia* is how to convince members of a Reformed Church that moral reformation is an on-going process — "not without dust and heat," as that famous reader and misreader of these texts, John Milton, would put it. The dilemma is engagingly captured in a letter evaluating Martin Bucer's attempts to establish a strong conviction of a need for that process in the hearts and minds of his new students at Cambridge:

> Dr. Bucer incessantly clamors that we repent, that we give up the depraved customs of hypocritical religion, that we correct the abuses of feast days, that we more frequently give and hear sermons, that we apply some kind of discipline. He impresses on us many things of this kind *ad nauseum.*[2]

We can see, in this visceral response of one Cambridge student, Thomas Horton, the special nature of the challenge taken up by several individuals associated with the Sidney circle: how to impress upon readers specific instructions and general convictions about godly discipline without inspiring this kind of denial, this kind of nausea.

Both *The Faerie Queene* and *The New Arcadia* strategically employ pagan philosophy to achieve these goals; their approach to the problem constitutes, in effect, "pre-Christian apologetics." These works have often been studied in the context of the period's apologetics and also in the context of the apologetic use of the *prisca theologia;* the late D. P. Walker examined the *Arcadia* in this light[3] and Bieman has extended many of Walker's insights in addressing Spenser's oeuvre. But I would like to focus upon the use of yet more palpably pagan literature and lore to address what Sidney's friend, Philippe de Mornay, calls "the falles of the vertuous": that is, the unregenerate actions (and lack of action) of the regenerate, indeed of the saved.[4] Andrew Weiner, in his examination of Sidney and "the Poetics of Protestantism," notes the importance of the concept of ongoing repentence in the Reformed Church as these men understood it; citing the *Second Helvetic Confession,* Weiner suggests that "at the heart of the Reformed Protestant's notion about what makes a life 'holy' is the perhaps paradoxical formulation that the godly life is one of 'daiely' repentance."[5] Weiner's subsequent discussions of the *Defence of Poesie* and *The Old Arcadia,* though, focus more on Sidneyan *energeia* than *suasio.*

In the *Defence,* Sidney himself raises the issue of persuasion but does not stay for an answer. Instead he rushes on to consider how poets or teachers of any sort can change the behavior of their "students":

For who will be taught, if he be not moved with desire to be taught? And what so much good doth that teaching bring forth (I speak still of moral doctrine) as that it moveth one to do that which it doth teach? For, as Aristotle saith, it is not *gnosis* but *praxis* must be the fruit. And how *praxis* can be, without being moved to practise, it is no hard matter to consider.[6]

In similar fashion there are, in both *Arcadias,* several occasions in which the reader is meant to be moved toward virtue and away from vice, as Weiner argues; but it is not always clear how the reader is to be persuaded that he or she personally needs to be so moved. A partial answer can be found if we reexamine the emphases in Sidney's insistence that the poet must move the reader toward "the end of well doing and not of well knowing only."[7] It is in the manner of teaching — *how* one leads the reader to know well — that one might best succeed in motivating the reader to do well. Mornay, Sidney, and Spenser, despite the differences between prose tractates, prose fictions, and epic romances, do share in their works similar didactic and apologetic strategies which employ a pagan setting the better to comment upon Christian misdeeds and inactivity.

This tactic is implicitly stated at the outset of Mornay's *De la vérité de la religion chréstienne,* which was translated into English by the indefatigable Arthur Golding, at the behest (and perhaps with the assistance) of Sidney himself.[8] The title of the English translation is: *A woorke concerning the trewnesse of the Christian Religion, written in French: Against Atheists, Epicures, Paynims, Jewes, Mahumetists, and other Infidels.* One might reasonably wonder how effective this — or most other works in apologetics — might be in defending the faith or in persuading unbelievers to believe. But Mornay is less concerned with the unfaithful than with those within the faith who, in one way or another, are guilty of participation in the forms of infidelity represented by the targets of the title. In his "Preface to the Reader,"

Mornay seeks to involve the reader in recognizing the need for ongoing reformation and also seeks to establish pagan (and other) creeds and mores as a mirror in which Christians might see their own "falles." He asks the reader to consider

> how great either coldness in the things which they ought to follow most wholly, or doubting in the things which they ought to believe most steadfastly, he findeth even in those which professeth the Christian godliness . . . [this is] why I have taken this worke in hand, more needfull now adaies—yea even (which I am ashamed to saie) among those which beare the name of Christians than ever it was among the verie Heathen and Infidels.[9]

Operating on the principle of "by their fruits, ye shall know them," Mornay proceeds to demonstrate specifically how atheism and Epicureanism are evident in the conduct of so-called Christians: the first in "bemiring" God-given reason "in the filthie and beastlie pleasures of the world"; the second in "never alledging or pretending honestie or conscience, but to their owne profit."

The terms of the distinction Mornay draws between the Atheist and the Epicure may seem surprising; after all, we tend — rather inaccurately — to associate Epicurus with hedonism, and also to tend — with more justice — *not* to associate it with the self-serving duplicity of the Machiavel. But Mornay and Sidney both participate in the fairly widespread Renaissance conflation of Epicureanism with Machiavellianism, and I will return to the reasons for that conflation and to Sidney's fictional embodiment of it in the character of Cecropia. First, though, I want to stress what use is made of these systems of thought: they serve as ways of increasing the conviction of the need for reform within Christianity and within the Christian reader. The historical Epicurean, as well as the perennial atheist, cannot easily be accommodated to Christian belief. Epicureanism seemed impious to many pagans; it occupied a place well on the margins of the classical philosophic heritage. But the terms of impiety, such as those found in or attributed to atheism and Epicureanism, are used here to point out where Christian piety needs to be reformed, improved, disciplined. As Mornay suggests, this reformation needs to concentrate on both action (what Christians "ought to follow") and doctrine (what they "ought to believe"); Sidney's poetic objectives of "well doing" and "well knowing" similarly note that reformation has to concentrate on how action and doctrine are interrelated.

The figures of the Atheist and the Epicure can serve, then, as indirect representations of those aspects of the reformed Christian which remain unregenerate. They are, in both Mornay and Sidney, attempts at beginning the process by which the reader is convinced that reformation — including reform of manners as well as of creed — must continue, even within himself or herself. Such a strategy does, admittedly, have its pitfalls; any rhetorical maneuver which depends upon a recognition of the Self in the supposedly absolute Other is risky indeed. But it is, I believe, a way in which writers hope to stave off the reaction voiced by the Cambridge student, the dis-ease which marks the denial of one's own "naturall corruption," to use the term found in the *Helvetic Confession.* The tactic is intended to prevent the common refusal to accept that one's will, as Sidney argues in the *Defence,* remains infected.[10]

One symptom of infection, according to Mornay and Sidney, is what they term "Epicureanism." The association, already seen in Mornay's preface, between the Epicure and the Machiavel found some justification in the authentic Epicurean attitude toward religious ceremony. The ancient writer Philodemus had ascribed the following admonition to Epicurus:

> Let us at least sacrifice piously and rightly where it is customary, and let us do all things rightly according to the laws not troubling ourselves with common beliefs in what concerns the noblest and holiest of things.[11]

This teaching reflects the Epicurean belief that while religious ceremonies can have no effect on the gods, they can have either a good or a bad effect on the participants. Eschewing common beliefs, and certain that the gods do not respond to rites or prayers, the Epicurean sage can still observe religious ceremonies if he uses the occasion to emulate, inwardly, the true nature of the gods.

Such duplicity in a sphere as vital and — it was held — as dependent upon public testimony as religion shocked commentators through the ages and particularly shocked reform-minded Christians in the sixteenth century. This might help to explain Mornay's *animus* against Epicurus, as it appears in the passage which answers Epicurean objections to the idea of Providence:

> Let us see what things wickednes can alledge against so manifest a doctrine. First of all steppes me foorth *Epicurus,* and denyeth

that he sees any providence at all in the world, but thinks to marke many things to the contrarie in the whole world; whereby he will needs gather that there is no providence, no nor (if he durst say it) any God at al.[12]

The suspicion toward any false dealing in matters of religion is clear in Mornay's aside "(if he durst say it)," but we need to recall that his immediate concern is not toward those who consciously conceal skeptical or heterodox opinions. Mornay's primary audience consists of those who fail to realize and to acknowledge openly that such opinions are made manifest in their own actions. Through the strategy of pre-Christian apologetics, Mornay and Sidney can deal with more than the "two types of religious skeptics" which William R. Elton describes as constituting "a commonplace Renaissance convention." In his consideration of the *Arcadia,* Elton presents Cecropia not as "the 'outward atheist,' who gives vent freely to his doubts," but as "the more terrible 'inward atheist,' or Machiavellian hypocrite."[13] More than this, though, Cecropia's actions and the course of action she advocates to Pamela—if recognized as similar to one's own behavior—can reveal unwitting atheism or Epicureanism to the reader.

Cecropia's name may itself be a dark echo of a classical tribute to Epicurean philosophy: the author of the *Ciris* recalls his training in a "Cecropian [i.e., Athenian] garden," and since it was believed in the Renaissance that the author was Virgil himself, it could also be thought that Virgil here is equating the Epicurean school of Siro with Epicurus' own Garden in Athens.[14] A more overt signal of the associations Sidney intends the reader to attach to the character can be seen in her attempts to undermine Pamela's "replies upon conscience." Cecropia announces her allegiance to Epicurean and Machiavellian attitudes, at least as they were conventionally understood, as she tries to persuade Pamela to wed her son, Amphialus, and to her way of thinking:

"Dear niece (or rather, dear daughter, if my affection and wish might prevail therein), how much doth it increase—trow you—the earnest desire I have of this blessed match, to see these virtues of yours knit fast with such zeal of devotion!—indeed the best bond which the most politic wits have found, to hold man's wit in well doing . . . so are these bugbears of opinions brought by great clerks into the world to serve as shewels [scarecrows] to keep them from those faults whereto else the vanity of the world and weakness of sense might pull them—but in you, niece, whose excellency is such as it need not to be held up by the staff of vulgar opinions, I would not you should love virtue servilely, for fear of I know not what which you see not, but even for the good effects of virtue which you see. . . . Be wise, and that wisdom shall be a god unto thee; be contented, and that is thy heaven; for else, to think that those powers—if there be any such—above are moved either by the eloquence of our prayers or in a chafe by the folly of our actions carries as much reason as if flies should think that men take great care which of them hums sweetest, and which of them flies nimblest."[15]

In this passage, Sidney spells out the theological bases which could motivate, justify, or excuse the behaviors which Mornay characterizes as "Epicurean": "to make short waie to the atteinement of goods or honour, [to] overreach and betraie othermen, selling their freends, their kinsfolke, yea and their own soules, & not sticking to do anie euill, that may serue their turne."[16]

In their distrust of Epicurean theology, Mornay and Sidney follow the lead of Cicero, who in his own consideration of the gods' condition, the *De natura deorum,* takes great pains to point out what he considers to be the inconsistencies and dangers of Epicurean theology. Cicero, through the character of Cotta, the Academic representative in the discussion, also expresses deep concern over Epicureanism's potentially ill effects upon society in general. In Cotta's view, teaching that the divine nature is free from concern ("*Nihil habet . . . negotii*") and that such godly detachment should be cultivated by humanity simply encourages sloth: "*etiam homines inertis efficit, si quidem agens aliquid ne deus quidem esse beatus potest*" ("it also makes men lazy, when not even a god can be happy if he is in any way active").[17] Worse still, the doctrine of the gods' lack of concern for humankind tends to denigrate the role of benevolence in human behavior. Since even solicitude on the part of the gods is seen as an obstacle to their perfect happainess, then solicitude on the part of humanity—concern for the good of the society or of the individuals that make up that society—must also be considered a flaw in Epicurus' view. As Cotta challenges his Epicurean interlocutor:

Vos autem quid mali datis cum in inbecillitate gratificationem
et benivolentiam ponitis! . . . ne homines quidem censetis nisi
inbecilli essent futuros beneficos et benignos fuisse?[18]
(As for you, what mischief you cause when you account kind-
ness and benevolence as weaknesses . . . do you think that even
human beneficence and benignity are grounded only in human infirmity?)

At this point the Epicurean ideal of ataraxy—of perfect detachment
and impassivity—is presented as contributing to inhumane cal-
lousness.[19]

Disregard of others is of central concern throughout Spenser's
Fearie Queene. Early in his "Introductory Letter" to Sir Walter Ralegh, Spenser announces that his intention is to "fashion" his readers
in "vertuous and gentle discipline," and his didactic approach is to
embody such virtues and gentility in the actions of his characters:
"So much more profitable and gratious is doctrine by ensample, then
by rule."[20] Beyond this, though, Spenser hopes that his readers will
also participate in the endless work of making the Word flesh in their
virtuous and gentle actions. We have here, if we recall the Reformed
culture in which Spenser played an active role, another approach to
the problem Bucer tackled of ongoing reformation, of continuous
metanoia, through discipline. Self-discipline certainly seems of prime
importance in Book II, the "Legend of Temperance," and the titular
hero of the Book, the "Knight of Temperance" Sir Guyon, has
impressed several readers as the most rigorously disciplined of all
Spenser's characters—so much so, that he has struck many of them
as rather a cold, uncaring fish indeed.[21] Guyon has, however, attracted
his share of defenders who argue against seeing him as smug and self-
consciously superior, and many of these readers point to his compassionate responses to Amavia in canto one.

I want to expand upon such an argument and suggest how necessary Guyon's compassion is to Spenser's didactic strategies in providing his readers with ethical lessons and also in showing them, as
Sidney does, the relation between right doctrine and right action.
Spenser is, in short, preaching to the semi-converted here, trying to
reform his readers by reminding them that compassion is at the heart
of all truly "religious reuerence." Moreover, that reverence is presented as being grounded in both *gnosis* and *praxis*: it is doctrinal and
practical, ideational and active. This reminder comes through most
strongly in related passages found at the end of canto one, which

describes the fate of Amavia, and the beginning of canto eight, which reacts to Guyon's celebrated swoon after he emerges from the Cave of Mammon. When these two passages have been considered in relation to each other, their connection with the Christian apologetics of the period—including the strategy which conflates the ethical and the theological, and argues for their interaction—has often been neglected.[22]

As we have seen, Mornay asks his readers to consider those who are guilty of "either coldness in the things which they ought to follow most wholly, or doubting in the things which they ought to believe most steadfastly."[23] Sidney, in the character of Cecropia, uses Epicurean skepticism toward the popular conception of the divine to investigate the effects of doubting; while Spenser also addresses that issue, he is more concerned with the effects of coldness and therefore focuses upon Epicurean ataraxy as a means for exploring Christian inaction. In both cases, the authors stress the interrelation between action and doctrine, between "well doing" and "well knowing."

The Christian faith, especially in its reformist mode, shares the authentically Epicurean distaste for misconceptions of the divine. But from the Christian perspective, Epicureanism is itself guilty of excess in its conception of God. In its avoidance of the superstitious, Epicurean thought denies any direct interaction between the divine and the human. A supremely sarcastic account of the Epicurean conception of the gods is provided by a writer Spenser deeply admired, Guillaume Du Bartas, in his *La Semaine ou Creation du monde*. Du Bartas considers the significance of God's resting on the seventh day, arguing that a God who does not, through His power and providence, remain deeply involved in the workings of His Creation is merely

une Divinité
Qui languisse là haute en morne oisiveté
Qui n'aime les vertus, qui ne punit les vices,
Un Dieu sourd à nos cris, aveugle à nos services,
Fay-neant, songe-creux, et bref, un Loir qui dort
D'un sommeil éternel, ou plustost un Dieu mort . . .
  Tu dormois Epicure encore plus que ton dieu,
Quand tu fantastiquois un léthargique au lieu
De la source de vie, ou, d'une ruse vaine
Des athées, fuyant non le crime, ains la peine,
Tu mettois en avant un Dieu tant imparfait
Pour l'avoeur de bouche et le nier de fait.

In Josuah Sylvester's widely-read translation, we are told of

> . . . an idle God
> That lusks in Heav'n and never lookes abroad,
> That crownes not Vertue, and corrects not Vice,
> Blind to our service, deafe unto our sighes;
> A Pagan Idol, void of power and pietie,
> A sleeping Dormouse (rather) a dead Deitie . . .
> Fond *Epicure,* thou rather slept'st thy selfe,
> When thou did'st forge thee such a sleepe-sicke Elfe
> For lifes pure Fount: or vainly fraudulent,
> (Not shunning th'*Atheists* sinne, but punishment)
> Imaginedst a God so perfect-lesse
> In works defying whom thy words professe.)[24]

While stressing the idleness and idolatry of such a conception of god, Sylvester misses some of Du Bartas' critique of Epicurean theology, although the final line returns to the central point. The vague term "service" may somewhat soften the Bartasian reference to the Epicurean attitude toward religious ceremony, but the emphasis on "works" over "words" indicates that not only religious services, but also actions in service of humankind perfect—in the sense of bring closer to fulfillment—one's profession of faith.

Many of the materials concerning the Epicurean theology present the questions of divine providence and human *pietas* as very closely related, and Spenser too ponders the questions and their interrelation. In canto one of Book II, there are recurring reflections on these issues and on their interconnection: from Amavia's resentment toward the "carelesse heauens," to Guyon's display of compassionate "ruth and fraile affection" and his somber confidence that "after death the tryall is to come" which determines one's eternal state. Guyon's response to Amavia's plight prepares us for the divine response to his helpless condition after he emerges from Mammon's cave. Amavia's death and Guyon's faint are parallel episodes combining to demonstrate Spenser's conviction that the heavens are not "carelesse" but actively compassionate, and that human beings should emulate that concern, should—as the parable of the Samaritan insists—go and do likewise.

Amavia's outcry, in fact, resembles Du Bartas' depiction of an Epicurean deity. She has been reunited with her beloved Mordant, who had been entrapped by Acrasia, only to lose him through one of the sorceress' deadly spells. In her anguish, Amavia decides the

celestial powers must indeed be indifferent to human suffering, and
may even derive some satisfaction at the difference between human
vulnerability to woe and their own tranquil condition:

> But if that carelesse heauens (quoth she) despite
>   The doome of just revenge, and take delight
>   To see sad pageants of mens miseries,
>   As bound by them to liue in liues despight,
>   Yet can they not warne death from wretched wight.
>   Come then, come soone, come sweetest death to mee,
>   And take away this long lent loathed light:
>   Sharpe be thy wounds, but sweet the medicines bee,
> That long captiued soules from wearie thraldome free.
>   (II.i.36)

If neither justice nor mercy are heavenly attributes, the example of
Amavia suggests, if God indeed is an idle onlooker, calmly watching
human suffering, then the peace the grave offers is indeed a consum-
mation devoutly to be wished.

Guyon's response to the "Pitifull spectacle" of the dying Amavia
and her bloodstained child beside the body of Mordant is anything
but detached:

> Whom when the good Sir *Guyon* did behold,
> His hart gan wexe as starke, as marble stone,
> And his fresh bloud did frieze with fearefull cold,
> That all his senses seemd bereft attone,
> At last his mightie ghost gan deepe to grone,
> As Lyon grudging in his great disdaine,
> Mournes inwardly, and makes to himselfe mone;
> Till ruth and fraile affection did constraine,
> His stout courage to stoupe, and shew his inward paine.
>   (II.i.42)

At first, Guyon's response is both deeply sensitive and, paradoxically,
insensitive: confronted with the enormity of the pitiable scene, he
is shocked and stunned into the lowest level of being, inanimate and
insensible. After this brief descent, he returns to the level of the noble
beast, who feels deep emotion, but resists displaying such feelings

openly. Finally, his human spirit and senses move him not only to showing "his inward paine" but also into compassionate action. He tends to Amavia's wounds, and when she regains consciousness, he tries to encourage her with "goodly counsell." The accusation, frequently heard, that Guyon is coldly detached from human feeling is not only unwarranted, but ignores the ethical point Spenser is making: the *imitatio dei* Christianity offers is compassionate, not ataraxic. As Kathleen Williams has observed, Guyon is "touchingly sympathetic" in this scene;[25] he shows quick and profound sympathy for Amavia's physical and spiritual ills. He becomes the Good Samaritan, by participating in an enactment of the parable.[26] Instead it is Amavia who, however, understandably, finds the burden of sympathetic love too heavy to bear, as she determinedly seeks to imitate the uncaring heavens: she not only claims her "dew rest" but also wants nothing to "trouble dying soules tranquilitee" (47.7–8), as she seeks release in the oblivion promised by the mortality of both body and soul. The memory of her beloved Mordant and the fate of her unfortunate child are too much for her, and she almost eagerly abandons both.

Guyon's grief at her death is profound; he can "vneath/From tears abstaine" (56.5–6). Refusing to question the care of heaven, he aims his accusations at lesser agencies: "Accusing fortune, and too cruell fate," he does not challenge providence itself. Indeed, "Religious reuerence" guides his thought and conduct throughout the aftermath of this episode. In endeavoring to make sense of Amavia's and Mordant's cruel fate, he provides rebuttals to a number of Epicureanism's irreligious tenets. In answer to the notion that pleasure is the true ruler of human morality, Guyon notes the dire consequences when "raging passion with fierce tyrannie/Robs reason of her due regalitie" (57.4–5). Against the Epicurean resignation that justice has no real part in the nature of things, Guyon insists there will be a just accounting in the next life, "When best shall be to them, that liued best." The notion of a future judgment also responds to the Palmer's confident assessment that Amavia deserves an "honourable toombe," because her death was due to anguish rather than crime (58.6–9). Guyon, less sure that we can judge what others deserve, still argues for the compassionate response:

> Palmer (quoth he) death is an equall dome
>   To good and bad, the common Inne of rest;
>   But after death the tryall is to come,
>   When best shall be to them, that liued best:
>   But both alike, when death hath both supprest,

Religious reuerence doth bury all teen,
Which who so wants, wants so much of his rest . . .

(II.i.59.1–7)

Whether the line is read as "buryall teene"—religious reverence itself
commands or compels proper burial—or as "bury all teen"—the
reverent observance of religious rites demands that one bury all
alike—Guyon's response is an apppropriate one.[27]

While he expresses doubt in the accuracy of human judgment,
Guyon nonetheless resolves that he will try to exact a form of justice
in this life: he will invert the divine promise of due reward, the best
to the best, and in retribution provide the worst to those that lived
worst. He swears vengeance upon Acrasia, the enchantress ultimately
responsible for the deaths of Mordant and Amavia, and will endeavor
to show the heavens more just by dedicating himself to the "doome
of just reuenge" for which Amavia cries out. Guyon will exercise
the power he has to avenge, if not to redress, the wrongs suffered
by Amavia.

Since neither human nor elfin dedication either to compassion or
to vengeance in itself guarantees the existence of a Providential order,
Spenser is not here providing any definitive answer to the question
of heavenly concern for earthly events. That answer is reserved for
the moment after Guyon's faint, when the knight is himself powerless
to prevent, avenge, or redress any wrong. As Guyon had shown
compassion for the plight of Amavia,[28] he is shown heavenly compassion in his time of need:

And is there care in heauen? and is there loue
    In heauenly spirits to these creatures bace,
    That may compassion of their euils moue?
    There is: else much more wretched were the cace
    Of men, then beasts.

(II.viii.1.1–5)

Spenser here confronts the question of whether godly qualities are
actually attributes of the Deity. If qualities like mercy and justice
have no place in heaven, then humankind, because it longs to see
these qualities as part of the nature of things, is doomed to the pain
of inevitable and inescapable disappointment. If this is the case, the
alternatives to the sorry condition of enforced disillusionment are a

foolish clinging to illusion or a conscious rejection of illusion. The first alternative constitutes a misuse of the human intellect and the other, it is implied, invites the individual to be less sensitive to the plight of others. Something in humanity insists on compassion toward others who suffer evils, and such a desire for loving concern surely has a genuine object elsewhere in the universe.

But what exactly *is* the "case of men"? How does providence intervene to offer in this life some tastes of mercy and justice? Spenser offers an answer which also serves as a rebuttal of Epicurean materialism: spiritual entities do exist, and they serve as the ministers of divine concern. As the narrator hastens to reassure us:

> But o th'exceeding grace
> Of highest God, that loues his creatures so,
> And all his workes with mercy doth embrace,
> That blessed Angels, he sends to and fro,
> To serue tro wicked man, to serue his wicked foe.
>
> (II.viii.1.5–9)

For the most part, though, God's presence and his agency in human affairs are mediated, not direct. Even in Spenser's fictive world, he remains *deus absconditus,* sending his angels to tend to human needs. But if their actions can show the heavens more just, then perhaps human actions can do the same. The angels leave "their siluer bowers," and we see them "with golden pineons, cleaue/The flitting skies" in order to combat the "foule feends" on the behalf of humankind (2.1–5). Their combat is not motivated by wrath, but is "all for loue"; they provide not only protection but "succour" at God's behest. The last line of the stanza—"O why should heauenly God to men haue such regard?"—serves as a statement of wonder that justice and mercy can be so conjoined, but it also serves as a direct challenge to the Epicurean precept that the divine has no regard for humankind. That there is care in heaven is no longer questioned: the divine motive for such care remains a mystery.

The angelic appeal to the Palmer recalls the voice from heaven which Christ invoked and which so many hearers interpreted as thunder, just as there are strong parallels between Guyon's guardian angel and the angel who appears at Christ's empty tomb, with "countenance . . . like lightning" and "raiment white as snowe." Through these biblical connections, Guyon is presented not so much as a

Christ figure but as the wayfaring, warfaring Christian (to echo Milton's conflation) for whom the gospel story provides exemplars—even in parables—for his own behavior and assurances for his destiny. The redemptive promise contained in Christ's resurrection sustains such confidence, and the appearance of Guyon's angel echoes that promise. The angel enlists the Palmer's aid, but also promises his own care and concern; he will both "succour, and defend" Guyon, making possible an individual pre-enactment of the general resurrection in the last days. A rigorously qualified comparison with a classical deity defines the role of charitable love here:

> Like as *Cupido* on *Idoean* hill,
>   When hauing laid his cruell bow away,
>   And mortall arrowes, wherewith he doth fill
>   The world with murdrous spoiles and bloudie pray,
>   With his faire mother he him dights to play,
>   And with his goodly sisters, *Graces* three . . .
>
>   (II.viii.6.1–6)

The desired end of heavenly love, of *caritas,* is carefully distinguished from the effects of the destructive passions Cupid commonly inspires. Spenser's simile describing the angel's winged form suggests a reformed Eros, one which seeks to heal and not to harm, to preserve and not to destroy. Other figures in canto eight will be interested in "murdrous spoiles," and against these enemies the vulnerable Guyon must be protected.

The description of the enemies underscores the didactic focus of the passage: the presentation of true doctrine about the divine nature and the refutation of false ideas about divinity. The episode comprises one of Spenser's most direct forays into apologetics. "Two Paynim knights," presented as willful unbelievers, turn out to be the attackers whom the angel describes as Guyon's "foe and mine" (8.6), as he quietly echoes the first stanza's reference to God's compassion toward his "wicked foe." As we have seen, Mornay addressed his treatise on the truth of the Christian religion against "Atheists, Epicures, [and] Paynims," and Spenser has similar targets in mind here: both Mornay's and Spenser's approach to apologetics is more concerned with reforming the believer than with refuting the infidel. In arguing for the connections between action and belief, he suggests that even an ostensibly Christian individual who behaves as Pyrochles and Cymochles do must have a misconception of his God. The behavior of the attacking knights shows them to be singularly lacking in compassion and in the "religious reuerance" that Guyon observed toward the remains of Amavia and Mordant, and that he asserted should be observed toward anyone.

Guyon has realized that "death is an equall doome/To good and bad" (i.59.1–2) and felt compelled to offset, somewhat, the shame and grief of the lovers' deaths by making certain they are not "vnburied bad" (59.9). Instead, Pyrochles sees Guyon's "slombred corse" and decides that death equals dishonor: "Loe," he cries, "where he now inglorious doth lye,/To proue he liued ill, that did thus foully dye" (viii.12.9) He and Cymochles are ready, in the Palmer's words, to "blot the honor of the dead" and even their own honor, since they will "with foule cowardize [Guyon's] carkasse shame" (13.3–4). This kind of "vile revenge" is nothing less than "sacrilege" (16.4–5), and the implication is that their misunderstanding of the divine nature contributes to their shameful behavior. The angelic promise and extension of divine agency are confirmed with the arrival of *Arturus ex machina*. Arthur prevents the unfaithful knights from exacting their unworthy revenge, and this defense rewards both Guyon's earlier piety and the Palmer's present fidelity.

The precise timeliness of Arthur's appearance can itself serve as a response to Epicurean forms of skepticism. In *De natura deorum,* the Epicurean Velleius mocks those who try to explain the workings of nature not by the interactions of necessity and chance, but by divine intelligence. He accuses those who believe in providence of using the same unsatisfactory strategy that inept playwrights use:

> ut tragici poetae cum explicare argumenti exitum non potestis confugitis ad deum . . .[29]

> (and so, like the tragic poets, being unable to bring the plot of your drama to a denouement, you have recourse to a god . . .)

As a response, Spenser stresses how the resolution of Book II relies upon divine intervention. Harry Berger has argued that the causational principle at work in Book II seems to move from Chance to Purpose,[30] and in this episode we witness a shift from the atomic swerve of the Lucretian *clinamen* writ large in nature and human action to the working out in time of the eternal will of God. Though even Reformed Christians might be tempted to see the agencies behind events as purely fortuitous, or as only human or elfin, the vision of the angel that begins canto eight serves as a reminder of the immanence of providential action. By exercise of Christian *pietas*—now infused, unlike the classical term, with the additional meanings conveyed by the Italian *pietà* or the English *pity*—one best fulfills one's duty to one's God.[31] Guyon's pious concern for Amavia is not only a reflection of heavenly compassion; it is also a participation in that love. The "Paynims'" disregard for "religious reuerence" toward the dead marks their refusal to take a participatory role.

Their behavior, with that of Cecropia, serves both as an indictment of an ethics based upon false ideas about divinity and as a call to readers that their actions more accurately reflect true doctrine about the divine nature. In arguing for the connections between action and belief, Spenser and Sidney suggest that ostensibly Christian individuals who behave as do Pyrocles, Cymochles, and Cecropia, must have a misconception of their God. That such behavior has all too frequent parallels in Christendom is acknowledged by the narrative explanation for Cecropia's response when Pamela demurs:

> as great persons are wont to make the wrong they have done
> to be a cause to do the more wrong, [Cecropia's] knowledge
> rose to no higher point but to envy a worthier, and her will
> was no otherwise bent but the more to hate, the more she
> found her enemy provided against her.[32]

The sad example set by "great persons," the need for higher knowledge, and the highly resistant infection of the will are all at work in this passage. The *Arcadia* and *The Faerie Queene* endeavor to address and to dramatize the essentials in moral reformation: action, doctrine and both the *energeia* and *suasio* of the preacher or poet to help in linking them together. Spenser's and Sidney's pre-Christian apologetics also enable the reader to consider his or her neediness at a distance.

The reader must then choose to close that gap, and many readers will of course decline to do so. Others might consider that openness itself a morally suspect quality. The Bishop of London, John King, found the *Arcadia*—along with that other experiment in moral reformation and refashioning, Spenser's *Faerie Queene*—to be "frivolous" and dangerous. In both pulpit and press, King lamented that "the sin of this land and age of ours (perhaps the mother of our atheism) [was] to commit idolatry with such books."[33] Given the nature of religious controversy, though, it was perhaps inevitable that a work endeavoring to extend the range and effectiveness of apologetics should be accused of fostering the very notions it was intended to refute. King's judgment may, in part, reflect the changing taste that Gabriel Harvey blamed for the *Arcadia*'s being out of fashion. But Harvey's words, in this context, suggest that Sidney's moral instruction still struck too close to home for some: Harvey also mentions that readers with "queasy stomachs" find the *Arcadia* not to their liking.[34] The nausea that Martin Bucer inspired in young Thomas Horton reminds us that Harvey may be describing not only aesthetic qualms. He may also glance at the uneasiness experienced by anyone reluctant to accept the Other as either neighbor or exemplar. Most of us are unwilling to admit that our actions often embody the systems of belief we claim to abjure; it is always difficult to recognize the recalcitrant goat in our (we like to think) sheepish selves.

University of Nebraska—Lincoln

NOTES

1. Elizabeth Bieman, *Plato Baptized: Towards the Interpretation of Spenser's Mimetic Fictions* (Toronto: University of Toronto Press, 1988), 143. See also Karl E. Morrison, *The Mimetic Tradition of Reform in the West* (Princeton: Princeton University Press, 1982), esp. 239. William Kerrigan makes a similar point in connection with Milton's and Blake's prophetic poetry in *The Sacred Complex: On the Psychogenesis of "Paradise Lost"* (Cambridge, MA: Harvard University Press, 1983), 95: "Symbols do not contain meaning. They begin it."

2. Letter from Thomas Horton to Francisco Dryander, May 15, 1550; translated by Amy Nelson Burnett in "Church Discipline and Moral Reformation in the Thought of Martin Bucer," *Sixteenth Century Journal* 22 (1991), 439. The Latin text of the letter appears in A. E. Harvey, *Martin Bucer in England* (Marburg: Bauer, 1906), 48–49.

3. D. P. Walker, *The Ancient Theology* (Ithaca, New York: Cornell University Press, 1972), 132–63.

4. Philippe de Mornay, *A woorke concerning the trewnesse of the Christian Religion* (London, 1587; rpt. Delmar, NY: Scholars' Facsimiles and Reprints, 1976), 210.

5. Andrew Weiner, *Sir Philip Sidney and the Poetics of Protestantism: A Study of Contexts* (Minneapolis: University of Minnesota Press, 1978), 15. See also Patrick Cullen, *Infernal Triad: The Flesh, the World, and the Devil in Spenser and Milton* (Princeton: Princeton University Press, 1974), 76: Guyon's travails demonstrate that "there remains even in the baptized Christian something of evil against which he contends."

6. Sir Philip Sidney, *Miscellaneous Prose,* ed. Katherine Duncan-Jones and Jan van Dorsten (Oxford: Clarendon Press, 1973), 91.

7. Sidney, *Miscellaneous Prose,* 83.

8.   The current consensus seems to be that the printed version is mostly, if not entirely, Goldring's work: see Duncan-Jones's comments in Sidney, *Miscellaneous Prse,* 155–57.

9.   Mornay, sig. **, fol. iiii.

10.   *Confession,* as cited by Weiner, p. 15; Sidney, *Miscellaneous Prose,* 79.

11.   As noted by Cyril Bailey, *Epicurus. The Extant Remains* (Oxford: Clarendon Press, 1926), 134–35. Diogenes Laertius also attests to Epicurus' observance of religious custom in *Lives of the Eminent Philosophers* X. 10. Kirk Summers considers whether Epicureans distinguished among ceremonial observances in "Lucretius and the Epicurean Tradition on Piety," *Classical Philology* 90 (1995): 32–57.

12.   Mornay, 175.

13.   William Elton, *King Lear and the Gods* (San Marino: Huntington Library, 1968), 53.

14.   *Ciris,* line 3. See *Virgil,* the Loeb Classical Library revised edition, 2 vols. (London: William Heinemann, 1967), II, 404. See also Norman DeWitt, *Virgil's Biographia Litteraria* (London: Oxford University Press, 1923), 47.

15.   Sir Philip Sidney, *The Countess of Pembroke's Arcadia,* ed. Victor Skretkowicz (Oxford: Clarendon Press, 1987), 358–59.

16.   Mornay, sig. **, fol. iiii.

17.   Cicero, *De natura deorum* I. xxxvii. 102. I have used the Loeb Classical Library edition and slightly adapted the translation by H. Rackham (London: William Heinemann, 1933).

18.   Cicero, I. xliv. 122.

19.   For a less antagonistic treatment of the philosophy, see Philip Mitsis, *Epicurus' Ethical Theory: The Pleasures of Invulnerability* (Ithaca: Cornell University Press, 1988). A useful overview of Epicurus and his interpreters is provided by Howard Jones, *The Epicurean Traditions* (London: Routledge, 1989).

20.   Edmund Spenser, *The Faerie Queene,* edited by Thomas P. Roche, Jr., with the assistance of C. Patrick O'Donnell (New Haven: Yale University Press, 1981), 15–16. All future references to *The Faerie Queene* will be drawn from this edition and cited in the text.

21.   Even C. S. Lewis, who is generally sympathetic to Guyon, argues that "the virtue [Spenser] here presents to us" through the character of Guyon "is a dull and pedestrian one to fallen man." He suggests that the character, too, must necessarily strike the reader as unprepossessing. See *The Allegory of Love* (London: Oxford University Press, 1939), 338.

22.   Hugh MacLachlan has argued for a strict separation of Spenser's ethical and theological considerations throughout Book II in "The 'carelesse heauens': A Study of Revenge and Atonement in *The Faerie Queene,*" *Spenser Studies* 1 (1980): 142. The use of pre-Christian apologetics suggests there could be exceptions in Renaissance texts both to this distinction and to the one frequently maintained between Pagan and Christian in Spenserian studies. Theresa M. Krier briefly but compellingly comments upon the moralizations upon desire that are under scrutiny in these two scenes; see *Gazing on Secret Sights: Spenser, Classical Imitation, and the Decorums of Vision* (Ithaca: Cornell University Press, 1990), 98.

23.   Mornay, sig. **, fol. iiii.

24.   Guillaume Du Bartas, "Le Septième Jour," lines 93–104 and 111–116. I have used the edition of Du Bartas' *Works* edited by Urban Tigner Holmes, Jr., et al., 3 vols. (Chapel Hill: University of North Carolina Press, 1935). The English version is taken from *The Divine Weeks and Works of Guillaume de Saluste, Sieur du Bartas, Translated by Josuah Sylvester,* edited by Susan Snyder, 2 vols. (Oxford: Clarendon Press, 1979). These are lines 103–108 and 117–122 of "The Seaventh Day."

25.   Kathleen Williams, *Spenser's World of Glass* (Berkeley and Los Angeles: University of California Press, 1966), 42.

26.   This resemblance has been noted by Carol V. Kaske in " 'Religious Reuerence Doth Buriall Teene': Christian and Pagan in *The Faerie Queene,*" *Review of English Studies* 30 (1979), 140.

27.   As her title indicates, Kaske accepts the former reading in persuasively relating this passage to Redcrosse's encounter with the fifth, sixth, and seventh beadsmen in Mercie's service (I.x.42). Our arguments differ, though, on how Spenser distinguishes between Christian and Pagan, and how he marks Guyon as either at this point in the narrative. Guyon's function as a Samaritan figure here should, I think, inspire hesitation in deciding the fold to which he belongs.

28.   The Reformed Church's teaching, of course, would resist any simple causality between human works and divine mercy. The marginal commentary in the Geneva Bible on the parable of the sheep and the goats mediates between ideas of reward and of freely given grace: "Christ meaneth not that our salvation dependeth on our workes or merites, but teacheth what it is to live justly according to godlines, & charitie, and that God *recompenseth* his [own] of his free mercie. . . ." (emphasis mine). See *The Newe Testament* in *The Bible and Holy Scriptures* (Geneva, 1560; rpt. [as *The Geneva Bible*] Madison: University of Wisconsin Press, 1969), fol. 14.

29.   Cicero, I. xx. 53.

30.   Harry Berger, Jr., *The Allegorical Temper* (New Haven: Yale University Press, 1957), 44–49.

31.   The vexed history of *pietas* in the Christian tradition has recently been outlined by James D. Garrison, *Pietas from Vergil to Dryden* (University Park: Pennsylvania State Press, 1992), esp. pp. 21–60. Garrison notes the role of pity in the occasion and the fulfillment of Guyon's campaign against Acrasia on 190–91.

32.   Sidney, *Countess of Pembroke's Arcadia,* p. 363.

33.   John King, *Lectures Upon Jonas* (London, 1597), sig Z. fol. 2; quoted by Skretkowicz in Sidney, *Arcadia,* p. xliii.

34.   Quoted by G. G. Smith, in *Elizabethan Critical Essays* 2 vols. (Oxford: Clarenton Press, 1904), II, 231; and by Skretkowicz in Sidney, *Arcadia,* xliii.

CHAUNCEY WOOD

"With Wit My Wit Is Marred": Reason, Wit, and Wittiness in Sir Philip Sidney's *Astrophil and Stella*

There is today widespread (although not universal) agreement
that readers should discriminate between the poet Sidney and
his creation Astrophil, who is presented in a negative light. This
essay attempts to analyze how Sidney effects this distinction and
how he undercuts Astrophil. The word "wit" is used in the
sequence to mean reason, right and wrong reasoning, cleverness,
and a witty person. In sonnet #34 Sidney portrays Astrophil as
a wit who complains that his reason/wit is undermined by his
thoughts of Stella—another use of wit—thereby leading him to
term himself an oxymoronic "foolish wit" and to complain that
Stella's powers "confuse my mind." Thus, some of the real
wittiness is at Astrophil's expense. Sonnets 2, 4, and 5 show
the divided mind of Astrophil arguing against himself, coming
to tortured conclusions/or rejecting sensible ones, while sonnet
10 has him invert the proper relationship between reason and
will. Stella, however, is portrayed very differently. Cupid never
prevails with her because, as is shown in sonnet 12, her heart
is "fortified with wit." Ultimately the wittiness with which
the poet treats the collapse of reason in his creation Astrophil
is designed to show that the infected will can erode the foundations of the erected wit.

IN SONNET 34 OF *Astrophil and Stella,* Astrophil holds a dialogue
with himself in which he argues on both sides of the issue of writing
poems in praise of Stella. On the one hand he argues that he should
write to "ease a burdened heart," but another part of his mind counters that the words he writes are the "glasses of [his] daily vexing

245

care."[1] The argument progresses until, in a remarkable pre–psycho-logical portrait of a conflicted self, Sidney supplies Astrophil with the line "Peace, foolish wit; with wit my wit is marred"—a line that not only plays on the meanings of wit and wittiness, but tells us the essence of Astrophil's dilemma: his "wit" or reason has, through his love for Stella, become a house divided against itself.[2] This witty treatment of what happens to the lover's wit as a result of his love for Stella operates as a major thematic device not just here but throughout the first sixty-three sonnets in *Astrophil and Stella.* So insistent is the device that one may argue that because Astrophil's wit is marred he has become someone who is both a wit and a fool—the oxymoronic "foolish wit" of the line under study, which can at once characterize Astrophil's conflicted reason, and, by synec-doche, the reasoner. Wit, then, can refer to a witty person, to the faculty of reason, and to the action of wit or wittiness—and to all of these in the same line.

Wittiness in *Astrophil and Stella,* one may assert, begins even before the sonnets themselves do, for there is considerable wit in the title, in which the star-lover, "Astrophil," a coinage with a terrible pun on the author's name, Philip, is equivocally joined with the star he professes to love, "Stella." The union is equivocal because the starry names, one derived from the Greek and the other from Latin, are perhaps selected to suggest that there is a fundamental incompatibility between the two "lovers"—"lovers" who never get together in the 108 sonnets and eleven songs that follow.[3] Indeed, they not only do not get together, there is not even a true dialogue between them since there are no songs or sonnets directed by Stella to Astrophil, while the only reports we have of her speech to him are not in the reciprocal mode. They begin with the unambiguous, discouraging refrain of the Fourth Song in which Stella is reported to say, " 'No, no, no, no, my dear, let be,' " and there is nothing more positive later in the sequence.[4] In the Eighth Song Stella asks him to cease in his attempts to prove her love and tells him " 'Now be still,' " while in the Eleventh Song she "ends" the dialogue that has never really begun by sending him about his business, saying " 'Well, be gone, be gone, I say.' " Given that all the sonnets and songs are directed from Astrophil to Stella, and given the complete absence of any posi-tive response from her, it is as though he is speaking to her in Greek.

Stella has no interest whatsoever in the love that Astrophil has for her; yet Astrophil persists. That irrational persistence is the occasion for some of the wittiness about wit in the sonnet we have already noted, while the key difference between Stella and Astrophil lies in their command of reason or wit, and that difference in wit becomes the occasion for a great deal of wittiness about wit itself. Sir Philip tells us in the wittiest manner possible that reason in his poetic creation, Astrophil, has been damaged by Cupid's arrow; yet he contrives to have Astrophil express his inner emotional and intellectual conflict with a poetical skill and witty playfulness that would be far beyond the ability of someone actually suffering from the effects of Cupid's arrow as they are described. In short, the circumscription of wit in Astrophil comes from his love for Stella, but the witty presentation of this continually reminds us of the need to distance Astrophil from Sidney; one Phil from the other.[5] That distance in turn permits Sir Philip to pun not only on his own name but also upon that of Penelope Devereux Rich without giving offense. But that is another story. Suffice to say that if *Astrophil and Stella* is approached as a series of poems on the uses of beauty, it is much more accessible than when approached as being a series of poems on a real or imagined love affair.[6]

In order to understand the relationships among wit, wittiness, and love in Astrophil and Stella we should normally begin at the beginning, but in the case of this particular sonnet sequence to do so is almost impossible. The first sonnet in *Astrophil and Stella*, with its injunction to Astrophil to look in his heart and write, is so well-known that to begin at the beginning is difficult. It is a sonnet that resists new analysis because it has passed into our general consciousness as an entire thing—sonnet and sense together—and we are so sure of its traditionally ascribed meaning as a sonnet reflecting upon the nature of art and love it is hard even to imagine that it could ever have been understood in any other way. So let us pass over the first sonnet for a moment to consider the second and some others—the sonnets that tell the story of Cupid's arrow, its effect on the lover, and Cupid's inability to make headway against Stella. Ringler has styled Sonnet 2 as the "second introductory sonnet . . ." and in many ways it introduces the themes of the sequence more clearly than does Sonnet 1: [7]

Not at first sight, nor with a dribbed shot,
    Love gave the wound which while I breathe will bleed:
    But known worth did in mine of time proceed,
Till by degrees it had full conquest got.
I saw, and liked; I liked but loved not;
    I loved, but straight did not what love decreed:
    At length to loves decrees I, forced, agreed,

Yet with repining at so partial lot.
   Now even that footstep of lost liberty
Is gone, and now like slave-born Muscovite
I call it praise to suffer tyranny;
And now employ the remnant of my wit
     To make myself believe that all is well,
     While with a feeling skill I paint my hell.

A terrible process is described here. The speaker has received a wound, it has festered, he has been forced to agree to decrees, he has become like a slave, and with what is left of his intellectual power, "the remnant of my wit," he describes the "hell" in which he finds himself. For a presumed love sonnet it is unpromising. Yet, the only note to this sonnet in the edition by Katherine Duncan-Jones follows Ringler in noting that Sidney, in contrast to Dante and Petrarch, does not love at first sight, to which she adds the phrase "exploiting this to the greater glory of Stella."[8] How falling in love slowly rather than quickly glorifies Stella is not clear, given that the emphasis in the sonnet is on the inexorable process of Cupid's arrow, resulting in a state the author describes as being in slavery and hell, a state that does not glorify Stella but rather underscores the *inglorious* nature of the love inspired by Cupid's arrow.

Sidney wittily describes a well-known process, the deprivation of reason as the result of wounding by Cupid's arrow, by having Astrophil use "the remnant of [his] wit" simultaneously to characterize yet transcend the effects of Cupid's arrow on him. Because Astrophil uses the remnant of his wit "To make myself believe that all is well," we see that his reason or wit is first reduced by Love and then the remnant is used by the speaker for his own self-deception even while the poems in which all this is expressed are witty both in terms of their presentation of the nominal subject and in the exquisite game that Sidney plays with Astrophil and the reader.[9] It is a game in which Astrophil is permitted to display some wit while at the same time despairing of its impairment by Cupid. To rhyme "all is well" with "paint my hell" creates an irony that is no doubt beyond the impaired abilities of Astrophil to perceive, but which Sidney has created for the reader's delight.[10]

While the speaker in *Astrophil and Stella* will be witty even as he speaks disparagingly of "dainty wits" in sonnet 3, his own wit or reason has been compromised by Cupid's arrow. In light of this, the opposition between "will and wit" that is set up in sonnet 4 is particularly instructive. Sidney dealt powerfully with the relationship between the wit and the will in an oft-quoted passage in *The Defence of Poesy:*

> Neither let it be deemed too saucy a comparison to balance the highest point of man's wit with the efficacy of nature; but rather gave right honour to the heavenly Maker of that maker, who having made man to His own likeness, set him beyond and over all the works of that second nature . . . with no small arguments to the incredulous of that first accursed fall of Adam, since our erected wit maketh us know what perfection is, and yet our infected will keepeth us from reaching unto it.[11]

Both wit and will come ultimately from the same maker, but the "erected wit" is still *able* to know perfection, while the "infected will" prevents man from reaching it. Postlapsarian wit is not automatically perfect, but properly used, rightly constructed or erected, it can recognize perfection. Improperly used, deconstructed or not erected, it may mistake something like female beauty for perfection itself. Thus the wit can be infected as readily as the will.[12] While man as a whole should be "beyond and over all the works of that second nature," the infected will makes such lordship problematic.

Reason and will should ideally operate together to move the individual forward, as in the medieval image of the two feet of the soul, the rational and the affective, in which the rational foot first perceives the good and then the foot of the will, the affective foot, moves after it.[13] In sonnet 4, however, Astrophil claims that "Virtue" has set "a bate between my will and wit." Since reason and will should be working together to pursue the good, it is remarkable that virtue, which should be sought through their agency, is perceived by the speaker as dividing the two. And, of course, it is Astrophil's perception that is mistaken as the sonnet makes fairly clear. The "bate" or debate that the reader might expect to find between wit and will is one in which the erected wit perceives perfection and urges the infected will through debate to move towards it. Astrophil, who styles himself as having only the remnant of wit, and that infected to the point that it works to deceive him as we have seen, nevertheless resents such rationality as remains with him. Rather than ask Virtue to move his will to join his wit, Astrophil asks Virtue to let his reason leave off altogether from debating his will. The debate between will and wit occurring in Astrophil is not caused by Virtue, but by virtue's absence.[14]

Virtue, alas, now let me take some rest:
Thou sett'st a bate between my will and wit.
If vain love have my simple soul oppressed,
Leave what thou lik'st not, deal not thou with it.
　　Thy sceptre use in some old Caton's breast;
Churches or schools are for thy seat more fit.
I do confess—pardon a fault confessed—
My mouth too tender is for thy hard bit.
　　But if that needs thou wilt usurping be
　　The little reason that is left in me,
And still the effect of thy persuasions prove:
　　I swear, my heart such one shall show to thee
　　That shrines in flesh so true a deity,
　　That, virtue, thou thyself shall be in love.

In lines 2–8 Astrophil asks Virtue to leave him alone if she does
not like what she finds in him, and the language in which this is
expressed is significant. He refers to "vain love," which may have
oppressed his "simple soul." Astrophil's love is vain in the sense that
it is born of vanity, and is also vain in the sense that it will come to
naught in the sequence. Pierced by Cupid's arrow, he suffers from
*cupid*ity, self-love, vanity. Given this problem, it is small wonder that
he goes on to say that if Virtue insists upon taking over "the little
reason that is left in me," then he will show Virtue someone who
"shrines in flesh so true a deity,/That, virtue, thou thy self shalt be
in love." Virtue can hardly "usurp" such reason as he has left since
Virtue is the objective that reason strives to perceive, not an invader
from outside. This kind of misperception on the part of Astrophil
shows just how little reason is in fact left in him. Of course Virtue
would love the virtuous Stella—what Astrophil does not understand
is that it is Stella's beauty and not her virtue that he himself loves.[15]
That Astrophil styles himself metaphorically as a horse whose mouth
is too tender for Virtue's bit is amusing, inasmuch as there exists a
long-standing iconographic tradition in which Virtue bridles Vice
with Temperance.[16] By having Astrophil overtly declare what he does
not want—the bridle of temperance—Sidney is able to show tacitly
precisely what he needs.

The next sonnet, number 5, sets all this out in some detail. The
speaker acknowledges that the "heavenly part" of man's nature should
be its "king"; that Cupid's arrow is merely an image for a choice we
make in our hearts, (and here he repeats the significant nomenclature

from sonnet 1: that the person who makes such a choice becomes a
"fool"); he notes that earthly beauty is merely a shadow of the true
beauty that resides in "virtue"; he concedes that we are pilgrims on
earth and should seek our heavenly home ("should in soul up to our
country move"), but in spite of all this he mistakenly believes that
he "must Stella love":

> It is most true, that eyes are formed to serve
> The inward light; and that the heavenly part
> Ought to be king, from whose rules who do swerve,
> Rebels to Nature, strive for their own smart.
>   It is most true, what we call Cupid's dart,
> An image is, which for ourselves we carve;
> And, fools, adore, in temple of our heart.
> Till that good god make Church and churchmen starve.
>   True, that true beauty virtue is indeed,
> Wherof this beauty can be but a shade,
> Which elements with mortal mixture breed;
> True, that on earth we are but pilgrims made,
>   And should in soul up to our country move;
> True; and yet true, that I must Stella love.[17]

It is Cupid, that is, his own choice, that compels him to love Stella's
beauty, not some external power that overcomes his reason. Virtue
would have him love the "true beauty" Stella encompasses by being
virtuous, but his reason has been reduced in its governing capacity
so that he has become one of the "fools" who worships "in temple
of our heart." In sonnets 4 and 5, Sidney demonstrates considerable
wittiness in acknowledging the theoretical truth of the proper domin-
ion in the soul of "the heavenly part," while simultaneously admitting the practical truth of Astrophil's need to love Stella, which
permits the use of the phrase "True; and yet true . . . ," to describe
the paradox that Astrophil can express but not overcome. Because
wounded by Cupid's arrow—that is, because he worships an image
he carved himself—Astrophil is condemned to love the shadow of
true beauty rather than the real thing, and so resents even the feeble
"bate" that remains between his misdirected will and his circum-
scribed wit. The excellent and witty verse in which all this is laid
out must therefore be credited to Sidney and not to Astrophil.

A similar play with the concept of Reason may be found in Sonnet
10, in which Astrophil's Reason is played off against love, will, and

the ambiguous word "sense," which seems to mean both sensibleness
and the perception of the senses:

> Reason, in faith thou art well served, that still
> Would'st brabbling be with sense and love in me.
> I rather wished thee climb the muses' hill,
> Or reach the fruit of nature's choicest tree,
> > Or seek heaven's course, or heaven's inside, to see.
> Why should'st thou toil our thorny soil to till?
> Leave sense, and those which sense's objects be:
> Deal thou with powers of thoughts, leave love to will.
> > But thou would'st needs fight with both love and sense,
> With sword of wit giving wounds of dispraise,
> Till downright blows did foil thy cunning fence:
> For soon as they strake thee with Stella's rays,
> > Reason, thou kneeld'st, and offered'st straight to prove
> > By reason good, good reason her to love.

Reason is used for sophistical purposes in this sonnet, just as wit was
in sonnet 2. Astrophil first upbraids Reason for "brabbling" with
sense and love in him. He would prefer that Reason confine itself
to poetry ("climb the muses' hill"), natural philosophy ("reach the
fruit of nature's choicest tree"), or astronomy ("seek heaven's
course"). In sum, he argues that Reason should confine itself to
abstract things: "Leave sense, and those which sense's objects be."
But while urging Reason to "Deal . . . with powers of thoughts,"
and to "Leave sense, and those [things] which sense's objects be," he
also asks Reason to "leave love to will."

In Astrophil's tortured split, Reason should confine itself to the
abstract, so that will may deal with the sensible world, the world of
man with his fallen nature. Sidney has prepared us to see Astrophil's
bizarre alignment in this sonnet, by having him urge Reason to
"reach the fruit of nature's highest tree," which inevitably reminds
us of the corruption of both reason and will that took place as the
result of reaching the fruit of another tree. Next, in an even bolder
hypothesis, Astrophil imagines his Reason yielding to love as he has
done, and kneeling before sense and love rather than "brabbling"
with them. The concluding couplet, with its elegant chiasmus in
the second line—"Reason, thou kneeled'st, and offered'st straight to
prove/By reason good, good reason her to love"—inverts the proper

relationship between the erected wit and the infected will; yet does so with a witty, rhetorical elegance that must be credited to Sidney rather than Astrophil.

No treatment of wit and wittiness in this sequence can overlook Sidney's repeated differentiation between Astrophil's reduced wit or reason, and Stella's unimpaired faculty. It is a contrast that informs the entire sequence, and gives the reader a perspective on Astrophil which in turn clarifies Sidney's objectives for his poem. By showing how Astrophil's rational faculty is distorted by his cupidinous attitude towards physical beauty, while at the same time showing Stella, beautiful in both her person and her virtue, resisting the love represented by Cupid, Sidney is able to tell an exemplary tale in a delightful form.

Stella's wit is not overcome by Cupid in spite of Cupid's assaults. In the twelfth sonnet, the speaker addresses Cupid and says that because Stella's breath "makes oft thy flames arise," that is, that she inspires a devotion to Cupid in others, that Cupid can claim her for himself "like those whose powers,/Having got up a breach by fighting well/Cry 'Victory'." This will not work, however, for Stella possesses not only wit but also "disdain"—presumably disdain for the love represented by Cupid and pursued in the sequence by Cupid's servant, Astrophil. Cupid has *not* conquered Stella and the importance of this fact is accordingly emphasized in this key sonnet:

Cupid, because thou shin'st in Stella's eyes,
    That from her locks, thy day-nets, none 'scapes free,
That her sweet breath makes oft thy flames to rise,
That in her breast thy pap well sugared lies,
    That her grace gracious makes thy wrongs, that she,
    What words so e'er she speaks, persuades for thee,
That her clear voice lifts thy fame to the skies;
    Thou countest Stella thine, like those whose powers,
Having got up a breach by fighting well,
Cry "Victory, this fair day all is ours!"
O no, her heart is such a citadel,
    So fortified with wit, stored with disdain,
    That to win it, is all the skill and pain.

Wit and disdain fortify Stella's heart in stark contrast with Astrophil's. There, we recall, the "remnant of [his] wit" is used for self-deception, and he had no original disdain for the works of Cupid. Indeed,

in his account of events it was looking and liking that brought him
into the purview of Cupid, where Cupid's arrow did the rest:

> I saw, and liked; I liked but loved not;
>> I loved, but straight did not what love decreed:
>> At length to loves decrees I, forced, agreed,
> Yet with repining at so partial lot.

We have already noted that Stella differs from Astrophil in that
her own "wit" fortifies her heart in such a way that it can withstand
Cupid's assaults. That Stella is different from him in that she has not
been harmed by Cupid's arrow, in spite of the fact that her beauty
can cause others to become vulnerable, is insisted upon in these early
sonnets. This is treated most directly in sonnet 8, in which Cupid is
described as having fled Greece to the colder climate of England,
where he seeks warmth. He imagines he will find it in Stella, whose
radiance appears to shed the kind of heat he seeks, but he is mistaken:

> At length he perched himself in Stella's joyful face,
>> Whose fair skin, beamy eyes, like morning sun on snow,
> Deceived the quaking boy, who thought from so pure light
> Effects of lively heat must needs in nature grow.
> But she, most fair, most cold, made him thence take his flight
>> To my close heart, where, while some firebrands he did
>>> lay,
>> He burnt unawares his wings, and cannot fly away.

Of course, as we have learned from sonnet 5, Cupid has no power
other than that we give him, so the business about burned wings may
be understood as the lover's own heat making him loathe to stop
loving Stella in a Cupidinous way.

Sonnets 9, 11, and 12 work together to show that while Stella is
beautiful, her beauty is not at the service of Cupid. Her heart remains
her own, unlike that of Astrophil, whose heart is captured by Cupid
through the agency of Stella's outward beauty. If we recall from
sonnet 5 that "true beauty virtue is indeed," then in sonnet 9 it is
not surprising that Stella's face appears to some to be the very court
of Virtue: "Queen Virtue's court, which some call Stella's face. . . ."
The closing sestet has occasioned some disagreement about the correct interpretation of the word "touch," which is important to work
out because of what it says about the nature of Cupid.

The windows now through which this heavenly guest
Looks o'er the world, and can find nothing such
Which dare claim from those lights the name of "best",
Of touch they are that without touch doth touch,
    Which Cupid's self from Beauty's mine did draw:
    Of touch they are, and poor I am their straw.

Stella's eyes are probably *both* touchstone and touchwood at the same time. In so far as they are touchstone, they attract without direct physical contact, just as virtue attracts the pilgrims who move "in soul up to our country" in sonnet 5. Those pilgrims can be inspired by earthly beauty to seek heavenly beauty or virtue, but only if they understand and bear in mind that "this beauty" is "but a shade" of the heavenly one. Stella's outward beauty is such that it should remind Astrophil of true beauty, Queen Virtue, whose court some can find in Stella's face. However, having already shown in the previous sonnet that his own heart is full of tinder that blazes up when Cupid lays down his firebrands, he here shows himself unable to find Queen Virtue in Stella's face. Rather, her eyes play in him the role of touchwood or fire-starter, and he again blazes up since "poor I am their straw." Stella is blameless in this. Her outward beauty should reveal the inward beauty of virtue, but Astrophil cannot see it. Cupid goes to "Beauty's mine," that is, Stella's face, and "draws" the light of Stella's eyes. Here "draw" is not used in the magnetic sense of attraction, but in the sense of drawing or taking away for his own purposes. Cupid, for which understand Astrophil's own heart, is touched by the rays of Stella's eyes but his heart wants to touch *her* and not the heavenly beauty to which her beauty should lead him. Accordingly, the touchstone of her eyes becomes touchwood in his heart and up blazes the straw.[18]

In sonnets 11 and 12, the relationship between Cupid and Stella's beauty is explored further. The conceit in 11 is that Cupid is "like a child," who finds a beautiful book or picture, but who "never heeds the fruit of writer's mind." That is, pays no attention to the purpose of the beauty that is discovered. Consequently, when Cupid finds Stella "in nature's cabinet" he immediately begins "playing and shining in each *outward* part." That is, like a child who can damage a fine book or painting by playing with it—a purpose for which it was not intended—Cupid, who is metaphorically Astrophil himself, takes Stella's external beauty and turns it to earthly, non-virtuous intentions. As noted earliler in the sonnet, "That when the heaven to thee his best displays/Yet of that best thou leav'st the best behind."

In spite of Cupid's misuse of Stella's external beauty he is warned
not to seek to "get into her heart," and, lest we miss the identification
of Astrophil and Cupid, Cupid is here styled a "fool" like Astrophil
himself in sonnets 1 and 5.

It would be a mistake for Cupid or Astrophil to attempt to win
Stella's heart, where her internal beauty lies, because, as we have
seen, her heart is a citadel fortified with wit and filled with disdain—presumably disdain for those who seek there something other
than virtue. Nevertheless, to those who perceive Stella's beauty
wrongly, it persuades powerfully but in the wrong direction. As
Astrophil puts it, "her grace gracious makes thy [i.e., Cupid's];
wrongs, that she,/What words so e'er she speaks, persuades for thee."

If Stella is blameless, Astrophil is not. If her beauty is misconstrued
by him, he has made it clear that the fault is his own: Cupid's darts
are merely an image he creates and worships in the temple of his
heart. In sonnet 14 he creates a "friend" who confronts him with
what he is doing:

> But with your rhubarb words you must contend
>> To grieve me worse, in saying that desire
>> Doth plunge my well-formed soul even in the mire
> Of sinful thoughts, which do in ruin end.

If we accept that Astrophil has foregone reason and loves only Stella's
external beauty, then, like Cupid, he has left the best behind. While
to modern ears this may seem only imprudent, not sinful, Astrophil
accepts that what the friend fears might happen—his desire could
plunge him into "the mire/Of sinful thoughts." His defense is interesting. He does not attempt to deny that desire can lead to sinful
thoughts; rather he argues that desire has created in him a new kind
of supposed virtue:

> If that be sin, which doth the manners frame,
> Well stayed with truth in word, and faith of deed,
> Ready of wit, and fearing nought but shame:
> If that be sin, which in fixed hearts doth breed
>> A loathing of all loose unchastity:
>> Then love is sin, and let me sinful be.

We shall have more to say about "truth in word," presently, but we
have already noted that Astrophil is scarcely "ready of wit" as he

contends except in the sense of being able to speak wittily. His wit or reason is not only not ready to do what it is supposed to do—perceive the good—but is doing the opposite: it is rationalizing his errors. That he fears shame is appropriate considering what he wants to do, and while his "fixed heart" may loathe "*loose* unchastity"—whatever that may be—that apparently leaves him free to pursue some other kind of as-yet-undefined unchastity. This love is sin, as he has observed before, and since he wants to end what little debate remains between his wit and will, he *will* be sinful as he avers.

Having established a little something about the nature and uses of beauty, about right order in the soul, and the sinful nature of Astrophil's love for Stella, we are now ready to venture a look at the opening sonnet in the sequence:

> Loving in truth, and fain in verse my love to show,
> That she (dear she) might take some pleasure of my pain;
> Pleasure might cause her read, reading might make her know;
> Knowledge might pity win, and pity grace obtain;
> I sought fit words to paint the blackest face of woe,
> Studying inventions fine, her wits to entertain;
> Oft turning others' leaves, to see if thence would flow
> Some fresh and fruitful showers upon my sunburnt brain.
> But words came halting forth, wanting invention's stay;
> Invention, nature's child, fled step-dame study's blows;
> And others' feet still seemed but strangers in my way.
> Thus great with child to speak, and helpless in my throes,
> Biting my truant pen, beating myself for spite,
> "Fool," said my muse to me; "look in thy heart, and write."

Given the sequential way in which the reader comes to understand what is going on in *Astrophil and Stella,* this first sonnet in the sequence can only be re-read. Upon re-reading it, the imagery for Astrophil is arresting. Biting his "truant" pen and beating himself for ignorance he is like an errant schoolboy; great with child he is not manly; helpless he is, well, helpless; yet all the while his proclaimed inability to show his love in verse is expressed in elegant and innovative Alexandrines. The "sunburnt brain" is Astrophil's not Sidney's, while the Muse's choice of the epithet "Fool" to address the protagonist seems very apt in the circumstances. Astrophil might as well look in his heart, since his brain will prove no help.[19]

In spite of the very unflattering picture that Astrophil paints of himself, he nevertheless is sure that he is someone who is "Loving in truth." The phrase can be read in several ways. In one sense it is true that he loves, and in another it is fair to say that he loves in truth in the sense of loving constantly. He is one who has a "fixed heart." Nevertheless, inasmuch as the love he has is described in Sonnet 4 as "vain love"—one both in vain and born of vanity—then it is a love that resists Virtue's "hard bit" in the same sonnet and therefore cannot be "true" as truth is defined in sonnet 5, which begins "It is most true, that eyes are formed to serve the inward light." That sonnet proceeds to declare that true beauty is virtue, and that it is true we are pilgrims who "should in soul up to our country move." No one in Sidney's audience would fail to know that the force that drew the pilgrim to the heavenly home was love, and that it and it alone is worthy of being called true love. In the largest sense, then, *Astrophil and Stella* beings with a statement about true loving that is false. And uttered by a fool.

When we permit the images we create to dominate our thoughts, our reason or "wit" operates irrationally, and our sunburnt brains lie dormant while our hearts respond. Sidney hints at this in the first sonnet; he depicts it eloquently in sonnet 47 in which Astrophil again has a dialogue with himself, expresses the rational thing, then follows the heart in irrationality:

> Virtue, awake: beauty but beauty is;
> I may, I must, I can, I will, I do
> Leave following that, which it is gain to miss.
> Let her go. Soft, but here she comes. Go to,
>   Unkind, I love you not—: O me, that eye
>   Doth make my heart give to my tongue the lie.

There are a great many instances in *Astrophil and Stella* in which the heart rules the tongue even when it would obey the head. To show this paradox in which wit or wittiness is expended even while wit or reason is subjugated is perhaps Sidney's greatest technical accomplishment in this brilliant set of poems.

McMaster University

Notes

1. *Sir Philip Sidney*, ed. Katherine Duncan-Jones (Oxford: Oxford University Press, 1989), 166. Subsequent quotations will be from this edition and will be cited by sonnet number in the text. Italicization has been introduced for emphasis.

2. While for many years critics have observed what Rudenstine, to take a typical example, calls the "playful wit" of *Astrophil and Stella,* until recently the analysis of what is witty and how it is so has been rare. See Neil L. Rudenstine, *Sidney's Poetic Development* (Cambridge, Mass.: Harvard University Press, 1967), 172. Daniel Traister has argued cogently that while most readers in recent years have found *Astrophil and Stella* to be "witty" and "essentially comic in structure and meaning," Sidney's wittiness and humor is not for its own sake. Drawing upon the *Defence of Poesy,* Traister argues that Sidney, like most people of the time, "believes that comedy is ultimately a didactic mode. . . . For Sidney, comedy is a negative exemplum . . ." (751). See "Sidney's Purposeful Humor: *Astrophil and Stella* 59 and 83," *ELH* 49 (1982): 751–64. For the negative example of Astrophil as "lust in action" (434), see Traister's " 'To Portrait That Which In This World Is Best': Stella in Perspective," *SP* 81 (1984): 419–437.

3. On the title's "disjunction" see Thomas P. Roche, Jr., "Astrophil and Stella: A Radical Reading," *Spenser Studies* 3 (1982): 143.

4. On the importance of Stella's negativity, see Roche, "Radical Reading," 141.

5. For an excellent account of the movement in Sidney criticism from purely autobiographical alignment of Astrophil with Sidney, through a disjunction that nevertheless found considerable sympathy on Sidney's part for his creation Astrophil, to the currently widespread view that Astrophil is offered by Sidney as a negative example, see Alan Sinfield, "Sidney and Astrophil," *SEL* 20 (1980): 25–41. Robert L. Montgomery comments that "in one sense, of course, all of the wit in the poems belongs to Sidney. But what is lent, so to speak, to Astrophil moves in one direction and is to be understood in one way, while that which creates the whole is to be taken entirely differently" (147). See "The Poetics of Astrophil," in *Sir Philip Sidney's Achievements,* ed. M. J. B. Allen, et al. (New York: AMS Press, 1990), 145–56.

While many writers in recent years have distinguished between Sidney the poet and his creation Astrophil on literary grounds, Katherine Duncan-Jones, in her Chatterton Lecture of 1980, more than a decade before her biography of Sidney was to be published, noted the profound biographical differences between Sidney, who was "passionately greedy for honour," and "his poet-lover Astrophil [who] collapses totally into a world of private and self-destructive emotion, neglecting his career at court and even ordinary forms of politeness." See "Philip Sidney's Toys," reprinted in *Sir Philip Sidney: An Anthology of Modern Criticism,* ed. Dennis Kay (Oxford: Clarendon Press, 1987), 76.

6. James J. Scanlon (p. 68) effectively cites Castiglione's *The Courtier* to provide a background on the correct understanding of beauty for an interpretation of *Astrophil and Stella.* See "Sidney's *Astrophil and Stella:* 'See what it is to Love' Sensually!" *SEL* 16 (1976): 65–74.

7. *The Poems of Sir Philip Sidney,* ed. William A. Ringler, Jr. (Oxford: Clarendon Press, 1962), 459.

8. Duncan-Jones, *Sidney,* 357–58; Ringler, *Sidney,* 459. Robert L. Montgomery argues with regard to sonnet 2 that "the fundamental irony of the sequence, which is evident in so many of its elements, is nowhere more pointed than here." See "Astrophil's Stella and Stella's Astrophil," in *Sir Philip Sidney and the Interpretation of Renaissance Culture,* ed. Gary F. Waller & Michael D. Moore (Totowa, N.J.: Barnes & Noble, 1984), 53.

9. Alan Sinfield takes this sonnet as the starting point of what he calls Astrophil's "programme of self-deception." See "Astrophil's Self-Deception," *EIC* 28 (1978): 1–18.

10. As Mary Jane Doherty succinctly puts it, "Astrophil's mind's eye is quite a muddy one." In so far as Astrophil defines his world as a hell, Professor Doherty notes that "from an Augustinian vantage, *Astrophil and Stella* is about a failed quest to come home—a journey to hell, not heaven." See *The Mistress-Knowledge: Sir Philip Sidney's Defence of Poesie and Literary Architectonics in the English Renaissance* (Nashville, Tenn: Vanderbilt University Press, 1991), xi; 124.

11. Duncan-Jones, *Sidney,* 217.

12. See Wendy Goulston, "The 'Figuring Forth' of Astrophil: Sidney's Use of Language," *SoRA* 11 (1978): 232 for the useful phrases "weak erected wit" and "infected wit." For a different approach to Astrophil's wit and will, which sees the reader "drawn to some degree into sympathy with Astrophel" (6), see C. Stuart Hunter, "Erected Wit and Infected Will: Sidney's Poetic Theory and Poetic Practice," *SNew* 5 (1984): 3–10.

13. See John Freccero, "Dante's Firm Foot and the Journey Without a Guide," *Harvard Theological Review* 52 (1959): 245–81.

14. Robert E. Stillman's work on the eclogues of *The Old Arcadia,* emphasizing Sidney's concern for "a harmonious balance between opposing elements, in this case between the wit and the will . . . ," which should stand in what the character Languet calls "jump concord" or just harmony, is very helpful for an understanding of *Astrophil and Stella* as well. While it may be argued that the wit and will are both injured in the fall, and so are not "opposing elements" but rather stronger and weaker elements of the same tarnished soul, nevertheless the general thrust of Stillman's argument for the meaning of these eclogues can profitably be applied to an understanding of Sidney's sonnet sequence. See Robert E. Stillman, *Sidney's Poetic Justice* (Lewisburg, Pa.: Bucknell University Press, 1986), 195–96.

Andrew D. Weiner, "Structure and 'Fore Conceit' in *Astrophil and Stella,*" *TSLL* 16 (1974): 1–25, cites the 39 Articles on the weakness of the will in order to argue that Astrophil becomes a "representation of fallen man, torn between the truths of reason, which he knows but cannot act upon, and the imperatives of passion, which he knows to be wrong, but from which he cannot refrain" (24). Here again it may be argued that it is the misuse of reason rather than the inability of the will that is the thrust of the sonnet sequence. If Astrophil, as fallen man, had no choices, there would be no point in showing the tragicomedy of his misfiring wit.

15. Alan Sinfield, in "Sidney and Astrophil," interprets this sonnet much as is done in the text here, seeing Astrophil claiming "to overwhelm virtue by producing

a deity incarnate and of course virtue would love the deity—but not a deity of the love religion, which is what Astrophil means" (30).

16. See D. W. Robertson, Jr., *A Preface to Chaucer* (Princeton: Princeton University Press, 1962), 23 and fig. 6, the statue by Paolo Veronese.

17. Robert H. Ray notes that the concept of pilgrims moving to their true heavenly home derives ultimately from Hebrews 11:13–16. Thus, Ray argues, "by accepting only a Chaucerian or generally medieval source for these lines of the sonnet, a reader misses the full thrust of Astrophil's statements. On the other hand, the reader who recognizes [the biblical source] also perceives the enormity of Astrophil's violation of the Biblical ideal when he casts it aside in line 14." See "Sidney's *Astrophil and Stella*, Sonnet 5," *Explicator* 41 (1983): 8–9.

18. On sexual puns on the word "touch" see Alan Sinfield, "Sexual Puns in *Astrophil and Stella*," *EIC* 24 (1974): 346.

19. The grammer of this sonnet, with its heavy use of the potential mood, the mood that indicates things that might occur, is very well analyzed by Margreta de Grazia, who argues that the potential mood normally should describe "how man should rule and direct himself" (23), but which in this sonnet leads not to the head but the heart. See "Lost Potential in Grammar and Nature: Sidney's *Astrophil and Stella*," *SEL* 21 (1981): 21–35. On the significance of the epithet "fool" here, compare the analysis of the word in sonnet 53 by Robert J. Dingley. He argues convincingly that sonnet 53 is "a complex and eloquent exposition of a mind out of harmony with itself" (109). The same may be said of sonnet 1. See " 'Sir Foole': *Astrophil and Stella* 53," Parergon: *Bulletin of the Australian and New Zealand Association for Medieval and Renaissance Studies*, n.s. 1 (1983): 105–112.

FORUM

JEAN R. BRINK

Spenser and the Irish Question: Reply to Andrew Hadfield

*F*OR A DISCUSSION OF additional evidence relating to the authorship of the *View*, see my article entitled "Appropriating the Author of the *Faerie Queene:* The Attribution of the *View of the Present State of Ireland* and *A Brief Note of Ireland* to Edmund Spenser," *Soundings of things Done: Essays in Early Modern Literature in Honor of S. K. Heninger, Jr.,* ed. Peter E. Medine and Joseph A. Wittreich. Newark: U of Delaware, 1997, Pp. 93–137.

As Andrew Hadfield points out, it is very difficult to document instances in which writers may have voluntarily engaged in self-censorship or have "concealed" comments on government policy, encoding their impolitic observations in subtle ways. Hadfield, however, remains convinced that writing about Ireland was a hazardous enterprise, especially if an author mentioned Ireland in the title of the work. He states that "virtually no books dealing with Ireland, or having Ireland in the title, appeared during Elizabeth's reign."

It is not clear why Hadfield downplays the importance of the publication of Holinshed's *Chronicles* (1577, 1587). The first edition of this influential chronicle of Ireland was dedicated to Sir Henry Sidney; its author, the Anglo-Irishman Richard Stanyhurst, was influenced by the Jesuit Edmund Campion, whose history of Ireland, interestingly, was later printed by James Ware in 1633. Both men were persecuted—not for writing on Ireland—but because of their religion; Campion was martyred, and Stanyhurst fled to the continent.

The poet Thomas Churchyard also wrote a number of works related to Ireland. In *A Generall Rehearsall of Warres* (1579), he vividly described Sir Humphrey Gilbert's methods of deterring rebellion. According to a well-known anecdote, Gilbert had the heads of his slain foes placed in a circle around his tent and forced the relatives of his victims to crawl through the circle. Churchyard also published works on the death of the rebel James Fitzmaurice and on the Essex expedition. In fact, he alluded specifically to Ireland in the title of *A Scourge for Rebels: wherein are many Notable Services truly set out Touching the Troubles of Ireland* (1584). Although military service, rather than poetry, may have earned him his pension, Churchyard was the only Elizabethan poet other than Spenser to receive this kind of official recognition. Churchyard's commentaries on Ireland did not adversely affect his career.

Hadfield also maintains that Barnaby Rich was the "only author in Jacobean England to represent Ireland in his book titles." If the publication of works with the word Ireland in the title was officially discouraged, then it is difficult to explain why Sir John Davies published *A Discoveries of the True Causes why Ireland was never entirely subdued, untill his majesties raigne* in 1612, presumably to further his career. In 1626 an E.C.S., yet another E.S., published *The Government of Ireland under Sir John Perrot,* the account of one of the least fortunate of many ill-fated deputies of Ireland in the sixteenth century.

Andrew Hadfield has rightly called attention to the complexity of the politics of Anglo-Irish relations in the sixteenth century and has acknowledged that twentieth-century tensions may color our perceptions of earlier periods. In this regard, it is important to note that politics may also have influenced the first editor of the *View*. James Ware claims that he is printing a copy of the *View* which he obtained from Archbishop Ussher's library. The copy of the *View* (TCD, MS 579), located at Trinity College, where Ussher's library was deposited, neither belonged to Ussher, nor was the copy text for Ware's edition. Once the right questions are asked, we may be able to determine which manuscript(s) Ware consulted and from this more informed position to assess the impact of politics on his editorial practice.

Arizona State University, Tempe

CAROL V. KASKE

The Word "Checklaton" and the Authorship of *A Vewe*

*A*S HAS SOMETIMES been remarked, while there is little external evidence that Spenser wrote *A Vewe of the Present State of Ireland*, there is much internal evidence. The most compelling is the rare word "checklaton," which occurs, as Hamilton notes in his edition of *The Faerie Queene*, both in the poem and in the *Vewe*, both times as the material of a "jacket" or "jacke." The chief torturer of Mirabella, Disdain, wears a "jacket quilted richly rare/Upon checklaton" (VI.vii.43.3–4). In the *Vewe*, Irenius says that the Irish wear "the quilted leather Jacke" as

> the proper wede of the horsemen as ye maye reade in *Chaucer* where he describeth: *Sr Thopas* apparrell and armour when he wente to fighte againste the Geaunt which Checklaton is that kinde of gilden leather with which they use to imbrother theire Irishe Jackes (ed. Gottfried, p. 121 = Renwick ed., p. 70).

The only other occurrence listed by the OED is the aforementioned one in Chaucer. Moreover, its context there, the *Tale of Thopas,* is the source for Arthur's vision of Gloriana in I.ix. This tips the balance of evidence towards Spenser's authorship.

Cornell University

267

A. KENT HIEATT

Male Boldness and Female Rights: What the Isle of Venus Proposes

*W*e are all in debt to Anthony Esolen ("Spenserian Chaos: Lucretius in *The Faerie Queene, Spenser Studies* XI: 31–51) for doing overdue justice to the more than Lucretian wildness at the base of Spenser's sexual reality in the Isle of Venus (IV.x): bulls bellowing, birds privily pricked, lusty bowers, fruitful laps, and all that. At the center of Esolen's picture is a Scudamour telling us in the first person how he was animated by love (and, I add, in IV.x.4 by the wish for honor and a place among the best) so as to overcome frightful odds and thrust indomitably to the center of the Isle and of Venus's Temple to get his Amoret.

But when I look back in the text to the account, in the third person, of Scudamour's subsequent failure to penetrate into the House of Busirane (III.xi), I relive the difference between Amer. Eng. "Attaboy!" and Brit. Eng. "a Very Young Person." Why does this paragon of boldness now (III.xi.7–27) lie wallowing, face down on the ground, blubbering his heart out (enough to occasion school-marmish injunctions from Britomart about constancy in misfortune); and then why, when Britomart has got him on his feet and put his armor on him, does he shortly throw himself down again, weeping and banging his head on the ground?

The contrast would make little difference to Esolen's position if it weren't that something about these two episodes shows us Spenser as a "philosophical poet," in Santayana's old term. Spenser is beyond the reach of Lucretius in a particular respect having to do with their highly original reactions to their two quite different cultures.

This something shows up most convincingly in the most powerful phrasal reinforcement that I know of in this poem renowned for its verbal pointers.[1] All of us know that the first two rooms in Busirane's House are signposted repeatedly "Be bold," Be bold," and then again "Be bold," but that as one comes to the third room where Busirane is torturing Amoret to make her love him, the sign reads "Be not too bold." Not all of us have noticed that the only other strong concentration in *The Faerie Queene* of words on the root "-bold-" offers itself in the Isle of Venus episode. Scudamour "*boldly* thought (so young mens thoughts are *bold*)" (IV.x.4) to take the shield of love because he wanted to win himself a place among the best. So he "*boldly* . . . encountered" (10) his first opponent. Then, face to face with Daunger, he recollected how others who had been stout and "*bold*" (18) had given in here. Finally, seeing Venus laughing at him, he was "*emboldned*" (56) to lead Amoret out of the Temple, contrary to her wish for freedom. But between the fourth and fifth of these instances, Womanhood, with Amoret in her lap, reproaches Scudamour for his forceful mastery in pulling Amoret away without the latter's own consent and accuses him of being "*ouer bold*" (54). He rejects her warning, of course; and, in fact, in the House of Busirane it is "*bold* Britomart" (III.xii.29.8) who ignores the similar previous warning "*Be not to bold*" and enters the utmost chamber.[2] Her modus operandi, however, is advised and mature (III.xii.28.1–2 and III. xi.23). Scudamour simply bulls ahead.

The agreement between the patterns *bold* vs. *overbold* / *too bold* in the two locales is too precise to be evaded. However much Spenser's thinking about closure of the Amoret-Scudamour story may have changed between the 1590 and 1596 editions, this verbal agreement did not change.

The cheerful Venereal chaos that we observe in our own and animal nature and that Spenser intensifies beyond Lucretius in the Isle of Venus is only half the story. It is reined in at a human, ethical level, where women are most likely to suffer from it, by an art of "friendship" in love which Spenser expresses in home-grown, Chaucerian terms. (There are no Lucretian terms for this). That is why there are companies of friends, not just lovers, on the Isle (and also why nature is complemented by an art of landscaping, not just counterfeited as in the Bower of Bliss). That is why Britomart and Arthur paraphrase Chaucer[3] on the friendly arts of finding agreement in love, and why the two of them bring Amoret friendship in rigorously parallel episodes, when she (mistaking Britomart in armor for a male) is fearful of more Busirane, or something like date-rape, from each of them (IV.i.5–15, IV.ix.18–19).

Amoret is in love with Scudamour, just as Britomart is in love with Artegal. The highlighted difference between the two cases resides in Scudamour's callow inability or unwillingness to court a beloved until she establishes in her own mind a paired interest beyond bold eros, as Artegal is able to do for Britomart (IV.vi.40–41). Because Scudamour cannot see beyond the advantages of boldly taking over—of doing what he has heard "men of worth" (IV.x.53.8) always do—it follows that Amoret, though married to him, is subject to being carried off by Busirane, much as she is subject to wandering off, in a reduplicative allegory, to be seized by Lust (IV.vii.4). Yet she surrenders to neither, because she loves the Scudamour who has brought that wild, Venereal chaos to her by means of Cupid's cruel dart (which Busirane also wounds her with).

It is possible to clarify Spenser's philosophical reach here by recalling some present-day -isms:

Is he p.c.? No. It's true that an ethical moment arises in his depicted sexual relationships, but it is only one end of a spectrum that encloses as well Lucretian intoxication with the erotic in human and biological life. If Amoret seems in need of a little help from a politically correct code, her avatars are well-known to us today and elicit our pity, but she is located along another spectrum on which Britomart also appears, who spurns protective codes and shatters the glass ceiling of her profession.

Is Spenser a feminist? Yes: he inhabits one of the many mansions in their house, but the first sexual harasser in *Faerie Queene* III is a woman: Malecasta.

What about lesbianism? If Josiane Balasko's movie *Gazon maudit* (*French Twist* in English) is taken into account, where a wife with a macho husband finds warmth and affection from a lesbian, and the husband begins to grow up, there is a sort of connection. Yet the erotic is banned from the warmly affectionate companionship of Britomart and Amoret, by the narrative, by the parallel to the rigorously non-erotic friendship of Arthur and Amoret, and by Britomart's heterosexual love for Artegal. As friends, the pair Britomart and Amoret (IV.i.15–16), the pair Spenser and Gabriel Harvey, and the pair teenage Kent Hieatt and one or another male friend sometimes slept together in the only available or affordable bed on their travels: nothing happened. And the same is true of the two Cambridge undergraduates in bed together in Chaucer's Reeve's Tale, except that one of them slipped into the first of two alternative, occupied beds standing in the same room, and the other one fooled an occupant of the second alternative bed into climbing in with him. Something happened then.

The University of Western Ontario, emeritus

NOTES

1.   I treated the substance of what follows in *Chaucer, Spenser, Milton . . .* , Montreal, 1975, Part I, and I refined my conclusions, with one or two changes, in

"Room of One's Own for Decision . . ." in *Refiguring Chaucer in the Renaissance,* ed. Theresa Krier, Gainesville, 1998, 147–64. The present more detailed discussion of one of its aspects was written in 1994 and scheduled for inclusion in *Renaissance Studies* XII, but was put off until now.

   2.   Cf. *"Be Bold"* and "her *bold* steps" in III.xi.50.

   3.   Hieatt, 1998, 156–58.

GLEANINGS

TOM PARKER

108 Uses of 108

SIDNEY'S *ASTROPHIL AND STELLA* is made up of 108 sonnets
interspersed with 108 song stanzas, and the arrangement of these
poetic units incorporates a variety of further groupings of 108 in an
intricate numerical pattern. The generally accepted explanation for
the presence of these groups of 108—first proposed by Adrian Benjamin, and followed by both Alastair Fowler and Thomas Roche[1]—is
that they allude to the number of suitors of Penelope and a game
that they are playing when they first appear in the *Odyssey,* (I, 107).
This game is described in Euthasius' commentary on the *Odyssey,*
and Benjamin sees it in a resemblance to the popular Elizabethan
game of bowls, allusions to which he then traces in *Astrophil and
Stella:* the game that Sidney plays to win the heart of Penelope, Lady
Rich, is thus woven into the structure of the sonnet sequence. This
suggestion is compelling, but leaves one to wonder why Penelope's
admirers are given this number in the first place. These suitors are
not counted until Book XVI of the *Odyssey* (II.245–53) where Tele-
machus adds them up in groups (52 + 24 + 20 + 12) amongst
various other hangers-on. This is surely more aristocrats than the
island of Ithaca could muster, and more than Odysseus' home could
hold—the authority of this passage has been questioned on these
grounds. Why, then, is this count made? Also, if Sidney's arrays of
108 are directly tied to Penelope Rich, what purpose would it serve
subsequent sonneteers to arrange their poems in similar groupings?

The sonnet sequences of Fulke Greville and Robert Sidney both
involve groups of 108 poetic units, and the arrangements of their
poems show such intimate knowledge of the formal arrangement of
Astrophil and Stella that it must be assumed that they shared Sidney's
creative intentions—but it stretches the limits of credibility to argue
that they also shared romantic interest in the Penelope story. Spenser's
Astrophell (not printed until 1595) contains 216 lines (or twice 108),
and while this may simply acknowledge respect for *Astrophil and
Stella,* the accompanying *Lay of Clorinda* (possibly by Sidney's sister,
the Countess of Pembroke, who was most likely to have been party

to Sidney's intentions) is an elegy of 108 lines in which an allusion to Penelope would be irrelevant. Both these elegies are cited by Fowler as evidence of the importance of the number in Sidney's circle,[2] but they cannot endorse the notion of a reference to Penelope. Likewise, the 108 poems (and eleven miscellaneous additions) in Alexander Craige's *Amorose Songes, Sonets, and Elegies* (1606), also cited by Fowler and Roche in support of the Penelope-game allusion because they contain ten poems to Lady Rich,[3] are deeply insulting to "*liberal* Penelope" in contrast with the Homeric type of continence and fidelity. While this sequence makes use of several of Sidney's important numerical structural referents (closely linked to Craige's "Idea" poems rather than to those for Penelope), Penelope is included as only one of eight semi-allegorized women, only one of whom receives fewer poems in her name, making it better employed as an example of a sequence in which 108 is not connected to Lady Rich.

A comparative study of the sequences of Fulke Greville and Robert Sidney makes it clear that none of Sidney's numbers is to be understood as independent of the others. Greville and Robert Sidney translate the patterns of *Astrophil and Stella* wholesale, adopting a number into their schemes only when they can incorporate all of its appropriate subdivisions in a manner that is truly to be described as proportional. These poets, both of whom shared the closest possible connection to Sidney in his literary experiments, do not write of Lady Rich and yet calculate to the most intricate detail the arrangements of their poems in the same structural units, employed in the same manner, as those in *Astrophil and Stella*. So close is their creative intent that their differing approaches to the same sets of proportions can even reveal previously unrecognised subtleties in the form of *Astrophil and Stella*.

It is not my intention here to provide a structural analysis of any of these sonnet sequences, nor does space allow for a full explanation of the nature and semantic value of their forms—suffice it to say that there is evidence to suggest that the formal patterns of *Astrophil and Stella* were calculated according to musical harmonies and that the use of 108 as the fundamental for division may derive from Plato's cosmological scheme laid out in the *Timaeus*. Such a scheme would set the tribulations of the misguided fool Astrophil against a divinely-ordained harmonious plan, and the mapping out of a Platonic world-soul in the proportions of the sequence might be intended to animate Sidney's Golden World of poetry—the form thus recasts the personal incidents of the individual poems, elevating them from the selfish concerns of worldly love to a profoundly moral universal perspective.

The reuse of this scheme by Robert Sidney reveals his manuscript collection to be a completed, and carefully calculated, sequence rather than the broken and incomplete miscellany suggested by Croft's edition.[4] Likewise, attention to the proportional form supports the authority of the Warwick manuscript version of *Caelica* (British Library Add. MS 54570) over the printed version of 1633 in most instances of their variance, but raises some interesting questions about the possibility of some intended typographical articulation of the buried formal structure of the sequence that has been blurred by the unauthorised addition of two poems. Even the gathering of *Certaine Sonets* appears to have been governed by a miniature version of the same scheme. A proportional form in the manner of *Astrophil and Stella,* using the same set of numbers, recurs in Mary Wroth's *Pamphilia to Amphilanthus,* both in the Folger Manuscript (MS V.a.104) and in the printed version (STC 26051) which represents a simplification and refinement of the same form. Beyond Sidney's family and closest friends, Henry Constable makes some use of the Sidneian harmonic scheme in the Todd Manuscript (V&A, MS. Dyce 44,ff.12 43), but it is Barnabe Barnes who appears to be Sidney's most accomplished imitator—the wild variety of *Parthenophil and Parthenophe* is contained in a precise and intricate homage to the formal sophistication of *Astrophil and Stella.*

So what of 108? The unfortunate coincidence of the publication of A. Kent Hieatt's groundbreaking study of Spenser's *Epithalamion*[5] with the dawn of the decade that saw the rise in popular enthusiasm for jumbled arcana and wooly mystical practice tarred scholarly literary numerologists with the same brush as spurious gurus who would find one's lost kaftan by counting the letters in one's name. Throughout my doctoral thesis I have been obliged to distance myself from any speculation that might smack of the bizarre in order to present a reasonable case for the use of number in the interpretation of literature. I am now free to indulge in broader discussion, with a view to the shedding of light on the question of where this particular number came from. If Homer's count is not merely arbitrary—an exaggeration to bring the number of suitors up to suitably epic proportions—could it be that 108 was picked for some symbolic value that it held? If Plato's ambiguous recipe for the World-soul is invoked, it may be that 108—with its harmonic subdivisions assumed—had come to be a shorthand expression for the world itself, with Penelope's suitors representing in their number a universal assault on her constancy.

According to Censorinus (*De Die Natali* (XVIII, 11) both Heraclitus and Linus believed that the duration of the Great Year—the

period spent by the heavenly bodies in returning to the same relative
position—was 108 centuries. For the Greeks, the shortest period for
human gestation was reckoned to be 216 days (2 x 108), and this is
connected by Plato to his calculation of the Great Year in *The Republic*
(546 BC.[6] The number appears frequently in ancient cosmolo-
gies—for example, Hipparchus, in the second century BC, counted
1080 stars of the first order of brightness—but its ultimate source
remains unclear, although it is most closely connected to the Pythagoreans who, according to Vitruvius *(De architectura* V, Pref. II.3–4),
went as far as to write down the rules of their brotherhood in groups
of 216 to make them more easy to remember.[7] The Pythagorean
origins of Plato's calculations in the *Timaeus* are lost, but even if a
direct source were extant, the problem would be little simplified: the
number, it appears, reaches far beyond Greek cosmology.

While remarkably accurate measures of the size of the Earth were
calculable—the Earth's mean circumference is 108 million times the
Roman half-pace (1.2165 foot)—it seems unlikely that such accurate
measure could have been made of other celestial bodies. However,
the distance of the Sun from the Earth divides by the Sun's diameter
108 times, and the Moon has a radius of 1080 miles. The atomic
weight of silver, the element associated with the Moon, is 108.[8] The
number 108 does seem to involve itself repeatedly in the ratios of
astronomy, and it may be that one such occurrence triggered its
symbolic resonance: often the seemingly arbitrary numbers of ancient
science, or magic, involve recurrent constants that have been confirmed since by modern mathematics, but that were extrapolated
upon in unpredictable ways by the long-gone priests and seers. One
such example may be seen in the vast units of Hindu chronology
that span from the moment of a blink (one *kāṣṭhā,* for example, equals
15 twinklings of an eye) to the ages of the gods. The Age of Brahma
is reckoned at 311,040,000 million solar years, which is said to be
100 years of Brahma; one Brahmic day is, by the Hindu reckoning
of 360 days to the year, 8,640 million solar years. By adding the
Brahmic Age to the Brahmic Year, and then adding the Brahmic
day, one achieves the digits of π correct to six significant figures:
314159040 million. While we cannot know if Vedic geometers made
use of this calculation, it may be that some cyclic measure was made
to give the original length of the Age of Brahma. The more usual
Hindu time measurement of the *Kali Yuga*—432,000 solar years; the
present one began in February 3101 BC—is one-third of a *Treta
Yuga* which, at 1,296,000 solar years is one-tenth of the Platonic
Great Year measured in days (see note 6). All these measures, from
the Age of Brahma to the *Treta Yuga,* are divisible by 108, and there

are also 10,800 *muhūrtta* (the thirtieth part of the Hindu day, used as an equivalent to the hour) in one year.

Further occurrences of 108 in the Hindu scheme of things include the 108 cowgirls who danced with Krishna (all at once!), the 108 shrines of extreme holiness, the 108 hymns of the *Ṛgveda,* the 108 *rudrākṣa* berries that make up the Śaivite *mālā* (or rosary), and the 10,800 bricks in the *agnicaya* or *uttaravedī*—the Northern high altar of the *śrauta* sacrifice at which the exhausted clreator god Prajāpati and all the cosmos is rejuvenated in the fire. The correspondence of the last example to the Platonic notion of a World-soul is accentuated by the fact that the altar itself is often built in the shape of a bird, representing the spiritual flight to heaven, which we may compare to Christian use of the dove as an image for the Holy Spirit. The urge to emphasize the number 108 is demonstrated in the opening lines of the *Muktika Upanishad,* which lists a supposedly canonical 108 Upanishads, although many more exist, and also in the otherwise arbitrary selection of 108 *mātrā* (a proportional unit of no fixed duration) as the limit for the retention of breath in ordinary *prāṇayāma* exercises.

The Buddhist tradition is also rife with groups that center on 108, from the fifty-four guests at the feast in the house of Yasa after the Buddha's first sermon—the "first turn of the Wheel of Truth"—to the 216 auspicious signs on the *Buddhapada* (or Buddha's footprint). Prayer beads are strung in groups of 108, which may either derive from, or be the root of, the apocryphal legend that the first set of prayer "beads" was made up from 108 severed fingers of the Buddha's followers: the rationale of this being that the pain it caused would be more than compensated for by the beneficial effect of subsequent mantras counted out in such groups. There were expected to be at least 108 lamas present at the funeral of a Tibetan prince, and Tibetan women often plait their hair into 108 braids. Rin-chen-bzan-po (958–1055 AD), the translator of some of the Sutras of Buddha that were gathered in the *Kanjur,* is said to have built 108 chapels, and the *Kanjur* itself was arranged in 108 volumes in the red-inked "Imperial Red" translation, commissioned by the Mongolian Emperor, that was distributed to the monasteries of the region to become the most common text from 1720 AD up to the desecrations of the Cultural Revolution.

In the West, the enthusiastic, but often unsightly, collision of the unfettered drug-culture of the Beat generation with Buddhist spirituality has led to some recent uses of gatherings of 108 in America: the poems of the expatriate Tibetan Chögyam Trungpa Rinpoche, founder of the "Jack Kerouac School of Poetics" in Boulder, Colorado, were published as *First Thought Best Thought: 108 Poems* (Boulder and London, 1983) with an introduction by Allen Ginsberg, and the filmmaker Gus Van Sant, chronicler of the doped-up "Grunge" subculture, has published a collection of *108 Portraits* (Santa Fe, NM, 1992) which includes photographs of Ginsberg and William S. Burroughs. There are also, it ought to be noted, 108 stitches on a baseball.

The system of gematria—the attention, in the absence of separate numerals, to the numerical value of the letters of a word, used extensively in the Gnostic and Kabbalistic traditions—yields some pertinent results to this enquiry. Appropriate to the Platonic formulation of the World-soul, both τὸ γαῖον πνεῦμ α (the Earth spirit) and ἡ ἁρμονία κόσμον (the universal harmony) have a numerical value of 1080. The relative paucity of occurrences of 108 in the Christian tradition may result from the suppression of the Gnostics, who would otherwise have carried such symbols into Western orthodoxy. Irenaeus, in *Contra Haereses,* casts scorn on such fatuous Gnostics "proofs" as that of the divinity of Christ being shown by the numerical equivalence of "Alpha and Omega" (= 801, Cf. Revelation 1: 8, 21:6 and 22:13) and περιστερα (dove, = 801), the symbol of the holy spirit, but his sustained—and eventually successful—effort to discredit this heterodox mode of exegesis attests to its power at the time. As specifically Christian examples of gematriac values, it is interesting to note that both τὸ ἅγιὸν πνεῦμα (the Holy Spirit) and the sum of M αριάμ (Mary, = 192) and Ἰήσονς (Jesus, = 888) come to 1080.[9] Although numerological fervour wilted as the One True Church succeeded in establishing its own canon of interpreters, Latin brought new means to generate numbers: IX, the initials of Jesus Christ in Greek, could read as Roman numerals to be multiplied by the number of the Apostles—9 × 12 = 108. The abbreviation of Jesus Christ often seen amongst the mysterious *gammata* of Byzantine iconography—IC XC, of which a prominent example is in the mosaic of Christ Pantocrator in the Hagia Sophia, Istanbul—may also be read as Roman numerals: 99 + 90 = 189. This latter number may be understood as 108 + 81 (81, or 9^2 being associated with the soul) or as 3 × 63—sixty-three being a harmonic subdivision of 108 (a perfect fifth in an octave of 108) and a number of great resonance in Elizabethan superstition as the so-called Grand Climacteric. Here the most obvious contemporary association of a number may be misleading, for although the number of the Climacteric was well known in Renaissance, England, the gathering of poems in groups of 63 by Henry Constable and Michael Drayton, and also the more lowly works of the flamboyant Thames bargeman John Taylor, may be related to what I have proposed as a Sidneian harmonic scheme—*Astrophil and Stella* is clearly divided after 63 sonnets by the First Song—rather than, or as well as, the Climacteric. Shakespeare's Sonnet 107 has been taken to be an allusion to the Queen's Climacteric year (i.e., the year of her sixty-third birthday, 1595–96), but because of its position in the sequence and the mention at its opening of the "soul/Of the wide world," it may have been intended as a sly nod towards Sidney's pattern and its World-soul origin.

Geometry was also involved in Gnostic calculations, and it is remarkable that the figure of a pentagon with sides of unit length—the internal angle between each adjacent pair of which is 108°—in its vertical height provides the side of a square with an area of 2.368:2368 being the numerical value of 'Ιησοῦς Χριστός (Jesus Christ). The related figure of a pentagram has at its points an internal angle of 72°: 72, the fifth part of 360,[10] also marks the division of a musical perfect fifth on a string of 108 units in length (cf. the harmonic division of *Astrophil and Stella* at the 72nd unit—the end of the First Song, and the beginning of the Second Song after Sonnet 72). Another potential geometric source for the attraction of symbols to 108 reflects the Babylonian origin of many of our contemporary measures: there are 10,800 minutes in a semicircle.

Spreading the net a little wider, we find that New Year in Japan is rung in with 108 chimes on a bell, to purge the 108 human desires (limit yourself to these if you can!). The Viking paradise of Vallhǫ, or Valhalla, is described by Snorri Sturluson as having 540 doors through each of which 800 warriors could pass at one time: thus 432,000 burly fellows might enter at once—the number of years in the Hindu *Kali Yuga,* 4,000 times 108.[11] In Britain, the great centers of mystical activity at Stonehenge and at St. Mary's Chapel, Glastonbury, both incorporate 108 into their ground plans. Arcane use has been made of microcosmic reflection of the macrocosm in the fact that man's average number of breaths per hour (1,080) adds up to 25,920 (or 240 × 108) breaths in a day, or the number of years for the sun to be in each successive sign of the Zodiac at the Spring Equinox—one formulation of the length of the Great Year. Although I have found no direct uses of 108 in the Islamic tradition, 108 is the product of two important numbers in Islamic number lore: 6 (the number of creation, derived from Zoroastrian mythology) and 18 (the consonants of the phrase with which every blessed act must begin: "In the name of Allah, the Merciful, the Compassionate"). The Chinese classic *Shui hu chuan* (or "Water Margin"), supposedly recast from folk-tales by Shih Nai-an (?1296–1370), concerns 108 colourful outlaws. Yuri Gagarin, becoming the first man to travel through the heavens, spent 108 minutes in the *Vostok's* single orbit of the Earth in 1961.

One might continue in this manner far beyond absurdity, but I hope that I have made it plain that a number such as 108 can reach out far beyond any purely rational means of study. Ancient astronomers or geometers may have made some relatively straightforward observation involving 108 that struck a chord with another measurement or observation, and a superstition was born. When number and superstition merge, and no clear intentions are recorded by the participants in a particular symbolic event, there is no way to discriminate between possible sources for the use of a particular number. Symbolilc associations will merge and change over time, until even those involved in a number-governed tradition will disagree over the value of the number itself. It cannot be assumed, for example, that the 10,800 bricks in the Hindu fire altar represent the hours in the Hindu year simply because the cultural locations of the two occurrences of the number are the same—whoever first piled together that number of bricks may have been thinking of the same formulation of the Great Year as was Heraclitus. Numbers are readily exportable, but leave no trace of their source: that 108 degrees here is considered or appropriate may result in 108 plaits being attractive there, or 108 chimes being auspicious in another place. It is only when an entire matrix, a patterned web of interlocking proportions, is translated from one medium to another that justifiable claims can be made concerning the influence of a particular instance of a number, and it is this type of translation that may be observed in the formal arrangements of the sonnet sequences of Sidney's circle. Although we are left to speculate about the exact symbolic value of various elements in the scheme, recurrent instances of the same complicated pattern in the same genre determine its importance to those that chose to shape their work in such a way.

Dulwich Art Gallery

Notes

1.   Benjamin's article was never published, but it is summarized and expanded upon in A. Fowler *Triumphal Forms* (Cambridge, 1970), pp. 174–80, and T. P. Roche, Jr. *Petrarch and the English Sonnet Sequences* (New York, 1989), p. 236–42, which works provide the most thorough interpretations of *Astrophil and Stella* from a numerological perspective.

2. Fowler *Triumphal Forms,* p. 175.

3. Fowler, loc. cit., and Roche, *Petrarch and the English Sonnet Sequences,* pp. 285ff.

4. P. J. Croft *The Poems of Robert Sidney.* (Oxford, 1984).

5. A. Kent Hieatt, *Short Time's Endless Monument: the Symbolism of the Numbers in Spenser's Epithalamion* (New York, 1960).

6. See J. Adam, *The Republic of Plato* (Cambridge, 1902), II, p.204f. Adam calculates Plato's Great Year as 12,960,000 days—120 thousand times 108. A more common calculation of the Great Year gives it as 25920 solar years, or 240 $\times$ 108.

7. Vitruvius was of the opinion that it was the cubic properties of 216 (= 6^3 that made it memorable as "when a cube is thrown, on whatever part it rests, it retains its stability" (trans. F. Granger (London and Cambridge, MA, 1955), p.253). Bongo (*Numerorum mysteria* (Bergamo, 1599), p.463) mentions some other properties of 216 (e.g. = $5^2 + 3^2$), and relates the number directly to the *Timaeus,* with various manipulations of the "Lambda" formula (which he draws out) also producing 216 (e.g., $4 \times 6 \times 9$ and 8×27).

8. For these observations, and several of those subsequent, I am indebted to J. Mitchell, *The Dimensions of Paradise* (London, 1988).

9. Mitchell (op. cit. pp. 178–85) connects the occurrences of 1080 together in a cosmic scheme in which 1080 is "the lunar number," with a symbolic value equivalent to the Chinese *yin.*

10. The Jewish and Christian Kabbalistic associations of 72 are myriad, from the 72 letters of the unpronounceable name of God to the languages of the world in which Christ's 72 disciples went out to spread his word.

11. Although it is possible that the old Germanic "long hundred" of 120 is intended (giving the number of doors as 640), this product may indicate a near-Eastern influence on Norse myth; see F. R. Schröder *Germanentum und Hellenismus* (Heidelberg, 1924).

ELIZABETH PORGES WATSON

Mr. Fox's Mottoes in the House of
Busirane

P ERRAULT AND GRIMM and Hans Andersen buried our native folk-
tales. Twenty people know *Cinderella* and *Rumpelstiltskin* and *Bluebeard*
for one that knows *Tattercoats* and *Tom Tit Tot* and *Mr. Fox*."[1] Kathleen
Briggs's ratio is now probably optimistic, but these and other native
versions of their story-types were those told to children of the Tudor
period and earlier. In what was almost entirely an oral tradition, any
literary handling of such material is of double interest: Peele for example
draws on it wholesale in *Old Wives Tale* and the play has been a quarry
for folklorists as well as for critics.[2] Less extensive references, made to
whatever effect and relying for this in the first instance on immediate
recognition by reader or audience, have tended to become obscured.

The third of Brigg's examples, *Mr. Fox,* was recognized in the early
nineteenth century by a Mr. Blakeway as providing Shakespeare's Bened-
ick with a passing quip in *Much Ado About Nothing* I i 200–201.[3] This
brought a version of the tale into print,[4] but its central and entirely
serious use by Spenser in FQ III xi–xii seems to have been almost unre-
marked and only lightly analyzed.[5]

Spenser's profound unease with the darker aspects of folklore belief
shows throughout his work. Occasionally it does so very noticeably,
being felt deeply enough to emerge against the contextual grain. For
example, Redcrosse and Artegall are both changelings (FQ I X 65; III
iii 26), and the pejorative term used by both Contemplation and Merlin
when explaining the knights' respective origins are those of the night-
fears of Spenser's own world, jarring with the finely realized idioms of
his Faerie Land.[6] More usually such discomfort is assimilated by its context, as in Fradubio's description of Duessa's naked ugliness,[7] FQ I ii
40–41, or, in a more personal generic context, the ritual banishing of
"euill sprights" and omens, in *Epithalamion* 333–52. The grim story of
Mr. Fox (see Note 1) is rather differently deployed in the Busirane episode: Spenser uses it deliberately to evoke childhood terrors, which he
can fairly assume he and his readers have in common.

Spenser's story line runs at an angle from that of *Mr. Fox:* Busirane
has never approached Britomart, and she enters his house not out of
curiosity but to rescue his captive victim Amoret. There is nothing
to tie in Lady Mary's adventure with Britomart's until the "utmoste
rowme" (FQ III ix 27) has been described in rich and claustrophobic
detail and Britomart has examined the statue of Cupid above the altar
set at its "upper end" (FQ III ix 47). She turns, and the reader's
memory is activated to color his own retrospect with nightmare:

> Tho as she backward cast her busie eye,
> To search each secret of that goodly sted,
> Over the dore thus written she did spye
> *Be bold:* she oft and oft it over-red,
> Yet could not find what sense it figured.
>
> (FQ III xi 50)

Spenser's readers would have had no such difficulty. There are no
factually horrific surprises in Busirane's House as there were in Mr.
Fox's: Scudamour's lament (FQ III xi 10–11) tells Britomart and the
reader pretty clearly what they may come upon in the way of sadistic
self-indulgence. One effect of this first citation of the motto is to
recall the brutal physicality of Lady Mary's story and in its present
context to give a literal edge to figurative expectation.

This is reinforced and given precise direction when Britomart has
entered the second room and marveled not only at its oppressive
spolendors but at the "wastefull emptinesse,/And solemne silence
over all that place." Ominous anticipation is aroused, and then specific dread made urgent by Britomat's inability to understand the
further warning that she presently sees over the last door:

> And as she lookt about, she did behold,
> How over that same door was likewise writ,
> *Be bold, be bold,* and euerywhere *Be bold,*
> That much she muz'd, yet ocild not construe it
> By any ridling skil, or commun wit.
> At last she spyde at that roomes upper end,
> Another iron dore, on which was writ,
> *Be not too bold;* whereto though she did bend
> Her earnest mind, yet wist not what it might intend.
>
> (FQ III xi 53–54)

The line between Britomart as a character and as an allegorical figure is nicely drawn here. Any young girl of Spenser's generation would recognize these mottos, with a familiar shudder. But a certain stage of feminine development is not ready to take in their meaning, then or now. Spenser leaves the last motto open-ended. The reader is to supply what should follow as part of his or her own response to Britomart's situation: "Lest that your Heart's Blood should Run Cold." This echo is free to resonate through the continuing action and no further reminders are needed or explicitly given. Once *Mr. Fox* has been brought to mind, at whatever level of recollection, parallels and contrasts between Lady Mary's situation and Britomart's become immediately perceptible, allowing Spenser certain emphases, from the moment that the respective solitudes of the two heroines are broken. Lady Mary, who has already looked into the bloody horrors of the innermost room, sees Mr. Fox come in, dragging his latest victim. She hides, making no attempt at what would be for her suicidal interference, only concealing the horrid evidence of the severed hand for future use. Britomart, who has not yet seen beyond the second chamber of the House, has no impulse to hide from the portents that precede Cupid's masque or from the masque itself, and even when she sees Amoret's agonizing involvement in it she makes no move to intervene on her behalf. Lady Mary's inaction is merely sensible: Britomart's detachment is strangely uncharacteristic. It demands explanation, whether she at once recognizes the masque as being phantasmagoric, merely symptomatic of its true origin, or because it expresses imaginings of her own that have to be brought under control before constructive action is possible. Time for thought is actually forced on her, since the last door locks fast against her as the masque vanishes through it.

When she finally enters the innermost chamber, "Neither of idle shewes, nor of false charmes aghast (FQ III xii 29)," Britomart does so in her expected role as rescuer; also as potential but self-defensive victim.[8] The slight wound Busirane is able to inflict on her arouses her only to angry revulsion, and this in turn has to be controlled through Amoret's intervention (FQ III xii 33). For just that moment of fury Britomart is close to Radigund: Busirane includes in his complexities of evil the capacity to provoke women into perceiving the masculine as essentially aggressive and loathsome.

A Freudian analysis of *Mr. Fox* and of the play Spenser makes with the story would be easy, and severely limiting. The psychological architecture of Busirane's House, its self-expressive ritual, expressed perversions of social, moral, spiritual, and imaginative registers that extend far beyond the sexual turmoils of adolescence and their control or resolution. But of all the ironies of reference, echoes and replayings of Ovid, Petrarch, Alciati, and many more, only *Mr. Fox* is likely to have provided the stuff of nightmare for Spenser's readers and for Spenser himself. There are never-ends that are activated in childhood, long before interpretative capacities of whatever kind can be educated into more sophisticated receptivity. Spenser touched on this familiar story so as to induce vibrations of unsophisticated and irrational horror, the synchronizing resonance of which should then operate subliminally through to the end of the episode.

University of Nottingham

NOTES

1. Kathleen Briggs; *The Anatomy of Puck: An Examination of Fairy Beliefs among Shakespeare's Contemporaries and Successors,* Routledge and Kegan Paul, London, 1959, p. 11. Her version of *Mr. Fox,* pp. 210–11, is given here. It is based on that of Blakeway (see below, n. 4), with minor changes where this departs from the traditional story-type. Blakeway gives the severed hand a bracelet instead of the more likely ring (tradition apart, a bracelet would probably fall off), and, more importantly, conflates the triple build-up of the ominous mottoes. *Mr. Fox* belongs to a story-type widely represented in England and elsewhere: "The Robber Bridegroom"; K 1916, Stith Thompson, *Motif Index of Folk-tale Literature,* Rosenkilde and Bagger, Copenhagen, 1955–58; 955 and H57.2.1, Antti Arne, *Types of the Folktale,* tr. Stith Thompson, Helsinki, 1964.

Mr. Fox

There was once a pretty girl called Lady Mary, who lived with her two brothers, and was courted far and wide. But the man she fancied most was Mr. Fox, a handsome, dashing man, but a stranger to those parts. He would often tell Lady Mary about his fine house, but she had never seen it; and one day, when he was away on business about their betrothal, she determined to go and see it for herself. She took a by-way, and tied up her horse to a little thicket gate, and walked up to the house. It was a fine, strong place, and over the doorway was carved: "Be Bold, Be Bold," Lady Mary went into a handsome hall, and over the great staircase was carved, "Be Bold, Be Bold, but not Too Bold." Lady Mary went up the staircase and along a passage, which narrowed to a heavy stone door, and over it was carved:

"Be Bold, Be Bold, but not Too Bold,
Lest that your Heart's Blood should Run Cold."

She stooped down and peeped in at the keyhole, and there was a great room, and seated round the table were the bodies of a great many young women in their bridal clothes. As she looked she heard a clattering in the courtyard, and she turned and ran, by the only way open, towards the staircase. When she reached the bottom Mr. Fox was at the door, and she had only time to hide behind a great barrel that stood under the staircase, before he came into the house, dragging a beautiful girl behind him. As he pulled her up the stairs she caught hold of the banisters, and he whipped out his sword and cut off her hand, which fell straight into Lady Mary's lap. No sooner was he out of sight that Lady Mary leapt up and ran from the house; but she took the hand with her.

Next day at the great betrothal feast Lady Mary proposed that they should all tell stories around the table. When it came to her turn she said: "I know no new stories, but I will tell a strange dream I had last night.' And she began to tell how she had visited Mr. Fox's house. And when she got to the carving over the door she said:

> "But it is not so, nor it was not so,
>   And God forbid it should be so."

And so she said at each pause until the end; when Mr. Fox, who had grown paler as the tale went on, took up the refrain. Then she answered him:

> "But it is so, and it was so,
>   And here the hand I have to show!"

And she drew forth the hand and pointed it at him. At that the guests leapt to their feet; and they chopped Mr. Fox into small pieces.

---

2.   Peele's extended play with folk-tale narrative in *The Old Wives Tale* allows easy identification of such motifs as the Two Sisters at the Well, the Magician's External Soul and The Grateful Dead Man. The second of these, as it is used in the play's climax, has often been cited as a likely source of Milton's handling of the same motif in *Comus* from the nineteenth century on: see *The Works of George Peele,* ed. A. H. Bullen, London 1888, vol. I, Introduction, p. xxxix. Whether or not he knew Peele's delightful play, it seems to me very likely that Milton first heard a version of the story in childhood. Exposure to folk-tale, told with much or little expertise, must have been almost universal, except perhaps in extreme Puritan households. Sidney makes his own use of such experience in *New Arcadia* II 14; Mopsa's carefully garbled analogue to the Cupid and Psyche story. See my article, "Folklore in Arcadia: Mopsa's 'Tale of the Old Cut' " re-cut and set, *Sidney Journal* 16:2 (1998): 3–15.

3.   *Claudio:* If this were so, so were it uttered.
Benedict: Like the old tale, my lord: 'It is not so, nor 'twas not so; but indeed, God forbid it should be so!' *Much Ado About Nothing,* Arden Edition, ed. A. R. Humphreys (Methuen, London, 1981), 98.

4.   Mr. Blakeway said that he had heard the tale from his aunt, who was born in 1715 and whom he thought had had it told to her by a narrator born under Charles II. It is the earliest surviving version, contributed to the Boswell-Malone Variorum Edition of Shakespeare, 1821, VII. 164–65. It is reprinted in the Arden Edition, Appendix V, pp. 232–33.

5. The *Variorum* edition of Spenser gives E. B. Fowler's unexpanded citation of "the old English nursery Tale" in Blakeway's version, see above, n. 4: E. B. Fowler, *Spenser and the Courts of Love,* originally a PhD thesis presented at Chicago, 1919, published by George Banta, Manasha, Wisconsin, 1921, 56, n. 76, *The Faerie Queene Book Three, Variorum Edition,* Special Editor, F. M. Padelford, (Baltimore: John Hopkins University Press, 1934), 208. Joseph Jacobs, *English Fairy Tales,* London, 1890, includes *Mr. Fox,* 148–151, and in a note cites Blakeway, 247. In the second edition, 1898, he adds a note, startingly unhelpful however derived; " 'Be Bold' is Britomart's motto in the Fairy Queen" (sic).

6. Contemplation glosses his reference to the 'base Elfin brood', left in place of the infant Redcrosse, quite explicitly. "Such men do Chaungelings call, so chaunged by Faeries theft," and Merlin tells Britomart that Artegall was, "whilome by false Faries stolne away." The vicious amorality suggested in these passages accords with the grim superstition referred to, but has no allegorical dimension to lift it into Spenser's Faerie Land, nor any relevant analogy in its experience. Spenser himself seems to have felt this, at least as far as Artegall was concerned. At the beginning of his Book Artegall's abduction into Faerie Land is revised into allegorical decorum. Astraea herself notices, "this gentle childe," "Whom seeing fit, and with no crime defilde,/She did allure with gifts, and speaches milde,/To wend with her" (FQ V I 6).

7. Fradubio says that he saw Duessa in her "proper hew," on a day (that day is every Prime, When Witches wont do pennance for their crime). Prime can refer to spring, or to their new moon. The tradition that witches "do pennance," or lose their powers, at certain times is widespread. The "time" is usually midwinter: the winter solstice. The new moon is associated with Hecate, patron Goddess of witchcraft: "Prime" here may refer to the new moon following the solstice; alternatively this belief may here be extended to apply to every new moon.

8. The closely related story type where the last of the murderer's intended victims herself avenges her predecessors is also widely distributed. An example of this is the ballad *Lady Isobel and the Elf Knight,* Child, *The English and Scottish Popular Ballads,* Cambridge, Mass. 1882; repr. Folklore Press, New York 1957, Vol. I. 4, A-F, pp. 22–62. The European versions cited by Child indicates the same development as those in English: that the false lover was originally an "elphin knight" (A), who descends into psychopathic humanity through later reworkings of the story. Spenser may have known some version of this or one of its many analogues, in all of which the lady tricks her seducer. Usually death is by drowning, but in A she lulls him asleep and stabs him with his own dagger:

"If seven king's daughters here ye hae slain,
Lye ye here, a husband to them 'a."

Index

291

DATE DUE			
			Printed in USA